JOURNEYS TO SELFHOOD

JOURNEYS
TO SELFHOOD

Hegel & Kierkegaard

MARK C. TAYLOR

UNIVERSITY OF CALIFORNIA PRESS
Berkeley • *Los Angeles* • *London*

University of California Press
Berkeley and Los Angeles, California
University of California Press, Ltd.
London, England

Library of Congress Cataloging in Publication Data

Taylor, Mark C   1945—
    Journeys to selfhood, Hegel and Kierkegaard.

    Bibliography: p. 277
    Includes index.
    1. Kierkegaard, Søren Aabye, 1813-1855.
    2. Hegel, Georg Wilhelm Friedrich, 1770-1831.
    3. Self (Philosophy)
    4. Individuation. I. Title.
B4378.S4T38   126   80-18802

Printed in the United States of America

1 2 3 4 5 6 7 8 9

For
Thelma Kathryn Cooper Taylor
and
Noel Alexander Taylor

CONTENTS

Acknowledgments

The real dwelling plight lies in this, that mortals
ever search anew for the nature of dwelling,
that they *must ever learn to dwell*. What if
man's homelessness consisted in this, that man
still does not even think of the *real* plight of
dwelling as *the* plight?
—*Heidegger*

This book represents a homecoming that is a leavetaking—at once an end and a beginning. The journey would not have been possible without the generous support of various institutions and the constant encouragement of family, friends, and colleagues. I wish to express my gratitude to the John Simon Guggenheim Memorial Foundation, the Deutscher Akademischer Austauschdienst, the Universities of Bochum, Freiburg, Heidelberg, and Copenhagen, and Williams College. My indebtedness to others is substantial; the I speaking in these pages is truly a we. To explain the unique contribution of each participant in this dialogue is both impossible and unnecessary. Naming alone speaks: Jørgen K. Bukdahl, John W. Chandler, Stephen Crites, Hermann Deuser, Ray L. Hart, Dieter Henrich, Gordon D. Kaufman, Peter Kemp, Rosemary Lane, H. Ganse Little, John D. Maguire, John A. Miles, Richard R. Niebuhr, Otto Pöggeler, George E. Rupp, Eileen Sahady, and Niels Thulstrup. To my family, Dinny, Aaron, and Kirsten, a special word of thanks for repeatedly reminding me that this project was important enough to complete, but not important enough to have completed sooner. And finally, my sincere appreciation to the two individuals without whom this sojourn never would have begun: my parents, Thelma and Noel Taylor, to whom this book is dedicated.

M. C. T.

Williams College
November 22, 1979

These are private words addressed to you in public.
T. S. Eliot

|1|

CONCLUDING PREFACE

In my beginning is my end. . . .
—*T. S. Eliot*

The result is the same as the beginning, only
because the *beginning* is the *end*. . . .
—*Hegel*

Only when reflection comes to a halt can a
beginning be made, and reflection can be
halted only by something else, and this something else is something quite different from the
logical, being a resolution of the will.
—*Kierkegaard*

BEGINNING

Introductions tend to be awkward, embarrassing affairs—coy games of hide-and-seek, revelation and concealment, appearance and disappearance. Mastering the art of beginning requires cultivating the ability to be sufficiently suggestive to interest and allure without becoming overt enough to bore and dissuade. Long explicit introductions usually are about as seductive as the people who offer them.

In matters philosophical and theological, where at least a semblance of argumentative rigor is to be expected, the problem of beginning is further compounded. Hegel begins his first major philosophical work, *Phenomenology of Spirit*, itself initially intended to be an introduction to his entire system, by pointing out the dilemma the philosopher faces.[1]

> It is customary to preface a work with an explanation of the author's aim, why he wrote the book, and the relationship in which he believes it to stand to earlier or contemporary treatises on the same subject. In the case of a philosophical work, however, such an explanation seems not only superfluous but, in view of the nature of the subject matter, even inappropriate and misleading. For whatever might appropriately be said about philosophy in a preface—perhaps a historical *assertion* of the main drift of the point of view, the general content and results, a string of random statements and assurances about truth—none of this can be accepted as the way in which to present philosophical truth.[2]

By forcing the author to state in an assertorial manner conclusions whose validity depends upon an argument yet to be unfolded, claims advanced in a preface appear to be as one-sided and debatable as the contrary viewpoints they seek to supplement or to correct. Such partiality seems to stand in tension with the systematic completeness that Hegel insists is characteristic of philosophical truth.

Though for quite different reasons, Kierkegaard is also wary of prefaces and introductions. Beginnings, he maintains, arise from the

---

1. The difficulties scholars have encountered in attempting to establish the proper relationship between the "introductory" *Phenomenology of Spirit* and the system as a whole amply illustrate Hegel's insistence on the complexity of the problem of beginning. This issue is probed in chaps. 3 and 6.

2. *Phenomenology of Spirit*, trans. A. V. Miller (New York: Oxford University Press, 1977), p. 1; 9. Hereafter cited as *Phenomenology*. Throughout this study I have, where necessary, altered or retranslated the English version of German texts. For the *Phenomenology* I have used Hoffmeister's edition, *Phänomenologie des Geistes* (Hamburg: Felix Meiner Verlag, 1952). Unless otherwise indicated, I have worked with the Suhrkamp edition: G. W. F. Hegel, *Werke*, 20 vols. (Frankfurt: Suhrkamp Verlag, 1969-1971). Notes to Hegel's writings include reference to the English edition, followed by citation of the corresponding German text.

abyss of free resolution, and consequently can be neither adequately understood nor satisfactorily explained. Creation, be it human or divine, is always *ex nihilo*. The freedom of beginning defies systematic comprehension. Moreover, the problem of beginning is particularly complex in the case of philosophical and theological works. Here, prefaces intended to aid the prospective reader by revealing the author's motive and purpose are especially misleading and inevitably disclose basic methodological confusion. The philosopher or theologian who attempts to explain his work in this direct manner mistakenly identifies essential meaning with authorial intention rather than with the effect wrought upon the reader by a decisive encounter with the written text.[3] Even if an author could fathom his own motivation, this consideration would be extrinsic to what Kierkegaard regards as the fundamental significance of the work. Under the guise of Johannes Climacus, Kierkegaard reflects upon his own authorship:

> It gives me pleasure to see that the pseudonyms, presumably aware of the relation subsisting between the method of indirect communication and the truth as inwardness, have themselves said nothing, nor misused a preface to assume an official attitude toward the production, as if an author were in a purely legal sense the best interpreter of his own words; or as if it could help a reader that an author had intended this or that, if it were not realized; or as if it were certain that it was realized because the author himself says so in the preface; . . . or as if an author were served by having a reader who precisely because of the author's clumsiness knew all about the book.[4]

For Kierkegaard, anticipatory summation breeds confusion. Philosophical and theological works ought to offer the reader an occasion for self-clarification and provide an opportunity for decisive response. In matters so closely related to human existence, meaning

---

3. Kierkegaard's analysis of this problem implies a critique of reductive modes of interpretation which anticipates the position formulated by Heidegger and developed most thoroughly by Gadamer. See Hans-Georg Gadamer, *Wahrheit und Methode: Grundzüge einer philosophischen Hermeneutik* (Tübingen: J. C. B. Mohr, 1965) and *Philosophical Hermeneutics*, trans. D. E. Linge (Berkeley, Los Angeles, London: University of California Press, 1976). Compare Paul Ricoeur's discussion of the relationship between the hermeneutics of suspicion and of belief in his *Freud and Philosophy: An Essay on Interpretation*, trans. D. Savage (New Haven: Yale University Press, 1970).

4. *Concluding Unscientific Postscript*, trans. David Swenson and Walter Lowrie (Princeton: Princeton University Press, 1968), pp. 225-226; 7:212. In checking and correcting the English translations of the Danish texts, I have used the following editions: *Søren Kierkegaards Samlede Værker*, ed. A. B. Drachmann, J. L. Heiberg, and H. O. Lange (Copenhagen: Gyldendalske Boghandel, 1901 ff.) and *Søren Kierkegaards Papirer*, ed. P. A. Heiberg, V. Kuhr, and E. Torsten (Copenhagen: Gyldendal, 1968 ff.). The Danish reference follows the English citation in each note. Both *Samlede Værker* and *Papirer* are cited in Arabic numerals.

and truth cannot be objectively expressed and directly communicated but must emerge indirectly through a subjective appropriation
process effected by each individual reader. Therefore philosophical
and theological writings are necessarily fragmentary, inconclusive,
open-ended, and unsystematic. Prefaces can suggest no conclusions,
summarize no results, for conclusions and results are unscientific
postscripts provided by the reader.

Despite the problematic nature of beginning, prefaces do have a
place in philosophical-historical studies of the sort undertaken in this
book. Even Hegel concedes that "since the presentation of a general
ideal in outline, before any attempt to follow it out in detail, makes
the latter easier to grasp, it may be useful at this point to give a
rough idea of it, at the same time taking the opportunity to get rid of
certain habits of thought which impede philosophical cognition."[5]
Our beginning is a "prefatory conclusion" in which we sketch the
"general idea in outline, before any attempt to follow it out in
detail," and identify the relationship of this investigation "to other
earlier or contemporary treatises on the subject." Preliminary reflection on beginning, however, underscores the abstract and incomplete
nature of the claims initially advanced. Beginning contains end as
purpose awaiting realization. The conclusion of the journey undertaken in this study will bring us back to our point of departure, for,
as Hegel recognizes, the true "is its own becoming, the circle that
presupposes its end as its aim and thus has it for its beginning."[6]
With Eliot,

> We shall not cease from exploration
> And the end of all our exploring
> Will be to arrive where we started
> And know the place for the first time.[7]

But if "the *beginning* is the *end*,"[8] the end must likewise be the
beginning.

> The end is where we start from. And every phrase
> And sentence that is right (where every word is
>   at home ...)
> Every phrase and sentence is an end and a beginning. ...[9]

---

5. *Phenomenology*, p. 9; 19.
6. Ibid., p. 10; 20.
7. T. S. Eliot, *Little Gidding*, Collected Poems, *1909-1962* (London: Faber and
Faber, 1963), p. 222.
8. *Phenomenology*, p. 12; 22.
9. T. S. Eliot, *Little Gidding*, p. 221.

Thus, while our beginning is a "concluding preface," our end will be a "prefatory conclusion."

JOURNEYS TO SELFHOOD

"Our hearts, O Lord," confessed Augustine, "are restless till they find their rest in Thee."[10] From the time of Augustine's account of human existence as a pilgrimage from sin to salvation, from the city of man to the city of God, Christians have imagined their lives to be a journey and have viewed themselves as sojourners. Life, as Frank Kermode suggests, is lived in the "middest,"[11] betwixt'n between Genesis and Apocalypse, creation and redemption. To represent experience as such a spiritual journey is to "map"[12] the time of biblical history onto the time of one's own life; it is "to internalize apocalypse by transferring the theatre of events from the outer earth and heaven to the spirit of the single believer, in which there enacts itself, metaphorically, the entire eschatological drama of destruction of the old creation, the union with Christ, and the emergence of a new creation—not *in illud tempus* but here and now in this life."[13] "The Pharisees asked Him, 'When will the kingdom of God come?' He said, 'The kingdom of God is not coming with signs to be observed; nor will they say, "Lo here it is!" or "there it is!"; for in fact the kingdom of God is in the midst of you' " (Luke 17:20-21). From this perspective Christ is envisioned as the way and life as wayfaring—*imitatio*: Anthropos becoming microcosmos and cosmos becoming macroanthropos. The inwardization of the apocalyptic drama consummates the wedding of *Heilsgeschichte* and *Bildungsgeschichte*, the union of Bridegroom and Bride.[14]

To comprehend human existence in these terms is to discover the "narrative quality of experience"[15] through a process of recollecting the chapters of one's spiritual autobiography. Though the life of the

---

10. Augustine, *The Confessions*, trans. J. G. Pilkington, in *The Basic Writings of Saint Augustine*, ed. W. J. Oates (New York: Random House, 1948), p. 1.

11. Frank Kermode, *The Sense of an Ending: Studies in the Theory of Fiction* (New York: Oxford University Press, 1975).

12. John Donne, *The Way of All the Earth* (New York: Macmillan Co., 1972).

13. M. H. Abrams, *Natural Supernaturalism: Tradition and Revolution in Romantic Literature* (New York: W. W. Norton and Co., 1971), p. 47. I have been instructed in many ways by Abrams's brilliant study and have drawn on it directly and indirectly throughout this investigation.

14. Ibid., pp. 188 ff.

15. Stephen Crites, "The Narrative Quality of Experience," *Journal of the American Academy of Religion* 39 (1971), 291-311. Crites's original and provocative discussion bears careful analysis.

wayfarer is inexpugnably temporal, experience need not be a chaotic succession of unintelligible occurrences, but can be informed, or- dered, patterned, plotted. As H. Richard Niebuhr points out, "to be a self is to have a god; to have a god is to have a history, that is, events connected in a meaningful pattern; to have one god is to have one history."[16] The particular images, metaphors, and symbols used to plot the labor through the *Stationen des Weges*[17] or the *Stadier paa Livets Vei*[18] vary considerably from period to period and from author to author. In an important sense, however, the story line re- mains constant. Variations are symphonic modulations of an ever re- curring theme. *Heimweb* becoming *Heimweg*—prodigals returning. The Alpha and the Omega of the pilgrimage remain the sojourner's own self. The story narrates the pilgrim's progress from sin to salvation, despair to faith, sickness to health, death to life, darkness to light, corruption to purity, dissipation to integration, ignorance to knowl- edge, spiritlessness to spirit. For such wayfarers, the world becomes "the vale of Soul-making."[19] Pilgrims repeatedly confess the narrow- ness of the way and the difficulty of the passage. But the persistence of the struggle reveals that "the life of spirit is not the life that shrinks from death and keeps itself untouched by devastation, but rather the life that endures it and maintains itself in it. It wins its truth only when, in utter dismemberment, it finds itself."[20]

The journey to selfhood, so deeply rooted in the Christian tradi- tion, has assumed renewed vitality marked by seemingly increased urgency in modern times. As individuals become more and more deeply entangled in a rapidly changing and ever more diverse world, the business of soul-making appears to be at once more pressing and less certain than in earlier eras. Change becomes an abiding feature of experience and raises doubts that obscure guideposts that previously had directed journeying pilgrims. Sojourners, left to wander aim- lessly, are stricken with a sense of homelessness and can confess little

---

16. H. Richard Niebuhr, *The Meaning of Revelation* (New York: Macmillan Co., 1967), p. 59.

17. In a self-conscious allusion to the *Leidenstationen*, the stations of the cross, Hegel used this phrase to describe the *Phenomenology*. See Hoffmeister's introduction to his edition of *Phänomenologie des Geistes*, p. xxxviii.

18. This is the title of the only work in which Kierkegaard explores each of the major stages of existence.

19. John Keats, *The Letters of John Keats*, ed. H. B. Forman (London: Reeves and Turner, 1895), p. 326. For an interesting contemporary elaboration of this point see James Hillman, *Re-visioning Psychology* (New York: Harper and Row, 1975).

20. *Phenomenology*, p. 19; 29-30.

more than *dubito ergo sum*. Yeats captures the mood of many moderns when he writes:

> Turning and turning in the widening gyre
> The falcon cannot hear the falconer;
> Things fall apart; the center cannot hold;
> Mere anarchy is loosed upon the world.[21]

And, we must add, upon the self.

The peculiarity of the modern dilemma is, at least in part, of our own making. Writing toward the turn of the last century, Friedrich Schiller developed what since has become an extremely influential analysis of the impact of industrial society upon individual persons. Casting a wistful glance toward Periclean Athens, Schiller explains that the

> character of the Greek states, in which every individual enjoyed an independent existence but could, when need arose, grow into the whole organism, now made way for an ingenious clock-work, in which, out of the piecing together of innumerable but lifeless parts, a mechanical kind of collective life ensues. State and Church, laws and customs, were now torn asunder; enjoyment was separated from labor, the means from the end, the effort from the reward. Everlastingly chained to a single little fragment of the whole, man himself develops into nothing but a fragment; everlastingly in his ear the monotonous sound of the wheel that he turns, he never develops the harmony of his being, and instead of putting the stamp of humanity upon his own nature, he becomes nothing more than the imprint of his occupation or of his specialized knowledge.[22]

Enslaved by his own creations, man's experience is fragmented, his self dissipated. To use a term whose popularization frequently obscures its precise philosophical meaning, man becomes alienated, estranged from self and world.[23]

In the twentieth century the journey to selfhood has taken a variety of forms. Exclusively religious perspectives increasingly have given way to categories of self-interpretation shaped by modern philosophy, science, and social science: the existential quest for authen-

---

21. W. B. Yeats, "The Second Coming," in *The Collected Poems of W. B. Yeats* (New York: Macmillan Co., 1956), p. 184.

22. Friedrich Schiller, *On The Aesthetic Education of Man in a Series of Letters*, trans. E. M. Wilkinson and L. A. Willoughby (New York: Oxford University Press, 1967), p. 35. As we shall see in chaps. 2 and 3, Hegel was deeply impressed by Schiller's analysis of modernity.

23. Although the term *alienation* or *self-alienation* originally derives from Stoic philosophy, Hegel gives the category its uniquely modern definition.

ticity; the Marxist pursuit of social revolution; the psychoanalytic search for a therapeutic method. Despite obvious and often superficial differences, such secularized searches for self bear the mark of their common spiritual ancestor: biblical pilgrimage. Life continues to be understood as a journey whose way leads from sickness to health, *salus*, salvation. While not always fully aware of it, latter-day wayfarers frequently engage in a process of rewriting Script-ure.

> The poem of the mind in the act of finding
> What will suffice. It has not always had
> To find: the scene was set; it repeated what
> Was in the script.
>   Then the theatre was changed
> To something else. Its past was a souvenir.
> It has to be living, to learn the speech of the place.[24]

The difficulty of the way and the obscurity or absence of any guiding script notwithstanding, many individuals seem to agree with Walker Percy's "moviegoer," Binx Bolling, when he concludes: "The search is what anyone would undertake if he were not sunk in the everydayness of his own life. . . . To become aware of the possibility of the search is to be onto something. Not to be onto something is to be in despair."[25]

HEGEL AND KIERKEGAARD

Few thinkers have contributed more to shaping the modern sense of self than the German philosopher G. W. F. Hegel (1770-1831) and the Danish philosopher-theologian Søren Kierkegaard (1813-1855). In the years immediately following his death, it appeared unlikely that Hegel's influence would be so lasting. Writing in 1844, the biographer Karl Rosenkranz commented on the response to Hegel's philosophy: "One would have to be astounded by the vehemence with which it is attacked precisely by those who declare it dead."[26] Such criticism was not one-sided but was leveled from both left and right

---

24. Wallace Stevens, "Of Modern Poetry," in *The Collected Poems of Wallace Stevens* (New York: Knopf, 1972), pp. 239-240.

25. Walker Percy, *The Moviegoer* (New York: Knopf, 1961). Percy has been profoundly influenced by Kierkegaard: see Bradley Dewey, "Walker Percy Talks about Kierkegaard: An Annotated Interview," *Journal of the American Academy of Religion* 54 (1974), 273-298.

26. Karl Rosenkranz, *Georg Wilhelm Friedrich Hegel's Leben: Supplement zu Hegel's Werken* (Berlin: Duncker und Humblot, 1844), p. xii. Quoted in Emil Fackenheim, *The Religious Dimension of Hegel's Thought* (Bloomington: Indiana University Press, 1967), p. 4.

ends of the intellectual spectrum. Subsequent history, however, has supported Lichtenberg's shrewd observation: "To do just the opposite is also a form of imitation." Hegel's impact on twentieth-century life and thought has, for the most part, been mediated by left-wing critics such as Ludwig Feuerbach, Arnold Ruge, Max Stirner, Bruno Bauer, David Friedrich Strauss, and, most importantly, Karl Marx. The ongoing Marxist critique of Hegelianism should not obscure the fact that Marx's interpretation of *homo oeconomicus* would have been impossible apart from the philosophical foundation laid by Hegel. Marx's implicit and explicit appropriation of tenets initially advanced by Hegel has been a crucial factor in firmly establishing Hegel's significance for our time. Nevertheless, the influence of Hegel cannot be restricted to Marx's use and abuse of his ideas. The breadth and complexity of Hegel's system have made it a continuing source of insight for authors of various persuasions who are preoccupied with a wide range of problems. The pioneering work of Hegel has left an indelible impress upon areas of inquiry as distinct as the history of philosophy and religion, sociology, phenomenology, hermeneutics, existentialism, structuralism, and liberal Protestantism. As is so often the case with a truly great thinker, Hegel's philosophy has forced later generations to recast the very terms in which they pose their questions. Though not as extensive, Kierkegaard's influence has been no less significant. Largely ignored in his own day, Kierkegaard's writings surfaced during the early decades of this century to become a dominant intellectual and social force. Nowhere is the importance of Kierkegaard's seminal work more evident than in the fields of philosophy and theology. The rediscovery of fundamental Kierkegaardian themes by Martin Heidegger and Jean-Paul Sartre played an essential role in the development of one of the most innovative post-Enlightenment movements of thought—existentialism. Throughout the period of the World Wars, philosophers, psychologists, and artists drew freely on Kierkegaard's insight in an effort to arrive at a distinctively modern interpretation of the human condition. The theological analogue to existential philosophy is neo-orthodox theology. When Karl Barth sounded his epoch-making *"Nein!"* (*The Epistle to the Romans*, 1919) in the face of then dominant *Kultur-Protestantismus*, Kierkegaard's voice was sounding in the not too distant background.[27] Though Barth was less inclined to

---

27. For a very helpful account of this frequently misunderstood chapter of European intellectual history see George Rupp, *Culture-Protestantism: German Liberal Theology at the Turn of the Twentieth Century* (Missoula, Mont.: Scholars Press, 1977).

draw on Kierkegaard after his decisive shift in 1930, Kierkegaard continued to guide theological reflection indirectly through the work of Rudolph Bultmann. Bultmann's version of neo-orthodoxy rests upon Heidegger's creative reformulation of central features of Kierkegaard's point of view. To numerous individuals struggling to come to terms with the dislocations and incongruities of twentieth-century experience, Kierkegaard's prophetic vision has proved compelling.

It would be a mistake, however, to view the legacy of Hegel and Kierkegaard solely in terms of their contribution to intellectual history. Their work is not so far removed from the vitality and confusion of everyday life. The ideas of Hegel and Kierkegaard so pervade the modern mind that they have transformed the way in which many people understand themselves and live their lives. All too often this influence is so subtle that it goes undetected. But to the tutored eye the continuing importance of these two extraordinary nineteenth-century figures is clearly visible. To understand ourselves is, at least in part, to comprehend the worlds of, and the world created by the thought of, Hegel and Kierkegaard. While Hegel is the genius whose vision inspires recent forms of socialism, Kierkegaard remains the greatest theoretician of contemporary individualism. From this perspective Hegel and Kierkegaard define the poles between which most moderns are destined to journey to selfhood.

Despite the enduring significance of the work of Hegel and Kierkegaard, the relationship between their philosophical and theological positions has rarely been the subject of careful and thorough discussion. Though the reasons for this oversight are many, the very nature of their writings is surely partly to blame. The works of Hegel and Kierkegaard are so extensive and so complex that often the effort to deal adequately with one or the other body of literature is a sufficiently demanding task for the aspiring analyst. Not uncommonly the price exacted by the prolonged study necessary to master the Hegelian or Kierkegaardian corpus is the conversion of the interpreter into a disciple. Frequently such devotion brings with it a blurring of evaluative vision. Criticism becomes heresy and commentary degenerates into justification. These developments render impossible the creation of a responsible dialogue between the contrasting positions of the two authors. As a result of such tendencies the philosophical and theological issues joining and separating Hegel and Kierkegaard have too long been shrouded in a mist of partisan polemics. Their points of view are often unintentionally misinterpreted or purposefully misrepresented.

To some extent this unfortunate situation is a consequence of Kierkegaard's own works. Throughout his diverse writings Kierkegaard's barbed and often vehement attacks on Hegel are couched in terms of witticisms, aphorisms, and fragmentary asides. Having understood the contradiction of a systematic critique of systematic thought, Kierkegaard assiduously avoids direct Hegel commentary. The opponent of the system must proceed ironically and humorously, writing philosophical fragments and concluding unscientific postscripts in which he points to discontinuities and contradictions where others believe they see continuities and mediations. The problem with systematizers who attempt all-inclusive explanations is that they do not see that the joke is on them. "If there be such a thing as a Danish philosophy," Kierkegaard writes, "it will differ from the German in not beginning with nothing. Neither will it be presuppositionless, nor explain everything by mediation. Let it rather begin with the sentence, 'There are many things in heaven and earth which no philosopher has explained.' "[28] More often than not, Kierkegaard's comments serve to obscure the significance and to oversimplify the nature of his relation to Hegel. This effect, of course, is not unintended. As Emil Fackenheim points out, "if thinkers such as Marx and Kierkegaard attack Hegel, it is not because he is irrelevant or absurd, but rather because he is too close for comfort."[29] But what Fackenheim and so many others do not seem to recognize is that Kierkegaard, at least, understands this all too well. Expressing his debt to Hegel, Kierkegaard goes so far as to admit:

> I feel what for me at times is an enigmatic respect for Hegel; I have learned much from him, and I know very well that I can still learn much more from him when I return to him again. . . . His philosophical knowledge, his amazing learning, the insight of his genius, and everything else good that can be said of a philosopher I am willing to acknowledge as any disciple. Yet, no, not *acknowledge*—that is too distinguished an expression—willing to admire, learn from him.[30]

---

28. *Søren Kierkegaard's Journals and Papers*, trans. Howard and Edna Hong (Bloomington: Indiana University Press, 1967 ff.), 3299; 5:A 46. My citations to the English translation of Kierkegaard's Journals list the *number* of the selection in the Hong translation, followed by the reference to the Danish *Papirer*.

29. Fackenheim, *Religious Dimension*, p. 7.

30. *Journals and Papers*, 1608; 6:B 54. 12.

To be sure, Kierkegaard uses what he learns to develop a spiritual vision that stands in tension with important aspects of Hegel's system. But evident differences distinguishing the viewpoints of Hegel and Kierkegaard should not overshadow the profound and, in many ways, more interesting similarities they share. Kierkegaard's ostensibly hostile response to Hegel conforms to what literary critic Harold Bloom labels "poetic misprision"—the willful misreading of an antecedent author which has as its purpose the formulation of a "creative correction."[31] Always aware of his role as a "corrective," Kierkegaard, unlike so many of his detractors and supporters, realizes that his own work would have been neither possible nor necessary apart from Hegel's philosophical system.

In the following pages we shall explore the intricate relationship between the positions of Hegel and Kierkegaard by developing a comparative analysis of their philosophical and theological perspectives. The inquiry is guided by the conviction that the distinctive features differentiating their viewpoints can emerge clearly only within the framework of their shared presuppositions, assumptions, and intentions. Briefly stated, the relationship between these two great dialecticians is itself thoroughly dialectical.

Hegel and Kierkegaard regard their work as the outgrowth of and response to dominant intellectual tendencies and social forces of the day. Their common point of departure is the development of a diagnosis of the philosophical, religious, and existential ills they believe to be plaguing their time. Their common destination is the formulation of a prescription to remedy what they regard as the sickness of the age. Hegel and Kierkegaard agree that the malaise peculiar to modernity is "spiritlessness"[32]—the condition of self-alienation or estrangement in which authentic selfhood remains unrealized and seems unrealizable. Behind this common diagnosis, however, lurk conflicting interpretations of the nature of the illness. Hegel insists that modern man faces the difficult task of finding the way from fragmentation and disintegration among and within individuals to a harmonious intra- and interpersonal unification or integration. Kierkegaard concludes that the way to selfhood in nineteenth-century Europe requires the negation of the dissipation of concrete existence

---

31. Harold Bloom, *The Anxiety of Influence: A Theory of Poetry* (New York: Oxford University Press, 1973), pp. 19, 30.

32. Hegel uses the German expression *das Geistlose*, and Kierkegaard the Danish term *Aandløshed*. As the argument progresses, it will become apparent that this category is an unusually useful "bridge concept" that facilitates a comparison of Hegel's and Kierkegaard's apparently different positions on a broad range of topics.

which results from the thoroughgoing identification of the individual with the sociocultural milieu through a long process of distinguishing person and world. While Hegel calls for a movement from oppositional differentiation to reconciliation of self and other, Kierkegaard stresses the importance of advancing from nondifferentiation to differentiation of self and other. For both, nonetheless, the question becomes: How can spiritlessness be cured? How can the movement, development, advance necessary for the realization of spirit be facilitated? In the confusing theater of modernity whose strange scenery obscures the way and where innovative playwrights constantly revise the script, how *is* one to journey to selfhood?

The difficult and seemingly abstract philosophical writings of Hegel and Kierkegaard are, in large measure, extended efforts to answer this fundamental question. The central thesis underlying our investigation is that Hegel and Kierkegaard develop alternative phenomenologies of spirit that are designed to lead the reader from inauthentic to authentic or fully realized selfhood.[33] While Hegel undertakes this task explicitly in his *Phenomenology of Spirit*, Kierkegaard unfolds his analysis indirectly in a series of pseudonymous writings composed over a period of years. Although the styles of the two authors differ widely, their methodological procedures share important features. Hegel's *Phenomenology* and Kierkegaard's pseudonymous writings present detailed interpretations of various figures of spirit, shapes of consciousness, forms of existence, or types of selfhood. In both cases the contrasting spiritual configurations are elaborated in a dialectical progression that advances from less complete to more complete forms of life. The structure of and movement through Hegel's *Stationen des Weges* and Kierkegaard's *Stadier paa Livets Vei* display many suggestive parallels. We shall examine in considerable detail the striking similarities and significant differences in the courses they map.

It is essential to stress at the outset of our exploration of the journeys to selfhood plotted by Hegel and Kierkegaard that though both authors are acutely aware of the serious existential dilemmas posed by the modern experience of spiritlessness, the contrasting therapies they propose are profoundly influenced by their respec-

---

33. This is not, of course, to reduce their writings to this single issue. Certainly these works are too rich and diverse to be viewed simply in terms of any one theme. But I shall attempt to demonstrate that the effort to define the structure and development of genuine selfhood is a central concern of both Hegel and Kierkegaard and forms an effective point of comparison for their overall positions.

tive interpretations and appropriations of certain elements in the Christian tradition. Most important for our purposes, Hegel and Kierkegaard see an inextricable bond between Christology and anthropology. Each, in his own way, maintains that the central figure of the Christian religion is, in some sense, revelatory of authentic human existence. Jesus embodies and discloses the normative structure of selfhood to be realized in the life of the believer. Consequently, for Hegel and for Kierkegaard the journey to selfhood is a spiritual pilgrimage that reenacts "the entire eschatological drama of destruction of the old creation, the union with Christ, and the emergence of a new creation."[34] The wayfarer's *imitatio Christi* becomes a recollection or a repetition of the way charted by Jesus. The end of the sojourn is the reconciliation of the Heilsgeschichte of the Pattern and the Bildungsgeschichte of His follower. Only in this union can the journey to selfhood find its completion.

The recognition of the deep-going similarities between the philosophical projects of Hegel and Kierkegaard must not, however, obfuscate the basic differences between their contrasting positions. In the final analysis their journeys lead in different directions. What Hegel regards as self-realization Kierkegaard sees as self-alienation, and what Hegel interprets as self-estrangement is for Kierkegaard self-fulfillment. Conversely, what Kierkegaard views as authentic selfhood Hegel believes to be inauthentic selfhood, and what Kierkegaard sees as inauthenticity is for Hegel authenticity. Kierkegaard believes Hegel's "voyage of discovery"[35] to be an odyssey back to "the Fatherland . . . whence we have come."[36] The course of this latter-day Odysseus is "immer nach Hause,"[37] his compass a philosophy that is "eigentlich Heimweh—Trieb überall zu Hause."[38] For Hegel, Kierkegaard's lonely sojourner remains estranged, "a stranger on

---

34. Abrams, *Natural Supernaturalism*, p. 47. See above, text corresponding to n. 14.

35. Hegel uses this phrase to describe the *Phenomenology*.

36. This is a quotation from Plotinus's commentary on Odysseus's plea in the *Iliad* (2. 140): "Let us flee then to the beloved Fatherland," See Plotinus, *The Six Enneads* (trans. S. MacKenna and B. S. Page [Chicago: Encyclopaedia Britannica, 1952] 1.6.8.) For a very helpful discussion of the considerable influence of Plotinus and Neoplatonism on Hegel see Abrams, *Natural Supernaturalism*, pp. 146-154. Abrams underscores the importance of this particular text from Plotinus for many nineteenth-century romantics and idealists.

37. Novalis, *Heinrich von Ofterdingen*.

38. Novalis, *Briefe und Werke* (Berlin, 1943), 3:172. Theodor Haering claims that Novalis's poetry is a direct precursor of Hegel's philosophy: see his *Hegel: Sein Wollen und sein Werk*, vol. 1 (Leipzig: B. G. Teubner, 1929). For other helpful accounts of the relation between Novalis and Hegel see Abrams, *Natural Supernaturalism*, p. 195, and Jack Forstman, *A Romantic Triangle: Schleiermacher and Early German Romanticism* (Missoula, Mont.: Scholars Press, 1977), pp. 47 ff.

earth, a stranger to the soil and to men alike."[39] With Abraham he cries, "Ich bin nicht zu Hause."[40] Condemned to suffer the homesickness born of exile and wandering in a foreign land, the faithful servant believes "finite experience as such is homeless."[41] For neither philosopher does the other's journey to selfhood lead to salvation, the realization of the authentic form of existence revealed in the person and life of Christ. Stranded either in the peaceful groves of Athens or on the frightful heights of Moriah, the pilgrim fails to reach Calvary, where peace is found amid the most frightful spiritual tensions.

The elaboration and support of this interpretation of the relationship between Hegel and Kierkegaard will require a detailed investigation of their most important philosophical and theological writings. Clearly the scope of this undertaking precludes a complete analysis of the entire corpus of each author. We shall restrict our attention to those works that bear most directly on the issue of the structure and development of selfhood. In the case of Hegel, we shall concentrate primarily on the *Phenomenology of Spirit*. As recent Hegel scholarship has increasingly realized,[42] however, the argument of the *Phenomenology* is undergirded by logical principles Hegel identifies during his years in Jena and elaborates most completely in his mature *Science of Logic*.[43] Therefore, any adequate understanding of Hegel's view of the structure of spirit and the dialectic of its actualization presupposes a satisfactory grasp of the fundaments of his speculative logic.[44] My brief remarks about the close connection

---

39. Hegel describes Abraham in these terms: see "The Spirit of Christiantiy and Its Fate," in *Early Theological Writings*, trans. T. M. Knox (Philadelphia: University of Pennsylvania Press, 1971), p. 186.

40. I borrow this phrase from Heidegger.

41. William James, *Pragmatism*. Quoted in Abrams, *Natural Supernaturalism*, p. 197.

42. The relation between the *Phenomenology* and the *Science of Logic* has been the subject of lively debate in Hegel scholarship. Discussions of this problem in the German literature have been particularly helpful. The most important studies include Wolfgang Bonsiepen, *Der Begriff der Negativität in den Jenaer Schriften Hegels*, Hegel-Studien, Beiheft 16 (Bonn: Bouvier Verlag Herbert Grundmann, 1977); H. F. Fulda, *Das Problem einer Einleitung in Hegels Wissenschaft der Logik* (Frankfurt: Suhrkamp Verlag, 1965); Dieter Henrich, *Hegel im Kontext* (Frankfurt: Suhrkamp Verlag, 1971); and Otto Pöggeler, *Hegels Idee einer Phänomenologie des Geistes* (Munich: Alber, 1973).

43. Throughout the text I indicate the *Wissenschaft der Logik* with the abbreviation *Logic*, and refer to the first part of *The Encyclopaedia of the Philosophical Sciences* as the *Lesser Logic*.

44. This reading of Hegel implies a greater continuity between his earlier and later work than is commonly assumed in much of the secondary literature. Although it is clear that there are noteworthy developments in Hegel's thinking, it is misleading to oppose the young enthusiastic supporter of the French Revolution to the old conservative defender of the Prussian state. For further discussion of this issue see chaps. 2 and 6.

Hegel sees between Christology and selfhood underscore the need to examine aspects of his interpretation of the Christian tradition. Although Hegel analyzes Christianity in the *Phenomenology*, his remarks are so condensed that they remain frustratingly cryptic. Hence, if we are to understand Hegelian Christology, it will be necessary to draw on the more extended discussions in the *Lectures on the Philosophy of Religion* and the *Philosophy of History*. Our consideration of Kierkegaard will focus chiefly on his pseudonymous writings.[45] It is apparent that the edifying discourses, *Papirer*, and more popular writings contribute significantly to our understanding of Kierkegaard's position. But his most important philosophical and theological ideas receive their fullest treatment in the pseudonymous literature.[46] Viewed as a whole, the diverse pseudonymous writings form a coherent analysis of what Kierkegaard believes to be the stages on life's way.[47]

The overriding concern to establish a dialogue between Hegel and Kierkegaard in which their philosophical similarities and differences emerge constantly will guide the selection of texts to be studied and problems to be examined.[48] Much of interest and importance in the

45. The pseudonymous literature, written and published under various names between 1841 and 1850, consists of nine major works: *Either-Or, Fear and Trembling, The Concept of Dread Repetition, Philosophical Fragments, Stages on Life's Way, Concluding Unscientific Postscript, The Sickness unto Death,* and *Training in Christianity.* The first seven of these works make up the chief part of the literature. *Concluding Unscientific Postscript* was originally intended to complete the pseudonymous writings. Here Kierkegaard, for the first time, publicly acknowledges that he is the author of the other pseudonymous works. But this admission does not come until the end of the book, and throughout the text itself, Kierkegaard treats the other works as if he were not their author. The last two pseudonymous writings, *The Sickness unto Death* and *Training in Christianity*, were published under the name of Anti-Climacus (vs. Johannes Climacus, the fictitious author of *Philosophical Fragments* and the *Postscript*) and represent a more explicitly Christian point of view than the first seven.

46. In the first chapter of *Kierkegaard's Pseudonymous Authorship: A Study of Time and the Self* (Princeton: Princeton University Press, 1975), I have presented a more extensive rationale for this procedure and have contrasted this method with different approaches illustrated in the vast secondary literature.

47. This line of argument represents an effort to find a mean between the extremes of viewing the pseudonymous literature as either systematically integrated or deliberately disorganized. For an example of the former approach see Paul Sponheim, *Kierkegaard on Christ and Christian Coherence* (New York: Harper and Row, 1968). The latter point of view is exemplified by Josiah Thompson's *Kierkegaard* (New York: Knopf, 1973), and "The Master of Irony," in *Kierkegaard: A Collection of Critical Essays,* ed. J. Thompson (New York: Doubleday and Co., 1972), pp. 103-163.

48. It is important to stress the obvious point that while Kierkegaard presents a lengthy account and critique of the Hegelian system, Hegel had no opportunity to respond to Kierkegaard's point of view. In attempting to create the ensuing exchange, I shall try to reconstruct the manner in which Hegel most likely would have interpreted Kierkegaard's position. The best guide in this undertaking is Hegel's phenomenological analysis of forms of experience similar to those Kierkegaard describes in his pseudonymous writings.

rich writings of each author must of necessity go undiscussed. Moreover, the search for a common ground of comparison always runs the risk of creating artificial juxtaposition or strained relations between these two intellectual titans. Doubtless our method of proceeding opens us to attack from at least two sides: for Hegelians we render Hegel too Kierkegaardian, and for Kierkegaardians we cast Kierkegaard in too Hegelian a light. As I have suggested, however, when treating dialecticians as subtle as Hegel and Kierkegaard, we must proceed dialectically. The threat of double assault cannot be avoided.

It should be evident that the interpretation of the Hegel-Kierkegaard relationship developed in this book stands in tension with most other treatments of the topic. By way of concluding this preface, it might prove helpful to fulfill the second requirement Hegel identifies as essential to any adequate introduction: the explanation of the relation of the present inquiry to "earlier or contemporary treatises on the subject."[49]

We have noted that secondary literature devoted to comparing and contrasting the positions of Hegel and Kierkegaard tends to be highly polemical. Either Hegel is viewed through the eyes of his Danish critic, or Kierkegaard's worst fears are confirmed and his insights are reduced to a paragraph in an all-encompassing Hegelian perspective. The most extensive treatment of the issue yet to have appeared is Niels Thulstrup's *Kierkegaards forhold til Hegel og til den spekulative Idealisme indtil 1846.*[50] Thulstrup's book presents a helpful account of the intellectual climate of Kierkegaard's Denmark. His discussion of usually ignored nineteenth-century authors such as Heiberg, Sibbern, Clausen, Martensen, and Poul Møller makes it possible to understand more completely Kierkegaard's response to Hegelianism in general and to Danish Hegelians in particular. When Thulstrup turns his attention to Kierkegaard's relation to Hegel him-

---

49. My remarks at this point are not intended to offer anything like a complete consideration of the material available on this subject. My purpose is to set this study in the context of the most important previous treatments of Hegel and Kierkegaard and to indicate different works that exemplify the range of *typical* approaches to the problem. There will be more specific discussion of relevant secondary works in the following pages.

50. Niels Thulstrup, *Kierkegaards forhold til Hegel og til den spekulative Idealisme indtil 1846* (Copenhagen: Gyldendal, 1967). An English translation recently has been published: *Kierkegaard's Relation to Hegel*, trans. Stengren (Princeton: Princeton University Press, 1980). Related works by Thulstrup include "Kierkegaard og den filosofiske Idealisme," *Kierkegaardiana* 4 (1962), 88-104; "Le désaccord entre Kierkegaard et Hegel," *Kierkegaard-Studiet* 4 (1964), 112-124; and "Søren Kierkegaard, historien de la philosophie de Hegel," *Tijdschrift voor Filosofie* 27 (1965), 521-572. In a second volume Thulstrup presents a summary of previous studies of Hegel and Kierkegaard: *Kierkegaards Verhältnis zu Hegel: Forschungsgeschichte* (Stuttgart: W. Kohlhammer, 1969).

self, however, his analysis is less useful and more problematic. He summarizes the primary conclusion of his argument when he writes: "Hegel and Kierkegaard have in the main nothing in common as thinkers, neither as regards object, purpose or method, nor as regards what were for each indisputable principles. This can be designated as this investigation's chief and major thesis."[51] Thulstrup defends this claim largely through the collation of the critical remarks Kierkegaard directed against Hegel in his published writings and private journal and papers up to 1846. While such a chronological approach lends an element of thoroughness to Thulstrup's study, the absence of any systematic or thematic focus creates a bothersome lack of coherence in the book as a whole. More disturbing, however, is the tendency throughout the work to view Hegel from Kierkegaard's perspective. Thulstrup's understanding of Hegel's system has been decisively shaped by his appropriation of Kierkegaard's insights and by his reading of Ivan Iljin's controversial right-wing interpretation of Hegel spelled out in *Die Philosophie Hegels als kontemplative Gotteslehre.*[52] As a result, Thulstrup's discussion never advances from a recounting of the obvious differences separating Hegel and Kierkegaard to reflection upon the deeper philosophical and theological issues at stake in the encounter.[53]

Hegel scholars have shown remarkably little interest in or understanding of Kierkegaard's writings. It would seem that most students of Hegel agree with Walter Kaufmann's indefensible assertion that "Kierkegaard did not understand Hegel."[54] Richard Bernstein's discussion of Kierkegaard in *Praxis and Action: Contemporary Philoso-*

---

51. Thulstrup, *Kierkegaard's Relation to Hegel*, p. 12.

52. Ivan A. Iljin, *Die Philosophie Hegels als kontemplative Gotteslehre*, trans. I. A. Iljin (Bern: A Francke Verlag, 1946). For further indication of Thulstrup's reading of Hegel see his short book, *Hegel* (Copenhagen: G. E. C. Gads Forlag, 1967). Fackenheim's discussion of the "Hegelian middle" (*Religious Dimension*, pp. 75-115) is very helpful when one is attempting to avoid the errors of right-wing readings of Hegel such as those represented by Iljin and Thulstrup and left-wing interpretations such as the one developed by Alexandre Kojève (see n. 64 below).

53. Thulstrup's book is the best representative of the approach to the Hegel-Kierkegaard controversy which is most common in the secondary literature. Even the brief remarks expressed in this introductory chapter indicate the very different orientation of the present work. The full extent of my disagreement with this recurrent view of Hegel and Kierkegaard can emerge only in the course of the study as a whole.

54. Walter Kaufmann, *Hegel: Reinterpretation, Texts, and Commentary* (New York: Doubleday and Co., 1965), pp. 85, 289 f. Richard Kroner anticipates Kaufmann's conclusion when he claims that "Kierkegaard never understood Hegel": see "Kierkegaards 'Hegel-Verständnis,' " *Kant-Studien* 46 (1954-55), 19-27. Kaufmann bases his conclusion on the assertion that Kierkegaard's knowledge and critique of Hegel derive from Schelling's 1840-41 Berlin lectures, rather than from a direct knowledge of Hegel's own texts. This

phies of Human Activity is illustrative of the propensity of commentators to attempt to answer questions raised in the Hegel-Kierkegaard debate by trying to place Kierkegaard's point of view within the Hegelian dialectic.[55] When this is done, Kierkegaard is regarded as a paradigm of Hegel's notion of the unhappy consciousness. Kierkegaard's inability to progress to further stages of spiritual development described by Hegel is seen as a manifestation of continuing self-alienation. Usually this approach aims at the perfunctory dismissal of Kierkegaard rather than at a serious exploration of his relation to Hegel.[56] But Sartre's contention that "Kierkegaard makes Hegel's system lie by showing that a past form of consciousness can be reborn"[57] should at least raise the suspicion that matters are not quite as neat and simple as these Hegelian critics would like to believe.[58]

Analysts who attempt to establish a positive relation between Hegel and Kierkegaard often concentrate on the early works of each author. The young Hegel is presented as a virtual Kierkegaardian, and the early Kierkegaard is described as a budding Hegelian. As if to underscore Löwith's claim that "the criticism of the Young Hegelians repeated the crisis which Hegel himself had gone through before overcoming it in his system,"[59] Jean Wahl presents insightful discus-

---

position cannot be supported by a careful study of Kierkegaard's intellectual biography. In fact, Kierkegaard was deeply disappointed with Schelling's lectures. He found little new in them and soon ceased attending them. His acquaintance with Schelling's lectures came through reading notes taken by other students. Kaufmann's position represents a common tendency to exaggerate the importance of the late Schelling for the development of Kierkegaard's thought, a tendency that is chiefly the consequence of Tillich's preoccupation with Schelling. See, for example, Paul Tillich, "Estrangement and Reconciliation in Modern Thought," *Review of Religion* 9 (1944), 5-19; idem, "Existential Philosophy: Its Historical Meaning," in *Theology of Culture*, ed. R. Kimball (New York: Oxford University Press, 1964), pp. 76-126; and idem, *The Courage to Be* (New Haven: Yale University Press, 1952).

55. Richard J. Bernstein, *Praxis and Action: Contemporary Philosophies of Human Activity* (Philadelphia: University of Pennsylvania Press, 1971), pp. 84-125.

56. This is unfortunate, for it prevents the cultivation of the kernel of truth this position contains. Bernstein is not as guilty of this offense as many less perceptive authors. For a consideration of the relation between Hegel's interpretation of unhappy consciousness and Kierkegaard's point of view, see below, chap. 7.

57. Jean-Paul Sartre, "The Singular Universal," in *Kierkegaard: A Collection of Critical Essays*, p. 239.

58. Some works written from a more Kierkegaardian perspective also suggest the applicability of Hegel's notion of the unhappy consciousness to Kierkegaard's outlook. See, for example, James Collins, "The Attack on Hegelianism," in *The Mind of Kierkegaard* (Chicago: Henry Regnery Co., 1967), pp. 220-250; Jean Wahl, *Études kierkegaardiennes* (Paris: Librairie Philosophique, 1949), p. 134; and idem, *Le malheur de la conscience dans la philosophie de Hegel* (Paris: Les Editions Rieder, 1929).

59. Karl Löwith, *From Hegel to Nietzsche: The Revolution in Nineteenth-Century Thought*, trans. D. E. Green (New York: Doubleday and Co., 1967), p. 162. In general,

sions of parallels between Hegel's early theological writings[60] and Kierkegaard's mature works.[61] Yet in his eagerness to demonstrate similarities between two thinkers so often seen as antithetical, Wahl is insufficiently sensitive to Hegel's early critique of the "Kierke-gaardian" perspective he so uncannily anticipates.[62] The converse argument is advanced by Jens Himmelstrup in his work entitled *Søren Kierkegaards Opfattelse af Sokrates*. Throughout the period 1838-1840, Himmelstrup argues, Kierkegaard was essentially a Hegelian.[63] He offers as proof of this claim the "Hegelian" charac-ter of Kierkegaard's Magister dissertation, *The Concept of Irony with Constant Reference to Socrates*. According to Himmelstrup, Kierke-gaard breaks decisively and irrevocably with Hegel shortly after the completion of this book. Himmelstrup's argument is open to criti-cism on at least two counts. The early Kierkegaard is not as Hegelian and the late Kierkegaard is not as anti-Hegelian as Himmelstrup would have us believe. Himmelstrup neither perceives the irony of Kierkegaard's use of Hegel throughout the thesis nor adequately grasps the explicit critique of Hegel developed in *The Concept of Irony*. While Wahl does not recognize the polemic against a generally Kierkegaardian stance in the early Hegel, Himmelstrup does not dis-

Löwith presents a convenient survey of post-Hegelian thought. But his account of Kierke-gaard within the context of the left-wing reaction to Hegel's system sometimes has the effect of obscuring important differences between Kierkegaard, on the one hand, and Feuerbach and Marx, on the other.

60. *Hegels theologische Jugendschriften*, ed. Herman Nohl (Tübingen: J. C. B. Mohr, 1907). Selections from Nohl's collection are translated into English under the title, *Early Theological Writings* (see n. 39 above). Wahl is a surer guide through this portion of the Hegelian corpus than either Kaufmann, who characterizes these fragments as "anti-theological" ("The Young Hegel and Religion," in *Hegel: A Collection of Critical Essays*, ed. Alastair MacIntyre [New York: Doubleday and Co., 1972], pp. 61-99), or Lukács, who dismisses Hegel's early interest in religion as a "reactionary legend" (*The Young Hegel: Studies in the Relation between Dialectics and Economics*, trans. R. Livingstone [Cam-bridge, Mass.: MIT Press, 1976]).

61. See Wahl, *Études kierkegaardiennes*; idem, "Hegel et Kierkegaard," *Revue philo-sophique de la France et de l'étranger* 112 (1931) 321-380; idem, "Hegel et Kierkegaard," in *Verhandlungen des dritten Hegelkongresses von 19. bis 23. April 1933 in Rom*, ed. B. Wigersma (Tübingen: J. C. B. Mohr, 1934), pp. 235–249; and idem, *Malheur de la con-science*.

62. Especially important in this connection is Hegel's essay, "The Spirit of Christian-ity and Its Fate," in *Early Theological Writings*, pp. 182-301. For further elaboration of my disagreement with Wahl see "Journeys to Moriah: Hegel vs. Kierkegaard," *Harvard Theologi-cal Review* 70 (1977), 305-326. Interestingly enough, when Wahl turns from Hegel's early to his later works, he insists on the differences between Hegel and Kierkegaard in a manner consonant with the more widespread view of their relationship described above.

63. Jens Himmelstrup, *Søren Kierkegaards Opfattelse af Sokrates* (Copenhagen, 1924), pp. 42-84. Himmelstrup gives particular emphasis to the Hegelian character of Kierkegaard's ethics.

cern the criticism of Hegelianism already present in the youthful Kierkegaard. Furthermore, Himmelstrup's insistence on the thoroughness of Kierkegaard's break with Hegel cannot do justice to the continuing influence Hegel's work exercised upon Kierkegaard's thinking.

These critical remarks are not intended to suggest that previous discussions of the Hegel-Kierkegaard relationship are of little or no value.[64] To the contrary, some useful insights can be garnered from works currently available. But none of the existing studies seems to be sufficiently sympathetic to and understanding of the positions of *both* Hegel and Kierkegaard to have succeeded in creating a dialogue between them which plumbs the depths of the issues they jointly probe.[65] No doubt this reading of earlier scholarship involves my own act of "misprision," though I hesitate to characterize it as "poetic." But the critical debate with other interpreters which runs throughout this work also rests upon a conviction gained from prolonged wrestling with these two extraordinary figures: affirmation is inseparable from negation, or to put the same point in other terms, identity is mediated by relation to difference.

My goal, in sum, is to bring Hegel and Kierkegaard closer together so that their differences can emerge more clearly. Kierkegaard rightly suggests that "in order to see one light determinately, we always need another light. For if we imagined ourselves in total dark-

---

64. Alexandre Kojève's idiosyncratic reading of the *Phenomenology* suggests interesting parallels between Hegel's work and central themes in twentieth-century existentialism. Kojève does not explicitly discuss Kierkegaard's writings, but his analysis points to fascinating links between Hegel and Kierkegaard. One must exercise great caution, however, in accepting Kojève's interpretation for Hegel's own position. The book is a striking example of Bloom's "misprision" and is, in many ways, more interesting when viewed as an original philosophical treatise than as a commentary on Hegel. *Introduction à la lecture de Hegel: Leçons sur la Phénoménologie de l'esprit, professées de 1933 à 1939 à l'Ecole des hautes-études*, ed. Raymond Queneau (Paris: Gallimard, 1947); abbreviated English translation: *Introduction to the Reading of Hegel*, ed. Alan Bloom, trans. J. H. Nichols (New York: Basic Books, 1969).

65. The work that comes the closest to achieving this goal is Stephen Crites's brief monograph *In the Twilight of Christendom: Hegel vs. Kierkegaard on Faith and History* (Chambersburg, Pa.: American Academy of Religion, 1972). Crites centers his discussion around Hegel's and Kierkegaard's "divergent reactions to the religio-cultural phenomenon of Christendom" (p. 2). He has developed his reading of Kierkegaard more fully in a series of articles (cited in my Bibliography) and is completing a lengthy study of Hegel soon to be published under the title *Christianity in the Development of Hegel's Thought: Dialectic and Gospel in the Philosophy of Hegel*. I have benefited greatly from Crites's fine analysis of Hegel and Kierkegaard and have drawn on his insights frequently in formulating and refining my argument. Mention of Crites's work calls attention to the dearth of English studies on Hegel and Kierkegaard. Other than Crites's monograph and the translation of Thulstrup's book there are no extended treatments of this issue available in English.

ness and then a single spot of light appeared, we would be unable to determine the position of the first light in relation to the other."[66] This concluding preface implies, however, that the journey undertaken in the following pages is not motivated by purely historical interest. I hope that the effort to illuminate the writings of Hegel and Kierkegaard in and through each other will yield insights that shed light upon the "rose within the cross of the present"[67] and thus brighten the too often dark and confusing way along which we all must journey to selfhood.

---

66. *Journals and Papers*, 2240; 1:A 1.
67. *Philosophy of Right*, trans. T. M. Knox (New York: Oxford University Press, 1969), p. 12; 7:26.

|2|

SPIRITLESSNESS OF THE AGE

> . . . we become
> An Anarchy of Spirits! Toy-bewitched,
> Made blind by lusts, disinherited of soul,
> No common centre Man, no common sire
> Knoweth! A sordid solitary thing,
> Mid countless brethren with a lonely heart
> Through courts and cities the smooth savage
>   roams
> Feeling himself, his own low self the whole.
> —*Coleridge*

> Earlier, the infinite sorrow existed only histori-
> cally in the culture. It existed as the feeling
> upon which the religion of more recent times
> rests, the feeling that God himself is dead; the
> same feeling that was, so to speak, only empiri-
> cally expressed by Pascal: "la nature est telle
> qu'elle *marque* partout un Dieu *perdu* et dans
> l'homme et hors de l'homme." . . . Good Friday
> must be speculatively restored in the full truth
> and harshness of its Godforsakenness. Since the
> more serene, superficial, and individual style of
> the dogmatic philosophies and of the natural re-
> ligions must disappear, the highest totality can
> and must be resurrected solely from this harsh
> consciousness of loss, encompassing everything,
> and ascending in all its seriousness out of its
> deepest ground to the most serene freedom of
> its form.
> —*Hegel*

> . . . to be lost in spiritlessness is the most ter-
> rible thing of all.
> —*Kierkegaard*

   Hegel and Kierkegaard are deeply committed existential thinkers whose writings are firmly rooted in and carefully calculated responses to what they regard as the most significant and distressing social, intellectual, and spiritual movements of the day. Although each author develops an extremely complex and highly theoretical body of literature, neither is interested in technical philosophical and theological problems that are divorced from fundamental human concerns. As I have stressed in the opening chapter, Hegel and Kierkegaard are preoccupied with the exploration of the malaise they label spiritlessness. While their characterizations of this condition differ significantly, they agree that any modern individual who undertakes the journey to selfhood faces difficulties unknown to previous pilgrims. Post-Enlightenment man has crossed a spiritual Rubicon that makes it impossible simply to follow the course mapped by earlier travelers along life's way. Since Hegel and Kierkegaard regard their writings as attempts to come to terms with dilemmas created by modern experience, they remain keenly aware of the historically relative character of their undertakings. Although Kierkegaard repeatedly satirizes the speculative philosopher who has "forgotten, in a sort of world-historical absent-mindedness, what it means to be a human being,"[1] Hegel insists that forms of reflection, be they naive or scientifically sophisticated, are inseparably bound to the historical situation within which they arise. In the preface to his late work, *Philosophy of Right*, Hegel expresses a conviction that informs his thinking from the outset: "Whatever happens, every individual is a child of his time; so too is philosophy its own time apprehended in thoughts. It is just as absurd to fancy that a philosophy can transcend its contemporary world as it is to fancy that an individual can overleap his own age, jump over Rhodes."[2] For his part, Kierkegaard never loses sight of the historical nature of all knowing and consistently emphasizes the partiality of alternative human perspectives. Indirectly voicing agreement with the author he so freely attacks, Kierkegaard, through Judge Wilhelm, claims that "every individual, however original he may be, is still a child of God, of his age, of his nation, of his family and friends. Only thus is he truly himself."[3] The unusual sensitivity of Hegel and Kierkegaard to the situational character of reflection and their common effort to offer a diagnosis

---

   1. *Postscript*, p. 109; 7:99.
   2. *Philosophy of Right*, p. 11; 7:26.
   3. *Either-Or*, vol. 1, trans. D. F. and L. M. Swenson (Princeton: Princeton University Press, 1971), p. 143; 1:123.

of and prescription for the existential problems peculiar to modernity combine to suggest the advisability of beginning our comparative investigation of their positions by probing their analyses of the social, intellectual, and spiritual worlds within which they find themselves.

FRAGMENTATION

Society and Politics: Disintegrating Reich

M. H. Abrams correctly points out that "no thinker was of greater consequence than Friedrich Schiller in giving a distinctive Romantic formulation to the diagnosis of the modern malaise, and to the overall view of the history and destiny of mankind of which the diagnosis was an integral part."[4] For Hegel and his generation, Schiller's *On the Aesthetic Education of Man* (1795) provided a definitive interpretation of the personal and social problems created by the industrialization and commercialization characteristic of modern society. Schiller's influential study effectively synthesizes a broad range of ideas circulating throughout Europe during the closing decades of the eighteenth century. By drawing on works as diverse as Goethe's *Wilhelm Meister* (1795), Ferguson's *Essay on the History of Civil Society* (1767), Lessing's *The Education of the Human Race* (1780), Herder's *Ideas on the Philosophy of the History of Mankind* (1784-85), and Kant's *Conjectural Origin of the History of Man* (1785), Schiller forges a comprehensive argument in which he maintains that the distinctive feature of modern experience is its fragmentation. In a world governed by the competitive laws of an industrial economy, class divisions emerge which create conflict among and within individuals. A particularly penetrating passage previously cited describes the consequences of the disintegration endemic to the age: "Everlastingly chained to a single little fragment of the whole, man himself develops into nothing but a fragment." Such personal and social fragmentation is all the more disconcerting for Schiller and his Romantic followers when it is compared to their idealized picture of the harmonious life enjoyed by the Greeks. Schiller recognizes, however, that the loss of Arcadia was neither accidental nor inexplicable. "It was civilization itself which inflicted this wound upon modern man. Once the increase of empirical knowledge, and more exact modes of thought, made sharper divisions between the sciences

---

4. Abrams, *Natural Supernaturalism*, p. 199.

inevitable, and once the increasingly complex machinery of state necessitated a more rigorous separation of ranks and occupations, the inner unity of human nature was severed too, and a disastrous conflict set its harmonious powers at variance."[5] Having irrevocably lost the primitive organic relation between subjective purpose and objective forms of life, individuals eventually begin to experience social structures in general, and the "machinery of state" in particular, as coercive—as alien to private interests and intentions.[6] Rather than spontaneously arising from the interplay of free individuals, social and political structures come to be regarded as externally and authoritatively imposed in a way that stifles creativity and represses liberty. Bound in such a "meagre fragmentary association," individuals suffer inward dissociation, "dismemberment of their being." Schiller admits:

> With us too the image of the human race is projected in magnified form into separate individuals—but as fragments, not in different combinations, with the result that one has to go the rounds from one individual to the other in order to be able to piece together a complete image of the race. With us, one might almost be tempted to assert, the various faculties appear as separate in practice as they are distinguished by the psychologists in theory, and we see not merely individuals but whole classes of men, developing but one part of their potentialities, while of the rest, as in stunted growths, only vestigial traces remain.[7]

---

5. Schiller, *Aesthetic Education*, p. 33.

6. Unlike so many others during this period, Schiller is not possessed of an unrealistic nostalgia to return to an Athenian paradise. This past is forever gone, and present division, painful though it is for particular persons, represents an advance for the race as a whole. He argues: "If the manifold potentialities in man were ever to be developed, there was no other way but to pit them one against the other. This antagonism of faculties and functions is the great instrument of civilization—but it is only the instrument; for as long as it persists, we are only on the way to becoming civilized" (p. 41). Schiller's interpretation of modern experience in terms of a historical dialectic of paradise lost and regained exercises a decisive influence on Hegel's thinking. Although Hegel presents important criticisms of Schiller's "aesthetic education" in his mature philosophy, his grasp of the nature of the modern predicament and the general structure of his proposed resolution remain profoundly Schillerian. G. A. Kelly, therefore, is essentially correct when he argues that "the *Phenomenology*, Hegel's greatest work, is at once a vast and genial reduplication of Schiller's theme and a bitter, yet affirmative, surpassing of Schiller's prescriptions for the healing of divided humanity" (*Hegel's Retreat From Eleusis* [Princeton: Princeton University Press, 1978], p. 79). Kelly provides an extended discussion of Hegel's relation to Schiller (see pp. 8-109). Other useful studies of this issue include Kaufmann, *Hegel: Reinterpretation, Texts, and Commentary*, pp. 46 ff.; Richard Kroner, *Von Kant zu Hegel* (Tübingen, 1921-1924), 2:52 ff.; and Raymond Plant, *Hegel* (Bloomington: Indiana University Press, 1973), pp. 22 ff., 74 ff.

7. Schiller, *Aesthetic Education*, p. 33. Compare Herder's remark in *Vom Erkennen und Empfinden der menschlichen Seele*: "Since together with the classes, ranks and professions, the inner faculties have unfortunately become separated . . . no single fragment partakes of the whole any more" (cited in Plant, *Hegel*, p. 21).

Inwardly and outwardly torn, individuals seek reintegration of their splintered selves. Schiller concludes that the fundamental question facing the age is: "How are we to restore the unity of human nature?"[8]

In a letter to Schelling dated 16 April 1795, Hegel expresses unreserved respect for Schiller by describing *On the Aesthetic Education of Man* as a "masterpiece."[9] For Hegel, struggling to come to terms with his puzzling times, Schiller's analysis provides unusual insight into the complex dynamics joining sociopolitical and personal fragmentation. In an extended passage near the end of his *Lectures on the Philosophy of Religion*, Hegel summarizes his view of the age.

> Just as in the time of the Roman Empire, because universal unity in religion had disappeared, the Divine was profaned, and further, because political life was universally devoid of principle, of action, and of confidence, reason took refuge only in the form of private right, or to put it differently, because that being which exists in and for itself was forsaken, individual well-being was elevated to the rank of an end, so too, is it now. Moral views, individual opinion, and conviction without objective truth have attained authority, and the pursuit of private rights and enjoyment is the order of the day. When the time is fulfilled and what is needed is *justification by means of the Notion*, then the unity of outer and inner no longer exists in immediate consciousness, in the world of actuality, and in *faith*, *nothing is justified*. The rigidity of an objective command, an external direction, the power of the state, can effect nothing here; the process of decay has gone too deep for that. When the Gospel is no longer preached to the poor, when the salt has lost its savor, and all the foundations have been tacitly removed, then the people for whose ever solid reason truth can exist only in a representation no longer know how to assist the impulses and emotions they feel within them. They are nearest to the condition of infinite sorrow; but since love has been perverted [*verkehrt*] to a love and enjoyment from which all sorrow is absent, they seem to themselves to be deserted by their teachers. These latter have, it is true, brought help to themselves by means of reflection, and have found their satisfaction in finitude, in subjectivity and its virtuosity, and consequently in what is empty and vain, but the substantial kernel of the people cannot find its satisfaction here.[10]

This is a particularly helpful account, for it at once highlights the similarities Hegel sees between his day and the years of the late Roman Empire and suggests what he regards as parallels between the

---

8. Schiller, *Aesthetic Education*, p. 85.
9. *Briefe von und an Hegel*, ed. J. Hoffmeister and R. Flechsig (Hamburg: Felix Meiner Verlag, 1952-1960), 1:24.
10. *Philosophy of Religion*, 3:150; 17:342-343.

coming of Christianity and the rise of speculative philosophy. Under-
scoring this point, G. A. Kelly notes that "turn-of-the-century Germany was indeed the land of the 'unhappy consciousness.'"[11]
Hegel's conclusions regarding the present age do not, however, represent a flight of Romantic imagination. They are based upon the
detailed study of social, economic, and political conditions of the
German *Reich*, carried out during his early years in Bern and Frankfurt. Though never intended for publication, the writings that resulted from this investigation laid the groundwork for much of
Hegel's mature work. He presents his most devastating critique of the
current social and political climate in a work that has come to be
known as "The German Constitution."[12] Hegel makes his basic
point concisely and incisively: "Every center of life has gone its own
way and established itself on its own; the whole has fallen apart. The
state exists no longer" (146; 7). In fact, this is a fair reading of the
German situation. Events traceable to the breakdown of the Holy
Roman Empire, the emergence of the Protestant Reformation, and
the subsequent Thirty Years' War left German society fragmented.
By the closing years of the eighteenth century, the once powerful
Reich had dissolved into an aggregate of diverse kingdoms, principalities, duchies, and territories, lacking any central authority or admin-
istration and barely held together by formal and often merely cere-
monial ties. To some people, mostly members of the intelligentsia,
events leading up to the French Revolution seemed to bode an era of
reform during which the political injustice and socioeconomic back-
wardness of Germany could be surmounted.[13] In some parts of
Germany a superficial alliance between Absolutism and *Aufklärung*
resulted in modest reforms. Hegel's native Württemberg was one of
the more advanced duchies in this regard. But as Avineri points out,

---

11. Kelly, *Hegel's Retreat*, p. 55.

12. The original manuscript, which dates from 1799-1802, is untitled. The present
title was supplied by later editors. The standard English translation is included in *Hegel's
Political Writings*, trans. T. M. Knox, with an introduction by Z. A. Pelczynski (New York:
Oxford University Press, 1968). Throughout this section of the essay, references to this
work are given in the body of the text. Following Knox, the German edition I have used is
Hegel's *Schriften zur Politik und Rechtsphilosophie*, ed. G. Lasson (Leipzig, 1923).

13. The best account of the impact of the French Revolution on Germany is J. Droz's
L'Allemagne et la Révolution française (Paris, 1949). For helpful studies of Germany during
this period see Klaus Epstein, *The Genesis of German Conservatism* (Princeton: Princeton
University Press, 1966) and Reinhold Aris, *History of Political Thought in Germany from
1789 to 1815* (London: George Allen and Unwin, 1936). On the face of it, José Ripalda's
The Divided Nation: The Roots of a Bourgeois Thinker: G. W. F. Hegel (Amsterdam: van
Gorcum, 1977) would seem to be especially relevant to this problem. But the Marxist slant
of Ripalda's argument distorts his account of Hegel's development.

"at the close of the eighteenth century the Diet, originally a bastion against ducal absolutism, became a stronghold of oligarchical privileges, corrupt practices and entrenched 'positive' rights, jealously guarded by an army of lawyers, clerks and place-men and defended by a fossilized procedure, making any reform in the sociopolitical structure impossible."[14] Opposition to reform was hardened by the violent turn of events in France and by the French invasion of the Rhineland in 1792. As we shall see, Hegel, initially an enthusiastic supporter of the French Revolution, never lost his appreciation for the world-historical significance of this event and never relinquished his commitment to the original principles from which it arose. In the present context, however, it must be emphasized that for Hegel the German defeat at the hands of the French was a "fate" revelatory of the inner "spirit," or perhaps more accurately inner spiritlessness, of the German people. The conclusion of the Franco-German war provides the occasion for Hegel to gather his thoughts on prevailing social and political conditions. "The peace," he writes, "makes it appropriate to consider carefully what are the inner causes, the spirit, of these results, and in what way the results are only the external and necessary appearances of that spirit" (144; 4).[15]

Throughout his inquiry, Hegel is preoccupied with the exploration of the nature and origin of the fragmentation and conflict plaguing his age. He regards the overt loss of territory to the French invaders as the outgrowth of the covert process of disintegration that began with the Peace of Westphalia in 1648. The decline of the Reich is attributable to at least two distinguishable forms of loss:

> There is the actual subjection of German territory to a foreign power and its emancipation from all Imperial rights and duties; but we must also regard it as a loss to the state that so many territories, though remaining in all their former legal and ostensible relationship to Emperor and Empire, have retained monarchs who, while being or having become members of the Empire, are simultaneously rulers of independent states. This is apparently no loss; apparently things are left as they were; but actually it has undermined the foundations upon which the cohesion of the state rests, because it has made these territories independent of the authority of the state." [175; 51-52]

---

14. Shlomo Avineri, *Hegel's Theory of the Modern State* (New York: Cambridge University Press, 1976), p. 37.

15. This remark illustrates Hegel's conviction that there is a dialectical relation between the spirit and the fate of a people. He explores this issue in more depth in his early theological writings as well as in the *Phenomenology* and the *Philosophy of History*.

With the loss of centralized authority and effective governing structures, individual principalities are left to go their separate ways,
seeking particular, and frequently conflicting, ends rather than pursu-
ing the common weal. The Reich dissolves into a "congeries of
independent states" (179; 58), creating a situation Hegel labels "legal
anarchy" (152; 15). The state loses its vitality and actually becomes
what, in his mature political philsophy, Hegel calls the *Not- und
Verstandesstaat.*[16] *Res publica* become *res privata*. According to
Hegel, "the German political edifice is nothing but the sum of rights
which the individual parts have wrested from the whole, and this
[system of] justice, which carefully watches to see that no power is
left over to the state, is the essence of the constitution" (150-151;
13-14). Constituent members turn to the state in an effort to satisfy
individual needs, desires, and interests or to mediate inevitably recurrent conflicts. From Hegel's point of view these developments bring
the death of the body politic. Outward defeat is but the manifestation of inward decay. In a rare resort to imagery he explains:
"Associations of this sort are like a heap of round stones which are
piled together to form a pyramid. But they are perfectly round and
have to remain so without any dovetailing; and so, as soon as the
pyramid begins to move toward the end for which it has been built,
it rolls apart or at least can offer no resistance [to disintegration]"
(180; 58-59).

This already difficult situation is worsened by the failure of
German sociopolitical structures to change with or adapt to altered
historical circumstances. Hegel maintains that "the old forms have
remained, but the times have changed, and with them manners,
religion, wealth, the situation of all political and civil estates, and the
whole condition of the world and Germany. This true condition, the
old forms do not express; they are divorced from it, they contradict
it, and there is no true correspondence between form and fact" (202;
92). Germany is nothing but a *Gedankenstaat*—"a state in theory and
not in reality; formality and reality differ; empty formality belongs
to the state, reality, however, to the nonexistence of the state" (180;
59). Persisting language of the Reich, the "German Nation," or the
"Empire" reflects the memory of a bygone age and does not present
an accurate description of social and political conditions in the late
eighteenth century. With historical changes, vestigial political structures fail to address the needs of the time and are experienced as

---

16. *Philosophy of Right*, par. 183; 7:340. Many of the insights first expressed in "The
German Constitution" are incorporated in Hegel's later interpretation of civil society: see
pars. 182-256; 7:339-398.

coercive and repressive. Onetime habitable forms of life become strange and estranging, and can be maintained only through "super-stitious adherence to purely external formalities" (197; 87). Echoing Schiller, Hegel describes this opposition between subjective purpose and objective sociopolitical structures as the state of alienation.

In his search for the underlying causes of this bewildering situation Hegel first points to the "German character's stubborn insistence on independence," which, he believes, "has reduced to a pure formality everything that might serve toward the erection of a state power and the union of society in a state" (196; 86). As a result of further reflection on the sociological and economic analyses of Ferguson[17] and the philosophical and poetic works of Schiller, Hegel expands his understanding of the source of the problem to include a recognition of the significance of the emergence of the bourgeois class. The advent of a manufacturing and commercial economy brought with it an increased division of labor and greater social pluralization. Hegel surmises that "with the change in manners and way of life, each individual was more preoccupied with his own necessities and his own private affairs. By far the greater number of free men, i.e. the strictly *bourgeois* class, must have had to look exclusively to their own necessities and their own living. As states became larger, those people who must have had to concern themselves exclusively with their own affairs formed a class of their own" (202; 92-93). In Hegel's eyes, the combination of this development and certain character traits he takes to be peculiar to the German people made the dissolution of the Reich unavoidable.

> But when, through the growth of the Imperial cities, the *bourgeois* sense, which cares only for an individual and not self-subsistent end and has no regard for the whole, began to become a power, this individualization of dispositions would have demanded a more general and more positive bond. When, through the advance of culture and industry, Germany was now pushed into the dilemma of deciding whether to obey a universal power or break the tie [between the estates] forever, the original German character swung it preponderantly toward insistence on the free will of the individual and on resistance to subjection to a universal, and it thus determined Germany's fate in accordance with its old nature. [190; 73-74]

Constantly aware of the social dimensions of selfhood, Hegel concludes his analysis of the disintegration of the German Reich by

---

17. Ripalda (*Divided Nation*, pp. 17 ff.) points out that while still a Gymnasium student in Stuttgart, Hegel became acquainted with Ferguson's work through the writings of Christian Garve.

stressing that sociopolitical dissolution inevitably brings with it personal fragmentation. "Once man's social instincts are distorted and he is compelled to throw himself into interests peculiarly his own, his nature becomes so deeply perverted that it now spends its strength on variance from others, and in the course of maintaining its separation it sinks into madness, for madness is simply the complete separation of the individual from the race" (242; 136). In less prosaic terms:

> . . . we become
> An Anarchy of Spirits! Toy-bewitched,
> Made blind by lusts, disinherited of soul,
> No common centre Man, no common sire
> Knoweth! A sordid solitary thing,
> Mid countless brethren with a lonely heart
> Through courts and cities the smooth savage roams
> Feeling himself, his own low self the whole.[18]

Fragmented, isolated, inwardly divided, spiritless. So Hegel describes the land of unhappy consciousness—the land where dissatisfied, sorrowful sojourners wander.

The Oppression of Objectivity: Religion and Self-alienation

In the same letter to Schelling cited earlier, Hegel writes: "Religion and politics have played under one blanket, the former has taught what despotism wanted, contempt for the human race, its inability to accomplish any good, or to be something on its own." This brief remark rests upon Hegel's lifelong conviction that the religious life of a people is intrinsically related to its sociocultural matrix. Preferring dialectical complexity to reductionistic simplicity, Hegel insists that religious thought and practice simultaneously reflect and are reflected in the historical world of which they are a part.[19] Throughout the 1790s Hegel complements his political and sociological analyses with a series of careful and imaginative studies of religion. While his aim in the former undertaking is to arrive at an adequate interpretation of the nature and origin of social and personal fragmentation, the latter inquiry represents an effort to grasp the most important features of religious experience in late-

---

18. Samuel Taylor Coleridge, "Religious Musings," lines 146 ff., in *The Poems of Coleridge* (New York: John Lane, n.d.).

19. While Hegel's analysis of religion in these writings anticipates many of the most important insights of his left-wing followers such as Marx, and Feuerbach and of twentieth-century sociologists and psychologists, his steadfast adherence to the dialectical interpretation of the genesis and function of religion prevents his argument from becoming one-sided and reductionistic.

eighteenth-century Germany. Since Hegel couches his reflection on religion in terms of an investigation of Judaism and early Christianity, commentators frequently overlook the close relation between his early political and theological writings.[20] However, having recognized the similarities Hegel sees between his day and the late Roman Empire, we are in a position to appreciate the relevance of his youthful writings on religion for his understanding of modernity and his ongoing concern with problems related to human selfhood.

Through numerous tentative and experimental writings Hegel is led to conclude that personal disintegration suffered as a result of social dissolution is both embodied in and perpetuated by prevailing religious ideas and conduct.[21] Instead of healing the wounds inflicted by modern experience, religious life all too often contributes to the inward distention of the personality and leads to further unraveling of the social fabric. But even in these early writings Hegel does not see such deleterious effects as endemic to religion. Religion, like other aspects of culture, assumes forms that are more or less fitted to the realization of genuine social and personal existence. In order to make this point as forcefully as possible, Hegel develops a series of binary oppositions, the most important of which are living versus dead religion, religion versus theology, and public (or civil) versus private religion. Although each pair of terms represents a specific emphasis and a different stage in Hegel's treatment of the issue, our purpose will be served best by concentrating on the closely related polarities of subjective versus objective religion and folk versus positive religion.

In a fragment dating from 1793, Hegel explains that "objective religion is *fides quae creditur*, understanding and memory are the powers that are operative in it, they examine evidences, think it through and preserve it or, if you like, believe it. . . . objective religion suffers itself to be arranged in one's mind, organized into a system, set forth in a book, and expounded to others in dis-

---

20. Since the publication of Nohl's edition of *Hegels theologische Jugendschriften* there has been a tendency to concentrate either on Hegel's early writings on religion or on his political works. The tradition of focusing on the early theological writings was initiated by Dilthey in *Die Jungendgeschichte Hegels* (Berlin, 1905) and has been developed most completely in Haering's *Hegel: Sein Wollen und sein Werk*. Lukács's *The Young Hegel* is the best example of the latter approach. As will become apparent in what follows, these two parts of Hegel's early work must be considered together. Moreover, in the next section we shall see that Hegel's critique of leading philosophical movements of his day is of a piece with his political and theological reflection.

21. Hegel's way to this conviction is long and circuitous. For a step-by-step account of his early thinking on religion see H. S. Harris, *Hegel's Development toward the Sunlight, 1770-1801* (New York: Oxford University Press, 1972), and Haering, *Hegel*, 2:59-582.

course."[22] In other words, objective religion consists of the outward aspects of religious life which can be codified in discursive doctrines, historical traditions, and formal ceremonies. This dimension of religion is essential to any living faith. What interests Hegel, however, is the tendency of objective features of religion to become divorced from and opposed to the subjective lives of believers. Objective religious structures can linger long after their soul has fled. This circumstance creates a conflict similar to the opposition between subjectivity and objectivity which Hegel discovers in his analysis of the process of social and political disintegration. When this occurs, objective religious forms can be maintained only through coercive repression exercised by powerful authorities or by "superstitious adherence to purely external formalities." Hegel labels such spiritless belief "fetishism."[23] In a startling anticipation of Kierkegaard's image of speculative philosophers who, in relation to their grand systems, "are like a man who builds an enormous castle and himself lives alongside it in a shed,"[24] Hegel describes the estrangement arising from fetishistic attachment to dead objective religion:

> The man who builds himself a palace on the model of the great house—lives in it like Louis XIV in Versailles, he hardly knows all the rooms in his property, and occupies only a very small sitting room—whereas the father of a family is better informed in every way about his ancestral home, and knows every screw and every tiny cupboard, and can explain its use and tell its story—Lessing's *Nathan*—"In most cases I still can tell how, where, and why I learned it."[25]

Subjective religion, by contrast, "is alive, is effective in the inwardness of our being, and is active in our outward behavior. Subjective religion is fully individuated, objective religion is abstraction. . . ."[26] The opposition between the subjectivity of the believer

---

22. "The Tübingen Essay of 1793," translated in Harris, *Hegel's Development*, p. 484.

23. This term and the process it represents play an essential role in Marx's analysis of the dynamics of self-alienation operative in the labor process. See Günter Rohrmoser, *Subjektivität und Verdinglichung: Theologie und Gesellschaft im Denken des jungen Hegel* (Gütersloh: Verlagshaus Gerd Mohn, 1961).

24. *Journals and Papers*, 3308; 7-1: A 82. Such similarities between Hegel and Kierkegaard are all the more striking when one realizes that Kierkegaard had no knowledge of Hegel's early theological writings, which were not published until this century.

25. "The Tübingen Essay," pp. 494-495. Always in the background of Hegel's characterization of "theology" and "objective religion" during this period is the work of his teacher at Tübingen, Gottlob Christian Storr. Storr attempted to use Kant's critical philosophy to establish the viability of supernatural faith based on revelational positivism.

The brief reference to *Nathan the Wise* in this passage suggests the decisive influence Lessing's writings exercised on the development of Hegel's thought.

26. Ibid., p. 484.

and the objectivity of established religion is overcome through a process of personal appropriation in which outward form and inward feeling and intention are reconciled. No longer experienced as oppressive, external structures effectively objectify internal dispositions and creatively guide individual and corporate activities of all members of the community.

Hegel develops his interpretation of vital religiosity that nourishes the social body and directs believers in their quest for wholeness most fully in his account of folk religion. The image of a perfect *Volksreligion* grows out of Hegel's idealized picture of the integrated life enjoyed by the Greeks. A living folk religion is the objective embodiment of the shared life animating people who participate in a common history and enjoy ethical and cultural consensus. There are three fundamental features of any genuine folk religion: "its doctrines must be grounded on universal reason"; "fancy, heart, and sensibility" must be satisfied; and "it must be so constituted that all the needs of life—the public affairs of the state—are tied in with it."[27] This form of religion plays an essential role in the common life of a people by enabling individuals to become integrated within their social world and attuned to sustaining natural rhythms.[28] Thoroughly rooted in the experience of the community, folk religion imaginatively objectifies group ideals and effectively elicits the voluntary assent of particular members. In this way folk religion unifies social and personal existence and counterbalances centrifugal forces that constantly threaten disintegration.

This account of folk religion is designed to contrast with the prevailing religious climate in late-eighteenth-century Germany. Hegel distinguishes "folk religion, which generates and nourishes noble dispositions" and "goes hand in hand with freedom," from the religion of his own day, which

> aims to educate men to be citizens of heaven whose gaze is ever directed thither so that human feelings become alien to them. At our greatest public festival, one draws near to enjoy the heavenly gifts, in a garb of mourning and with lowered gaze—at the festival, which ought to be the feast of universal brotherhood, many a man is afraid he will catch from the common cup the venereal infection of the one who drank before him, so that his

---

27. Ibid., p. 499.

28. In addition to his concern about the social conflict generated by the division of labor, Hegel is also sensitive to the perversion of the man-nature relation brought by modern industrialization. Throughout his philosophical career, Hegel attempts to bind the rift separating man and nature. He believes the religious festivals tied to seasonal changes serve this end in folk religion.

mind is not attentive, not occupied with holy feelings, and during the function itself he must reach into his pocket and lay his offering on the plate—unlike the Greeks with the friendly gifts of nature—crowned with flowers and arrayed in joyful colors—radiating from open faces that invited all to love and friendship—so they approached the altars of their benevolent gods.[29]

Over against folk religion, Hegel sets positive faith. Positivity, in all the forms Hegel eventually will identify, is characterized by unmediated opposition between subjectivity and objectivity. In the present context, he explains that

a positive faith is a system of religious propositions which ought to have truth for us because it is commanded us by an authority to which we cannot refuse to subject our belief. In this concept there first appears a system of religious propositions or truths which, independent of our convictions, ought to be regarded as truths; even if they had never been known by any person, had never been held as true by any person, they would still remain truths, and in that way are frequently called objective truths. . . . But belief in the authority of the positive teaching is nothing that lies within our will, and the confidence in it must be established prior to all acquaintance with or evaluation of the contents of the given teaching. God's rule over us and the obligation of our obedience to him now rest upon the fact that he is our mighty Lord and Master and we are his creatures and servants, upon his good deeds to us and our duty of gratitude, and further upon the fact that he is the source of truth and we are ignorant and blind.[30]

So described, positive faith is thoroughly authoritarian. It does not arise spontaneously from lived experience, but is encountered as foreign to subjective purpose and imposed upon personal disposition. Rather than being generated by the ongoing life of a community, moral values and spiritual truths are revealed by an alien other. Before this unknown transcendent Lord, one is "to renounce one's will in one's conduct; to subject one's self throughout like a machine to given rules; to abandon intellect altogether in action or renunciation, in speech or silence. . . ."[31]

In his initial discussion of religious positivity Hegel distinguishes a degenerate Christianity based upon historical accident, the person of Jesus, and heteronomous commands, from the morally pure

29. "The Tübingen Essay," pp. 505-506.
30. *Hegels theologische Jugendschriften*, pp. 233-234.
31. *Early Theological Writings*, pp. 169-170; 141. Remaining references to this work in this section are given in the body of the text. German references are to Nohl's *Hegels theologische Jugendschriften*.

religion of its founder.[32] The most complete account of the nature of religious positivity, however, is reserved for the depiction of Judaism offered in the pivotal essay, entitled "The Spirit of Christianity and Its Fate."[33] Here Hegel compares the spiritless and repressive character of the Jewish religion of law with the spiritual vitality of the Christian religion of love. This is a particularly important work for our investigation, for it both bears the impress of many of the ideas of Schiller we have previously considered and anticipates significant aspects of Hegel's relation to Kierkegaard.[34]

From Hegel's point of view, the faith of Abraham represents an effort to come to terms with the conflict engendered by the separation of human consciousness from its natural milieu, a separation mythically depicted in the Old Testament flood narrative. Prior to the estrangement of man from nature, Hegel posits a state of harmonious unification in which humankind finds itself at home in and at one with the world. With the unleashing of dissolutive flood waters, "formerly friendly or tranquil nature abandoned the equipoise of her elements, requited the faith the human race had in her with the most destructive, invincible, irresistible hostility" (182; 244). Hegel suggests three alternative reactions to the breach between man and nature. The characteristic Greek response is captured by the beautiful pair Deucalion and Pyrrha, who, "after the flood in their time, invited men once again to friendship with the world, to nature, made them forget their need and their hostility in joy and pleasure, made a peace of *love*, were the progenitors of more beautiful peoples, and

32. In the course of developing his early analysis of the connection between religion and self-alienation, Hegel's relationship to Kant takes a variety of forms, ranging from the support evident in his *Life of Jesus* and "The Positivity of the Christian Religion" to the critical stance presented in "The Spirit of Christianity and Its Fate." Even the works that display the strongest Kantian influence, however, suggest important corrections of Kant's position. Most importantly, Hegel insists on a closer relation between the self's affectional and rational faculties and grounds Kant's abstract categorical imperative in the shared standards and common mores of the social group. Further comments on Hegel's critique of Kant are developed in the next section.

33. This work (1799) marks a decisive turning point in Hegel's thinking. Under the renewed influence of his former classmate Hölderlin and other outstanding members of the German Romantic movement in Frankfurt and Jena, Hegel reevaluates his estimate of Kantianism and develops a position that anticipates the basic structure of his mature system. In following this line of argument, I side with Dieter Henrich and oppose Harris's overemphasis on the uninterrupted continuity of Hegel's thinking during his early years. See Harris, *Hegel's Development*, pp. 294-295 n., and Henrich, "Hegel und Hölderlin," in *Hegel im Kontext*, pp. 9-40.

34. Hegel's appropriation of Schiller's insights is most evident in his use of the historical dialectic of the loss and recovery of unity. Thus the disintegration represented by Abraham stands between primitive Greek harmony and the reunification effected by Christianity.

made their age the mother of newborn natural life which maintained its bloom of youth" (184-185; 245). In contrast with this effort to restore harmony lost, the Jewish reaction to the flood maintains the hostility between man and nature by attempting to establish human mastery over natural forces. Two possibilities of domination emerge. Nimrod "persuaded men that they had acquired all good things for themselves and by their own courage and strength" (184; 245) and hence could rule nature by means of their own activity. Uncertain of the efficacy of human agency, Noah sought mastery over nature through a creation of his own reflection. "It was in a thought— product that Noah built the shattered world together again; his thought-produced ideal [*gedachtes Ideal*] he turned into a [real] Being and then set everything else over against it, so that in this opposition realities were reduced to thoughts, i.e., to something mastered" (183; 244). Abraham rendered explicit the implications of Noah's attempted resolution of the human dilemma brought about by man's alienation from the natural domain.

Abraham's entire existence was a testimony to his servile devotion to the radically transcendent Lord whom he believed to be the ground of all reality. Since he had suffered separation from the natural whole of which he had been an integral member,

> mastery was the only possible relationship in which Abraham could stand to the infinite world opposed to him; but he was unable himself to make this mastery actual, and it therefore remained ceded to his Ideal. He himself also stood under his Ideal's domination, but the Idea was present in his mind, he served the Idea, and so he enjoyed his Ideal's favor; and since its divinity was rooted in his contempt for the whole world, he remained its only favorite. [188-189; 248]

Abraham did not seek immediate reconciliation with the totality from which he had fallen, but tried to establish domination over the surrounding world which was mediated by an exclusive relation to the Lord of nature and history. Hegel expresses the heart of Judaism represented in Abraham as "the spirit of self-maintenance in strict opposition to otherness" (186; 246). There were, however, multiple opposites requisite for Abraham's self-maintenance. On the most basic level, there was the antithesis between man and nature.[35] In addition to this, there was the opposition between God and world,

---

35. This opposition can also be expressed in terms of the contrast between consciousness and world or between subject and object. This way of viewing the problem Hegel is treating in this context suggests the implications of his reflections on religious positivity for his later consideration of epistemology.

Creator and created, or Master and mastered. Hegel explains: "The whole world Abraham regarded as simply his opposite; if he did not take it to be a nullity, he looked on it as sustained by the God who was alien to it. Nothing in nature was supposed to have any part in God; everything was simply under God's mastery" (187; 247). Through the relationship to God, Abraham attempted to maintain himself over against the hostile powers of nature. In this process a further opposition developed. As a member of the created order, Abraham stood opposed to the wholly other God upon whom he was absolutely dependent. The positive relation to the divine for which Abraham yearned could be established only by unqualified obedience to God expressed in a thoroughly negative relation to world and to self. Negation of world and self, and affirmation of God, stood in a completely dialectical relationship. From this perspective it becomes apparent that the Abrahamic "solution" to the alienation of man from nature replaced one form of slavery with a more profound servitude. The price of mastery over nature was bondage to a transcendent Lord whose demands upon the individual are infinite.

Abraham's heteronomous obedience to transcendent authority deepened his separation from God and heightened his opposition to the world. Hegel points out that "the first act which made Abraham the progenitor of a nation was a disseverance which snapped the bonds of communal life and love. The entirety of the relationships in which he had previously lived with men and nature, these beautiful relationships of his youth he spurned" (185; 245-246). Abraham became a faithful wanderer, a lonely nomad who "was a stranger on earth, a stranger to the soil and to men alike. Among men he always was a foreigner" (186; 246). The struggle to avoid constricting ties to the surrounding world sometimes became violent. At certain junctures in Jewish history, obedience to God manifested itself in the effort to slay infidels. For Abraham, the highest expression of faith was his willingness to suspend the supreme social bond by obeying the divine command to sacrifice his own son. Only in such an extraordinary act of negation could complete devotion to God be affirmed. Hegel goes so far as to assert of Abraham: "Love alone was beyond his power; even the one love he had, his love for his son, even his hope of posterity—the one mode of extending his being, the one mode of immortality he knew and hoped for—could depress him, trouble his all-exclusive heart and disquiet it to such an extent that even this love he once wished to destroy" (187; 247). From the viewpoint represented by Abraham, individual selfhood is most completely actualized in the isolation from other persons and the opposition to the natural realm established by total devotion to the transcendent Lord over against whom the individual always stands. This is the end toward which "the spirit of self-maintenance in strict opposition to everything" is directed.

What for Abraham was the goal of human striving is for Hegel the negative moment of alienation which itself must be negated if reconciliation is to become actual. Instead of healing the breach between man and nature, Abraham's type of faith exacerbates the opposition between the individual and his social-natural world. The faithful wanderer continues to be alienated from his natural environment and from the rest of the human race. Even the ostensibly sustaining relationship to God really represents a further dimension of spiritlessness. The wholly other God remains separate from and opposed to finite persons. Moreover, the infinity of the demands placed upon the individual by this authoritarian Master necessarily leads to the final and most excruciating aspect of estrangement—the alienation of the self from itself. The devotee believes he is not what he ought to be. Reality and ideality clash in his own personality and deepen the inward dismemberment he has been attempting to overcome. According to Hegel, Judaism

> poses essence beyond existence and God outside of man. By recognizing the duality of the extremes, I stand with the nonessential. I am merely nothingness; my essence is transcendent. But that my essence is not in me but posed outside of me necessarily entails an effort on my part to rejoin myself so as to free myself from nonessence. Human life, thus, is an unceasing effort to attain itself. But this effort is futile, because immutable consciousness is posed as transcendent *a principio*.[36]

Consequently, for Abraham, "melancholy, unfelt unity was the supreme reality" (194; 252). Hegel summarizes his interpretation of Abraham when he suggests that the guiding principle of the Jewish religion

> was the spirit inherited from its forefathers, i.e., was the infinite object [*das unendliche Objekt*], the essence of all truth and all relations, which thus is strictly the sole infinite subject. . . . the antitheses are the Jewish nation, on the one hand, and, on the other, the world and all the rest of the human race. These antitheses are the genuine pure objects; i.e., this is what they become in contrast with an existent, an infinite, outside them; they are

---

36. Jean Hyppolite, *Genesis and Structure of Hegel's Phenomenology of Spirit*, trans. S. Cherniak and J. Heckman (Evanston: Northwestern University Press, 1974), p. 192.

without intrinsic worth and empty, without life; they are not even something dead—a nullity—yet they are a something only insofar as the infinite
object makes them something, i.e., makes them not something which *is*, but
something *made* which for itself has no life, no rights, no love. [191; 250]

As we have seen, Hegel's analysis of the relationship between religion
and self-alienation remains bound to his understanding of processes
of social and personal fragmentation. Hence he concludes that the
oppressive notion of God's objectivity which lies at the heart of
religious positivity "is a counterpart to the corruption and slavery of
man, and it is strictly only a revelation, only a manifestation of the
spirit of the age" (163; 227-228).

Abrahamic faith, Hegel insists, is essentially spiritless and inevitably leads to the form of experience he describes as "unhappy
consciousness [*das unglückliche Bewusstsein*]." By reifying dualisms
into unsurpassable oppositions, religious positivity renders reunification unattainable and makes self-alienation unavoidable. Not only is
the individual set in opposition to the natural and social world, but
he also suffers inner fragmentation that alienates him from God. In
such a condition the faithful pilgrim, left to wander in a foreign land,
labors under the "infinite sorrow" of separation and loss and can
only "yearn" for the everlasting peace of reconciliation.

The Reflective Philosophy of Subjectivity

In the foreword to a book by a former student, Hegel describes
the "evil of the *present time*" as "the *fortuitousness* and *caprice* of
subjective feeling and its opinions associated with the *culture of
reflective thought* which has proved to its own satisfaction that spirit
is *incapable of knowing the truth*."[37] Hegel provides the fullest
explanation and defense of this claim in his first two major philosophical works written some twenty years earlier. Originally published in the *Critical Journal of Philosophy*, which he edited jointly
with Schelling, *The Difference between the Fichtean and Schellingian Systems of Philosophy* (1801) and *Faith and Knowledge*
(1802)[38] supplement Hegel's political and religious analyses by de-

---

37. Hegel, foreword to H. Fr. W. Hinrich, *Die Religion im inneren Verhältnisse zur
Wissenschaft* (1822), trans. A. V. Miller, in *Beyond Epistemology: New Studies in the
Philosophy of Hegel*, ed. F. G. Weiss (The Hague: Martinus Nijhoff, 1974), p. 240.
38. English translations of these works have recently appeared: *Faith and Knowledge*,
trans. W. Cerf and H. S. Harris (Albany: State University of New York Press, 1977); *The
Difference between Fichte's and Schelling's System of Philosophy*, trans. W. Cerf and H. S.
Harris (Albany: New York University Press, 1977). Hereafter the latter work is cited as
Differenzschrift.

veloping a critical interpretation of the most significant philosophical movements of his day. By concentrating on the writings of Kant, Fichte, and Jacobi, Hegel attempts to demonstrate that eighteenth- and nineteenth-century philosophy gives theoretical expression to the social, political, and religious fragmentation of modern life.

Although distinguishable from each other in subtle and significant ways, Hegel groups the works of Kant, Fichte, and Jacobi under the common heading "Reflective Philosophy of Subjectivity."[39] Pointing to the close relation between prevailing sociocultural conditions and philosophical thought, Hegel maintains that "these philosophies have to be recognized as nothing but the culture of reflection raised to a system."[40] In order to grasp the gist of Hegel's argument, it is essential to note the precise meaning of the term *reflection*. "Reflection is the action that establishes oppositions and goes from one to the other, but without effecting their combination and realizing their thoroughgoing unity."[41] Reflection, therefore, is primarily an analytical activity by which one makes distinctions and establishes antitheses. Hegel also refers to this mental function as understanding (*Verstand*). In contrast with the integrative activity of reason (*Vernunft*), understanding is antinomic. Analytic understanding represents the capacity of the mind to dissolve concrete totalities into discrete parts and to identify specific differences definitive of isolated particulars. Its guiding rules are abstract self-identity and the law of noncontradiction. According to these principles, "the determinations of thought are absolutely exclusive and different and remain unalterably independent in relation to each other."[42] Hegel summarizes his point when he writes: "Thought, as *understanding*, sticks to

---

39. It is important to note that while Hegel does not concentrate on Schleiermacher in this study, he believes his critique of Jacobi to be applicable to Schleiermacher's position. Hegel explains his misgivings about Schleiermacher's theology more extensively in his forward to Hinrich's work. In one of his more infamous remarks Hegel writes: "When feeling is said to constitute the fundamental character of a man's nature, then he is put on the same level as the animal, for the peculiarity of the animal is to have its determination in feeling and to live in accordance with feeling. If religion in man is based only on a feeling, then the nature of that feeling can be none other than the *feeling of his dependence*, and so a dog would be the best Christian, for it possesses this in the highest degree and lives mainly in this feeling" (foreword to Hinrich, *Religion*, p. 238).

40. *Faith and Knowledge*, p. 64; 2:298. Hegel's relationship to these thinkers is extremely complex. In this context it is not, of course, possible to offer a detailed analysis of the problems involved in Hegel's response to Kant, Fichte, and Jacobi. Instead we shall attempt to come to a more adequate understanding of Hegel's view of his philosophical task by placing his reading of these philosophers within the framework of the issues we have been considering in the foregoing sections.

41. *Philosophy of Religion*, 1:191; 16:197.

42. Ibid., 3:18-19; 17:228.

fixed determinations and to the distinction of one thing from another: every such limited abstraction it treats as having a subsistence
of its own."[43] As the cognitive counterpart of a fragmented world
and the intellectual expression of divided selves, reflective philosophy separates (*entzweit*) but cannot integrate, divides (*trennt*) but
cannot unite, alienates (*entfremdet*) but cannot reconcile.

This form of thought, which is rooted in the Cartesian opposition
between the independent *res cogitans* and the mechanically determined *res extensa*, pervades Enlightenment philosophy from British
empiricism to French materialism and atheism. Hegel believes that
the most complete and provocative statement of this position is
developed in Kant's critical philosophy. In matters theoretical, practical, and aesthetic, Kantian philosophy remains suspended between
the fixed opposites reified by reflective understanding. Although
Kant glimpses the rational interplay of contraries, his confinement of
this unity to the realm of ideality or conceptuality and the correlative denial of its concrete actuality are testimony to the dualism
inherent in his perspective.

Hegel argues that the reflective character of Kantian philosophy
is particularly evident in the epistemology defended in the *Critique
of Pure Reason*. In his search for the necessary conditions for the
possibility of experience, Kant presupposes a primordial bifurcation
between subject and object. Subject is set over against object, and
the problem of knowledge becomes one of bridging this gap. In fact,
Kant fails, and, according to Hegel, necessarily so. The very nature of
his starting point implies the impossibility of knowledge. Kant opposes universal a priori forms of intuition (space and time) and
categories of understanding to the particular data of empirical (a
posteriori) experience. Apart from the encounter with the sensible
manifold of intuition, cognitive structures are purely formal and
completely abstract. Without the imposition of the forms of intuition and categories of understanding, the data of sensation remain
utterly formless. Knowledge, according to Kant, involves the conjunction of universal a priori structures of cognition and particular a
posteriori sensible data. The fundamental heterogeneity of these
opposing elements, however, creates problems for their attempted
unification. Since the structures of reflection actively contribute to
the formation of the manifold of experience into a comprehensible

43. *Lesser Logic*, trans. W. Wallace (New York: Oxford University Press, 1968),
par. 80; 8:169.

object, Kant is forced to distinguish the object-as-known (*für uns*) from the object taken apart from the knowing relation, the thing-in-itself (*Ding an sich*). The thing-in-itself remains opposed to and an absolute limit upon the activity of the knowing subject. It is a sheer beyond (*ein Jenseits*), completely inaccessible to human understanding. Subject and object are, in the final *analysis*, alien to each other. Despite this unavoidable stricture imposed upon knowledge, Kant refuses to draw a skeptical conclusion from the argument he develops. He maintains that even though reality itself is impenetrable, knowledge is not merely subjective. The universality of cognitive structures insures the objectivity of human knowledge. Kant argues that any attempt to extend the categories of understanding beyond the strict limits he establishes inevitably leads to the illusions identified in the "transcendental dialectic" of the first *Critique*.[44] In the *Critique of Judgment* he does suggest the possibility of an *intellectus archetypus* or "intuitive intellect" for which subjectivity and objectivity are not irrevocably opposed.[45] But Kant insists that such an intellect is neither actual nor humanly actualizable. This notion simply serves as a regulative idea that can effectively direct the subject's ceaseless search for knowledge.

From Hegel's point of view, Kant's failure to unite subject and object leads to a subjectivism that makes knowledge, *sensu eminentiori*, impossible. What Kant calls objectivity is, according to Hegel, "to a certain extent subjective. Thoughts, . . . although universal and necessary categories, are *only our* thoughts—separated by an impassable gulf from the thing, as it exists apart from our knowledge. But the true objectivity of thinking means that the thoughts, far from being merely ours, must at the same time be the real essence of the things, of whatever is an object to us."[46] If subject and object remain antithetical, the object becomes an unknowable other, and the subject "a noumenal monad," a "fixed noumenal unit conditioned by infinite opposition."[47] In another context, Hegel explains:

44. Kant, *Critique of Pure Reason*, trans. Norman Kemp Smith (New York: St. Martin's Press, 1965), pp. 297 ff. Hegel finds the analysis of the antinomies of pure reason one of the most important aspects of Kant's philosophy.

45. Kant, *The Critique of Judgment*, trans. J. C. Meredith (New York: Oxford University Press, 1973), esp. pars. 76-77. Kant's notion of the archetypal intellect proved enormously important for the emergence of post-Kantian idealism. Here as elsewhere, Kant's followers boldly affirm the actuality of what Kant defines conceptually but denies ontologically.

46. *Lesser Logic*, par. 41; 8:116.

47. *Faith and Knowledge*, p. 83; 2:319.

"In its relation to the object, therefore, thinking does not go out of itself to the object; this, as a thing-in-itself, remains a sheer beyond of thought."[48] The subject, enclosed within its own subjectivity, is alienated from the strange, unintelligible world within which it finds itself. "This reason," Hegel writes, "remains a restless searching, and its very searching declares that the satisfaction [Befriedigung] of finding is a sheer impossibility."[49] Dieter Henrich captures the implication of Hegel's argument when he observes that Kant's transcendental theory results in "the homelessness of the mind."[50]

Kant's analysis of man's practical activity is formally analogous to his interpretation of the theoretical sphere of human life. In his Lectures on the History of Philosophy, Hegel provides a concise summary of Kant's main line of argument in the second Critique:

> As theoretical reason is opposed to objective sensuousness, so practical reason is opposed to practical sensuousness, to impulses and inclinations. Perfected morality must remain a beyond [ein Jenseits]; for morality presupposes the difference of the particular and universal will. It is a struggle, the determination of the sensuous by the universal; the struggle can only take place when the sensuous will is not yet in conformity with the universal. The result is, therefore, that the aim of the moral will is to be attained only in infinite progress."[51]

The bifurcating character of Kant's reflective philosophy is further illustrated for Hegel by the continuing opposition it posits between the universality of the moral law and the particularity and plurality of sensuous inclination. While theoretical reason constantly seeks to unite a priori categories of cognition and a posteriori sense-data, practical reason involves the unending effort to join moral ideality and empirical reality. The opposition that previously separated knowing subject from intended object now is internalized as the conflict between the universal or objective categorical imperative and the particular or subjective desire of the individual. With this development, alienation becomes self-alienation. Furthermore, since universality and particularity are intrinsically opposed, reconciliation

---

48. Logic, par. 45; 5:37.
49. Phenomenology, p. 145; 182. Hegel frequently plays on the etymological connection between the German words for satisfaction (die Befriedigung) and peace (der Friede).
50. Dieter Henrich, "Between Kant and Hegel: Post-Kantian Idealism—An Analysis of Its Origins, Systematic Structures and Problems" (Lectures delivered at Harvard University Spring 1973, ed. S. Dunning, D. Pacini, and C. Ream), p. 14.
51. Hegel's Lectures on the History of Philosophy, trans. E. S. Haldane and F. H. Simson (New York: The Humanities Press, 1968), 3:461; 20:369-370.

can never be concretely realized. At best, one can hope for an infinite approximation to moral perfection made possible by the postulation of human immortality. It is true that Kant imagines a holy will that exhibits a perfect harmony between universal law and particular predilection. But as in the case of the archetypal intellect, this holy will is an unreal idea with solely subjective significance. Moreover, the actuality of such a holy will would involve the abolition of morality. Hegel points out that Kant's view of practical activity as entailing an essential conflict between universal moral law and particular sensuous desire implies a fundamental contradiction. The realization of morality is simultaneously its negation. Apart from the split between *is* and *ought*, moral action is impossible. Duty, therefore, necessarily remains an unrealizable *Sollen* or an unreachable *Jenseits*. Life becomes a ceaseless struggle to arrive at an end that in principle is unattainable. Hegel insists that conflict is deepened as it becomes more inward.

Not unlike faithful Abraham, the Kantian knowing subject and moral actor are sundered by oppositions within and without. By the time of the third *Critique*, Kant realizes that the possibility of genuine knowledge and effective moral action requires a closer relation between man and nature, subject and object, thought and being, universality and particularity, and ideality and reality than he previously had allowed. In an effort to define the dialectical relation of opposites, Kant undertakes an investigation of the faculty of judgment. Judgment, he argues, entails the unification of universality and particularity either determinatively, through the subsumption of the particular under the universal, or reflectively, through the discovery of the universal in the particular. Kant's consideration of judgment in relation to organic and aesthetic phenomena leads to the formulation of his principle of "immanent purpose" or "inner teleology." "Purpose [*Zweck*]," as Hegel explains, "is the notion [*Begriff*], which is immanent; not external form and abstraction as distinguished from a fundamental material, but penetrating, so that all that is particular is determined by this universal itself."[52] Such a concrete universal joins opposites, previously separated by Kant, in an integral, organic unity. With the notion of inner teleology, Hegel believes Kant rises to genuinely speculative heights. In fact, Kant identifies the dialectical structure of what Hegel eventually calls the onto-logical speculative

---

52. Ibid., p. 467; 20:376.

Idea. But Kant avoids the radical implications of his argument. He insists that the idea of immanent purpose is simply a "subjective maxim" that guides judgment but is not definitive of things-in-themselves. Hegel acknowledges that Kant

> characterized the substratum of nature as intelligible, recognized it to be rational and identical with all reason, and knew that the cognition in which concept and intuition are separated was subjective, finite cognition, a phenomenal cognition. Nonetheless, there the matter must rest; we must absolutely not go beyond finite cognition. Although the cognitive faculty is capable of [thinking] the Idea and the rational, it simply must not employ it as a cognitive standard; it must regard itself as absolute only when it knows the organic and itself finitely, phenomenally.[53]

In other words, even Kant's third *Critique* finally remains limited by the bifurcating propensity of understanding.

Hegel's painstaking investigation of the Kantian corpus leads him to conclude that "Kant's philosophy ends with a dualism, with the relation that is an essential 'ought,' with unreconciled contradiction."[54] Although Kant envisions a unification of opposites through notions such as the intellectus archetypus, the practical postulates, and inner teleology, he refuses to admit that these ideal constructs are real. Hence he leaves the self fragmented, painfully suspended between opposing extremes.

Hegel is convinced that the major tendencies in post-Kantian thought, represented primarily by Fichte and Jacobi, fail to overcome the estrangement inherent in Kant's interpretation of existence. Fichte makes grand claims for his work. "My system," he declares, "is the first system of liberty. As the French nation liberated man from external chains, my system liberates him from the chains of the thing-in-itself, or of external influence, and sets him forth in his first principle as a self-sufficient being."[55] For Hegel, however, Fichte's philosophy falls far short of its exalted aim. Fichte attempts to do away with Kant's thing-in-itself by regarding nonego (objectivity) as a product of an ego (subject) that is engaged in an infinite process of self-realization. Nonego represents the necessary self-limitation through the negation of which the ego affirms itself. Rather than reconciling subjectivity and objectivity, Fichte's argu-

---

53. *Faith and Knowledge*, pp. 91-92; 2:328.
54. *History of Philosophy*, 3:476; 20:384.
55. *J. G. Fichte: Briefwechsel*, ed. H. Schulz (Leipzig, 1925), 1:449.

ment inwardizes the opposition characteristic of Kant's theoretical philosophy. Hegel explains that

> now the limitation is something immanent, for it is the ego that limits itself. The objects are only posited in order to explain this limitation; and the self-limiting of intelligence is the only real. Thus the absolute opposition which empirical consciousness sets up between subject and object is suspended; but it is transferred in another form into intelligence itself, and intelligence finds itself closed in by incomprehensible limits; its law of self-limitation is absolutely incomprehensible to it.[56]

Such inner dissociation is even more dramatically illustrated in Fichte's practical philosophy. For Fichte, as for Kant, *is* and *ought* remain opposed; ideality ever again confronts reality with a task to be completed. Slavery, not freedom, Hegel argues, is the conclusion to which Fichte unwittingly is driven: "Once the commander is transferred within man himself, and the absolute opposition of the command and the bondage is internalized, the inner harmony is destroyed; disunion and absolute bifurcation constitute the essence of man."[57] Self-integration is forever sought, never attained.

The implications of Jacobian intuitionism are equally problematic. Having accepted the strictures Kant places upon reason, Jacobi resorts to immediate feeling as the locus of truth and the source of the awareness of God. Such feeling is necessarily individual, idiosyncratic, and indeterminate. This position discloses most clearly the dangers inherent in the subjectivism of reflective philosophy. Hegel points out that

> understanding, having dissipated all this content, has again veiled God from human knowledge and reduced Him to the status of something merely yearned for, something unknown. Consequently, all that remains as material for thought is the finite material already mentioned, only with the *consciousness* that it is merely temporal and finite in character; it is to such material that thinking is restricted, and it must find its satisfaction in the vain elaboration in various ways of a subject matter lacking any substantial import.[58]

The effect of this type of intuitionism on practical social life is as distressing as the self-confessed vanity of all human knowledge. The

---

56. *Differenzschrift*, p. 131; 2:66-67.
57. Ibid., p. 150; 2:88. Hegel levels the same criticism at Kant in his *Early Theological Writings*: see pp. 214-215; 246.
58. Foreword to Hinrich, *Religion*, p. 232. Hegel treats Jacobi's position as typical of a main current in Romantic philosophy, literature, and theology. Later Schleiermacher and Schelling fall prey to the same critique. See also *Lesser Logic*, pars. 61-78; 8:148-168.

idiosyncrasy and indeterminacy of feeling render vacuous distinctions between truth and falsehood and between virtue and vice. Feeling remains an "absolute indefiniteness that constitutes the standard and authority, i.e., the caprice and inclination of the individual, to be and to do what pleases him and to make himself the oracle for what shall be accepted as true as regards religion, duty, right, and what is fine and noble."[59] When truth and virtue become so privatized, community disintegrates into a plurality of self-enclosed subjects, each 'claiming to be possessed of wisdom in isolation from and opposition to others. The social, political, and religious fragmentation of Hegel's Germany and the corresponding personal disintegration here are absolutized and philosophically justified. This is a further sign of the spiritlessness of the age.

Firmly rooted in the finitude of understanding, the reflective philosophy of subjectivity establishes oppositions but is impotent to effect reconciliation. "The fundamental principle common to the philosophies of Kant, Jacobi, and Fichte is, then, the absoluteness of finitude and, resulting from it, the absolute antithesis of finitude and infinity, reality and ideality, the sensuous and the supersensuous, and the beyondness of what is truly real and absolute."[60] As with religious positivity, reified dualisms make reunification impossible and self-alienation inevitable. Subject and object, self and other, remain estranged. There is, of course, "on the one hand, a going out from my finitude to a Higher; on the other hand, I am determined as the negative of this Higher. The latter remains an Other, which cannot be determined by me, insofar as determination is to have an objective meaning. What is present is only this going out on my part, this aiming to reach what is remote; I remain on this side, and have a yearning [Sehnsucht] after a beyond [Jenseits]."[61] In Hegel's graphic image, sojourners following this way "stay immovably impaled upon the stake of absolute opposition."[62] But the "unending pain" of this dismemberment, the "infinite sorrow" of Godforsakenness, Hegel maintains, is the passion heralding a reconciliation that "can and must be resurrected solely from this harsh consciousness of loss, encompassing everything."[63]

---

59. Foreword to Hinrich, *Religion*, p. 239.
60. *Faith and Knowledge*, p. 62; 2:295-296.
61. *Philosophy of Religion*, 1:177; 16:171.
62. *Faith and Knowledge*, p. 65; 2:299.
63. Ibid., p. 191; 2:432-433. The last sentence of this work is quoted more fully in one of the quotations prefacing this chapter.

"The Need of the Time"

Hegel believes that "the evil of the *present time*" reveals "what the *need of the time* is."[64] The need of the time is to find a satisfactory answer to the question Schiller had posed: "How are we to restore the unity of human nature?" Ever aware of the close relation between self and society, Hegel, like so many of his contemporaries, initially invests his hope in the French Revolution.[65] But the failure of the Revolution combined with further philosophical reflection to persuade Hegel of the futility of any effort to bind together fractured existence by violent radical change. The very presupposition of a rift between reality and ideality upon which such action is based is itself a manifestation of persisting alienation. If reconciliation is to be realized, it must be within, not beyond, fragmented life. Gradually Hegel becomes convinced that philosophy is the means by which to discover the rose in the cross of the present. He explains to Schelling: "In my intellectual development [*Bildung*], which began from the more subordinate needs of men, I was bound to be driven on to science, the ideal of my youth had at the same time to be transformed into a reflective form, into a system."[66] People cannot become whole apart from the capacity to see things whole. Having defined the integrative role of philosophy, Hegel can say with Blake:

> The war of swords departed now
> The dark Religions are departed and sweet
> Science reigns.[67]

---

64. Foreword to Hinrich, *Religion*, p. 240.

65. Helpful studies of Hegel's relation to the French Revolution include G. A. Kelly, *Idealism, Politics, and History: Sources of Hegelian Thought* (London: Cambridge University Press, 1969), esp. pp. 83 ff.; F. Nauen, *Revolution, Idealism, and Human Freedom: Schelling, Hölderlin, and Hegel—The Crisis of Early German Idealism* (The Hague: Martinus Nijhoff, 1971); and J. Ritter, *Hegel und die französische Revolution* (Cologne: Westdeutscher Verlag, 1957). Plant's remark is particularly helpful in this context: "It was Hegel's achievement that he always kept in mind the social dimension of the problem of individual fragmentation. His ideal like that of most of his contemporaries was that of the *recreation of a whole man in an integrated, cohesive, political community*. Despite several changes in analysis and prescription, this humanistic moral and social concern was to remain at the very centre of his thought and constitutes the key to its identity" (Plant, *Hegel*, p. 25).

66. *Briefe von und an Hegel*, 1:59-60. Abrams notes that disappointment with the turn of events in France led many intellectuals to shift the locus of expected change from the sociopolitical arena to the domain of poetry and philosophy: "Faith in an apocalypse by revelation had been replaced by faith in an apocalypse by revolution, and this now gave way to faith in an apocalypse by imagination or cognition" (*Natural Supernaturalism*, p. 334).

67. Blake, "The Four Zoas." Quoted in Abrams, *Natural Supernaturalism*, p. 355.

Hegel comes to see the labor of infinite sorrow during his time as the stirring of an imminent spiritual rebirth, whose midwife will be speculative philosophy. In the preface to the *Phenomenology* he writes:

> Ours is a birthtime and a period of transition to a new era. Spirit has broken with the world it previously has inhabited and imagined, and is of a mind to submerge it in the past, and in the labor of its own transformation. Spirit is indeed never at rest, but always engaged in moving forward. But just as the first breath drawn by a child after its long, quiet nourishment breaks the gradualness of merely quantitative growth—there is a qualitative leap, and the child is born—so likewise the self-forming spirit [*der sich bildende Geist*] matures slowly and quietly into its new shape, dissolving bit by bit the structure of its previous world, whose tottering state is only hinted at by isolated symptoms.[68]

The resurrection of spirit from spiritlessness can be brought about only by reconciling the oppositions sundering self and society through unifying philosophical comprehension. Fragmentation, "bifurcation, is the source of *the need of philosophy*." "When the might of union vanishes from the life of men and the oppositions lose their living relation and reciprocity and gain independence, the need of philosophy arises."[69] Though typified by the fundamental antithesis between subjectivity and objectivity, the disintegration unique to modernity is, as we have seen, multifaceted. It has social, political, psychological, religious, and philosophical dimensions. If philosophy is to restore the unity of man, it must effectively mediate the full range of conflicts in which the age is mired. "The sole interest of reason," Hegel maintains,

> is to transcend such rigid opposites. But this does not mean that reason is altogether opposed to opposition and limitation. For the necessary bifurcation is *one* factor in life. Life eternally forms itself by setting up oppositions, and totality at the highest vitality of living energy is only possible through its own restoration out of the deepest separation. What reason opposes, rather, is just the absolute fixity which the understanding gives to

---

68. *Phenomenology*, p. 6; 15. This aspect of Hegel's position reveals the other side of his reaction to current philosophy. The major philosophical positions he criticizes not only embody contemporary disintegration; they also *implicitly* express the philosophical principles necessary for the reintegration of oppositions. Hence Hegel's task does not require the introduction of a radically new philosophical perspective but involves the clear articulation of philosophical wisdom already at hand. This dimension of Hegel's argument will become more evident when we consider the *Phenomenology*.

69. *Differenzschrift* pp. 89, 91; 2:20, 22.

the dualism; and it does so all the more if the absolute opposites themselves originated in reason.[70]

In these few lines Hegel expresses a conviction that underlies his entire philosophical enterprise. The reconciliation that overcomes self-alienation requires neither a mystical reversion to a primordial or infantile state of nondifferentiation that takes the world to be illusory nor a "monkish flight"[71] from mundane conflict to transcendent calm that regards all human endeavor as vain. In Hegel's mature vision, peace must be found in the midst of strife through the apprehension of the union of union and nonunion, or, in other terms, the identity of identity and difference.[72] Expressed theologically, reconciliation, decisively revealed in the Christian religion, is not utterly transcendent but is at hand. The task of the philosopher is to render implicit unification explicit, through rational recollection. Only in this way can wandering pilgrims overcome the sense of homelessness and complete the journey to selfhood. Along with Hölderlin's sojourner, Hyperion, Hegel discovers: "Like the strife of lovers are the dissonances of the world. In the midst of conflict is reconciliation, and all things that are parted find one another again. The veins separate from and return into the heart, and all is one eternal glowing life."[73]

DISSIPATION

Society and Politics: Leveling Crowd

As a master diagnostician of the ills and pitfalls awaiting pilgrims who undertake the journey to selfhood, Kierkegaard realizes that "proper diagnosis and prognosis of a disease are more than half the battle . . . and likewise no ability, no care and vigilance, is of any avail when the case has not been correctly diagnosed."[74] We have noted that Kierkegaard, in agreement with Hegel, identifies the malaise of the age as "spiritlessness." But his understanding of the etiology of this disease and his prescription for a "radical cure"

---

70. Ibid., pp. 90-91; 2:22-23.
71. I am indebted to Fackenheim for this phrase: *Religious Dimension*, p. 79.
72. For an elaboration of these points, see below, chap. 5, 1st sec. ("Relationship: Both-And").
73. Quoted in Abrams, *Natural Supernaturalism*, p. 243.
74. *Kierkegaard's Attack upon Christendom*, trans. W. Lowrie (Princeton: Princeton University Press, 1968), p. 139; 14:169.

distinguish Kierkegaard's interpretation of the existential dilemmas
of modernity from Hegel's reading of the human condition. Kierkegaard does not hesitate to assert that "to be lost in spiritlessness is
the most terrible thing of all." He attempts to explain this important
point when he writes:

> This is its [spiritlessness's] misfortune, that it has a relation to spirit which
> proves not to be a relation. Spiritlessness may therefore to a certain degree
> possess the whole content of spirit—not as spirit, be it noted, but as jest,
> galimatias, phrase, etc. It may possess truth—not as truth, be it noted, but as
> rumor and old wives' tales. . . . In fact, spiritlessness can utter the same
> words the richest spirit has uttered, only it does not utter them by virtue of
> spirit. When man is characterized as spiritless, he has become a talking-
> machine [Talemaskine], and there is nothing to prevent him from learning a
> philosophical rigmarole just as easily as a confession of faith and a political
> recitative repeated by rote.[75]

Spiritlessness, in other words, is not simply the absence of spirit,
but is "the stagnation of spirit and the caricature of ideality."[76]
Spiritlessness can emerge as an existential possiblity only over against
its opposite, genuinely spiritual existence. Since Kierkegaard believes
that authentic selfhood is revealed solely in the person of Christ, he
regards spiritlessness as a problem unique to the Christian West.[77]
More specifically, the condition of spiritlessness is bound to the
complex religiocultural phenomenon known as Christendom, which,
from Kierkegaard's point of view, reaches its most complete expression in the bourgeois life of nineteenth-century Europe. This malady
is not characterized by fragmentation that threatens to dismember
self and society through the conflict of contradictory forces. Kierkegaardian spiritlessness entails the dissipation of concrete human existence through a relaxation of spiritual tensions essential to authentic
individuality. This loss of selfhood arises within bourgeois social
institutions, whose primary function is, as Crites stresses, "to stabilize human relationships, to establish procedures and patterns of
decorum, to protect its members from unexpected contingencies and
to enable them to make prudent provision for the future: to modulate the demands and perils of temporal existence so far as possible

---

75. *The Concept of Dread*, trans. W. Lowrie (Princeton: Princeton University Press,
1957), pp. 84-85; 4:364-365.
76. Ibid., p. 85; 4:365.
77. This does not imply that authentic existence can be achieved apart from the
Christian form of life. Kierkegaard clearly denies this. The point to be stressed here is that
though people living in ignorance of Christian revelation remain inauthentic selves, it is
incorrect to label their condition "spiritless."

into an ordered social space."[78] When sociocultural forms function effectively, people begin to feel at home in the world. But, Kierkegaard insists, though usually unnoticed, spiritlessness thrives in the homey atmosphere of the family parlor.[79] Sojourners cease wandering, settle down, and become securely wrapped in the everydayness of familiar custom and routine. From Kierkegaard's perspective, this style of life signals that people have *"forgotten* what it means to *exist*, and what *inwardness* signifies."[80] Such a form of existence is not simply pagan but is a kind of "paganism within Christendom," which "lacks spirit in a direction away from it, or by apostasy, and hence is, in the strictest sense, spiritlessness."[81] It is the illusion that Christendom is Christian.

Although this understanding of the spiritlessness of nineteenth-century Europe is presupposed in all of his writings, Kierkegaard formulates his critique of modernity most explicitly in a work published in 1846, *Two Ages: The Age of Revolution and the Present Age*. Ostensibly this essay is a review of a book entitled, significantly, *A Story of Everyday Life*, written by Thomasine Christine Gyllembourg-Ehrensvärd, wife of P. A. Heiberg and mother of Johan Ludwig Heiberg. The period with which Kierkegaard concerns himself is the decade of the 1840s. During this time Denmark was emerging as a modern industrial capitalist state.[82] Having been ruled by a relatively conservative monarchy since 1660, the hierarchical structure of Danish society remained clearly defined, with monarch and bishop (of Sjælland) atop the social pyramid. Unrest caused by the Napoleonic wars, and renewed economic activity throughout the 1830s, gradually led to social changes that resulted in the democratic constitution of 1849. These developments brought a shift of real political power to the rapidly enlarging bourgeoisie.

In an effort to come to terms with the situation in his native Denmark, Kierkegaard constructs an imaginative comparison of "The Present Age" and "The Age of Revolution." His purposefully ideal-

---

78. Crites, *Twilight of Christendom*, p. 76.

79. Crites organizes much of his comparison of Hegel and Kierkegaard around their contrasting intepretations of "domesticity." See, for example, *Twilight of Christendom*, pp. 1 ff.

80. *Postscript*, p. 223; 7:210.

81. *Sickness unto Death*, trans. W. Lowrie (Princeton: Princeton University Press, 1970), p. 180; 11:159.

82. This brief account is, for the most part, drawn from Kresten Nordentoft's *Kierkegaard's Psychology*, trans. B. Kirmmse (Pittsburgh: Duquesne University Press, 1978), pp. 245 ff. The most complete discussion of Kierkegaard's Denmark is Bruce Kirmmse, "Kierkegaard's Politics: The Social Thought of Søren Kierkegaard in its Historical Context" (Ph.D. diss., University of California, 1977).

ized account depicts the era of the French Revolution as "essentially passionate."[83] It was a time in which "fossilized formalisms" and "narrow-hearted custom" were overcome through the impassioned devotion to an idea or a cause. Events of the time confronted individuals with unreconciled alternatives and evoked irreversible decisions. Kierkegaard points out that "the presence of the crucial either-or depends upon the individual's own impassioned desire directed toward acting decisively, upon the individual's own intrinsic competence, and therefore a competent man covets an either-or in every situation because he does not want anything more" (67; 63). In the eyes of Kierkegaard, this is the stuff of selfhood.

In contrast to the vitality of the age of revolution, "the present age is essentially a *sensible, reflecting age, devoid of passion, flaring up in superficial, short-lived enthusiasm and prudentially relaxing in indolence*" (68; 64). Kierkegaard, with Hegel, defines his time as an age of reflection, burdened by the oppression of objectivity. For Kierkegaard, however, "reflection" in this context does not signify the analytic act of abstracting particular entities from constitutive relations and opposing isolated individuals to one another. The form of reflection about which Kierkegaard has misgivings abstracts from unique particularity and dissipates concrete individuality. As Kant distinguishes between theoretical and practical reason, Kierkegaard similarly contrasts the detached and disinterested orientation of objective reflection with the concerned and interested stance of subjective reflection and personal decision.[84] The reflective quest for universally valid truth leads one to become essentially an observer or spectator for whom subjective interest and individual decision cloud the objectivity of universal vision. Consequently, "the urge to decision is precisely what reflection dispels or wants to dispel" (76; 72). During an era governed by the ideal of objective reflection, "the single individual . . . has not fomented enough passion in himself to tear himself out of the web of reflection and the seductive ambiguity of reflection. The environment, the contemporary age, has neither

---

83. *Two Ages: The Age of Revolution and the Present Age, A Literary Review*, trans. Howard and Edna Hong (Princeton: Princeton University Press, 1978), pp. 68 ff.; 8:64 ff. Throughout the remainder of this section, references to this work are given in the body of the text.

84. For further discussion of the similarities between Kant and Kierkegaard on this point see Stephen Crites, introduction to *Crisis in the Life of an Actress and Other Essays on Drama* (New York: Harper and Row, 1967), pp. 19 ff. and idem. *Twilight of Christendom*, pp. 21 ff. Compare Emil Brunner, "Das Grundproblem der Philosophie bei Kant und Kierkegaard," *Zwischen den Zeiten*, 2, 6 (1924), 31-47; and Jerry H. Gill, "Kant, Kierkegaard, and Religious Knowledge," in *Essays on Kierkegaard*, ed. J. H. Gill (Minneapolis: Burgess Publishing Co., 1969), pp. 58-73.

events nor integrated passion, but in a negative way creates a reflective opposition which toys for a moment with the unreal prospect
and then resorts to the brilliant equivocation that the smartest thing
has been done, after all, by doing nothing" (69; 65-66).

The existential consequences of such reflection are, according to
Kierkegaard, devastating. The reflective observer finally becomes a
spectator of his own life. Concerns vitally related to concrete existence are regarded as a mere "shadow-play" and selves become more
and more "unreal." This "objective tendency . . . proposes to make
everyone an observer, and in its maximum to transform one into so
objective an observer that one becomes almost a ghost. . . ."[85] The
observer "stares at the world-historical play until he is lost in it; he
dies and leaves the scene, and nothing of him remains; or rather, he
himself remains like a ticket in the hands of the usher, a sign that the
spectator has gone."[86] At best, reflection can lead to the discovery
of possibilities which the individual might attempt to embody in his
own life. But since the observer consistently refrains from intentional
activity, reflection simply leads to further dissipation of concrete
individuality by the endless proliferation of possibility. Finally, "possibility . . . appears to the self ever greater and greater, more and
more things become possible, because nothing becomes actual. At
last it is as if everything were possible—but this is precisely when the
abyss has swallowed up the self."[87]

In large measure, Kierkegaard attributes the dissipation of selfhood characteristic of his age to the tendency of reflection to
obscure passionate disjunctions that are the *conditio sine qua non* of
spiritual existence. Unlike revolutionary times, the sensible present
age *"has abrogated the principle of contradiction"* (97; 90). The
opposition of silence and speaking dissolves in idle chatter (*snak*);
philandering emerges from the confusion of love and debauchery;
superficiality (*overfladiskhed*) is the consequence of the disintegration of the distinction between inwardness and outwardness. Most
importantly, Kierkegaard argues that reason's search for a harmonious integration of opposites leads to "the abrogation of the passionate disjunction between subjectivity and objectivity. As abstract
thought, reason is not sufficiently profound dialectically; as concep-

85. *Postscript*, p. 118; 7:107. The analysis of reflective aesthetic existence will treat
this form of life in more detail: see chap. 6, 2d sec. ("Stages on Life's Way"), 2d subsec.
("Ethical Selfhood").

86. Ibid., p. 142; 7:131.

87. *Sickness unto Death*, p. 89; 11:149.

tion and conviction, it lacks full-blooded individuality" (103; 96). [88]
The problem of the relation between subjectivity and objectivity is
no more narrowly epistemological for Kierkegaard than it is for
Hegel. Kierkegaard also sees clearly the social, political, religious, and
philosophical ramifications of the issue. But whereas Hegel is preoccupied with the disintegration generated by the opposition of subjectivity and objectivity, Kierkegaard is concerned with the existential
consequences resulting from the identification of subjectivity and
objectivity.

Nowhere is the loss of "full-blooded individuality" more apparent for Kierkegaard than in the dominant social currents of the day.
"The dialectic of the present age," he argues, "is oriented to equality, and its most logical implementation, albeit abortive, is leveling
[Nivellementet], the negative unity of the negative mutual reciprocity of indivduals." Put differently, "leveling is an abstract power
and is abstraction's victory over individuals" (84; 79). [89] Through
this process, the individual becomes so identified with or integrated
within the social totality of which he is a member that all sense of
personal uniqueness and self-responsibility evaporate. The result is
mass, herd, or crowd existence. [90] Convinced that universality is
superior to particularity, the crowd man lacks the "superior intellect" that "sees only individuals," [91] and thus fails to recognize that
" 'the single individual' is a spiritual definition of being a human
being; the crowd, the many, the statistical or numerical is an animal
definition of being a human being." [92] As the power of the crowd
waxes, the strength of the individual wanes. The race becomes

88. In translating this passage, Hong renders at raisonere as "to be loquacious." He
points out that although the term can be translated "to reason," Kierkegaard's intention is
better conveyed by "to be loquacious." In the present context, however, the use of "to
reason" is more accurate, and suggests the critique of Hegelianism implicit in Kierkegaard's
remarks.

89. William Hazlitt's comment on Wordsworth (The Spirit of the Age, 1825) reflects a
similar sentiment. "Mr. Wordsworth's genius is a pure emanation of the Spirit of the
Age. . . . It partakes of, and is carried along with, the revolutionary movement of our age:
the political changes of the day were the model on which he formed and conducted his
poetical experiments. His Muse . . . is a leveling one. It proceeds on a principle of equality,
and strives to reduce all things to the same standard" (quoted in Abrams, Natural Supernaturalism, pp. 395-396). As previous references to Romantic poets suggest, Hegelianism
shares many commitments with Romanticism. There are particularly interesting parallels
between the standpoint of Hegel and that of Wordsworth. A case could be made to support
the claim that Hegel's Phenomenology and Wordsworth's Prelude are philosophical and
poetic versions of a common journey to selfhood.

90. The Danish word Kierkegaard uses is Mængde, which can mean quantity, number,
multitude, crowd, mass, or herd.

91. So Kierkegaard describes Socrates: Papirer, 10-3:A 476.

92. Journals and Papers, 2050; 11-1:A 81.

essential or substantial, and the individual becomes inessential or accidental. Rather than attempting to define unique individuality through resolute decision, people allow themselves to be swept along by mass movements swirling in the social mainstream. "Everything must attach itself so as to be a part of some movement; men are determined to lose themselves in the totality of things, in world-history, fascinated and deceived by a magic witchery; no one wants to be an individual human being."[93] The public, a bloodless abstraction of "insubstantial individuals," becomes the ruling power. Kierkegaard predicts that "in this age of indolent laxity, more and more individuals will aspire to be nobodies in order to become the public" (94; 87-88).

When public opinion holds sway, truth and value, no longer established authoritatively, lose their moorings and drift with the ever changing currents of the day. Issues of import are decided through the objectivity of majority rule, in which the quantitative dialectic of numerical accumulation replaces the qualitative dialectic of individual resolution. Everyone becomes "practiced in indecisiveness," for definitive action must be withheld until the last vote is counted. The crowd man degenerates into a thoughtless cipher for the viewpoints of others expressed impersonally in the mass media. Kierkegaard's tireless polemic against the press is not simply a reaction to the personal abuse he suffered, but is, more significantly, the outgrowth of his recognition of the power of public media to mold opinion, to direct conduct, and thus to mitigate individual responsibility. Devoid of personal opinion and lacking an individual point of view, "no one wants to be *I*, but pulls in his antennae and becomes third person, 'the public,' 'they.' "[94] Kierkegaard hints at the relationship between such depersonalization and the process of industrialization which Denmark was then undergoing when he concludes that "eventually human speech will become just like the public: pure abstraction—there will no longer be someone who speaks, but an objective reflection gradually will deposit a kind of atmosphere, an abstract noise that will render human speech superfluous, just as machines make workers superfluous" (103; 96).[95] Anonymity is the mark of the crowd man.

---

93. *Postscript*, p. 317; 7:308.
94. *Journals and Papers*, 2075; 11-1:A 533.
95. Recall Schiller's modern man, for whom "the monotonous sound of the wheel turns everlastingly in his ear" (*Aesthetic Education*, chap. 1, n. 25). Kierkegaard's emphasis, however, is less on the personal and social fragmentation wrought by modern industrial economy than on the dissipation of self through the individual's identification with machine and society. When he loses himself in the crowd, man becomes a machine, an automaton.

Since the present age regards the race as a substantial totality and the crowd as the locus of truth, the ideal of the nameless one becomes social adjustment or conformity. What he "fears more than death is reflection's judgment upon him, reflection's objection to his wanting to venture something as an individual" (86; 80). The crowd man seeks to repress all idiosyncrasies through conformity to established custom and identification with an objectively validated social role.[96] Immersed in the business and busyness of everydayness, he "constantly runs errands in life" but never seems to get anywhere. Such a person "acquires some little understanding of life, he learns to imitate the other men, noting how they manage to live, and so too he lives after a fashion. In Christendom he too is a Christian, goes to church every Sunday, hears and understands the parson, yea, they understand one another; he dies; the parson introduces him into eternity for the price of ten dollars."[97] But, Kierkegaard maintains, the crowd man is finally

> defrauded by "the others." By seeing the crowd of men about one, by getting engaged in all sorts of worldly affairs, by becoming wise about how things go in this world, such a man forgets himself, forgets his name (in the divine understanding of it), does not dare to believe in himself, finds it too venturesome a thing to be himself, far easier and safer to be like the others, to become an imitation, a number in the crowd.[98]

Important though he may appear, the man of the world is, in fact, a "nobody."

Kierkegaard sees the political developments of mid-nineteenth-century Europe as symptomatic of the modern malaise he so carefully diagnoses. "In these times," he sighs, "politics is everything."[99] Recognizing the danger of what Paul Tillich aptly labels "democratic conformism,"[100] Kierkegaard stresses the totalitarian potential of the modern state. The absorption of insubstantial individuals in the essentiality of the race foreshadows the loss of divine transcendence and the deification of the state. People define themselves and articulate their aims solely in terms of finite ends mediated by sociopolitical structures. Consequently, social change and institutional reform are believed to cure all ills. But this extraordinary veneration of political power simply compounds confusion. *Res privata* become *res*

---

96. Nordentoft gives a helpful analysis of this tendency: see "Spiritlessness: The Social Complex," in his *Kierkegaard's Psychology*, pp. 240 ff.
97. *Sickness unto Death*, p. 186; 11:165.
98. Ibid., pp. 166-167; 11:147.
99. "The Individual," *Point of View*, p. 107; 13:589.
100. *The Courage to Be*, pp. 103-112.

publica, and the improvement of the individual's lot is viewed in terms of outward change rather than inward transformation. When the journey to selfhood exhausts itself in merely finite ends, human existence itself is finitized, trivialized. Selves become spiritless. It is clear that in this situation a revitalization of social life offers no remedy for the ills of spiritlessness. In opposition to Hegel, Kierkegaard holds that "the idolized principle of sociality in our age is the consuming, demoralizing principle which, in the thralldom of reflection, transforms even virtues into *vitia splendida*" (86; 80). Developing this crucial insight, he continues, "in our age the principle of association . . . is not affirmative but negative; it is an evasion, a dissipation, an illusion, whose dialectic is as follows: as it strengthens individuals, it vitiates them; it strengthens by numbers, by sticking together, but from the ethical point of view this is a weakening" (106; 99).

For Kierkegaard, as for Hegel, the spiritlessness of the age ends in "madness." During a predominantly reflective era, Kierkegaard writes,

> the objective way deems itself to have a security which the subjective way does not have . . . ; it intends to escape a danger which threatens the subjective way, and this danger at its maximum is madness. In a merely subjective determination of the truth, madness and truth become in the last analysis indistinguishable, since they may both have inwardness. Nevertheless, perhaps I may here venture to offer a little remark, one which would seem to be not wholly superfluous in an objective age. The absence of inwardness is also madness.[101]

In contrast with Hegel, for whom "madness is simply the complete separation of the individual from the race," Kierkegaard regards the insanity of spiritlessness as grounded in the dissipation of the individual in the race. When pilgrims become irrepressibly reflective and inordinately objective, they lose sight of the stages on life's way. Anonymous sojourners are strangers, even to themselves. Stricken with spiritlessness, selves become "mirages," "ghosts," "shadows," "living dead." In a significant allusion to Hegel's notion of unhappy consciousness, Kierkegaard describes the one suffering this peculiarly modern disease as "the unhappiest man." Absent to and estranged from himself, the unhappiest man

> cannot become old, for he has never been young; he cannot become young, for he is already old. In one sense of the word he cannot die, for he has not

---

101. *Postscript*, pp. 173-174; 7:161-162.

really lived; in another sense he cannot live, for he is already dead. He cannot love, for love is in the present, and he has no present, no future, and no past; and yet he has a sympathetic nature, and he hates the world because he loves it. He has no passion, not because he is destitute of it, but because simultaneously he has the opposite passion. He has no time for anything, not because his time is taken up with something else, but because he has no time at all.[102]

In a spiritless age haunted by estranged crowd men, the people of the world become little more than *symparanekromenoi.*[103]

The Oppression of Objectivity: Religion and Self-alienation

From his earliest pseudonymous writings to his final "Attack upon Christendom," Kierkegaard maintains that the religious life of nineteenth-century Denmark feeds the disease of spiritlessness. The unholy alliance between the kingdom of God and the kingdom of man initiated by Constantine culminates in modern Europe's identification of religious commitment with participation in a banal form of cultural Protestantism. Christendom's zealous effort to sacralize the profane ends with the profanation of the sacred. The most alarming instance of the confusion of the two kingdoms is, for Kierkegaard, the Danish state church. Drawing a distinction that strictly parallels the Hegelian polarity of objective and subjective religion, Kierkegaard argues that the wedding of the secular and the sacred creates a dead, objective religiosity that lacks the vitality generated by subjective appropriation. In Christendom, the church no longer is made up of individuals struggling to sustain the tensions of genuinely spiritual selfhood. Having betrayed its original mission, the church has become a bourgeois social institution whose primary role, as we have seen, is nothing more than "to stabilize human relationships" and "to modulate the demands and perils of temporal existence." Priests become civil servants paid by the state to tend the "spiritual" affairs of the citizenry. In a characteristically biting passage, Kierkegaard remarks:

> Among the many various things which man needs on a civilized plane and which the state tries to provide for its citizens as cheaply and comfortably as possible—among these very various things, like public security, water, lighting, roads, bridge-building, etc., etc., there is also . . . an eternal blessed-

---

102. *Either-Or,* 1:224; 1:200.
103. Kierkegaard coins this word and uses it in the first volume of *Either-Or.* Following Geismar, Lowrie suggests the Greek term can be best translated as "the fellowship of buried lives." *Either-Or,* 1:450 n. 1.

ness in the hereafter, a requirement which the state ought also to satisfy (how generous of it!) and that in as cheap and comfortable a way as possible.[104]

With their worldly well-being hanging in the balance, priests seek mass acceptance for their teachings. In fact, "the 'priest' is monetarily interested in having people call themselves Christians, for every such person actually is (through the state as intermediary) a contributing member, and at the same time contributes to the power of the clerical order."[105]   For such a priest, the actual content of the doctrine he preaches is of little consequence. He detaches himself from the teaching and makes no effort to embody Word in deed. Promotion of religious life is simply one more way of winning one's daily bread. Kierkegaard continually satirizes the urbane philistinism of the Danish clergy which masquerades as sincere religious piety. He confesses:

> This I do not understand: to be able to be objective in this way about the religious. On Saturday a person takes out the religious (about the way a lawyer takes out his law books) and "puts himself into it," works out a sermon that he delivers on Sunday—but otherwise has nothing to do with the religious; it does not overwhelm him, never grips him suddenly—no, it is a business like the merchant's, the attorney's, the administrator's.[106]

The oppressive objectivity of the religious establishment is matched by the lifeless formalism inherent in the belief and practice of Christendom's nominal Christians. People become convinced that the essence of religious faith can be objectively defined in formal doctrines and discursive teaching presented by priests and professors. From this perspective, the task of the believer involves, at most, the mastery of objective doctrine and teaching. "In an age of knowledge," writes Kierkegaard, "when all men are Christians and know what Christianity is, it is only too easy to use the sacred names without attaching any thought to them, to recite the Christian truth by rote without having the slightest impression of it."[107]   Such formal learning, however, bears no necessary relation to the subjective life of the individual. We have seen that Kierkegaard believes spiritlessness may "possess the whole content of spirit—not as spirit . . . but as jest, galimatias, phrase, etc. It may possess truth—not

---

104. *Attack upon Christendom*, p. 99; 14:121.
105. Ibid., p. 84; 14:110.
106. *Journals and Papers*, 4557; 10-3:A 22.
107. *Postscript*, p. 252; 7:242.

as truth . . . but as rumor and old wives' tales. . . . In fact, spiritlessness can utter the same words as the richest spirit uttered, only it does not utter them by virtue of spirit."[108] In contrast with subjective reflection, which "turns its attention inwardly to the subject, and desires in this intensification of inwardness to realize the truth,"[109] Christendom's objective religiosity effects no inner transformation of individuals. Kierkegaard maintains that, appearances to the contrary notwithstanding, objective religious forms actually oppose the subjective experience of individuals and are maintained by "superstitious adherence to purely external formalities." Having become as mechanized as the world in which they dwell, people are transformed into spiritless "talking-machines." Christians roaming Christendom remind Kierkegaard of the asylum inmate who, after escaping, is warned: "When you come to town, you will be recognized, and you will at once be brought back here again; hence you need to prepare yourself fully to convince everyone, by the objective truth of what you say, that all is in order as far as your sanity is concerned." To persuade everyone that he no longer is deranged, the escapee parades back and forth through the center of town, bouncing a ball in his coattails and proclaiming, "Bang, the earth is round . . . . Bang, the earth is round."[110] Such is the madness of the "spiritual" life of Christendom.

Kierkegaard does not deny that religion serves a purpose in Christendom. He stresses that the Christianity of Christendom attempts to tranquilize the restlessness of human spirit by providing people with a false sense of security and certainty. This illusion is created by the assumption that all existential dilemmas are resolved through mere birth into a Christian world. Religious faith ministers to the bourgeois ideal of a peaceful, harmonious, mundane existence. Or as Kierkegaard puts it, "Christendom is comfortable—from this comes this tendency toward unity. The Christian categories, valid for the whole life, are made into something transitory, a thoroughfare. It begins with being incomprehensible, but gradually we smuggle in the natural man's inclination to comprehend and then get unity into its essence—and coziness. For with the coming of this unity, restlessness and striving, and fear and trembling, which should obtain for the entire life, go out."[111] In Christendom there is such a close relation-

---

108. *Concept of Dread*, pp. 84-85; 4:364-365.
109. *Postscript*, p. 175; 7:164.
110. Ibid., p. 174; 7:163.
111. *Journals and Papers*, 77; 10-3:A 186.

ship between the kingdom of God and the kingdom of man that the established order actually is regarded as divine. *Vox dei* is confounded with *vox populi* by "the indolent worldly spirit which would put itself at rest and imagine that all is sheer security and peace."[112] "The fundamental derangement at the root of modern times, which," for Kierkegaard, "branches out into logic, metaphysics, dogmatics, and the whole of modern life, consists in this: that the deep qualitative abyss in the difference between God and man has been obliterated. . . . The derangement has come about in many ways, and has many forms, but mainly as follows. As the crowd intimidates the king, as the public intimidates counselors of state and authors, so the generation will ultimately want to intimidate God, constrain him to give in, become self-important before him, brazenly defiant in their numbers, etc."[113]

With the loss of belief in divine transcendence, the journey to selfhood founders. Unlike faithful Abraham, sojourners forget that "finite experience as such is homeless." Pilgrims become rooted in finitude by settling into a comfortable and homey life governed by accepted custom and daily routine. Having mediated the oppositions, abrogated the contradictions, and relaxed the tensions of selfhood, the life of spirit is "domesticated."[114] Lost in the triviality of the quotidian, individuals strive for nothing other, long for nothing different. Restlessness stilled, yearning satisfied, selves become spiritless.

The Reflective Philosophy of Objectivity

In *Either-Or* Kierkegaard, through the persona of Judge Wilhelm, suggests that the thought of certain German philosophers "is tranquilized, the objective logical thought is brought to rest in its corresponding objectivity, and yet they are in despair, even though they distract themselves with objective thinking; for a man can distract himself in many ways, and there is hardly any anaesthetic so powerful as abstract thinking, because here it is a question of behaving as impersonally as possible."[115] For Kierkegaard, Hegelian

---

112. *Training in Christianity*, trans. by W. Lowrie (Princeton: Princeton University Press, 1967), p. 89; 12:84.

113. *Journals and Papers*, 6075; 8:A 414.

114. I borrow this term from Crites (*Twilight of Christendom*, pp. 4 ff.).

115. *Either-Or*, vol. 2, trans. W. Lowrie (Princeton: Princeton University Press, 1971), p. 216; 2:190. Issues touched in a preliminary way in this section will be the subject of further consideration in the remainder of the study. My present purpose is not to enter into a detailed consideration of Kierkegaard's critique of Hegel but to examine his understanding

philosophy gives theoretical expression to the dissipation of individual selfhood so common in modern life. Kierkegaard does not dispute Hegelianism's claim to represent the self-consciousness of the *Zeitgeist*. Speculative philosophy does provide the objective comprehension of Christendom. What Kierkegaard denies, however, is that Hegelianism provides an accurate representation of spiritual existence which can guide sojourners struggling through the stages on life's way. As the conceptual articulation of a spiritless age, Hegelianism likewise is spiritless, a symptom of the sickness unto death. The terms with which Kierkegaard describes Hegelianism are the same as those he uses to characterize his de-spirited time: *reflective, objective, speculative, abstract, pagan,* and *unhappy.*

Recalling Hegel's definition of the spiritless philosophies of his day as the "Reflective Philosophy of Subjectivity," we can categorize Kierkegaard's interpretation of Hegelianism under the heading: "Reflective Philosophy of Objectivity." Hegelianism, as Judge Wilhelm stresses, is inseparably bound to the ideal of objective reflection. Elsewhere Kierkegaard explains that

> the way of objective reflection makes the subject accidental, and thereby transforms existence into something indifferent, something vanishing. Away from the subject, the objective way of reflection leads to the objective truth, and while the subject and his subjectivity become indifferent, the truth also becomes indifferent, and this indifference is precisely its objective validity; for all interest, like all decisiveness, is rooted in subjectivity. The way of objective reflection leads to abstract thinking, to mathematics, to historical knowledge of different kinds; and it always leads away from the subject, whose existence or non-existence, and from the objective point of view quite rightly, becomes infinitely indifferent.[116]

When the goal of reflection is universally valid objective truth, the particularity of subjective interest, passion, and decision can only confuse matters. I have stressed that Kierkegaard consistently opposes theoretical reflection to personal resolution. As a loyal citizen of the state of reflection, the Hegelian philosopher is essentially an observer, "a dispassionate spectator" who "apprehends the world-historical in terms of purely metaphysical categories, and views it

---

of the relationship between Hegelianism and the sociocultural phenomenon of Christendom. In this chapter, therefore, we are more concerned with the general outlines of the Hegelianism popular during Kierkegaard's day than with the details of Hegel's own position. The analysis of the adequacy of Kierkegaard's representation of Hegelianism will be left for subsequent chapters.

116. *Postscript*, p. 173; 7:161.

speculatively as an immanent system of relationships between cause and effect, ground and consequence."[117]   In Kierkegaard's vocabulary, the term *speculation* carries negative connotations when applied to matters of existential concern. The word suggests a form of detachment, disinterestedness, and disengagement in which subjective passion evaporates and concrete individuality dissipates. Anesthetized by his own reflection, the speculative philosopher "becomes too objective to talk about himself."[118]   With the anonymous one, "he has in his distraction forgotten his own name."[119]

To say that objective reflection dissipates concrete individuality is to admit that it is essentially abstract. Speculative philosophy, Kierkegaard contends, gives ontological and epistemological priority to universality over particularity. Truth emerges only when the particular is subsumed under or consumed by the universal. Given this basic presupposition, Hegelian philosophy consistently "turns from concrete men to consider pure man."[120]   Kierkegaard emphasizes this point by his repeated insistence that speculation concentrates on the abstraction of the human race to the exclusion of its particular members. As "one becomes more and more objective, . . . subjectivity is held in contempt, the category of the individual is despised, and comfort is sought in the category of the race."[121]   In the realm of political theory, this leads to the deification of the state. Kierkegaard is persuaded that in Hegelian philosophy, individual citizens are little more than means to the all-consuming ends of the social organism.

The abstraction of speculative philosophy is further illustrated by its tendency toward *systematic* comprehension. Through the synthetic activity of reason, Hegelianism attempts to integrate the oppositions of finite experience within a self-enclosed system. Truth, it is argued, presupposes such an all-encompassing rational totality. But Kierkegaard cautions against this lofty ideal. The effort to achieve the systematic comprehension of concrete experience is fundamentally misguided and further perplexes human self-understanding. The philosopher is forced to try to view everything *sub specie aeterni*. Vision struggles to become theocentric, creating a comedy of errors occasioned by the philosopher's "having forgotten, in a sort of

117. Ibid., p. 138; 7:127.
118. Ibid., p. 50; 7:38.
119. Ibid., p. 130; 7:118.
120. Ibid., p. 315; 7:305.
121. Ibid., p. 248; 7:238.

world-historical absentmindedness, what it means to be a human being."[122]   Furthermore, since any system presupposes closure, Hegelianism seemingly must deny the open-endedness of historical existence. This results in the dissolution of the temporal tensions unique to human becoming. The stance of the world-historical observer is consistently retrospective. He can only understand "behindhand," and must turn his back to the uncertainties of the future. For speculation, time effectively ceases, and though the spectacle might go on, the spectator "dies and leaves the scene, and nothing of him remains." Hegelian philosophers are charter members of Kierkegaard's *symparanekromenoi*.

For Kierkegaard, however, the most pernicious aspect of Hegelianism's spiritlessness is its misrepresentation of Christianity. We have noted that Kierkegaard sees spiritlessness as a peculiarly modern malaise. It is not simply the absence of spirit but the "stagnation of spirit, . . . the caricature of ideality" which constitutes "apostasy." Spiritlessness is the paganism that lies at the heart of Christendom. Hegelianism both expresses and perpetuates the illusion of "Christian" paganism. "Speculative philosophy," Kierkegaard argues, "deduces paganism logically from Christianity."[123]   While purporting to unfold the conceptual truth hidden within Christian symbols, speculation actually transmutes the distinctively Christian understanding of selfhood into a Greek interpretation of human existence. Christendom sprinkles holy water on an unconverted Athens.

In sum, the reflective philosophy of objectivity absolutizes and philosophically justifies the dissipation of individual selfhood characteristic of the social, political, and religious life of Kierkegaard's Denmark. Hegelianism is a sign of the spiritlessness of the age, "the culture of reflection raised to a system." With his fellow citizens of Christendom, the speculative philosopher no longer knows what it means to exist. The dispassionate, disinterested, objective, absentminded professor finally forgets his own name—becomes estranged—*l'étranger*. He is the unhappiest man, a stranger who is merely a shadow, walking death.

"What the Age Needs"

In a note appended to his posthumous work, *The Point of View for My Work as an Author: A Report to History*, Kierkegaard

---

122. Ibid., p. 109; 7:99.
123. Ibid., p. 329; 7:319.

remarks: "What the age *needs* in the deepest sense can be said fully and completely with one single word: it needs ... eternity. The misfortune of our time is just this, that it has become simply nothing else but 'time,' the temporal, which is impatient of hearing anything about eternity."[124] Kierkegaard recognizes that for most people, "the age of distinctions is past, the system has overcome it." Moreover, he acknowledges that "he who in our age loves distinctions is an eccentric man whose soul clings to what has long vanished."[125] Nevertheless, Kierkegaard continues to love distinctions, clings to what apparently has vanished, and follows, though in a way quite different from Hölderlin, the *exzentrische Bahn* that alone leads to authentic selfhood.[126] Differentiation, separation, individualization, bifurcation is what the age needs. Only by reestablishing the oppositions, rediscovering the contradictions, and reaffirming the tensions obscured by Christendom and its philosophy, Hegelianism, can settlers be unsettled sufficiently to undertake anew the journey to selfhood.

Since Kierkegaard believes the leveling that dissipates individual selfhood "can be halted only if the individual in individual separateness [*i individuel Udsondring*] gains the intrepidity of religiousness," he insists that "rescue comes only through the essentiality of the religious in the single individual."[127] Kierkegaard takes as his fundamental task the "reintroduction of Christianity into Christendom."[129] He is fully aware of the difficulty of administering the "radical cure" he prescribes, for he knows that "what the sick man most desires is just what feeds the disease."[129] Yet Kierkegaard is convinced that beneath the façade of bourgeois complacency and respectability lurks a hidden melancholy which he describes as the "hysteria of spirit" latent in dissipated selfhood. In a manner reminiscent of Hegel's interpretation of the infinite sorrow of dismembered spirit which forebodes imminent spiritual renewal, Kierkegaard believes this melancholy is a "presentiment of a metamorphosis." "There comes an instant in a man's life," he writes, "when his immediacy is, as it were, ripened and spirit demands a higher form in which it will apprehend itself as spirit. Man, so long as he is immedi-

---

124. *Point of View*, p. 108; 13:590.
125. Preface to *Concept of Dread*.
126. Hölderlin describes the course pursued by Hyperion as "eine exzentrische Bahn."
127. *Two Ages*, pp. 86, 88; 8:81, 82.
128. *Training in Christianity*, p. 139; 12:130.
129. *Attack upon Christendom*, p. 139; 13:169.

ate spirit, coheres with [*sammen med*] the whole earthly life, and now the spirit would collect itself [*samle sig*] , as it were, out of this dissipation [*Adspredthed*] and explain itself to itself—the personality would be conscious of itself in its eternal validity."[130] By means of his pseudonymous writings. Kierkegaard endeavors to assume the role of a Socratic midwife who attends this spiritual rebirth.

---

130. *Either-Or*, 2:193; 2:170. *Adspredthed* also implies distraction, preoccupation, and absentmindedness.

|3|

AESTHETIC EDUCATION

Not to keep men from error is the duty of the
educator of men, but to guide the erring one,
even to let him swill his error out of full cups—
that is the wisdom of teachers.
                            —*Goethe*

The philosopher must possess just as much aesthetic power as the poet. Men without aesthetic
sense is what philosophers of the letter of our
time are. The philosophy of the spirit is an aesthetic philosophy.
                            —*Hegel*

It is not wrong of the spectator to want to lose
himself in poetry, this is a joy which has its reward, but the spectator must not mistake the
theatre for reality, nor himself for a spectator
who is nothing else but a spectator at a comedy.
                            —*Kierkegaard*

A method is a way. The search for a method[1] is the search for a
way—a way through the "middest" that at once separates and joins
beginning and end, Genesis and Apocalypse. To have a method is to
be underway, to be on a journey leading from origin to destination.
In the previous chapter we have explored the worlds from which
Hegel and Kierkegaard embark upon their respective journeys to
selfhood. In the two succeeding chapters we shall examine the
destinations of their pilgrimages. For the moment our concern is
method, the means—*die Mittel*—between the extremes of *archē* and
telos, spiritlessness and spirit. Only "impatience demands the impossible, to wit, the attainment of the end without the means—*die
Mittel*."[2]

In his ninth letter *On the Aesthetic Education of Man*, Schiller
admonishes: "Live with your century; but do not be its creature.
Work for your contemporaries; but create what they need, not what
they praise."[3] Hegel and Kierkegaard attempt to follow Schiller's
advice: they seek to confront people with what is required rather
than with what is desired. Careful analysis of their different ages
yields a common conclusion: what is most needed is a remedy for
the disease of spiritlessness—the sickness unto death. Hegel contends
that the ills of fragmentation and disintegration can be cured only
through the rational reintegration of the oppositions and mediation
of the conflicts sundering modern man's personal and social life. For
Kierkegaard, overcoming the dissipation of concrete existence requires the definition of individual uniqueness through the arduous
process of distinguishing self and world. In more abstract terms,
while Hegel prescribes a movement from oppositional differentiation
to reconciliation of self and other, Kierkegaard points to the need to
advance from the nondifferentiation to the differentiation of self and
other. Despite this essential difference Hegel and Kierkegaard face
the same fundamental question: How can spiritlessness be cured?
How can lost sojourners be shown the stations of the way or stages
on life's way? How can despairing pilgrims make progress?

After considerable deliberation, Hegel and Kierkegaard decide
that the need of the age can best be met by means of an "aesthetic

---

1. This reference, of course, is to Sartre's *Search for a Method*, trans. H. E. Barnes
(New York: Random House, 1968).
2. *Phenomenology*, p. 17; 26. Hegel's most extensive treatment of *die Mittel* is
developed in his analysis of the syllogism. See *Logic*, pp. 664 ff.; 6:351.
3. Schiller, *Aesthetic Education*, p. 61.

education." Reflecting the continuing influence of Schiller, Hegel writes, "the philosopher must possess just as much aesthetic power as the poet. Men without aesthetic sense is what philosophers of our time are. The philosophy of the spirit is an aesthetic philosophy."[4] The one who is able to formulate such an aesthetic philosophy of spirit becomes a *Volkserzieher*, "educator of the people," "teacher of mankind."[5] With the transformation of the ideal of his youth into a reflective form, Hegel is able to assert: "To embrace the whole energy of the suffering and discord that has controlled the world and all forms of its culture for some thousand years, and also to rise above it—this can be done by philosophy alone."[6] Hegel's confidence that philosophical reflection can bind the wounds modern experience inflicts upon the human spirit motivates and sustains his enormous philosophical enterprise. In 1808 he writes: "Daily I am more convinced that theoretical work accomplishes more in the world than practical. Once the realm [*Reich*] of representation is revolutionized, actuality cannot hold out."[7] Kierkegaard suggests his understanding of his task when he explains: "I am the last stage of the development of a poet in the direction of a small-scale reformer. I have much more imagination than a reformer as such would have, but then again less of a certain personal force required for acting as a reformer."[8] Or as he puts it elsewhere, "my whole life is an epigram to make men aware."[9] Hegel and Kierkegaard share a common sense of mission: they believe themselves called to assume the role of reformer, educa-

---

4. "Earliest System-Programme of German Idealism," trans. in Harris, *Hegel's Development*, p. 511; 1:235. Although the authorship of this fragment has been the subject of lively scholarly debate over the years, evidence now strongly supports analysts who argue that Hegel, rather than Schelling, penned the work. For a convenient summary of this discussion see Harris, pp. 249-257.

5. Ibid., p. 511; 1:235. In his detailed reconstruction of Hegel's early years, Harris argues that "the ambition to be a *Volkserzieher*" (*Hegel's Development*, p. xix) provides a focus around which to organize Hegel's otherwise disparate youthful philosophical wanderings. Although Harris's study is generally quite helpful and insightful, his effort to view all of Hegel's work prior to 1801 from the perspective of his intention to become a Volkserzieher distorts important aspects of his development and creates needless interpretative problems. Harris's recognition of the importance of this ideal of Hegel is correct but need not be pursued with such relentlessness to be persuasive. For a suggestive, though limited, discussion of Kierkegaard's pedagogical preoccupations see Ronald J. Manheimer, *Kierkegaard as Educator* (Berkeley, Los Angeles, London: University of California Press, 1977).

6. Quoted in Richard Kroner's introduction to Hegel's *Early Theological Writings*, p. 38.

7. *Briefe von und an Hegel*, 1:253. A text such as this underscores Hegel's continuing commitment to the ideals of his youth.

8. *Journals and Papers*, 6061; 8-1:A 347.

9. Ibid., 6108; 8-1:A 549.

tor, teacher of humanity. Their diverse philosophical and theological writings are consistently informed by the pedagogical purpose of leading individuals from (*e-ducare*) spiritlessness to spirit.

Beneath the significant differences distinguishing their interpretations of spiritlessness lies an agreement that this sickness is contracted from having *forgotten* the nature of authentic selfhood. Aesthetic education, therefore, involves *anamnesis*—the recollection of genuine spiritual existence.[10] In forming their mnemonic therapies Hegel and Kierkegaard draw heavily upon their interpretations of Socratic and Platonic dialectic. Through their writings they attempt to engage the reader in a dialogue that eventually will unmask ignorance, sublate "apparent knowledge,"[11] and dispel illusion. The beginning and end of the educational journey Hegel and Kierkegaard bid the reader to undertake can be expressed in various terms. These educators of humanity attempt to enable people to move from inauthenticity to authenticity, from bondage to freedom, or from abstract to concrete individuality. They are fully aware of the difficulty and the delicacy of the task. "There is nothing that requires such gentle handling," Kierkegaard states, "as an illusion, if one wishes to dispel it."[12] The educator who attempts "to totter what is firmly fixed" encounters resistance at every turn.

Since they both recognize the importance of proper educational technique, Hegel and Kierkegaard agree that "it would help very little if one persuaded millions of men to accept the truth, if precisely by the method of their acceptance they were transferred into error."[13] In spite of significant stylistic differences the pedagogical methods employed by Hegel and Kierkegaard are remarkably similar. They attempt to provide a therapeutic aesthetic education by developing alternative phenomenologies of spirit which chart the

---

10. For the twentieth-century reader, Hegel's and Kierkegaard's recognition of the therapeutic value of recollection suggests interesting parallels with Freud's psychoanalytic method. Consider Jean Hyppolite, "Hegel's Phenomenology and Psychoanalysis," in *New Studies in Hegel's Philosophy*, ed. W. E. Steinkraus (New York: Holt, Rinehart and Winston, 1971), pp. 57-70; Paul Ricoeur, *Freud and Philosophy*; idem, "Hegel aujourd'hui," *Études théologiques et religieuses* 49 (1974), 335-355; J. Preston Cole, *The Problematic Self in Kierkegaard and Freud* (New Haven: Yale University Press, 1971); Kresten Nordentoft, *Kierkegaard's Psychology*; and Mark C. Taylor, "Psychoanalytic Dimensions of Kierkegaard's View of Selfhood," *Philosophy Today* 19 (1975), 198-212.

11. The German term *erscheinendes Wissen* connotes apparent and illusory, as well as phenomenal and appearing, knowledge. Hegel repeatedly plays on the multiple meanings of the term.

12. *Point of View*, p. 25; 13:531.

13. *Postscript*, p. 221; 7:208.

course and identify the stations or stages along the way from inauthentic to authentic selfhood. As we have noted, this is Hegel's
primary task in the *Phenomenology of Spirit* and Kierkegaard's chief
purpose in the pseudonymous writings. "Instruction begins," Kierkegaard writes, "when you, the teacher, learn from the pupil, put
yourself in his place so that you may understand what he understands and in the way he understands it, in case you have not
understood it before."[14] Löwenberg's account of Hegel's phenomenological method in terms of a suggestive comparison with the
aesthetics of drama clarifies the point Kierkegaard is making:

> The manner of reconstructing the phenomenon, the phenomenon in each
> case being a unique way of knowing, analogous as it is to the actor's art of
> impersonation, may not inaptly be described as *histrionic*. There is no
> impropriety in the description; for what is the art of impersonation if not
> the art of entering *ab intra* into a character foreign to the impersonator's?
> The actor must be able to hide his real face behind an alien mask. He must
> play a part. He must mimic with fidelity the appearance of another being,
> "suiting the action to the word and the word to the action." He cannot do
> this without identifying himself for the moment with the inner life of the
> character he is portraying.[15]

Any effective therapist, like any good teacher, must be part actor. By
means of imaginative role-playing, Hegel and Kierkegaard assemble a
cast of characters that includes representatives of different styles of
selfhood, forms of existence, or shapes of consciousness. Through
these dramatis personae, they stage the drama of the journey to
selfhood. The characters enact contrasting spiritual configurations
which the directors arrange in a dialectical progression that advances
from less to more complete forms of life.

---

14. *Point of View*, p. 30; 13:534.
15. Jacob Löwenberg, "The Exoteric Approach to Hegel's *Phenomenology*," *Mind* 43
(1934), 440. Schrag's comment on Kierkegaard draws the parallel neatly. "This method of
phenomenological description was already part and parcel of Kierkegaard's existentialism,
although it was never systematically elaborated. The existential thinker must penetrate his
concrete, lived experience with thought and describe this existence in its immediate
disclosure. Kierkegaard's profound descriptions of the various modifications of anxiety and
his elucidation of the three 'stages of existence' indicated an underlying awareness and use
of the phenomenological method. It is through the use of the phenomenological method
that one penetrates the structures of human subjectivity. Only in this way can the
existential thinker discover the universal possibilities of his lived concreteness" (*On Existence and Freedom: Towards an Ontology of Human Finitude* [Evanston, Ill.: Northwestern
University Press, 1961], p. 11). Gregor Malantschuk labels this technique Kierkegaard's
"experimental psychology" (*Kierkegaard's Thought* [Princeton: Princeton University Press,
1971], p. 33).

Educational goals, of course, influence pedagogical method. Since the telos of the journey mapped by Hegel and Kierkegaard is free concrete individuality, they must proceed in a way that does not violate the integrity and autonomy of the student. Their teaching must be subtly Socratic rather than overtly didactic. Most importantly, instruction must begin from the standpoint of the pupil and proceed to disclose the internal inconsistencies and contradictions of the learner's perspective in such a way that the student is enabled to move step by step through the stages from error and bondage to truth and freedom. Aesthetic education is a "pedagogy for the oppressed" which calls each reader to "self-examination" and demands that he "judge for himself" the form of life he is leading. Undertaking this educational journey exacts a price. Hegel admits that "the decision to philosophize casts itself purely into thinking . . . as into an ocean without beaches; all bright colors, all mainstays have vanished, all friendly lights otherwise present are extinguished. Only one star still shines, the inner star of spirit. . . . It is natural that, thus alone, spirit is assailed . . . by dread."[16] Recalling Hegel's image, Kierkegaard repeatedly stresses that the journey to selfhood finally thrusts one into a dangerous suspension "above seventy thousand fathoms of water, many, many miles from all human help."[17] Critical reflection discloses old certainties to be untenable illusions. Perplexed and bewildered, the voyager tosses and turns on a sea of doubt (*Zweifel, Tvivl*) and despair (*Verzweiflung, Fortvivlelse*). Hegel and Kierkegaard go so far as to argue that every station along life's way short of the final destination remains a form of inauthentic existence that must be described as "despair." According to Kierkegaard,

> it is ordinarily assumed that a man is well when he does not himself say that he is sick, and still more confidently when he says that he is well. The physician, on the other hand, regards sickness differently. . . . The physician knows that just as there is a sickness that is only imaginary, so there is such a thing as apparent health. In the latter case, therefore, the physician first employs medicines to cause the disease to become manifest.[18]

For Hegel and Kierkegaard, aesthetic education is the medicine that brings to light the disease of spiritlessness. They admit that their

---

16. *Berliner Schriften, 1818-1831*, ed. J. Hoffmeister (Hamburg: Felix Meiner, 1956), pp. 19-20.

17. *Stages on Life's Way*, trans. W. Lowrie (New York: Schocken Books, 1967), p. 425; 6:438.

18. *Sickness unto Death*, p. 156; 11:137.

pedagogy leads the pupil along a distressing "highway of despair."[19] But the tonic that reveals the illness also effects the cure of the sickness unto death. Though the highway of despair plunges the wayfarer into a dark night of the soul, completion of the journey holds the promise of realized selfhood.

When the pedagogical intent of these writings is perceived, Hegel's *Phenomenology of Spirit* and Kierkegaard's pseudonymous writings appear to be Bildungsromane.[20] This genre, which was particularly fashionable during the latter half of the eighteenth and first half of the nineteenth century, is illustrated by works of authors as different as Rousseau (*Emile*), Goethe (*Wilhelm Meisters Lehrjahre*), Novalis (*Heinrich von Ofterdingen*), and Hölderlin (*Hyperion*). In such *Romane*, the author follows the circuitous path of the hero's Bildung—development, education, cultivation, self-formation. The journey usually leads through various educative experiences in the course of which the protagonist progresses from the naiveté and illusion of youth to the sobriety of mature selfhood. The experiences recounted are of interest less for their individual uniqueness than for their representative character. Josiah Royce points out that

> such romances are prone to lay stress upon some significant process of evolution, through which the hero passes. He himself represents a type of personal experience, or development of character. The effect of such work is rather to present to us the world, or some portion of it, as seen from a typical or characteristic, and in so far personal point of view, rather than to interest us directly in the passions or in the tragedy of the hero's life."[21]

The hero is conceived as an Everyman in whom each reader can see his own life reflected. In its entirety, the way of the latter-day pilgrim represents an *ordo salutis,*[22] an ascent of the *scala*

---

19. *Phenomenology*, p. 49; 67. Throughout the remainder of this chapter, references to the *Phenomenology* are given in the body of the text.

20. Other authors who have recognized the similarities between Hegel's *Phenomenology* and the genre of Bildungsroman include Abrams, *Natural Supernaturalism*, pp. 225-237; Hyppolite, *Genesis and Structure*, pp. 11-12; and Josiah Royce, *Lectures on Modern Idealism* (New Haven: Yale University Press, 1964), pp. 147 ff. See also W. H. Bruford, *The German Tradition of Self-cultivation: From Humboldt to Thomas Mann* (New York: Cambridge University Press, 1975). The only author who has suggested a connection between Kierkegaard's works and the Bildungsroman tradition is Louis Mackey: see his *Kierkegaard: A Kind of Poet* (Philadelphia: University of Pennsylvania Press, 1972), pp. 273 ff. Mackey, however, restricts the relation to certain parallels between Goethe's *Wilhelm Meister* and *Either-Or*. Compare Aage Henriksen, *Kierkegaards Romaner* (Copenhagen: Gyldendal, 1969).

21. Royce, *Modern Idealism*, p. 148.

22. Hermann Diem writes: "Retrospectively we might consider and elucidate the whole Socratic existential dialectic as being, from the point of view of the Christian

paradisa.[23] The Bildungsroman "translates the painful process of Christian conversion and redemption into a painful process of self-formation, crisis, and self-recognition, which culminates in a stage of self-coherence and self-recognition."[24]   As I previously have suggested, this way of interpreting personal experience tends "to internalize apocalypse by transferring the theatre of events from the outer earth and heaven to the spirit of the single believer, in which there enacts itself, metaphorically, the entire eschatological drama of the destruction of the old creation, the union with Christ, and the emergence of a new creation."[25]

When viewing Hegel's *Phenomenology* and Kierkegaard's pseudonymous writings from this angle, it is necessary to distinguish three narrative strands woven together in each Bildungsgeschichte. In the first place, Hegel's and Kierkegaard's works are quasi-autobiographical. They summarize the phases through which the authors have passed in their personal, religious, and philosophical development. Hegel describes the *Phenomenology of Spirit* as his "voyage of discovery" and indicates that there is nothing of importance in his own history which is not, in one way or another, incorporated in this work.[26]   Kierkegaard is even more explicit on this point: "The fact is that in the works under my own name or that of pseudonyms, I have treated and described fundamentally, as I always do, the various stages through which I passed before reaching the point where I now am."[27]   Particularly in the case of Kierkegaard, preoccupation with the relation of author to text frequently obscures important aspects of the writings themselves.[28]   Second,

---

revelation, the necessary *ordo salutis*, constituting the path of Christian existence" (*Kierkegaard's Existential Dialectic*, trans. H. Knight [New York: Frederick Ungar Publishing Co., 1965], p. 52).

23.   The image of the ladder is important for both Hegel and Kierkegaard. Hegel claims that the *Phenomenology* offers the reader a "ladder" to the scientific perspective (14: 25). Kierkegaard's pseudonym Johannes Climacus is taken from a mid-seventh-century compendium of monastic spirituality entitled the *Ladder of John*, a work that identifies thirty steps that lead the monk to perfection.

24.   Abrams, *Natural Supernaturalism*, p. 96.

25.   Ibid., p. 47. See above, chap. 1 text corresponding to n. 14.

26.   In *Repetition*, Kierkegaard alludes to Hegel's *Phenomenology* when he satirically describes the young man's journey to Berlin as a "voyage of discovery": see *Repetition: An Essay in Experimental Psychology*, trans. W. Lowrie (New York: Harper and Row, 1964), p. 54; 3:191. For similar references see *Either-Or*, 1:36; 1:22; and *Philosophical Fragments*, p. 54; 4:210.

27.   *Attack upon Christendom*, p. 52; 14:76. In his Journal he explains: "My writing is essentially my own development" (*Journals and Papers*, 6390; 10-1:A 273.

28.   For a critique of the biographical-psychological approach to Kierkegaard's works see Taylor, *Kierkegaard's Pseudonymous Authorship*, pp. 26 ff.

each phenomenology of spirit recapitulates the stages of racial development. Hegel stresses that the dialectical course he plots represents the Bildung of the universal individual (*allgemeine Individuum*) or world spirit (*Weltgeist*).[29] Although less often emphasized, Kierkegaard does suggest that the stages on life's way can be viewed as "the different stages of the evolution of world-consciousness."[30] Finally, the forms of spirit depicted by Hegel and Kierkegaard describe the stages that must be traversed by the reader if he is to reach the goal of authentic individuality. From this perspective, the chief protagonist of these contrasting Bildungsromane becomes the reader himself. Hegel's and Kierkegaard's phenomenologies encourage the reader to educate himself or to cultivate himself in such a way that he emerges from spiritlessness and rises to spiritual existence. The dramas unfolded never lose sight of the audience to which they are directed. Here the pedagogical intention of Hegel and Kierkegaard is most evident.[31] The aesthetic education they develop seeks to provide a remedy for the disease plaguing modern man—spiritlessness. Each author, however, fashions the prescribed cure in a distinctive manner.

THEORIA

The Drama of Experience

In his "Introduction" Hegel describes the *Phenomenology* as "the path of the natural consciousness which presses forward to true knowledge; or as the way [*der Weg*] of the soul which journeys through the series of its own configurations as though they were the stations appointed for it by its own nature, so that it may purify

---

29. See, for example, *Phenomenology*, p. 16; 26.

30. *Either-Or*, 1:60; 1:45. This point is more fully developed in *The Concept of Irony with Constant Reference to Socrates*, trans. L. Capel (Bloomington: Indiana University Press, 1968), pp. 222-240; 13:279-297. The only other commentator who has recognized this tendency in Kierkegaard's work is Gregor Malantschuk: see his *Kierkegaard's Way to the Truth* (Minneapolis: Augsburg Publishing Co., 1963), pp. 25 ff., 46 ff.; and *Frihends Problem I Kierkegaards Begrebet Angest* (Copenhagen: Roskenkilde og Bagger, 1971), chap. 2.

31. By way of anticipation, it should be noted that Hegel's interpretation of finite spirit as the incarnation of infinite spirit leads him to conclude that the world-historical process also represents the Bildung of Absolute Spirit. The basis for this claim will become more understandable after we consider Hegel's use of central Christian symbols.

Surely each of these ways of viewing Hegel's *Phenomenology* and Kierkegaard's pseudonymous writings is illuminating. But in light of the previous chapter, it should be apparent that the third point of view is most in keeping with each author's own intentions. Moreover, this line of analysis discloses most completely the nature of the relationship between the positions of Hegel and Kierkegaard.

itself for the life of the spirit, and achieve finally, through a completed experience of itself, the awareness of what it really is in itself"
(49; 67).[32] The book attempts to provide its reader with a "ladder"
(14; 25) by which to ascend to the scientific perspective from which
spirit can grasp its own actuality. I have already suggested that Hegel
believes the journey from inauthenticity to authenticity has both
universal or generic and individual or personal dimensions. "The task
of leading the individual from his uneducated standpoint [*unge-
bildeten Standpunkt*] to knowledge," Hegel maintains, "had to be
seen in its universal sense, just as it was the universal individual,
self-conscious spirit whose formative education [Bildung] had to be
studied" (16; 26). Hegel proceeds to argue that "the single individual
must also pass through the formative stages [*Bildungsstufen*] of
universal spirit so far as their content is concerned, but as shapes that
spirit has already left behind, as stages on a way that has been made
level with labor" (16; 27). As the analysis unfolds, it becomes
apparent that the education of universal and individual spirit, in fact,
forms two aspects of a single pedagogical process.

> This past experience is the already acquired property of universal spirit
> which constitutes the substance of the individual, and hence appears exter-
> nally to him as his inorganic nature. In this respect formative education
> [Bildung], regarded from the side of the individual, consists in his acquiring
> what thus lies at hand, devouring his inorganic nature, and taking possession
> of it for himself. But, regarded from the side of universal spirit as substance,
> this is nothing but its own acquisition of self-consciousness, the bringing
> about of its own becoming and reflection into itself. [16-17; 27]

Hegel's educational journey begins with "the standpoint of consciousness which knows objects in their opposition to itself, and
itself in opposition to them" (15; 25). By initially focusing on the
form of experience in which subject and object or self and other are
sundered, Hegel takes as his point of departure the condition he
refers to as "spiritlessness." The individual subject sets himself over
against an alien object that he then attempts to grasp. "Knowledge in
its first phase, or *immediate spirit*," Hegel asserts, "is spiritlessness

---

32. Hegel's undertaking is not without historical precedent. As Werner Marx points
out, in the work of both Fichte and Schelling "we find the idea of a genetic presentation of
the build-up of self-consciousness in its various capacities, conceived as a 'sequence of
reflection,' in which consciousness increasingly improves in self-discernment" (*Hegel's
Phenomenology of Spirit: Its Point and Purpose—A Commentary on the Preface and
Introduction*, trans. P. Heath [New York: Harper and Row, 1975], p. xvii). See Fichte's
Science of Knowledge and *Foundations of the Entire Science of Knowledge*, and Schelling's
System of Transcendental Idealism.

[*das Geistlose*]" (15;26). The demanding "initiation of the unscientific consciousness into science," which is necessary for the actualization of spirit, involves the sublation of this opposition through the
incremental reconciliation of subjectivity and objectivity. The goal of
this voyage of discovery is a mediation of self and other which
involves "*pure* self-recognition in absolute otherness" (14; 24). Hegel
expresses the final insight toward which he leads the pupil in more
technical language when he writes: "The spiritual alone is the *actual*;
it is essence, or that which has *being in itself*; it is that which *relates
itself to itself* and is *determinate*, it is *other-being* and *being-for-self*,
and in this determinateness, or in its self-externality, abides with
itself; in other words, it is *in and for itself*" (14; 24).[33] Taken
together, the different dimensions of this reconciliation of subject
and object form a unification of self and other which Hegel sees as
overcoming the fragmentation and disintegration characteristic of
alienation. The dialectical reintegration of subjectivity and objectivity negates determination by alien otherness and realizes authentic
self-relation that is mediated by relation to other. This, for Hegel, is
the freedom unique to concrete individuality; it is the restoration of
the unity of man.

The very nature of the end Hegel sets for himself creates a
methodological dilemma. In order to lead the reader from inauthentic to authentic existence, it would seem necessary to employ a
criterion to discriminate inadequate forms of life and to arrange
competing structures of consciousness in a progressive sequence. And
yet if the point of the educational journey is the emergence of free
autonomous selfhood, no measure can be externally or coercively
imposed in a heteronomous manner. Hegel attempts to solve this
problem by arguing that every form of consciousness provides itself
with a standard for self-evaluation and hence need not be subjected
to an alien norm. Consciousness distinguishes itself from its object,
which it takes to exist independently of the cognitive relationship.
The apparently self-subsistent object is the criterion by which consciousness judges itself.

> In consciousness one thing exists *for* another, i.e., consciousness regularly
> contains the determinateness of the moment of knowledge; at the same
> time, this other is to consciousness not merely *for it*, but is also outside of

---

33. The precise meaning of this definition of spirit will become clearer after we have
considered Hegel's interpretation of the principles of identity, difference, and contradiction.
See below, chap. 4, 1st sec. ("Mediation").

this relationship, or exists *in itself*: the moment of truth. Thus in what consciousness affirms from within itself as *being-in-itself* or the *True* we have the standard that consciousness itself sets up by which to measure what it knows. If we designate *knowledge* as the Notion, but the essence or the *True* as what exists, or the *object*, then the examination consists in seeing whether the Notion corresponds to the object. But if we call the *essence* or in-itself of the *object* the *Notion*, and on the other hand understand by the *object* the Notion itself as *object*, viz. as it exists *for an other*, then the examination consists in seeing whether the object corresponds to the Notion. It is evident, of course, that these two procedures are the same. [53; 71]

If consciousness's comparison of itself with its standard yields a negative conclusion concerning the correspondence of subjectivity and objectivity, consciousness is forced to change itself in order more adequately to grasp its object. But, Hegel argues, "in the alteration of the knowledge, the object itself alters for it [i.e., consciousness] too, for the knowledge that was present was essentially a knowledge of the object: as the knowledge changes, so too does the object, for it essentially belonged to this knowledge. Hence it comes to pass for consciousness that what it previously took to be the *in-itself* is not an *in-itself*, or that it was only an in-itself for consciousness" (54; 72). As a result of this process of self-correction, consciousness is doubly confounded: subjective certainty becomes doubtful, and what had been seen as an objective measure now seems all the while to have been a subjective appearance. The apprehension of the illusory character of its criterion is inseparable from consciousness's recognition of a new standard of evaluation. From the viewpoint of consciousness itself, this new norm is encountered as a novel object whose origin is unknown but which beckons consciousness to attempt to grasp it.[34] This situation, of course, constitutes the occasion for further dialectical development.

It is necessary to stress that Hegel regards the critique of consciousness by which it moves from less to more adequate forms as "immanent." Consciousness engages in a protracted dialogue with itself in which it subjects itself to constant questioning, revision, and reform. Hegel makes this point emphatically when he writes: "Thus consciousness suffers this violence at its own hands; it spoils its own limited satisfaction" (51; 69). The conviction that consciousness

---

34. Hegel explains: "But it is just this necessity itself, or the *origination* of the new object, that presents itself to consciousness without its understanding how this happens, which proceeds for us, as it were, behind the back of consciousness" (p. 56; 74).

engages in immanent self-criticism forms an essential presupposition of Hegel's phenomenological method. In a crucial passage Hegel explains that "not only is a contribution by us superfluous, since Notion and object, the criterion and what is to be tested, are present in consciousness itself, but we are also spared the trouble of comparing the two and really *testing* them, so that, since what consciousness examines is its own self, all that is left for us to do is simply to look on [*nur das reine Zusehen bleibt*] " (54; 72). In other words, Hegel conceives his task as basically *descriptive*.[35] He attempts to re-present accurately the stages through which consciousness progresses by its own internal dialectic. The phenomenologist cannot arbitrarily instruct consciousness in the errors of its ways but must sink his "freedom in the content, letting it move spontaneously of its own nature, by the self as its own self, and then contemplate [*betrachten*] this movement" (36; 48). When understood in this way, Hegel's method is radically empirical.[36] He immerses himself in the observed perspective as completely as possible in order to describe it from within in a manner that simultaneously fathoms its inherent principles and discerns its latent contradictions. Only through such a dialectic of immanent self-examination and self-judgment does Hegel think consciousness can be led from error and illusion to truth and knowledge.

Spectator and Spectacle

Hegel's "empiricism," however, is of an unusual sort; it is both theoretical and speculative. To arrive at the "immanent contemplation of the object," he assumes the stance of a spectator who observes and records the drama of experience unfolding before him.[37] The education he attempts to provide through such careful observation and speculation is, properly speaking, "aesthetic." As

---

35. A similar reading of Hegel's phenomenological method is developed insightfully and persuasively by Kenley Dove: see his "Hegel's Phenomenological Method," in *New Studies in Hegel's Philosophy*, pp. 34-56, and "Toward an Interpretation of Hegel's *Phänomenologie des Geistes*," (Ph.D. diss., Yale University, 1965), esp. chaps. 2-3. Compare Kojève's assertion that Hegel's method is "purely contemplative and descriptive or better, phenomenological in Husserl's sense of the term" (*Introduction to the Reading of Hegel*, p. 171; cf. pp. 183-184).

36. George Schrader offers an illuminating discussion of the contrast between Hegelian and British empiricism: see his "Hegel's Contribution to Phenomenology," *The Monist* 48 (1964), 18-33.

37. Given Hegel's careful use of the term *experience* in the *Phenomenology*, it is instructive to note the connection between the German *Erfahrung* and the word for "travel," *fahren*.

Stephen Crites points out, the term *aesthetic* derives from the Greek verb αἰσθάνομαι, which in its sense of "to observe" is related in meaning to both *theory* (*Theoria*) and *theater*.[38] In the *Phenomenology* Hegel offers a narrative account of the drama of human consciousness for the reader's contemplation. It is his hope that the observation of this spectacle will provide an aesthetic education that is cathartic.

This educational method involves an essential distinction between observed and observing consciousness. Hegel is no mere chronicler of consciousness's experience as it moves from standpoint to standpoint. His narrative perspective affords him an angle of vision that is not immediately accessible to the form of life which he is describing. Having grasped the overall plot of the drama he recounts, Hegel understands the experiences of the actors better than the players themselves. He does not suffer Oedipus's tragic blindness. This comprehensive vision enables Hegel to be the educator who can serve as the reader's guide. Throughout the narrative Hegel communicates *directly* with his reader in an effort to provide a map for the perilous journey along the highway of despair. His method for offering such guidance is the employment of a device that can best be described as "the phenomenological we."[39] By means of repeated remarks interspersed throughout the text which explicitly reflect the viewpoint of "us" or of the "we," Hegel attempts to help the reader anticipate the peripeteias and avoid the pitfalls to which observed consciousness inevitably succumbs. But Hegel's direct identification with the reader through the use of the "we" should not obscure the significant difference between the points of view of instructor and pupil. When regarded as observing consciousness, both author (i.e., Hegel) and reader are distinguished from observed consciousness.

---

38. Stephen Crites, introduction to Kierkegaard's *Crisis in the Life of an Actress and Other Essays on Drama* (New York: Harper and Row, 1967), p. 21. Compare W. Barrett, *Irrational Man: A Study in Existential Philosophy* (New York: Doubleday and Co., 1962), p. 164.

39. Hegel's use of the "we" throughout the *Phenomenology* has received considerable attention in the secondary literature. See, for example, Dove, "Toward an Interpretation," chap. 2; John Findlay, *Hegel: A Reinterpretation* (New York: Collier Books, 1962), pp. 87 ff.; Martin Heidegger, *Holzwege* (Frankfurt: V. Klostermann, 1957), pp. 173 ff.; Hyppolite, *Genesis and Structure*, pp. 3 ff.; R. Kroner, *Von Kant bis Hegel*, vol. 2, *Naturphilosophie zur Philosophie des Geistes* (Tübingen: J. C. B. Mohr, 1924), pp. 369 ff.; Lukács, *The Young Hegel*, pp. 474 ff.; and Herbert Marcuse, *Reason and Revolution: Hegel and the Rise of Social Theory* (Boston: Beacon Press, 1960), pp. 94 ff. None of these commentators, however, adequately distinguishes the viewpoint of the author from that of the reader.

Nevertheless, Hegel's perspective and that of the reader are not identical; they differ as does the initiator from the initiate. The reader occupies a position suspended between the forms of life examined and the comprehensive vision of the instructor—he "hovers *between* the viewing and the viewed standpoints."[40] Habermas correctly points out that "the phenomenologist's perspective from which the path of knowledge in its manifestations presents itself 'for us,' can only be adopted in anticipation until this perspective itself is produced in phenomenological experience. 'We,' too, are drawn into the process of reflection, which at each of its levels is characterized anew by a 'reversal of consciousness.' "[41] Hegel's pedagogy, therefore, involves a triplicity of consciousness: the consciousness of the instructor, of the instructed, and of the object of instruction.[42]

After establishing the distinction between the perspectives of teacher and student *within* observing consciousness, it is possible to analyze the precise way in which Hegel distinguishes viewing from viewed consciousness. The basis of the difference between these two forms of awareness lies in the nature of their respective objects. We have noted that observed consciousness sees itself involved in an effort to establish knowledge by relating to an object that it believes to be both independent of consciousness and true in itself. Since this very knowledge is the object of observing consciousness, observed consciousness's contrast between subject and object, being-for-consciousness and being-in-itself now is seen as a distinction that falls *within* consciousness. The criterion that consciousness encounters as external to and imposed upon itself is, for the phenomenologist, immanent in consciousness itself. In other words, "consciousness provides its own criterion within itself, so that the investigation becomes a comparison of consciousness with itself" (53; 71). Hegel stresses that "the essential point to bear in mind throughout the whole investigation is that these two moments, 'Notion' and 'object,' 'being-for-another' and 'being-in-itself,' both fall *within* that knowledge which *we* [emphasis added] are investigating" (53; 71). Having

---

40. Fackenheim, *Religious Dimension*, p. 36.
41. Jürgen Habermas, *Knowledge and Human Interests*, trans. J. Shapiro (Boston: Beacon Press, 1971), p. 17.
42. The emphasis on the threefold nature of consciousness in the *Phenomenology* distinguishes my line of analysis from interpretations such as that of Abrams (*Natural Supernaturalism*, pp. 225 ff.) in which consciousness is seen as merely double. If the tripartite distinction is allowed to slip into simple duality, Hegel's pedagogical purpose becomes overshadowed by autobiographical preoccupations.

recognized the inextricable relation between subjectivity and objectivity, the phenomenological observer realizes that

> there is no mind-versus-nature, or mind-versus-the-world. The mind implies the world, at least in the sense that the mind is a self-grasping entity. Each way, however, in which it grasps itself is necessarily connected with a certain image of a structure of something which is not the mind itself, to which it is rather opposed in various ways. . . . Thus, a certain concept of the mind implies a concept of the world: we cannot have the concept of the mind, unless we see that in the self-understanding of the mind, the concept of the world is already implied.[43]

This insight is central to Hegel's entire argument.

Observed consciousness initially believes the progressive experiences it undergoes result from a series of contingent encounters with different external objects. Hegel argues that the reflective description of the experience of consciousness eventually sublates both the externality of the subject-object relation and the contingency of the stages of development from error to truth. Empathetic identification with other forms of consciousness discloses the inherent contradictions that lead to the self-negation of every partial viewpoint. Each perspective is internally related to its opposite in such a way that it bears within itself the seeds of its own destruction. Put differently, every particular point of view is inwardly contradictory and therefore inherently unstable. Hegel insists that the dissolution that inevitably results from such self-contradiction is at the same time a resolution. With the discovery of the illusory character of its previous "knowledge," the subject meets a new object. It is evident to Hegel and his pupil that this novel object encountered by consciousness is not a creation *de novo* but is resurrected from the ashes left by consciousness's own negation of its prior object.

> Consciousness knows *something*; this object is the essence or the *in-itself*; but it is also for consciousness the in-itself. . . . We see that consciousness now has two objects: one is the first *in-itself*, the second is the *being-for-consciousness of this in-itself*. The latter appears at first sight to be merely

---

43. Dieter Henrich, "Between Kant and Hegel," p. 10. Although it had been suggested in Kant's critical philosophy, Henrich credits Fichte with this discovery. He stresses the lasting significance of this point when he writes: "This insight into the connection between concepts of the mind on the one side and images of the world on the other is the origin of the modern method of historical interpretation. It is the very origin of the word *Weltanschauung*, image of the world—the word was not there before Fichte started his theory; it was invented by him" (p. 10).

the reflection of consciousness into itself, i.e., what consciousness has in mind is not an object, but only its knowledge of the first object. But . . . the first object, in being known, is altered for consciousness; it ceases to be the in-itself, and becomes something that is the *in-itself* only *for-consciousness*. And this then is the true: the being-for-consciousness of this in-itself. Or, in other words, this is the *essence*, or the *object* of consciousness. This new object contains the nothingness of the first, it is what experience has made of it. [55; 73]

The previous errors of consciousness, therefore, are neither acciden- tal aberrations nor inconsequential mistakes but form essential moments in the dialectical development of truth. For Hegel, as for the Goethe of *Wilhelm Meister*, "not to keep from error is the duty of the educator of men, but to guide the erring one, even to let him swill his error out of full cups—that is the wisdom of teachers."[44] Truth is imbibed only by draining dry the cup of error.

The sequence of experiences undergone by consciousness is gen- erated by a continuous process that Hegel calls "determinate nega- tion." The distinguishing characteristic of any particular object is mediated by the specificity of the object through whose negation it arises. Since each object is inherently related to its antithesis, the progressive unfolding of the experience of consciousness is not arbi- trary and inflicted in an external manner but grows out of a *neces- sary* process of immanent dialectical development. In the *Science of Logic* Hegel offers an abstract description of the method concretely applied in his *Phenomenology*. In the course of realizing itself, each form of consciousness

at the same time dissolves [*auf-löst*] itself, has for its result its own negation—and so passes into a higher form. All that is necessary to achieve scientific progress . . . is the recognition of the logical principle that the negative is just as much positive, or that what is self-contradictory does not resolve itself into a nullity, into abstract nothingness, but essentially only into the negation of its *particular* content, in other words, that such a negation is not all and every negation, but the negation of a determinate thing which resolves itself, and consequently is a determinate negation [*bestimmte Negation*], and therefore the result essentially contains that from which it results. . . . Because the result, the negation, is a *determinate* negation it has a *content*. It is a fresh Notion but higher and richer than its predecessor; for it is richer by the negation or opposite of the latter,

44. This is Walter Kaufmann's translation (*Hegel: Reinterpretation, Texts, and Com- mentary*).

therefore contains it, but also something more, and is the unity of itself and its opposite.[45]

The stages through which spirit passes in moving toward its full realization form a *necessary* progression in which beginning and end are implicitly one. The apprehension of the necessity of this dialectical development is the lesson taught by the reader's phenomenological guide. Hegel stresses the significance of this point when he writes:

> Our account implied that our knowledge of the first object, or the being-*for-*consciousness of the first in-itself, itself becomes the second object. It usually seems to be the case, on the contrary, that our experience of the untruth of the first notion comes by way of a second object which we come upon by chance and externally, so that our part in all this is simply the pure *apprehension* of what is in and for itself. From the present viewpoint, however, the new object shows itself to have come about through a *reversal of consciousness itself*. This way of looking at the matter is something contributed by *us*, by means of which the succession of experiences through which consciousness passes is raised into a scientific progression—but it is not known to the consciousness we are observing. [55-56; 73-74][46]

Inwardizing: Recollection

In the closing paragraph of the *Phenomenology* Hegel maintains that the fulfillment of spirit

> consists in perfectly *knowing* what *it is*, in knowing its substance; this knowing is its *withdrawal into itself* [*Insichgehen*] in which it abandons its outer existence and gives its existential shape over to recollection [*Erinnerung*]. Thus absorbed in itself, it is sunk into the night of its self-consciousness; but in that night its vanished outer existence is preserved, and this transformed existence—the former one, but now reborn of spirit's knowledge—is the new existence, a new world and new shape of spirit. In the immediacy of this new existence the spirit has to start afresh to bring itself to maturity as if, for it, all that preceded were lost and it had learned nothing from the experience of the earlier spirits. But the recollection, the

---

45. *Logic*, p. 54; 5:49. Hegel believes that the content generated by the process of determinate negation prevents his dialectic from becoming skeptical.

46. In an important related remark, Hegel observes that "because of this necessity, the way to science is itself already *science*, and hence, in virtue of its content, is the science of the *experience* [*Erfahrung*] *of consciousness*" (p. 56; 74). In recent years the question of the relationship between the *Phenomenology* and Hegel's mature system has provoked heated debate among German commentators. The best discussion of the problem is Fulda's *Problem einer Einleitung*. Kierkegaard was already aware of this difficulty in Hegel's philosophy: see *Postscript*, p. 160; 7:149.

inwardizing [*Er-Innerung*] of that experience, has preserved it and is the inner being, and in fact the higher form of the substance. [492:563-564]

This important text underscores an essential conviction that informs Hegel's pedagogy: spiritlessness is implicitly spirit; or expressed differently, in itself inauthentic selfhood is authentic selfhood. The aesthetic education Hegel offers his reader involves the act of re-collecting or re-membering the spiritual existence that has dis-integrated in forgetfulness. Insofar as this method is designed not only to disclose the error inherent in apparent truth but also to reveal the truth implicit in manifest error, it is, properly speaking, Socratic. In one of the best-known passages in the *Phenomenology* Hegel explains that truth

> includes the negative also, what would be called the false, if it could be regarded as something from which one might abstract. The evanescent itself must, on the contrary, be regarded as essential, not as something fixed, cut off from the true, and left lying who knows where outside it, any more than the true is to be regarded as something on the other side, positive and dead. Appearance is the arising and passing away which does not itself arise and pass away, but is "in itself," and constitutes the actuality and the movement of the life of truth. The true is thus the Bacchanalian revel in which no member is sober; yet because each member collapses as soon as he drops out, the revel is just as much transparent [*dursichtig*] and simple repose. Judged in the court of this movement, the single shapes of spirit do not persist any more than determinate thoughts do, but they are as much positive and necessary moments as they are negative and evanescent. In the *whole* of the movement, seen as a state of repose, what distinguishes itself ... and gives itself particular existence is preserved as something that *recollects* itself, whose existence is self-knowledge, and whose self-knowledge is just as immediately existence. [27-28; 39]

With the recognition of Hegel's interpretation of the dialectical interplay of error and truth, and correlatively of spiritlessness and spirit, it becomes clear that the educational journey he invites the reader to undertake eventually leads to the contemplative re-cognition of the ideality of actuality brought about by cognitive recollection. As Hyppolite observes, "the rise of empirical conscious-ness to absolute knowledge is possible only if the necessary stages of its ascent are discovered *within it*. These stages *are* still within it; all that is needed is that it descend into the interiority of memory by an action comparable to Platonic recollection."[47] Through this process

---

47. Hyppolite, *Genesis and Structure*, p. 39. Emphasis added.

of recollection (*Er-Innerung*) the individual who accepts Hegel's invitation and follows his guidance inwardizes or appropriates as his own the stages necessary for full self-realization. Prior to this inwardization the phases of spirit's cultivation remain external to one another in outward temporal dispersion (*Entäusserung*). Recollection renders spirit transparent (*durchsichtig*) to itself and brings a fulfillment that "consists in perfectly *knowing* what *it is*, in knowing its substance."

Despite his persistent pedagogical purpose, Hegel, in an important sense, has nothing to teach his pupil. The journey to which he calls the reader turns out to be a voyage of *self*-discovery whose destination is spirit's adequate comprehension of the actuality it has become. "Here the old saying of Plato has its place," Hegel concludes; "man learns nothing, he only recollects [*erinnert sich*]; the truth is something which man originally carries within himself; . . . he is in himself [*an sich*] spirit, the truth lies in him, and what has to be done is merely to bring it to consciousness."[48] Through his speculative philosophy Hegel seeks to become the midwife who attends the pupil's spiritual rebirth.

It would be a mistake, however, to attribute Hegel's pedagogical method exclusively to his interpretation of Greek philosophy. Equally important is his acceptance of what he regards as the heart of the Christian message. Hegel believes that Christ reveals reconciliation to be at hand. Christ has overcome estrangement and self-alienation, not by flight from, but by immersion in, the conflicts and tensions of temporal experience. For the Christian, peace is found within strife and unity is discovered within opposition. Truth is incarnate in a man "impaled" upon a cross. The wayfarer's recollection becomes an imitatio Christi in which Bildungsgeschichte and Heilsgeschichte are reconciled.[49]

Poiesis

A Pseudonymous Production

In *Concluding Unscientific Postscript*, Kierkegaard writes: "If it is the misfortune of the age to have forgotten what inwardness is, it is, of course, not the task to write for 'paragraph-eaters,' but existing

---

48. *Philosophy of Religion*, 1:165; 16:160.
49. The elaboration of these claims forms the substance of the first part of the next chapter.

individuals must be represented in their distress, when their existence presents itself to them as a confusion, which is something different from sitting safely in the chimney corner and reciting *de omnibus dubitandum*. If the production is to be significant, it should always have passion."[50] Our consideration of Kierkegaard's analysis of his time has shown that he holds spiritlessness to arise from the dissipation of individual selfhood created by abstract reflection. When reflection obscures vital distinctions and "dispels the urge to decision," the individual becomes absent to himself—a mere spectator of his own life, devoid of the passionate inwardness essential to genuine individuality. Kierkegaard does not propose a thoroughgoing condemnation of all reflection. He recognizes that responsible deliberation is a presupposition of free selfhood. But when carried to extremes, reflection can paralyze the individual by infinitely delaying decisive action. "Reflection is not the evil," Kierkegaard insists, "but a standing state of reflection and a standstill in reflection are the fraud and the corruption, which by transforming the conditions for action into a means of escape lead to dissipation."[51] Although he acknowledges that "beyond a doubt there is no task and effort more difficult than to extricate oneself from the temptations of reflection,"[52] Kierkegaard believes precisely such an undertaking is required to overcome the spiritless dissipation of his day. The purpose of Kierkegaard's diverse writings is to engender inwardness by making people aware of the depths to which they have fallen and by creating the possibility for them to begin the journey from despair to realized selfhood. Since Kierkegaard is convinced that "rescue comes only through the essentiality of the religious in the single individual," his works have from the outset a religious orientation. More specifically, Kierkegaard's belief that concrete individuality can be fully actualized only through Christian existence leads him to conclude that the sole antidote to spiritlessness is the clarification of "how to become a Christian."[53]

Paradoxically, however, Kierkegaard can combat the problematic reflection of his day only reflectively. "My task," he explains, "was to cast Christianity into reflection, not poetically to idealize it (for the essentially Christian, after all, is itself the ideal), but with poetic fervor to present the total ideality at its most ideal—always ending

---

50. *Postscript*, p. 236; 7:224.
51. *Two Ages*, p. 96; 8:90.
52. Ibid., p. 77; 72.
53. *Point of View*, p. 13; 13:523.

with: I am not that, but I strive."[54]   An aesthetic age calls for an aesthetic education. Since he is aware of the potential danger of abstract thought, Kierkegaard carefully qualifies the kind of reflection that is needed. His pedagogy does not employ objective reflection, which "makes the subject accidental, and thereby transforms existence into something indifferent, something vanishing." Quite the opposite, aesthetic education presupposes subjective reflection, which "turns its attention inwardly to the subject, and desires in this intensification to realize the truth."[55]   "It is one thing," Kierkegaard argues, "to think in such a way that one's attention is solely and constantly directed towards an external object; it is something else to be so turned in thought that constantly at every moment one himself becomes conscious, in reflection, conscious of one's own condition or how it is with oneself under reflection. But only the latter is essentially what thinking is: it is, in fact, transparency [*Gjennemsigtighed*]."[56]

Kierkegaard no more than Hegel can accomplish his end by attempting to force his viewpoint on others. His understanding of the nature of free selfhood requires him to employ a method that constantly respects the integrity of the individual. Like Hegel, therefore, Kierkegaard decides that spiritlessness can be overcome most effectively by the depiction of alternative forms of life that provide the occasion for the reader's self-examination and self-judgment. The various personae of Kierkegaard's pseudonymous writings constitute the cast of characters through which he stages the dramatic struggle for authentic selfhood. Each pseudonym represents a particular shape of consciousness, form of life, or type of selfhood. In order to present every standpoint as completely and as accurately as possible, Kierkegaard, like Hegel, allows each persona to speak for itself. In the course of the ensuing dialogue the characters uncover the unique contours, nagging tensions, and destructive contradictions of their different perspectives. Taken together, the pseudonyms present a coherent account of what amounts to a phenomenology of spirit analogous, though alternative, to the course plotted by Hegel. The Kierkegaardian forms of life are arranged as dialectical stages in the development of genuine individuality. As educator, Kierkegaard tries to enable the reader to achieve more adequate self-knowledge and thus

---

54. *Journals and Papers*, 6511; 10-2:A 106.
55. *Postscript*, pp. 173, 175; 7:161, 164.
56. *Works of Love*, trans. Howard and Edna Hong (New York: Harper and Row, 1962), pp. 331-332; 9:342.

to provide the occasion for the movement from spiritlessness to spirit.

In contrast with Hegel's phenomenology of spirit, Kierkegaard's pseudonyms do not represent descriptions of the stages through which consciousness *has passed* in the process of self-actualization. His fictitious figures are *imaginative* projections of existential possibilities that *might be realized* in the course of becoming an authentic individual. In place of Hegel's theoretical description of the progressive development of spirit's actuality, Kierkegaard creates poeticized possibilities that confront the sojourner along life's way with decisive alternatives. *Poiesis*, not *Theoria*, is Kierkegaard's element. To understand more adequately the distinctive features of Kierkegaard's aesthetic education, it is necessary to consider his interpretation of the person of the poet and the nature of the poetic work of art.

Poet and Poetry

We have already noted that Kierkegaard regards himself as essentially a poet. Writing in his Journal, he describes the distinguishing characteristic of a poet: "What is it to be a poet? It is to have one's own personal life, one's actuality in categories completely different from those of one's poetic production, to be related to the ideal only in imagination, so that one's personal life is more or less a satire on the poetry and on oneself."[57] The poet's thought and being, language and life, ideality and reality, do not coincide, but contradict one another. Since he believes that his "purely ideal task" involves "casting Christianity completely and wholly into reflection,"[58] Kierkegaard always insists that he is not a Christian. The pedagogical poet who poses "the ideal picture of a Christian" must "confess that he is related only poetically to this ideal picture or *qua* poet to the *presentation* of this picture."[59] The disavowal of the poet masks a definite educational strategy. Kierkegaard is persuaded that if

> it is an illusion that all are Christians—and if there is anything to be done about it, it must be done indirectly, not by one who vociferously proclaims himself an extraordinary Christian, but by one who, better instructed, is ready to declare that he is not a Christian at all. That is, one must approach

---

57. *Journals and Papers*, 6300; 10-1:A 11. In his excellent study, Louis Mackey also stresses the importance of Kierkegaard's understanding of poetry and the poet: see his *Kierkegaard: A Kind of Poet*, esp. chap. 6.
58. *Journals and Papers*, 6237; 9:A 226.
59. *Armed Neutrality*, trans. Howard and Edna Hong (New York: Simon and Schuster, 1969), p. 37.

from behind the person who is under an illusion. Instead of wishing to have an advantage of being oneself that rare thing, a Christian, one must let the prospective captive enjoy the advantage of being the Christian, and for one's own part have resignation enough to be the one who is far behind—otherwise one will certainly not get the man out of his illusion, a thing that is difficult enough in any case.[60]

Kierkegaard's interpretation of the poet represents his version of the principle of Socratic ignorance. This becomes apparent when he contrasts his approach with the practices of the priests of Christendom.

In order to get men along, one may (out of consideration for what men are like these days and what one is himself) reduce the Christian requirements, reduce Christianity, make concessions in that direction. This way one gets to be the most earnest Christian himself and wins many such people over to Christianity. This does irreparable harm, and it is inconceivable that anyone has dared to take this responsibility upon himself, for it is winning men over to Christianity by doing away with Christianity. One may, however, do the reverse and present Christianity without such defense, and then, lest one seem to be juding others, judge oneself as being so far behind that one can scarcely claim the name of Christian, yet deeply desires to become a Christian and strives to be that. This is the right way. In due time it may have a resemblance to the relation of Socratic ignorance to the glut of human knowledge.[61]

Kierkegaard's educational technique is thoroughly informed by his appropriation of important aspects of Socratic method. While Kierkegaard's understanding of Socrates is profoundly influenced by Hegel's consideration of the Socratic position, his criticism of Hegel's analysis points to crucial differences between their views of selfhood and their methodological commitments. Kierkegaard's interpretation of Socrates consists of a radicalization of Hegel's insights. Kierkegaard ironically assumes Hegel's perspective in order to negate it.[62] He admits that Hegel correctly identifies the essence of the Socratic position as irony, and agrees with the Hegelian definition of irony as "infinite absolute negativity." Hegel's error lay in his failure to carry

---

60. *Point of View*, pp. 24-25; 13:531.
61. *Journals and Papers*, 6237; 9:A 226.
62. This interpretation directly opposes analysts who maintain that Kierkegaard's Magister dissertation is fundamentally Hegelian. See, for example, Vilhelm Andersen, *Tider og Typer af Dansk Aands*, part 2, vol. 2 (Copenhagen, 1961), pp. 65-108; Jens Himmelstrup, *Søren Kierkegaards Opfattelse af Sokrates*, pp. 42-84; and Harold Høffding, *Søren Kierkegaard som Filosof* (Copenhagen, 1892).

through his insight with sufficient rigor. Instead of allowing Socrates to remain "infinitely negative" Hegel urges him toward a positive resolution of the dilemmas he discovers. Consequently, irony becomes nothing more than a passing moment. The negativity essential to ironic vision ceases to be a permanent perspective and is itself negated by the "higher" positivity it is supposed to generate. In an important passage in *The Concept of Irony* Kierkegaard distinguishes his reading of Socrates from that of Hegel.

It is toward this point of exhibiting Socrates as the founder of morality that Hegel unilaterally allows his conception of Socrates to gravitate. It is the Idea of the good that he seeks to claim for Socrates, but this causes him some embarrassment when he attempts to show how Socrates has conceived the good. It is essentially here that the difficulty with Hegel's conception of Socrates lies, namely, the attempt is constantly made to show how Socrates has conceived the good. But what is even worse, so it seems to me, is that the direction of the current in Socrates' life is not faithfully maintained. The movement in Socrates is to come to the good. His significance for the development of the world is to arrive at this (not at one point to have arrived at this). His significance for his contemporaries is that they arrived at this. Now this does not mean that he arrived at this toward the end of his life, as it were, but that his life was constantly to come to this end and to cause others to do the same. . . . He did not do this once and for all, but he did this with every individual. He began wherever the individual might find himself, and soon he was thoroughly involved in issuing clearance papers for each one of them. But as soon as he had ferried one of them over he immediately turned back for another. No actuality could withstand him, yet that which became visible was ideality in the most fleeting suggestion of its faintest configuration, that is, as infinitely abstract. . . . Socrates ferried the individual from reality over to ideality, and ideal infinity, as infinite negativity, became the nothingness into which he made the whole manifold of reality disappear. . . . Actuality, by means of the absolute, became nothingness, but the absolute was in turn nothingness. In order to be able to maintain Socrates at this point, in order never to forget that the content of his life was to undertake this movement at every moment, one must bear in mind his significance as a divine missionary. Yet this has been ignored by Hegel, although Socrates himself places much emphasis upon it.[63]

---

63. *Concept of Irony*, pp. 254-255; 13:311-312. Throughout the remainder of this chapter, references to this work are given in the body of the text. For helpful discussions of the differences between Hegel's and Kierkegaard's views of Socrates, see Robert L. Perkins, "Hegel and Kierkegaard: Two Critics of Romantic Irony," in *Hegel in Comparative Literature* (Baltimore: St. John's University Press, 1970), pp. 232-254; idem. "Two Nineteenth-Century Interpretations of Socrates: Hegel and Kierkegaard," *Kierkegaard-Studiet* (International Edition) 4 (1967), 9-14; and Jean Wahl, "Hegel et Kierkegaard," *Revue philosophique de la France et de l'étranger* 112 (1931), 321-380.

Kierkegaard contends that Hegel does not adequately distinguish
Socrates' existential and Plato's speculative dialectic. Therefore, in
Hegel's hands Socratic questioning and irresolution become speculative answering and resolution. "One may ask a question," Kierkegaard
points out,

> for the purpose of obtaining an answer containing the desired content, so
> that the more one questions, the deeper and more meaningful becomes the
> answer: or one may ask a question not in the interest of obtaining an
> answer; or one may ask a question not in the interest of obtaining an
> an emptiness remaining. The first method naturally presupposes a content,
> the second an emptiness; the first is the speculative, the second the ironic.
> Now it was the latter method that was especially practised by Socrates. [73;
> 13:131].

To correct the errors into which Hegel's interpretation falls, it is
necessary to return to the notion of "infinite absolute negativity"
and apply it consistently to the person and position of Socrates.
Kierkegaard sees Socrates' standpoint as "exclusively ironic." Thus
he insists that Socrates never allows negativity to give way to a
"higher" positivity. For the existing individual, the disquiet of ignorance cannot be replaced by the peace of knowledge. "The reason
Socrates could content himself with this ignorance was that he had
no deeper speculative need. Instead of pacifying this negativity
negatively, he pacified it far more through the external unrest in
which he repeated the same process with each particular individual"
(201; 13:258). Unlike the systematic philosopher, the Socratic
educator neither provides solutions nor offers results. Question
marks, not periods, punctuate his dialogue. His goal is to disturb, to
unsettle, to dispel illusion—in short, not to make life easier but to
make it more difficult, though no harder than it really is.

Kierkegaard's preoccupation with Socrates becomes more understandable when we recall his conviction that the spiritlessness of
modernity arises from the thoroughgoing identification of the individual with the sociocultural milieu. The entire point of Socratic
questioning, Kierkegaard maintains, is to raise "the individual out of
immediate existence" through the decisive differentiation of self and
social totality (85; 13:143).[64] By means of his questions, Socrates

---

64. Kierkegaard's analysis at this point follows Hegel quite closely. Hegel contends
that the inward turn of consciousness brought about by Socrates' questioning precipitated
the disintegration of the substantial *Sittlichkeit* of the Greek world. See especially *Phenomenology*, pp. 266 ff.; 317 ff.; and *Lectures on the History of Philosophy*, trans. E. S. Haldane
(New York: Humanities Press, 1968), 1:384 ff.; 18:441 ff.

"sawed through the virgin forest of substantial consciousness in all quietude, and when everything was ready, all these formations suddenly disappeared and his mind's eye enjoyed a prospect such as it had never before seen" (215; 13:272). What is exposed is nothing less than the free individual which Socrates' art of midwifery seeks to bring to birth. Such a birth is possible, however, only if "the umbilical cord of substantiality" is severed. Kierkegaard contends that Socratic midwifery involves a justified deception intended to dispel the interlocutor's illusions. The ignorance resulting from this dis-illusionment forms "the nothingness from which a beginning must be made" (222; 13:278). Poetic or ironic dissimulation is never without pedagogical purpose, for it attempts "to mystify the surrounding world not so much in order to conceal itself as to induce others to reveal themselves" (268;13:325). The nature of this evoked self-revelation becomes evident when attention turns from the person of the poet to the nature of the poem.

"The speech of a poet," Professor Mackey points out,

> does not utter his inner states, but rather builds meanings into a free standing structure of language. Paradox, self-concealment, plural connotations, distentions of metaphor and the like are the shears by which he clips the umbilical of his fancy's child and sends it out on its own. His art is not the externalizing of himself, but the objectifying of a work of words: *poiesis*. What the poet produces is a verbal object (*poiema*) in which meanings, released from any personal interest he may vest in them, are neither affirmed nor denied, but simply placed. A poem in this sense does not *mean*—it does not urge the feelings and opinions of the poet on the reader. It *is*—as a thing made it is self-sufficient (*perfectum*) and bears no message not indigenous to its perfection. But the poetic object, however much it dispatches the poet's words from the poet, is nevertheless an object (*objectum*, *Gegenstand*) and as such commands a response.[65]

In an effort to elicit such a response, Kierkegaard produces his pseudonymous writings. He explains that "a pseudonym is excellent for accentuating a point, a stance, a position. It creates a poetic person."[66] The "poeticized personalities"[67] who act out the pseud-

---

65. Mackey, *Kierkegaard*, pp. 284-285.

66. *Papirer*, 10-1:510, in *Armed Neutrality*, p. 88.

67. The Journal entry in which Kierkegaard uses this phrase underscores the relationship he sees between his pseudonymous method and the spiritlessness of the age. "One of the tragedies of modern times is precisely this—to have abolished the 'I,' the personal 'I.' For this very reason real ethical-religious truth is related essentially to personality and can only be communicated by an I to an I. As soon as the communication becomes objective in this realm, the truth has become untruth. Personality is what we need. Therefore I regard it as

onymous production are "personified possibilities"[68] —imaginative projections of fantastic, fictitious forms of life that can serve as models for the despairing person's self-interpretation and self-judgment. The ideality of these imagined possibilities is essential to their function in Kierkegaard's aesthetic education.

Drawing on his understanding of Hegelian aesthetics, Kierkegaard maintains that a genuine work of art embodies an ideal form in the medium singularly appropriate to the idea it seeks to express. As Crites indicates, "the idea comes to consciousness only in the process of artistic creation itself, and only in the appropriate medium. The problem in art, as Hegel had shown, is to shape the material or medium in such a way that it will become as transparent as possible to its proper idea, so that the idea can, as it were, shine through the medium employed."[69] Such artistic transparency represents an abstraction from the tensions of finitude. The timeless ideality of the work of art articulates pure possibilities that stand in marked contrast with the bewildering options faced in temporal experience. This atemporal ideality provides the occasion for aesthetic education. Borrowing Hegel's term, Kierkegaard argues that a person apprehends the aesthetic object by a process of "recollection" (*Erindring*). In recollection, one grasps ideal forms that are antecedent to and the presupposition of temporal existence. Aesthetic education affords the opportunity for self-clarification by transporting the individual from the conflicts and confusions of actual life to the momentary repose and clarity of the ideal realm of pure possibility. Instead of

---

my service that by bringing poeticized personalities who say I (my pseudonyms) into the center of life's actuality I have contributed, if possible, to familiarizing the contemporary age again to hearing an I, a personal I speak. . . . But precisely because the whole development of the world has been as far as possible from this acknowledgment of personality, this has to be done poetically. The poetic personality always has a something which makes him more bearable for a world which is quite unaccustomed to hearing an I" (*Journals and Papers*, 657; 8-2:89).

68. Paul Holmer, "Kierkegaard and Ethical Theory," *Ethics* 63 (1952-53), 157-170. Compare Holmer's related articles: "Kierkegaard and Religious Propositions," *Journal of Religion*, 35 (1955), 135-146; and "On Understanding Kierkegaard," in *A Kierkegaard Critique*, ed. H. A. Johnson and N. Thulstrup (Chicago: Henry Regnery Co., 1962), pp. 135-146. In these essays Holmer gives a helpful interpretation of Kierkegaard's theory of communication.

69. Stephen Crites, introduction to *Crisis in the Life of an Actress*, p. 29. Crites provides an excellent account of Kierkegaard's aesthetic theory in relation to Hegel's position. See also his "Pseudonymous Authorship as Art and as Act," in *Kierkegaard: A Collection of Critical Essays*, pp. 183-229. I have benefited greatly from these two essays and have drawn on them in formulating my interpretation of Kierkegaard's aesthetics. Another study of considerable importance is Theodor Adorno's *Kierkegaard: Konstruktion des Aesthetischen* (Frankfurt: Suhrkamp Verlag, 1966). Adorno's analysis effectively relates Kierkegaard's notion of aesthetics to his general understanding of aesthetic existence.

re-present-ing actual personalities or real forms of life, Kierkegaard's pseudonymous characters pro-ject idealized, unrealized existential possibilities. It is precisely the ideality of the characters enacting the Kierkegaardian drama that is illuminating for the observer. But art's strength is also its weakness. "It is not wrong of the spectator to want to lose himself in poetry, this is a joy which has its reward, but," warns Kiekegaard, "the spectator must not mistake the theatre for reality, nor himself for a spectator who is nothing else but a spectator at a comedy."[70] To wish to remain in aesthetic repose is to fall victim to spiritlessness.

Inwardizing: Repetition

For Kierkegaard, aesthetic education is not an end in itself, but has a nonaesthetic, ethical purpose. "To understand and to understand are two things," Kierkegaard insists. "Inwardness is an understanding, but *in concreto* it is a matter of how this understanding is to be understood. To understand a discourse is one thing; to understand the element in it which points to one personally is something else. To understand what one says is one thing; to understand oneself in what one has said is something else."[71] Over against the speculative mediation of thought and being, ideality and reality, and possibility and actuality, Kierkegaard reasserts their lasting contrariety. He maintains that "man thinks and exists, and existence separates thought and being, holding them apart from one another in succession."[72] The opposites between which human existence is ever suspended can be brought together only momentarily through the passionate exercise of the individual's will. The difference between thought and being or possibility and actuality forms the basis of Kierkegaard's distinction between aesthetics and ethics. "The aesthetic and intellectual principle is that no reality is thought or understood until its *esse* has been resolved into its *posse*. The ethical

---

70. *Stages on Life's Way*, p. 417; 6:429. Elsewhere Kierkegaard remarks, "in paganism the theatre had reality as a sort of divine worship" (*Concept of Dread*, p. 16; 4:289). He is thinking not only of the ancient world, of course, but more importantly of the modern-day "paganism" at the heart of Christendom and Hegelianism.

71. *Concept of Dread*, pp. 126-127; 4:408.

72. *Postscript*, p. 296; 7:287. Recalling our discussion of Hegel's critique of the reflective philosophy of subjectivity in chap. 2, 1st sec. ("Fragmentation"), 3rd subsec. ("The Reflective Philosophy of Subjectivity"), it is interesting to note that Kierkegaard underscores his rejection of the Hegelian mediation of thought and being by defending Kant's analysis of the ontological argument against Hegel's attack. See *Postscript*, p. 297 f.; 7:288 f. As will become increasingly apparent, Kierkegaard's position is a paradigm of Hegel's *Verstandsphilosophie*.

principle is that no possibility is understood until each *posse* has really become an *esse*."[73]

Upon the basis of this contrast Kierkegaard argues that reflection must be doubly reflected and recollection must lead to repetition. Explaining his poetic production through the persona of Johannes Climacus, Kierkegaard stresses that "a communication in the form of a possibility compels the recipient to face the problem of existing in it, so far as this is possible between man and man."[74] By means of his pseudonymous writings, Kierkegaard attempts to extricate his reader from "the temptations of reflection" by occasioning a crisis of decision. His poeticized personalities force the reader to confront difficult choices posed by irreconcilable alternatives. The dramatis personae lay a claim upon the will as well as upon the imagination of the audience. Pure possibilities, of course, must initially be grasped reflectively. But this reflective apprehension of imagined ideality is the propaedeutic to the existential act of "double reflection" in which possibility becomes actual and ideality is reflected in reality by means of the individual's free decision. A person does not achieve transparency (Gjennemsigtighed) simply by the appreciation of an ideality already implicit in his reality, but by volitional activity in which he struggles to become a living expression of the ideal he has reflectively conceived. In striving to "reduplicate" concept in being, one attempts to " 'exist' in what one understands."[75] To the extent that Kierkegaard's undertaking is successful, the ideality of truth becomes actual as the actuality of the individual becomes truthful.

With respect to human existence, the identity of thought and being definitive of truth is not primordial but is historically emergent. It is born of the individual's free activity. This is the point of Kierkegaard's oft-misunderstood claim that in ethical and religious matters, "truth is subjectivity." He explains: *"An objective uncertainty held fast in an appropriation-process of the most passionate inwardness is truth*, the highest truth attainable for an *existing*

---

73. *Postscript*, p. 288; 7:279.
74. Ibid., p. 320; 7:310.
75. *Training in Christianity*, p. 133; 12:125. In another context, Kierkegaard elaborates: "However, coming into existence may present a reduplication, i.e., the possibility of a second coming into existence within the first coming into existence. Here we have the historical in the stricter sense, subject to a dialectic with respect to time. The coming into existence that in this sphere is identical with the coming into existence of nature is a possibility, a possibility that for nature is its whole reality. But this historical coming into existence in the stricter sense is a coming into existence within a coming into existence" (*Philosophical Fragments*, p. 94; 4:240).

individual."[76] The most important phrase in this definition is "appropriation-process" (*Tilegnelse*). Because the concrete individual is in a state of becoming in which possibility and actuality are separate, his life can never be more than a constant approximation of the ideals he conceives. "Subjectivity" indicates the process by which an individual appropriates what he thinks, or constitutes his actuality by realizing his possibilities. Kierkegaard identifies subjectivity with truth for the existing individual: "the truth consists in nothing else than the self-activity of personal appropriation."[77] Through this process of appropriation an individual renders himself truthful. In this sense, truth is edifying (*opbyggelse*). It builds up (*bygge op*) the personality as it is built up in the individual.[78] It should be obvious that Kierkegaard's argument is not intended to deny the notion of truth as the conformity of thought and being. His point is that since the existing individual is always engaged in becoming, such conformity cannot finally be actualized as long as life continues, but must remain an ideal that is asymptotically approximated.

> Not for a single moment is it forgotten that the subject is an existing individual, that existence is a process of becoming, and that therefore the notion of truth as the identity of thought and being is a chimera of abstraction, in its truth only an expectation of the creature; not because truth is not such an identity, but because the knower is an existing individual for whom the truth cannot be such an identity as long as he lives in time.[79]

Temporal selves can only yearn and strive for the peace that this truth brings.

This understanding of the nature of religious truth further illuminates Kierkegaard's pedagogical strategy. Since true selfhood presupposes an individual's free actualization of possibility, the teacher must communicate with the pupil in an *indirect* manner. Instead of constantly identifying with and offering direct guidance to the reader,[80] the author must withdraw himself from the dialogic relation and leave the reader alone with the imagined possibilities expressed in the poetic work. "When in reflection upon the com-

---

76. *Postscript*, p. 182; 7:170.
77. Ibid., p. 217; 7:203. For further discussion of this point, see Taylor, *Kierkegaard's Pseudonymous Authorship*, chap. 2; and Louis Mackey, "Kierkegaard and the Problem of Existential Philosophy, II," *The Review of Metaphysics* 9 (1955-56), 569-588.
78. The English terms *edify* and *edifice* suggest Kierkegaard's wordplay.
79. *Postscript*, p. 176; 7:164.
80. As Hegel does through the "phenomenological we."

munication the receiver is reflected upon, then we have ethical communication. The maieutic. The communicator disappears, as it were, makes himself serve only to help the other to become."[81] By insisting upon the disparity between his ideas and his life, the poet directs the reader away from his person and toward his poetic creation. Kierkegaard's pseudonymity is the curtain separating him from the drama he stages. His multiple literary devices seek to focus the reader's attention on the play his personae enact rather than on the complex behind-the-scences maneuvres necessary to mount the production.

For Kierkegaard, however, observation of the drama is not itself cathartic. The purification of spirit which cures the sickness unto death lies not in passive speculation but in practical action. Theoretical reflection is a necessary but not sufficient condition of the development of inwardness. To recollection must be added repetition, a movement Kierkegaard argues Hegel never makes.

> The dialectic of repetition [*Gjentagelse*] is easy; for what is repeated has been, otherwise it could not be repeated, but precisely the fact that it has been gives to repetition the character of novelty. When the Greeks said that all knowledge is recollection they affirmed that all that is has been; when one says that life is a repetition, one affirms that existence which has been now becomes. If one has neither the category of recollection nor that of repetition, the whole of life is resolved into a vain and empty noise. Recollection is the pagan lifeview, repetition is the modern. Repetition is the *interest* of metaphysics, and at the same time the interest upon which metaphysics founders; repetition is the solution contained in every ethical view, repetition is a *conditio sine qua non* of every dogmatic problem.[82]

---

81. *Journals and Papers*, 654; 8-2:B 89.
82. *Repetition*, pp. 52-53; 3:189. An extended passage from the *Postscript* clarifies Kierkegaard's cryptic remarks about the limitations of metaphysical speculation. "What reality is cannot be expressed in the language of abstraction. Reality is an *inter-esse* between the moments of that hypothetical unity of thought and being which abstract thought presupposes. Abstract thought considers both possibility and reality, but its concept of reality is a false reflection, since the medium within which the concept is thought is not reality, but possibility. Abstract thought can get hold of reality only by nullifying it, and this nullification of reality consists in transforming it into possibility. All that is said about reality in the language of abstraction and within the sphere of abstract thought is really said within the sphere of the possible. The entire realm of abstract thought, speaking in the language of reality, sustains the relation of possibility to the realm of reality; but this latter reality is not one which is included within abstract thought and the realm of the possible. Reality or existence is the dialectical moment in a trilogy, whose beginning and whose end cannot be for the existing individual, since *qua* existing individual he is himself in the dialectical moment. Abstract thought closes up the trilogy. Just so. But how does it close the trilogy? Is abstract thought a mystical something, or is it not the act of the abstracting

In contrast with the "backwards" reflection of speculative philosophy, repetition is the category "by which one enters eternity forwards."[83] Kierkegaard readily admits that "philosophy is perfectly right in saying that life must be understood backwards." The problem arises when philosophers "forget the other clause—that it must be lived forwards. The more one thinks through this clause, the more one concludes that life in temporality never becomes properly understandable, simply because never at any time does one get perfect repose to take a stance: backward."[84] From Kierkegaard's perspective, therefore, the inwardness constitutive of authentic selfhood cannot be the result of a retrospective dialectic of recollection which grasps reality as the necessary outworking of an immanent dialectic of ideality.[85] Inwardness presupposes a prospective dialectic of repetition positing an abyss between ideality and actuality which can be bridged only by the *contingent* leap of the free individual. Kierkegaard's stages on life's way are not internally related and do not constitute a *necessary* progression. They represent distinct forms of life that can be realized only if they are willed by the individual. Kierkegaard's pseudonymous writings lead the reader to the brink of decision by presenting idealities to be actualized by the individual through decisive repetition.

In a sense, Kierkegaard too has nothing to teach his pupil. He questions but does not answer; his aesthetic education ends without result. He confesses that the

> result is not in my power; it depends upon so many things, and above all it depends upon whether he [i.e., the individual reader] will or not. In all eternity it is impossible for me to compel a person to accept an opinion, a conviction, a belief. But one thing I can do: I can compel him to take

---

individual? But the abstracting individual is the existing individual, who is as such the dialectical moment, which he cannot close or mediate, least of all absolutely, as long as he remains in existence. So that when he closes the trilogy, this closure must be related as a possibility to the reality or existence in which he remains" (279; 7:270).

83. *Concept of Dread*, p. 80 n.; 4:360. For a helpful account of Kierkegaard's notion of repetition see André Clair, "Médiation et repetition: Le lieu de la dialectique kierkegaardienne," *Revue des sciences philosophiques et théologiques* 59 (1975), 38-78. When considering the concept of repetition, it is important to realize that the literal meaning of the Danish word *Gjentagelse* is "a taking again."

84. *Journals and Papers*, 1030; 4:A 164.

85. Throughout his discussion of the subjectivity of truth, Kierkegaard uses the terms *subjectivity* and *inwardness* interchangeably. For Kierkegaard, as for Hegel, truth is inwardness. The Danish *Inderlighed* shares an etymological root with the German *Innigkeit* and *Erinnerung*. I am suggesting, however, that Kierkegaardian inwardness differs from Hegelian inwardness by adding repetition to recollection.

notice. In one sense this is the first thing, for it is the condition antecedent to the next thing, i.e., the acceptance of an opinion, a conviction, a belief. In another sense it is the last—if, that is, he will not take the next step.[86]

The journey to which Kierkegaard calls his reader is unending. Omega ever recedes, for the concluding chapter of the drama of selfhood can only be written after the final curtain falls.

Kierkegaard's unsettling maieutic seeks to keep the individual on the journey to selfhood by preventing the sojourner from sinking roots too deeply in finitude. Unlike Hegel, Kierkegaard's Socratic midwifery attends a spiritual rebirth effected by the volitional repetition of transcendent possibility, instead of the cognitive recollection of immanent ideality. Rather than only enabling the reader to discover what he is, Kierkegaard prods the individual to become what he is not. As with Hegel, however, it would be a mistake to attribute Kierkegaard's pedagogical method exclusively to his interpretation of Socrates. Equally important is Kierkegaard's acceptance of what he regards as the heart of the Christian message. For Kierkegaard, Christ reveals the authentic selfhood each individual is called upon to realize in his or her own life-time. The wayfarer's repetition becomes an imitatio Christi in which Bildungsgeschichte struggles toward the Heilsgeschichte for which it ever yearns.

---

86. *Point of View*, p. 35; 13:538.

|4|

CHRISTIANITY AND SELFHOOD

Awake! awake O sleeper of the land of shadows,
    wake! expand!
I am in you and you in me, mutual in love
    divine
Fibres of love from man to man thro' Albion's
    pleasant land.
I am not a God afar off, I am a brother and
    friend:
Within your bosoms I reside, and you reside in
    me.
             —Blake

The eternal life of the Christian is the very
Spirit of God, and the Spirit of God is precisely
this: to be self-conscious of oneself in the
Divine Spirit.
             —Hegel

Philosophy's idea is mediation—Christianity's,
the paradox.
             —Kierkegaard

The New Testament records that Jesus proclaimed: "I am the way, the truth, and the life; no man comes to the Father but by me." Hegel's and Kierkegaard's search for a method, a way, the means, *die Mittel*, by which to guide sojourners from spiritlessness to spirit is inseparably bound to their respective interpretations of Christ as the Way and the Truth, the Mediator—*der Mittler, Mellemmanden*—in whom the extremes of the divine and the human join to reveal the genuine nature of God and self. Only by following the Way can wayfarers overcome despair and discover the stations or stages that lead to authentic selfhood.

Effective spiritual physicians require "a definite and well thought out conception of what it is to be in sound health," by which to test the condition of the selves they examine.[1] Hegel and Kierkegaard agree that the normative structure of spirit is disclosed in the person and life of the central figure of the Christian religion. Hegel argues that humankind's religious awareness is the "self-consciousness of spirit." Spirit's explicit knowledge of itself, however, emerges gradually. The history of religion represents "the path of the education of spirit [*Weg der Erziehung des Geistes*]," which culminates in Christianity, "the perfect, *absolute* religion, in which it is revealed what spirit is."[2] Kierkegaard maintains that "religion is the true humanity."[3] He explains: "By the ideal picture of a Christian I understand in part a kind of human interpreting of Christ as the prototype [*Forbilledet*], a human interpreting which, although he is and remains the object of faith, contains all the middle terms in relation to derivatives and casts everything into becoming. . . ."[4] For despairing, dissipated selves, " 'the individual' is the category of spirit, of spiritual awakening." And, from Kierkegaard's point of view, " 'the individual' . . . is the decisive Christian category."[5]

In other words, the anthropologies of Hegel and Kierkegaard are thoroughly Christocentric. They both adhere to what they regard as a strictly orthodox Christology that steers a middle course between the Scylla of Docetism and the Charybdis of Ebionism. In keeping with tenets originally defined at the Council of Chalcedon, Hegel and Kierkegaard affirm that Christ is the God-Man—fully God and fully man. The *Gottmensch*, Hegel argues, represents "the union of the

---

1. *Sickness unto Death*, p. 156; 11:137.
2. *Philosophy of Religion*, 1:76, 84; 16:80, 87.
3. *Point of View*, p. 108; 13:590.
4. *Armed Neutrality*, p. 36.
5. *Point of View*, pp. 132, 133; 13:606.

most tremendous opposites," a "frightful combination [*ungeheure Zusammensetzung*] which absolutely contradicts the understanding [*Verstand*]."[6] Kierkegaard repeatedly insists that *Gud-Mennesket* is a *coincidentia oppositorum*, an Absolute Paradox, an absurdity that "is composed in such a way that reason has no power at all to dissolve it."[7] For Hegel, however, what remains a mystery for the understanding can be grasped by dialectical reason. Through the historical mediation of Christendom and the philosophical mediation of speculative philosophy, the conceptual truth implicit in the Incarnation is rendered explicit and becomes comprehensible. The result of this mediation process is "a conversion of consciousness" in which the individual is able to re-cognize the reconciliation revealed by Christ. Kierkegaard objects that while philosophy proposes mediation, Christianity insists upon paradox. One does not discover the structure of authentic selfhood through the internalization of results brought about by historical and philosophical mediation, but by a leap that vaults one over the eighteen hundred years of Christendom and thrusts one into a situation of contemporaneity with the Prototype whose life ought to be repeated in the concrete existence of every person. For the existing individual, reconciliation is an eschatological hope to be fully realized in the future rather than an accomplished fact to be appropriated in the present. In the final analysis this essential difference in perspective explains why Hegel's pilgrim can come to feel at home in the world, while Kierkegaard's sojourner is forever an unsettled, rootless wanderer.

MEDIATION

The Fullness of Time: The Present

In his survey of world history, Hegel maintains that "the identity of the subject and God comes into the world when the *fullness of time* has arrived: the consciousness of this identity is the recognition of God in his truth. The content of truth is *spirit* itself, the living movement in itself. The nature of God as pure spirit is revealed to man *in the Christian religion.*"[8] The "fullness of time" in which the revelation of spirit occurs is, for Hegel, the "hinge of history," the

---

6. *History of Philosophy*, 3:15; 19:506. *Philosophy of Religion*, 3:76; 17:277-278.
7. *Journals and Papers*, 7; 10-2:A 354.
8. *The Philosophy of History*, trans. J. Sibree (New York: Dover Publications, 1956), 323; 12:391.

turning point of the entire historical process. This moment at once takes up into itself the essential elements of all previous temporal development and anticipates events yet to be unfolded. Given its recollective and proleptic character, the fullness of time, Hegel argues, must be regarded as the "true present" in which time and eternity explicitly meet. "In the positive meaning of time, it can be said that only the present is, that before and after are not. But the concrete present is the result of the past and is pregnant with the future. The true present, therefore, is eternity."[9] To understand Hegel's notion of the Incarnation, it is necessary to come to terms with his interpretation of the past from which it results and the future gestating within it.

Throughout most of his philosophical career, Hegel remains convinced that "it is the nature of truth to prevail when its time has come, and . . . it appears only when this time has come, and therefore never appears prematurely, nor finds a public not ripe to receive it."[10] When the time is ripe, a given historical development necessarily takes place. In affirming such historical necessity, Hegel does not, as his detractors often suggest, intend to deny temporal contingency.[11] His point is considerably more limited. In the *Science of Logic*, he argues that *real* possibility and actuality are finally indistinguishable—the former immediately passes over into the latter. "When all the conditions of something are completely present, it enters into actuality; the completeness of the conditions is the totality as in the content, and *the something itself* is this content determined as being as actual as possible."[12]

The condition constituting the fullness of time, and hence necessitating the Incarnation, is the emergence of what Hegel regards as the unhappy consciousness of the Jewish religion and the late Greco-Roman world. Unhappy consciousness is, as we have seen, a form of experience characterized by fragmentation, isolation, and estrangement.[13] Self is set against nature, other selves, God, and

---

9. *Philosophy of Nature*, trans. A. V. Miller (New York: Oxford University Press, 1970), par. 259; 9:55.

10. *Phenomenology*, p. 44; 58.

11. The best treatment of this problem is Dieter Henrich's "Hegels Theorie über den Zufall," in his *Hegel im Kontext*, pp. 157-186.

12. *Logic*, p. 548; 6:210. This point will be considered in more detail in the next chapter.

13. See above, chap. 2, 1st sec. ("Fragmentation"), 2d subsec. ("The Oppression of Objectivity: Religion and Self-alienation"). I have already stressed the similarities Hegel sees between his time and the development of speculative philosophy on the one hand, and the late Empire and the development of Christianity on the other.

itself, creating the condition of spiritlessness. As descendants of Abraham the Jewish people labor under the infinite sorrow of unhappy consciousness. They suffer "self-conscious abjectness and depression" present when one is "inwardly conscious that in the depths of his being he is a contradiction."[14] For Hegel's Jewish believer, outward affliction generated by conflict with the socio-natural environment is mirrored in the inner sorrow of an individual who realizes that he is "the negation of himself—a divided and discordant being."[15] Hegel insists that estrangement is deepened by servile obedience to the transcendent Lord of the Jewish religion. The distraught believer expresses his own nothingness by humbling himself before an omnipotent Master. While the particular, finite individual is deemed inessential and insubstantial, the universal and infinite Lord is believed to be the essential substance of all reality. "What is highest here," Hegel argues, "is the inadequacy of the subject to express the universal, this bifurcation [*Entzweiung*], this sundering [*Zerreissung*] which is not healed, not harmonized—the standpoint of the opposition of the infinite on the one side, and on the other side a fixed finitude."[16] This form of faith leaves homeless sojourners to wander through a godless world in search of a worldless God.[17]

To Hegel's dialectical vision, however, this represents merely one side of unhappy consciousness. The infinite pain of self-alienation is not simply negative but also involves an implicit positivity that must be made explicit. "Sorrow is present only where there is opposition to an affirmative. What is no longer in itself an affirmative has no contradiction, no sorrow. Sorrow is just the negativity in the affirmative, the affirmative that suffers the wound of self-contradiction."[18] In the act of affirming the opposition between God and self, the devotee unknowingly absolutizes the finite and finitizes the Absolute. "This contradiction occurs," Hegel explains, "as a direct

---

14. *History of Philosophy*, 3:22; 19:510. *Philosophy of Religion*, 3:60; 17:263.
15. *Philosophy of History*, p. 321; 12:388.
16. *Philosophy of Religion*, 3:64; 17:268.
17. These terms are suggested by Fackenheim (*Religious Dimension*, pp. 200-201). My interpretation of the relationship between Hegel's view of the Jewish religion and the late Greco-Roman world bears some similarity to Fackenheim's analysis. I differ from Fackenheim, however, in stressing the dialectical character of Jewish and Greek experience in which each contains within itself its own opposite. Fackenheim's view of Christianity as the synthesis of the Jewish East (a worldless God) and the Greco-Roman West (a godless world) is insufficiently dialectical. Christianity reveals reconciliation in the midst of estrangement by discovering the unity implicit in the oppositions of unhappy consciousness.
18. *Philosophy of Religion*, 3:60; 17:263.

result of the circumstance that the finite remains a determinate being opposed to the infinite, so that there are *two* determinatenesses; *there are* two worlds, one infinite and one finite, and in their relationship the infinite is only the *limit* of the finite and is thus only a determinate infinite, an *infinite which is itself finite*."[19] When the infinite and the finite are seen as antithetical and mutually exclusive, the infinite is, in fact, limited and bounded by the finite. It is a "finite" and therefore a "bad" or "spurious infinite [*Schlecht-Unendliche*]*."* Whereas the believer intends to affirm the negativity (inessentiality) of finite existence and the positivity (essentiality) of the infinite, he ends by asserting the positivity of finitude and the negativity of infinitude. The infinite is the *in*-finite, the *non*-finite, the negation of firmly established finitude. Elaborating this dialectical reversal, Hegel writes:

> The infinite determined as such has present in it the finitude that is distinct from it; the former is the *in-itself* in this unity, and the latter is only determinateness, limit in it; but it is a limit which is the sheer other of the in-itself, is its opposite; the infinite's determination, which is the in-itself as such, is ruined by the addition of such a quality; it is thus a *finitized infinite*. Similarly, since the finite as such is only the negation of the in-itself, but by reason of this unity also has its opposite present in it, it is exalted and, so to say, infinitely exalted above its worth; the finite is posited as the *infinitized* finite.[20]

Unbeknown to the believer, overt humility expressed in self-negation involves covert pride of self-affirmation.

This hidden pride becomes manifest in the other religious precursor of Christian revelation: the Greek "religion of humanity." The development of Greek religion culminates in dramatic comedy for which "actual self-consciousness exhibits itself as the fate of the Gods."[21] Hegel maintains that the comic denial of the reality of the divine is at the same time the affirmation of the absoluteness of the self. This form of experience apparently overcomes the servility of unhappy consciousness.

> What this self-consciousness beholds is that whatever assumes the form of essentiality over against it, is instead dissolved in it—in its thinking, its

---

19. *Logic*, pp. 139-140; 5:152.
20. Ibid., p. 145; 5:159. The truth of the dialectical relation of infinitude and finitude implicit in unhappy consciousness is revealed in the Incarnation.
21. *Phenomenology*, p. 450; 517. By way of anticipation, it is important to note that while Hegel sees comedy as the form of life immediately antecedent to the revealed religion, Kierkegaard regards humor as the last stage prior to Christian faith. The similarities and differences of these two points of view will be discussed in chap. 6.

existence, and its action—and is at its mercy. It is the return of everything universal into the certainty of itself which, in consequence, is this complete loss of fear and of essential being on the part of all that is alien. This self-certainty is a state of spiritual well-being [*Wohlsein*] and repose, such as is not to be found anywhere outside of this comedy.[22]

The self-assurance that divinizes man also humanizes God, thereby bringing the lofty Jewish Lord down to earth. Hegel insists that, appearances to the contrary notwithstanding, comic awareness is likewise inherently self-contradictory. In itself this ostensibly happy consciousness is actually unhappy.

We see that this unhappy consciousness constitutes the reverse side and the fulfillment of the comic consciousness that is perfectly happy with itself. Into the latter, all divine being returns, or it is the complete *alienation* [*Entäusserung*] of *substance*. The unhappy consciousness, on the other hand, is, conversely, the tragic fate of the certainty of self that aims to be absolute. It is the consciousness of the loss of all *essential* being in this *certainty of itself*, and of the loss even of this knowledge about itself—the loss of substance as well as of the self, it is the sorrow, the pain that expresses itself in the hard saying that "God is dead."[23]

This godless world in which particular selves are absolutized assumes concrete form in late imperial Rome. The essential principle of the Roman Empire is "finitude and particular subjectivity exaggerated to infinitude."[24] In the person of the deified Emperor, isolated individuality gains "a perfectly unlimited realization." Through completely capricious activity the Emperor unravels the social fabric. "As when the physical body decays, each point gains a life for itself, which, however, is only the miserable life of worms, so the political organism is here dissolved into atoms—viz., private persons. Such a condition is Roman life during this epoch."[25] Isolated individuals who share no common life form an "anarchy of spirits" held together solely by the sheer power and force of the *monas monadum*, the earthly lord. Crushed by such overwhelming oppression, individuals become estranged from a state that now is regarded as coercive and repressive. When objective sociopolitical structures cease to satisfy subjective need and individual purpose, the opposition of subject and object definitive of self-alienation arises.

In an effort to retreat from the "universal misery of the world,"

22. Ibid., pp. 452-453; 520.
23. Ibid., pp. 454-455; 522-523.
24. *Philosophy of History*, p. 318; 12:386.
25. Ibid., pp. 315, 317; 12:382, 384.

people seek refuge by turning inward. This is evident, Hegel argues, in the philosophical and religious movements that emerge in the latter days of the Empire. For instance, "according to stoicism or skepticism, one is driven back into himself, should find satisfaction in himself. In this independence, this rigidity of being-with-self [*Beisichsein*], this accord with himself, one is to find happiness; one should rest in this abstract, present, self-conscious inwardness."[26] The stoic seeks stability and inner peace in abstract thought that is supposed to free him from surrounding flux and confusion. But this "independence" is established in a completely negative way. The freedom of the self is affirmed by attempting to sever any sustaining relationship with the environing world. For Hegel, this "negative relation to otherness" which lies at the heart of stoicism is finally indistinguishable from the negativity essential to the experience of the skeptic. In skepticism, the self-contradiction of stoicism becomes explicit. The effort to remain independent of the disintegrating social totality discloses the self's continuing dependence upon, and further involves the individual in, the broken world. Through the activity of negation, the self's identity becomes intrinsically bound up with the other from which it seeks to differentiate itself. Hegel explains that

> it is just in this process that this consciousness, instead of being self-identical, is in fact nothing but a purely accidental entanglement, the dizziness of a perpetually self-engendered disorder. It is itself aware of this; for it itself maintains and creates this restless confusion. Hence it also admits to it, it owns to being a wholly contingent, single, and separate consciousness—a consciousness which is *empirical*, which takes its guidance from what has no reality for it, which obeys what is for it not an *essential* being, which does those things and brings to realization what it knows has no truth for it.[27]

In this form of experience, the individual knows himself to be both independent and dependent, unchanging and changing, self-identical and self-alien. But since these extremes remain antithetical, self-awareness is "bifurcated, inwardly fragmented, unhappy consciousness [*unglückliches in sich entzweites Bewusstsein*]."[28] Recognizing

---

26. *Philosophy of Religion*, 3:63; 17:266. Although Hegel is thinking of the stoicism and skepticism that developed during the decline of the Empire, he is less interested in these particular philosophical positions than in the general form of experience they represent. Hegel might also have supported his argument by pointing to the flowering of exotic mystery cults that promised initiates personal salvation.

27. *Phenomenology*, pp. 124-125; 156-157.

28. Ibid., p. 126; 158.

its inner division and inevitable entanglement in ceaseless temporal flux, the despairing self sets the changeable and unchangeable in opposition to each other. The unchangeable "it takes to be the *essential* being [*Wesen*] ; but the other, the protean changeable, it takes to be the inessential. The two are, for unhappy consciousness, alien to or estranged from [*fremd*] one another; and because it is itself the consciousness of this contradiction, it identifies itself with the changeable consciousness, and takes itself to be the inessential."[29] Having established this opposition, unhappy consciousness is gripped by the "boundless energy of longing" and yearns to extricate itself from mutability by fleeing to the immutable. Sundered within and without, the Greco-Roman world shares the fate of Judaism—spiritlessness.

For unhappy consciousness, opposites remain unreconciled. Like Kierkegaard's unhappiest man, the fragmented self is "sunk in melancholy."[30] But as Hegel stresses in *Faith and Knowledge*, the infinite pain of dismemberment, the unbounded sorrow of Godforsakenness, is the harbinger of a reconciliation that "can and must be resurrected solely from this harsh consciousness of loss encompassing everything."[31] Suffering (*Leiden*) opposition is not simply an unfortunate accident but is essential to the process of reintegration. Hegel argues that "for the attainment of reconciliation, this standpoint of consciousness, of reflection, of bifurcation [*Entzweiung*] is just as necessary as its abandonment."[32] The atonement to which Hegel points does not shun opposition but is found in its midst; it is the union of union and nonunion revealed on a cross. Only sharply differentiated contraries can be re-membered. The passion (*Leidenschaft*) of spiritlessness creates the need for spirit. "The deepest need of spirit consists in the fact that the opposition in the subject itself has attained its universal, i.e., its most abstract extreme."[33] The awareness of this need brings unhappy consciousness full term and generates the "fullness of time"—the age is ripe for the birth of spirit. This birth, however, would not be possible were not spirit gestating in the womb of spiritlessness. "The very fact that this opposition is in itself [*an sich*] sublated [*aufgehoben*] constitutes the condition,

29. Ibid., p. 127; 148.

30. *Philosophy of History*, p. 278; 12:339.

31. *Faith and Knowledge*, p. 191; 2:432-433. See above, chap. 2, text corresponding to n. 63.

32. *Philosophy of Religion*, 1:278; 16:266.

33. Ibid., 3:66; 17:269.

the presupposition, of the subject's ability to sublate it explicitly [*für sich*]."[34] Once the pains of labor become acute, birth *cannot* be delayed.

Incarnation: Mediator

"When the fullness of time was come, God sent his Son." Hegel believes that Christ is the Mediator, *der Mittler*, in whom the extremes between which unhappy consciousness is torn are reunited. In Christ, "man appears as God, and God appears [*erscheint*] as man."[35] The Incarnation involves the divinization of the human and the humanization of the divine, or, expressed in other terms, the infinitizing of the finite and the finitizing of the infinite. As the revelation of the differentiated unity of opposites, the God-Man directly addresses the deepest need of unhappy consciousness. "What satisfies this need," Hegel writes, "we call the consciousness of reconciliation, the consciousness of the sublation, of the nullity of the opposition, the consciousness that this opposition is not the truth, but that rather the truth consists in reaching [*erreichen*] unity through the negation of this opposition, i.e., the peace, the reconciliation which this need demands. Reconciliation is the demand of this need, and lies within it as what is infinitely one, what is self-identical with itself."[36] Hegel insists that if the healing consciousness of reconciliation is to emerge, its certainty must be made immediately accessible to human awareness. This can occur only if the *universal* God becomes *present* in a *particular* self-conscious individual. In the person of Jesus, "the identity of divine and human nature attains the stage of certainty" by appearing in "the form of immediate sense intuition of external existence [*äusserliches Dasein*]."[37] For Hegel, "this Incarnation [*Menschwerdung*] of the divine being [*Wesen*], or the fact that it essentially and immediately has the shape of self-consciousness, is the simple content of the absolute religion. In this religion the divine being is known as spirit, or this religion is the

---

34. Ibid., p. 67; 17:269.
35. Ibid., p. 73; 17:275. Especially helpful studies of Hegel's Christology include Albert Chapelle, *Hegel et la religion*, 3 vol. (Paris: Éditions Universitaires, 1963 ff.), esp. vol. 2-3; Benoît Garceau, "Hegel et la christologie," *L'église et théologie* 4 (1973), 349-358; Hans Küng, *Menschwerdung Gottes: Eine Einführung in Hegels theologisches Denken als Prolegomena zu einer künftigen Christologie* (Basel: Herder, 1970); George Rupp, *Christologies and Cultures: Toward a Typology of Religious Worldviews* (The Hague: Mouton, 1974), esp. part 2; and James Yerkes, *The Christology of Hegel* (Missoula, Mont.: Scholars Press, 1978).
36. *Philosophy of Religion*, 3:66-67; 17:269. 37.
37. Ibid., p. 73; 17:275.

consciousness of the divine being that is spirit. For spirit is the knowledge of oneself in the externalization of oneself; the being that is the movement of retaining its self-identity in its otherness."[38] In order to understand the notion of spirit represented in the God-Man, it is necessary to grasp the relationship between the Incarnation and the Christian doctrine of the Trinity. Hegel goes so far as to declare that "God is recognized as *spirit* only when known as triune. This new principle is the axis upon which the history of the world turns. This is *the goal* and *the starting point* of history."[39]

Hegel suggests the inextricable relationship between Incarnation and Trinity when he writes: "The reconciliation believed to be in Christ has no meaning if God is not known as triune, if it is not recognized that he *is* but is at the same time the other, the self-differentiating, the other in the sense that *this other* is God himself, and has in himself the divine nature, and that the sublation of this difference, of this otherness, this return, this love, is spirit."[40] If Jesus is God, the divine can be neither the wholly transcendent and completely abstract One of Judaism, nor an undifferentiated Parmenidean identity, but must be an internally differentiated unity. The Christian God has to be triune, three-in-one and one-in-three, a multiplicity-in-unity and unity-in-multiplicity that forms the identity of identity and difference or the union of union and nonunion. Such is spirit—"*pure* self-recognition in absolute otherness."[41] "God is this," Hegel argues, "to differentiate himself from himself, to be an object to himself, but in this differentiation, to be absolutely identical with himself—this is spirit."[42] The Son is at once other than and one with the Father, and the Father is both other than and one with the Son. Each sees himself in the other and becomes himself through the other. "God beholds himself in what is differentiated; and when in his other he is united only with himself, he is there with no other but himself, he is in close union only with himself, he beholds *himself* in his other."[43] Hegel insists that in the spiritual relationship

38. *Phenomenology*, p. 459; 528.
39. *Philosophy of History*, p. 319; 12:386. Jörg Splett's *Die Trinitätslehre G. W. F. Hegels* (Freiburg: Alber, 1965) is a useful work on this issue. See also Chapelle, *Hegel et la religion*, vol. 3.
40. *Philosophy of Religion*, 3:99-100; 17:298.
41. *Phenomenology*, p. 14:24.
42. *Philosophy of Religion*, 3:327; 17:187.
43. Ibid., 3:18; 17:228. For a more extensive treatment of this issue see Traugott Koch, *Differenz und Versöhnung: Eine Interpretation der Theologie G. W. F. Hegels nach seiner Wissenschaft der Logik* (Gütersloh: Verlagshaus Gerd Mohn, 1967).

of Father and Son, otherness is both maintained and overcome. To fail to sustain this dialectical tension is to fall prey to the heterodoxy of either Docetism or Ebionism. Hegel explains this important point most clearly in the *Science of Logic*: "Father is the other of son and son the other of father, and each only *is* as this other of the other; and at the same time, the one determination only is, in relation to the other; their being is a *single* subsistence."[44]

The "single subsistence" that reconciles contraries or mediates opposites is spirit, *sensu eminentiori*. In himself, apart from Incarnation the Father remains abstractly universal. Through the otherness of the Son's particularity, the Father sublates this abstract indeterminacy by assuming specific existence in which he achieves self-actualization. So understood, spirit is concrete universality or individuality that is realized by the activity of self-differentiation and self-reconciliation. This process is the "movement of retaining self-identity in its otherness." "The three forms [here] indicated are: eternal being in-and-with itself, the form of universality [*Allgemeinheit*]; the form of appearance, being-for-other, particularization [*Partikularisation*]; the form of return from appearance into self, absolute individuality [*Einzelheit*]. In these three forms, the divine Idea explicates itself. Spirit is the divine history, the process of self-differentiation, diremption, and reappropriation."[45] The actuality of the divine presupposes such an incarnational process. In other words, the Incarnation meets a divine as well as a human need.

The two examples that Hegel most often cites to illustrate this complex notion of spirit are self-consciousness and love. In self-consciousness, the subject simultaneously distinguishes himself from himself and remains identical with himself. As will become apparent in our analysis of the *Phenomenology*, this self-awareness is not simply intrasubjective but is mediated by the self's relation to other. The intersubjectivity of spirit is explicit in love. Hegel maintains that

> love implies a differentiation between two who are, however, not merely different from one another. Love is this feeling of being outside of myself, the feeling and consciousness of this identity. I have my self-consciousness not in myself, but in another in whom alone I am satisfied and am at peace with myself—and I am only insofar as I am at peace with myself, for if I have not this, I am the contradiction that sunders itself.[46]

---

44. *Logic*, p. 441; 6:77.
45. *Philosophy of Religion*, 3:2; 17:214.
46. Ibid., pp. 10-11; 17:221-222. For an interesting anticipation of Hegel's interpretation of the Trinity in terms of the structure of self-consciousness and love, see Augustine's *On the Trinity*, Books 9-12.

As the concrete appearance of spirit, the God-Man seeks to effect a "conversion of consciousness [*Umkehrung des Bewusstseins*] ." In a manner analogous to Hegel's aesthetic education, Christ brings a "new consciousness," "the consciousness of absolute reconciliation," "the consciousness of the reconciliation of man and God." The unity of opposites incarnate in the Mediator discloses the inherent or implicit nature of all individuals. Though absolute reconciliation is decisively revealed in the *particular* person of Jesus, this truth is a *universal*, though unrecognized, characteristic of humankind. "Christ, man as man, in whom the unity of God and man has appeared, has in his death, and his history generally, himself presented the eternal history of spirit—a history that every man has to accomplish in himself, in order to exist as spirit, or to become a child of God, a citizen of his kingdom."[47] God's self-objectification in Christ creates the possibility of man's self-recognition. In the divine-human object, the subject can see himself reflected. Paradoxically, however, the very sensuous particularity necessary for the certainty of the unity of the divine and human natures inhibits the consummating wedding of subjectivity and objectivity in which self-alienation and estrangement are overcome. The believer sets himself over against the object of belief, that is, the God-Man, whom he regards as "an exclusive individual man, not representing all individuals, but as one from whom all are closed off."[48] To overcome this separation of subjectivity and objectivity, the truth revealed by the Mediator must itself be mediated.

Mediation

"The essence of the Christian principle," for Hegel, "is the principle of mediation." This fundamental religious tenet asserts that "the human and the divine nature are in and for themselves one, and that man, insofar as he is spirit, also possesses the essentiality and substantiality that belong to the notion of God. The mediation is dependent upon precisely the consciousness of this unity; and the *intuition* of this unity has been given to man in Christ."[49] We have seen that the recognition of the truth of spirit, like all other genuine knowledge, initially encounters the individual from without. Hegel argues that "the absolute religion is undoubtedly a positive religion in the sense that everything which exists for consciousness is for it an

---

47. *Philosophy of History*, p. 328; 12:397.
48. *Philosophy of Religion*, 3:73; 17:255.
49. *Philosophy of History*, p. 377; 12:453. Emphasis added.

objectification [*ein Gegenständliches*]. Everything must come to us in an outward, external way. The sensuous is something positive, and, to begin with, there is nothing so positive as what we have before us in immediate intuition."[50] Like all sensuous positivity, the God-Man is at first characterized by the exclusivity typical of abstract particularity. The process of mediation involves the universalization of Christ's particularity in such a way that the bifurcation of the object of belief and the subjectivity of the believer is sublated. Religion overcomes dead objectivity and becomes subjectively vital when the believer appropriates Christ's truth as his own. This mediation or "appropriation process" that establishes the "subjectivity of religious truth"[51] is threefold: it involves religious, sociocultural, and philosophical dimensions.

The mediation of Christ's unique particularity and positive objectivity begins during the lifetime of the historical Jesus. According to Hegel, the death of Christ is "the middlepoint [*der Mittelpunkt*]" around which all else turns. Christ's Crucifixion and Resurrection simultaneously affirm the full humanity of divinity and full divinity of humanity. By suffering the deepest extreme of finitude, death on a cross, God negates his abstract universality and reveals that humanity "is itself a moment in the divine life."

> "God Himself is dead," as it is said in a Lutheran hymn; the consciousness of this fact expresses the truth that the human, the finite, frailty, weakness, the negative, is itself a divine moment, is in God himself; that otherness or other being, the finite, the negative, is not outside of God; and that as otherness it does not hinder unity with God. Otherness, the negation, is consciously known to be a moment of the divine nature. The highest knowledge of the nature of the Idea of spirit is contained in this thought.[52]

For Christian vision, however, Crucifixion is inseparable from Resurrection. Christ's death is "the death of death, the negation of negation," in which the abstract particularity of the Son is reunited

---

50. *Philosophy of Religion*, 2:336; 17:194. For an excellent discussion of Hegel's notion of positivity in relation to his view of religion, see Stephen Crites, "The Problem of the 'Positivity' of the Gospel in the Hegelian Dialectic of Alienation and Reconcilation," (Ph.D. diss., Yale University, 1961). This argument is refined and expanded in Crites's forthcoming work entitled *Christianity in the Development of Hegel's Thought: Dialectic and Gospel in the Philosophy of Hegel*.

51. The reference, of course, is to Kierkegaard. We have seen the different meanings he gives these terms in the previous chapter. The significance of the contrast between Hegel and Kierkegaard on this issue for their distinctive interpretations of the Incarnation will become apparent in the next section.

52. *Philosophy of Religion*, 3:98; 17:297.

with the universality of the Father to form the concrete individuality of spirit—Holy Spirit. In the life and death of Jesus finitude is raised to infinitude, humanity resurrected as divinity.

> This death is love itself, posited as a moment of God, and this death is the reconciliation. In it we are able to intuit absolute love; God is *at home* with himself [*bei sich selbst*], and this finitude, as seen in death, is itself a determination of God. Through death God has reconciled the world and reconciled it eternally with himself. This coming back from estrangement [*Entfremdung*] is his return to himself, and through this He is spirit. The third point accordingly is that Christ has risen. Negation is consequently overcome, and the negation of negation is thus a moment of the divine life.[53]

As I have suggested, this incarnational process is not limited to the unique person of Jesus, but "represents the *absolute history of the divine Idea* that in itself had taken place and eternally takes place."[54] Having suffered on Golgotha, spirit is reborn in the Christian community.

Although the early church continues to represent (*vorstellen*) Jesus as an object of devotion, the community, through cultic activity, participates in divine presence by re-present-ing Christ in a way that sublates his historical particularity and alien objectivity. The ongoing life of the church is "the way [*der Weg*], the process of reconciliation, through which spirit unites with itself what it differentiated from itself in its diremption, its original separation [*Urteil*], and thus spirit is Holy Spirit, the spirit in its communitity [*Gemeinde*]."[55] The church becomes a spiritual community by means of the indwelling of divine spirit. In this community, the external objectivity of spirit is sublated by the appropriation process in which the believer inwardizes the object of belief and becomes one with Christ. This reconciliation is symbolized in the mass. Through the "eternal repetition" of this ritual, "the unity of the subject and the absolute object is offered directly to the individual for immediate enjoyment."[56] Sustained by the animating life of divine spirit, the church forms a community of love in which individual members

---

53. Ibid., p. 96; 17:295. Emphasis added.
54. Ibid., p. 94; 17:292.
55. Ibid., p. 1; 17:214. *Urteil* usually is translated "judgment." But in this context, the literal translation "original separation" (*Ur-teil*) is more suggestive of Hegel's meaning. It is also instructive to note the etymological connection between "community," *Gemeinde*, and "universal," *allgemein*.
56. Ibid., p. 132; 17:328.

reach fulfillment through active interrelation with one another. This spiritual community is nothing other than the kingdom (*Reich*) of God.

> What Jesus calls the "Kingdom of God" is the living harmony of men, their fellowship in God; it is the development of the divine among men, the relationship with God which they enter through being filled with the Holy Spirit, i.e., that of becoming his sons and living in the harmony of their developed many-sidedness and their entire being and character. In this harmony their many-sided consciousness chimes in with one spirit and their many different lives with one life; but, more than this, by its means the partitions against other godlike beings are abolished, and the same living spirit animates the different beings, who therefore are no longer merely similar but one; they make up not a collection, but a communion.[57]

Reconciliation, however, cannot be fully realized in the early church. By setting itself aloof from and in opposition to a spiritless world, the spiritual community and its members continue to suffer fragmentation. Hegel maintains that the disintegration of the sacred and the secular within the Christian tradition reaches its most extreme form in medieval Catholicism. The dissolution of self and society characteristic of the Middle Ages is most explicitly expressed for Hegel in the monastic vows of poverty, chastity, and obedience. The struggle to free oneself from spiritless entanglements issues in a "monkish flight" from the world in which the self remains inwardly and outwardly divided. Complete reconciliation presupposes an integration of the kingdom of God and the kingdom of the world. The pivot upon which this reunification turns is Luther's recognition that "the secular, the worldly is able to have the truth in it." Consequently, for Luther "secular pursuits are a spiritual occupation."[58] Hegel believes that Luther's insight implies that

> divine spirit must immanently pervade the entire worldly domain: thus wisdom is concrete within it, and determines its own justification. But that concrete indwelling is constituted by the . . . forms of ethical life [*Sittlichkeit*], the ethical life of marriage against the sanctity of the unmarried state; the ethical life of wealth and earning activity against the sanctity of poverty and its indolence; the ethical life of an obedience dedicated to the right of the state against the sanctity of an obedience from which law, right, and duty are absent, the enslavement of conscience.[59]

---

57. "The Spirit of Christianity," *Early Theological Writings*, p. 277; 321.
58. *Philosophy of History*, pp. 422, 355; 12:502, 427.
59. *Philosophy of Spirit*, trans. by W. Wallace (New York: Oxford University Press, 1971), par. 552; 10:359. Wallace's translation of *Sittlichkeit* as "morality" is misleading, for

It remains for the Teutonic[60] world to embody in concrete actuality the unity of the secular and sacred recognized in principle by Luther. The mediation of truth revealed in Christ culminates in the religious, social, cultural, and political life of Protestant Christendom. All that is necessary for the final realization of spirit is the philosophical comprehension of Mediator and mediation. Hegel believes this last step is taken in his system.

The mediation of religious truth by philosophical reflection is formally parallel to the religiocultural mediation effected by the history of the Christian West. Through speculative comprehension, sensual immediacy is grasped as mediated universality, and the opposition of subject and object is overcome. Hegel contends that the exercise of religious imagination issues in representations (*Vorstellungen*) that point toward, but finally fail to express, the universality of philosophical thought. Speculative philosophy seeks to articulate the conceptual content represented in religious images. Through rational reflection, religious Vorstellungen are translated into philosophical *Begriffe*. Hegel insists that the distinction between Vorstellung and Begriff is formal rather than substantive:

> Philosophy thus characterizes itself as a cognition of the necessity in the content of the absolute representation [*Vorstellung*]. . . . This cognition [*Erkennen*] is thus the recognition [*Anerkennen*] of this content and its form; it is the release from the one-sidedness of the forms, raising them into absolute form, which determines itself to content, remains identical with it, and is in that the cognition of that essential and actual necessity. This movement, which philosophy is, finds itself already accomplished, when at the close it grasps its own notion [*Begriff*], i.e., only reflects on its knowledge.[61]

Philosophy's conceptual mediation of the truth inherent in Christian symbols results in spirit's transparent self-consciousness.

---

it suggests that Hegel's term is *Moralität*. As will become apparent in chap. 6, *Sittlichkeit* and *Moralität* have different meanings for Hegel.

60. Professor Rupp correctly suggests that "Teutonic" rather than "Germanic" better expresses Hegel's meaning (*Christologies and Cultures*, chap. 6).

61. *Philosophy of Spirit*, par. 573; 10:378. Hegel's point is put in a more modern idiom when Paul Ricoeur argues that "the symbol gives rise to thought": see Ricoeur, "Hegel aujourd'hui," pp. 350 ff., and idem, *The Symbolism of Evil*, trans. E. Buchanan (Boston: Beacon Press, 1967), pp. 347 ff. Yerkes gives an unusually helpful account of the relationship between Hegel's view of religious Vorstellung and the mental activity of representation (*Christology of Hegel*, pp. 107 ff.). Dupré's analysis of Hegelian Vorstellung underscores the relationship between Hegel's argument on this point and the positions of Fichte and Schelling ("Religion as Representation," in *The Legacy of Hegel: Proceedings of the Marquette Hegel Symposium, 1970* [The Hague: Martinus Nijhoff, 1973], pp. 137-143).

In Protestant Christendom and speculative philosophy, the truth of spirit revealed in the historical figure of Jesus is fully incarnate and adequately comprehended. The reconciliation of the secular and sacred in personal and sociocultural life is the outworking of the union of the divine and human present-ed in Christ.[62] From Hegel's point of view, sojourners can feel at home only in a world in which the divine itself is at home. Heaven descends to earth and earth ascends to heaven, bringing the kingdom of God. This is a third *Reich*, characterized by neither the undifferentiated identity of childhood, nor the hostile antagonism of adolescence, but by the differentiated unity of mature individuals in communion with one another. To become a member of this kingdom, the individual must self-consciously retrace the steps or recollect the stages of spirit's self-development. This is the journey to selfhood undertaken in the *Phenomenology of Spirit*. In contrast with the spiritual results of the mediation process, Hegel argues, "it might almost be said that when Christianity is carried back to its first appearance, it is brought down to the level of spiritlessness, for Christ himself says that the spirit will not come until he himself has departed."[63]

PARADOX

The Fullness of Time: The Moment

Kierkegaard rejects Christendom's historical mediation and speculative philosophy's conceptual comprehension of the Incarnation. Christianity, he contends, "is no doctrine concerning the unity of the divine and the human, or concerning the identity of subject and object; nor is it any other of the logical transcriptions of Christianity. If Christianity were a doctrine, the relationship to it would not be one of faith, for only an intellectual type of relationship can correspond to a doctrine. Christianity, therefore, is not a

---

62. As should be evident by now, the reading of Hegel developed in this study rejects the interpretation of Hegel either as an atheistic humanist or as a pantheistic mystic. His position lies between these two extremes. In Christological terms, he accepts neither the Ebionite dissolution of divinity in humanity nor the Docetic dissolution of humanity in divinity, but insists on the Chalcedonian affirmation of the full humanity *and* full divinity of Christ. Kojève offers the most outstanding example of the former reading of Hegel, and Iljin and Thulstrup represent the latter line of argument. If one errs in the direction of either of these extremes, it becomes impossible to join the philosophical and theological issues at stake in the Hegel-Kierkegaard debate.

63. *History of Philosophy*, 3:14; 19, 505.

doctrine, but [is] the fact that God has existed."[64] The *fact* of the appearance of the transcendent, eternal God in the form of a particular temporal individual is an utterly contingent and thoroughly positive revelation event that can be neither historically nor rationally mediated. In relation to such sheer facticity, "mediation is mob rebellion."[65] Rather than bringing to full self-consciousness and complete realization the spiritual form of life initially disclosed in the God-Man, Christendom represents an "apostasy of spirit," a sinking into the stupor of spiritlessness. Kierkegaard writes: "It is eighteen hundred years since Christ lived, so he is forgotten—only his teaching remains—that is to say, Christianity has been done away with."[66] As I have suggested, Kierkegaard attempts to reestablish for a confused and de-spirited Christendom exactly what it means to be a Christian. This task requires the clarification of the central existential categories of Christianity which have been obscured by the march of worldly "spirit."[67] Since Kierkegaard attributes much of this confusion to Hegelianism, the formulation of his own Christological anthropology is inseparable from his critique of important features of the speculative exposition of Christianity. The two works in which Kierkegaard addresses this problem most directly are *Philosophical Fragments* and *Concluding Unscientific Postscript*, books whose very titles satirize the integrative scientific vision of the systematic philosopher.

For Kierkegaard, as for Hegel, the fullness of time is the moment in which time and eternity join "in a frightful combination" that reveals the true nature of God and self. Kierkegaard stresses the importance of establishing the proper interpretation of this central moment:

> The concept around which everything turns in Christianity, the concept that makes all things new, is the fullness of time, is the moment as eternity, and yet this eternity is at once the future and the past. If one does not give heed

---

64. *Postscript*, pp. 290-291; 7:281.

65. *Journals and Papers*, 1615; 10-2:A 431. By making the point in this way, Kierkegaard suggests the connection he sees between the philosophical principle of mediation and the depersonalization of individual existence brought about by identification with the public or the crowd. See above, chap. 2, 2d sec. ("Dissipation"), 1st subsec. ("Society and Politics: Leveling Crowd").

66. *Training in Christianity*, p. 127; 12:119.

67. Stanley Cavell has pointed out that Kierkegaard's work can be understood in a way analogous to the clarification of concepts attempted by recent linguistic analysts: see "Kierkegaard's *On Authority and Revelation*," in *Must We Mean What We Say?* (New York: Charles Scribner's Sons, 1969), pp. 163-179.

to this, one cannot save any concept from heretical and treasonable admixtures that destroy the concept. One does not get the past as a thing for itself, but in simple continuity with the future—and with that the concepts of conversion, atonement, redemption, are resolved in the significance of world-history, and resolved in the individual historical development.[68]

In contrast with the Hegelian fullness of time, the Kierkegaardian moment is not an integral part of a *continuous* historical process. Moreover, it does not arise *necessarily* through the immanent development of spirit, be that spirit human or divine. The moment is a "breach with immanence," a "breach of continuity."[69] The fullness of time represents the most radical accentuation of the contingency characteristic of all historical becoming.[70] *Øjeblikket* is neither the inevitable result of past occurrences nor the necessary anticipation of future events. It is at once immanent in and transcendent to the historical process. As such, the moment is "liminal";[71] it is the *limen* or boundary forming the ambiguous, tension-filled frontier that is the passageway between past and future, the point at which time and eternity meet.

Although Kierkegaard's understanding of the moment is a cornerstone of his entire philosophical position, he develops his most explicit and complete analysis of the nature of Øjeblikket in the "Interlude" in *Philosophical Fragments*. Between his discussion of "the contemporary disciple" of the God-Man and the latter-day believer, described as "the disciple at second hand," Kierkegaard addresses the question: "Is the past more necessary than the future? or, When the possible becomes actual, is it thereby made more necessary than it was?"[72] This problem provides the occasion for a

---

68. *Concept of Dread*, p. 81; 4:360. The Danish word Kierkegaard uses is *Øjeblikket*, which means "the glance of an eye." Kierkegaard notes that his term recalls Paul's phrase "in the twinkling of an eye." This word is the Danish equivalent of the German *Augenblick*. See *Concept of Dread*, p. 79; 4:358.

69. *Postscript*, p. 506; 7:496; *Philosophical Fragments*, p. 104; 4:247. For a helpful discussion of this point see Günter Rohrmoser, "Kierkegaard und das Problem der Subjektivität," *Neue Zeitschrift für systematische Theologie und Religionsphilosophie* 8 (1966), 289-310.

70. Although in this context our analysis of the moment focuses on the Incarnation, it will become apparent that this instant is prototypical of all historical events.

71. I borrow this term from Victor Turner's study, *The Ritual Process: Structure and Anti-structure* (Chicago: Aldine Publishing Co., 1969). Turner's analysis of the liminality of ritual rites of passage sheds interesting light on Kierkegaard's interpretation of the moment. H. Ganse Little offers an extraordinarily insightful and suggestive account of decision in which he creatively draws on Turner's argument: see his *Decision and Responsibility: A Wrinkle in Time* (Missoula, Mont.: Scholars Press, 1974).

72. *Philosophical Fragments*, p. 89; 4:235.

general consideration of historical becoming. Kierkegaard begins by asserting that all genuine becoming entails a change that amounts to "a transition from not existing to existing." With this claim, however, a dialectical puzzle immediately emerges. On the one hand, change presupposes something that changes. On the other hand, if becoming is to be understood in terms of "coming into existence," it would seem that the subject of change cannot exist prior to the becoming through which its determinate being is realized. Kierkegaard simultaneously ties and cuts this Gordian knot when he writes:

> This coming-into-existence kind of change, therefore, is not a change in essence, but in being, and is a transition from not existing to existing. But this non-being that the subject of coming into existence leaves behind must itself have some sort of being. Otherwise "the subject of coming into existence would not remain unchanged during the change of coming into existence," unless it had not been at all, and then the change of coming into existence would for another reason be absolutely different from every other kind of change, since it would be no change at all, for every change always presupposes something that changes. But such a being, which nevertheless is a non-being, is precisely what possibility is; and a being that is being is indeed actual being or actuality; and the change of coming into existence is a transition [*Overgangen*] from possibility to actuality.[73]

Having described becoming as the transition from possibility to actuality, it is incumbent upon Kierkegaard to define the exact nature of this elusive passage. He emphatically rejects any proposal that suggests that the actualization of possibility is effected by means of a necessary transition. From Kierkegaard's perspective, "everything that comes into existence proves precisely by coming into existence that it is not necessary, for the only thing that cannot come into existence is the necessary, because the necessary *is*."[74] Necessity characterizes purely atemporal relations of logical idealities and cannot be predicated of temporal reality. This is the basis of Kierkegaard's frequently repeated critique of the Hegelian introduction of movement into logic. "In logic," he argues, "no movement can *come about*, for logic *is*, everything logical simply is, and this impotence of logic is the transition to the sphere of becoming where existence and reality appear. . . . In logic every movement (if for a moment one would use this expression) is an immanent movement, which in a deeper sense is no movement, as one will easily convince

---

73. Ibid., p. 91; 4:237.
74. Ibid.

oneself if one considers that the very concept of movement is a transcendence that can find no place in logic."[75] Kierkegaard's denial that there is movement in logic implies, of course, that there is no logic in movement. This negative conclusion, however, does not adequately explain the nature of the transition Kierkegaard is exploring.

The direction of Kierkegaard's solution to the problem posed by the relation of the possible and the actual begins to emerge when it is recognized that he rejects the applicability of the conceptual coimplication of possibility and actuality to concrete existence. In the face of what he takes to be speculative philosophy's mistaken identification of possibility and actuality, Kierkegaard reasserts their abiding opposition.[76] Since possibility and actuality are inherently antithetical, they do not necessarily pass over into one another but can be brought together only through a third that is distinguishable from the extremes it struggles to join. This third is, for Kierkegaard, freedom. "The change involved in coming into existence," he argues,

> is actuality; the transition takes place with freedom. No coming into existence is necessary. It was not necessary before the coming into existence, for then there could not have been the coming into existence, nor after the coming into existence, for then there would not have been the coming into existence. All coming into existence takes place with freedom, not by necessity. Nothing comes into existence by virtue of a logical ground, but only by a cause. Every cause terminates in a freely effecting cause. The illusion occasioned by the intervening causes is that the coming into existence seems to be necessary; the truth about intervening causes is that just as they themselves have come into existence, they point back ultimately to a freely effecting cause.[77]

The free cause to which all becoming finally must be referred is God. Kierkegaard conceives God as a radically transcendent and completely free acting subject, whose omnipotent will is the ultimate

---

75. *Concept of Dread*, p. 12; 4:284-285.
76. Kierkegaard's argument attributes to Hegel a much stronger necessitarian position than Hegel intended to affirm. As we have seen, Hegel maintains that his interpretation of the dialectical relation of possibility and actuality does not destroy the contingent. Kierkegaard rejects Hegel's disclaimers and contends that the *logical* conclusion of the Hegelian position is the denial of all contingency. Kierkegaard's misprision of Hegel on this point has been largely responsible for the widespread misinterpretation of Hegel as an outright or undialectical determinist. Hegel's and Kierkegaard's contrasting views of possibility and actuality will be considered further in the next chapter.
77. *Philosophical Fragments*, p. 93; 4:238-239.

ground of reality.[78]   Unlike the Hegelian God, who is incomplete
apart from the world and hence is internally and necessarily related
to finitude, the Kierkegaardian God, who is possessed of perfect
aseity, is externally related to the world he infinitely transcends. The
relation between the infinite and the finite depends upon divine
freedom instead of divine need, and therefore is contingent rather
than necessary. If God chooses to relate himself to the finite domain
standing over against him, "He must indeed move himself, and
continue to exemplify what Aristotle says of him: ἀκίνητος πάντα
κινεῖ. But if he moves himself, it follows that he is not moved by
some need, as if he could not endure the strain of silence, but had to
break out in speech."[79] God's self-disclosure in Christ is an act of
divine freedom whose reason no person can know. In opposition to
the speculative effort to fathom the necessity of the fullness of time,
Kierkegaard insists that God "will have nothing to do with man's
pert inquiry about why, and why did Christianity come into the
world. . . . Therefore everything men have hit upon relatively to
explain the why and the wherefore is falsehood."[80]

The Kierkegaardian moment is the interface of possibility and
actuality in which the movement of coming into existence which
constitutes historical becoming originates. Kierkegaard stresses the
kinetic character of the moment by noting the derivation of
momentum from the Latin *movere* and by associating his interpretation of coming into existence with the Aristotelian notion of κίνησις.
In Øjeblikket, "history begins."[81] The historical process is not the
necessary unfolding of an ever present Idea, but is a contingent
sequence of events that arises through the free activity of independent agents. Rather than being a continuous and coherent progression, history is discontinuous, punctuated by surdity and novelty.
From the human perspective the course of history remains incoher-
ent, illogical, even absurd. Kierkegaard maintains that finite human

---

78. Some commentators contend that Kierkegaard really has two incompatible
notions of God: an impersonal Greek Absolute and a personal Christian God. Even when
Kierkegaard borrows the language of Greek metaphysics to accentuate the Absolute Para-
dox, however, he retains the personalistic or theistic image of the divine. See Torsten
Bohlin, *Kierkegaards dogmatiska aaskaadning i dess historiska sammanhang* (Stockholm:
Svenska Diakonistyrelses, 1925); Michael Wyschogrod, *Kierkegaard and Heidegger: The
Ontology of Existence* (London: Routledge and Kegan Paul, 1954), esp. pp. 42 ff.; and
Richard Kroner, "Kierkegaards Hegelverständnis," *Kant-Studien* 46 (1954-55), 19-27.
79. *Philosophical Fragments*, p. 30; 4:193.
80. *Training in Christianity*, p. 66; 12:59.
81. *Concept of Dread*, pp. 79, 80; 4:359. *Philosophical Fragments*, p. 90; 4:236.

beings cannot subsume this irrationality under a higher, more inclusive rationality. The brute facticity of unique occurrences remains utterly opaque—the rationale of history is not transparent to human eyes.[82]

This interpretation of historical events enables Kierkegaard to answer the question he raises at the outset of the Interlude: "Is the past more necessary than the future?" After acknowledging that what has been done cannot be undone, he argues that this unchangeableness is not identical with the immutability of necessity. Since it is rooted in free activity, the past might have been different. By contrast, what is necessary can never be other than it is. Kierkegaard contends that the predication of necessity to any part of the historical process dissipates genuine becoming. To view the past as necessary is to regard the future as closed and freedom as illusory. "If the past had become necessary," he writes,

> it would not be possible to infer the opposite about the future, but it would rather follow that the future also was necessary. If necessity could gain a foothold at a single point, there would no longer be any distinguishing between the past and the future. To assume to predict the future (prophesy) and to assume to understand the necessity of the past are one and the same thing, and only custom makes the one seem more plausible than the other to a given generation. The past has come into existence; coming into existence is the change of actuality brought about by freedom. If the past had become necessary it would no longer belong to freedom, i.e., it would no longer belong to that by which it came into existence. . . . Freedom itself would be an illusion, and coming into existence no less so; freedom would be witchcraft and coming into existence a false alarm.[83]

---

82. Kierkegaard does not deny that *sub specie aeterni* history assumes coherence and intelligibility. At one point he even suggests that while human beings can never reach the perspective of Hegelian philosophy, God is able to do so. In making this provocative statement, Kierkegaard intends to stress that finite selves cannot assume the viewpoint of the infinite. But he does not seem to realize that this way of stating the case runs the danger of making human freedom epiphenomenal, an illusion created by the limited viewpoint of individual selves. For further discussion of this problem see *Postscript*, pp. 127 ff.; 7:116 ff.

83. *Philosophical Fragments*, p. 96; 4:241. In a note appended to this passage, Kierkegaard makes it clear that Hegel is the target of his criticism. "A prophesying generation despises the past, and will not listen to the testimony of the scriptures; a generation engaged in understanding the necessity of the past does not like to be reminded of the future. Both attitudes are consistent, for each would have occasion to discover in the opposite the folly of its own procedure. The Absolute Method, Hegel's discovery, is a difficulty even in Logic, aye a glittering tautology, coming to the assistance of academic superstition with many signs and wonders. In the historical sciences it is a fixed idea. The fact that the method here at once begins to become concrete, since history is the concretion of the Idea, has given Hegel the opportunity to exhibit extraordinary learning, and a rare power of organization, inducing a quite sufficient commotion in the historical material. But it has also promoted a distraction of mind in the reader" (p. 96; 4:241).

Since becoming arises from the unfathomable abyss of freedom, history cannot be an object of knowledge but must be apprehended through belief. Kierkegaard argues that "the historical cannot be given immediately to the senses, for the *elusiveness* of coming into existence [*Tilblivelsens Svigagtighed*] is involved in it."[84] This elusiveness implies an element of uncertainty pertaining to historical events which can be overcome solely through a willful act of belief. If one is to grasp becoming,

> the organ for the historical must have a structure analogous to the historical itself; it must comprise a corresponding something by which it may repeatedly negate in its certainty the uncertainty that corresponds to the uncertainty of coming into existence. The latter uncertainty is two-fold: the nothingness of the antecedent non-being is one side of it, while the annihilation of the possible is another, the latter being at the same time the annihilation of every other possibility. Now faith has precisely the required character; for in the certainty of faith [*Tro*] there is always presented a negated uncertainty, in every way corresponding to the uncertainty of coming into existence. Faith believes what it does not see; it does not believe that the star is there, for that it sees, but it believes that the star has come into existence. The same holds true of an event.[85]

Kierkegaard denies that history can be adequately comprehended through rational reflection. The absentminded speculative philosopher forgets that the momentary transition from possibility to actuality remains impenetrable to his contemplative gaze. His understanding is, in fact, a misunderstanding that arises through man's tragicomic presumption to be divine.

The situation is even more complex when one considers the moment of God's Incarnation in the historical figure of Jesus. This event "is not an ordinary historical fact, but a fact based on a self-contradiction." It is, in short, "an eternal fact [*et evigt Faktum*]" or "an absolute fact [*et absolut Faktum*]."[86] This absolute fact is the unique revelation of the eternal God through which, paradoxically, the individual can discover for the first time what it means to be an authentic temporal self. Øjeblikket is not born of the past and is not pregnant with the future, but decisively disjoins "here" and "hereafter." Though in a way quite different from Hegel, the moment is, for Kierkegaard, the hinge upon which history

---

84. Ibid., p. 100; 4:244.
85. Ibid., pp. 101-102; 4:245. As Hong points out, *Tro* can translate as "faith" or "belief." I use these two terms interchangeably.
86. Ibid., pp. 108, 124-125; 4:250, 262-263.

swings. "Such a moment," he suggests, "has a peculiar character. It is brief and temporal indeed, like every moment; it is transient as all moments are; it is past, like every moment in the next moment. And yet it is decisive, and filled with the Eternal. Such a moment ought to have a distinctive name; let us call it the Fullness of Time [*Tidens Fylde*]."[87] From Kierkegaard's perspective, God does not necessarily become incarnate when time is fulfilled; rather, when God freely "chooses to become an individual man,"[88] the fullness of time arrives.

Incarnation: Absolute Paradox

In *Concluding Unscientific Postscript* Kierkegaard queries:

> But what other presupposition can, generally speaking, come into question for a so-called Christian philosophy, but that Christianity is the precise opposite of speculation, that it is the miraculous, the absurd, a challenge to the individual to exist in it, and not to waste his time by trying to understand it speculatively? If we are to have speculation within this presupposition, it will be the function of this speculation more and more profoundly to grasp the impossibility of understanding Christianity. . . . If Christianity is the opposite of speculation, it is also the opposite of mediation, the latter being a category of speculative thought; what then can it mean to mediate them? But what is the opposite of mediation? It is the Absolute Paradox.[89]

In place of Hegel's notion of the Mediator who reunites opposites in an inherently rational manner, Kierkegaard posits the God-Man as an absolutely paradoxical coincidence of opposites which resists all religious, historical, and philosophical mediation.[90] Kierkegaard goes

---

87. Ibid., p. 22; 4:188. Throughout *Philosophical Fragments*, Kierkegaard conducts a "thought experiment" in which he constructs a hypothetical religion that conforms to what in the *Postscript* he explicitly identifies as Christianity.

88. *Training in Christianity*, p. 131; 12:123.

89. *Postscript*, p. 338; 7:327-328.

90. Alastair McKinnon rightly argues that Kierkegaard's view of paradox is largely a response to his interpretation of Hegel's account of Christianity: see "Kierkegaard: 'Paradox' and Irrationality," in *Essays on Kierkegaard*, pp. 102-112. Surprisingly, Hegel's and Kierkegaard's Christologies have rarely been compared. In a recent work, L. M. Read undertakes this task. While there is much that is of interest in Read's study, the argument is flawed by a facile acceptance of Kierkegaard's critique of Hegel and by the preoccupation with a Buberian model of dialogic relation which is supposed to overcome the *apparent* monistic implications of Hegel's position ("Hegel and Kierkegaard: A Study in Antithetical Concepts of the Incarnation" [Ph.D. diss., Columbia University, 1977]). Although Hegel's relationship to Kierkegaard is not a major theme in Professor Rupp's study, his typological categories of "realist-processive" and "nominalist-transactional" illuminate Hegel's and Kierkegaard's respective interpretations of Christ (*Christologies and Cultures*, pp. 49 ff.).

so far as to argue that "the characteristic mark of Christianity is the paradox, the Absolute Paradox. As soon as so-called Christian speculation sublates the paradox and reduces this characterization to a transient factor, all the stages [of existence] are confused."[91] Kierkegaard's notion of the Absolute Paradox presupposes that the divine and the human are not implicitly one but are completely opposite, separated by a "yawning abyss" that reflects an "infinite qualitative difference." Only the conjunction of absolute antitheses can create an Absolute Paradox.

> That God has existed in human form, has been born, grown up, and so forth, is surely the paradox *sensu strictissimo*, the Absolute Paradox. As such it cannot relate itself to a relative difference between men. . . . But the absolute difference between God and man consists precisely in this, that man is a particular existing being . . . , whose essential task cannot be to think *sub specie aeterni*, since as long as he exists he is . . . essentially an existing individual, whose essential task is to concentrate on inwardness in existing; while God is infinite and eternal.[92]

The appearance of God in Christ does not abrogate the otherness of God so obediently acknowledged by Abraham, the father of faith. Against Hegel's claim that the Incarnation discloses the immanence of God and thus the homogeneity of the divine and the human, Kierkegaard affirms that the Absolute Paradox reveals the radical transcendence of God and the heterogeneity of the divine and the human.[93] The Incarnation is a unique and unrepeatable event. The fullness of time represents "that ambiguity in which time and eternity touch one another;"[94] it is the particular historical moment in which the universal, eternal God freely appears in the form of a particular, temporal individual. "The God-Man," Kierkegaard avers, "is the unity of God and an individual man. That the human race is

---

Hermann Deuser's *Søren Kierkegaard: Die paradoxe Dialektik des politischen Christen* (Munich: Chr. Kaiser Verlag, 1974) presents an unusually perceptive consideration of important implications of Kierkegaard's view of Christ. In a recent study of related interest, Deuser turns his attention to a comparison of Kierkegaard's late writings and the work of Adorno ("Dialektische Theologie: Studien zu Adornos Metaphysik und dem Spätwerk Kierkegaards" [Habilitationsschrift, University of Tübingen, 1977]). Other considerations of Kierkegaard's Christology include T. H. Croxall, "Facets of Kierkegaard's Christology," *Theology Today* 8 (1951), 327-339; Louis Dupré, *Kierkegaard as Theologian* (New York: Sheed and Ward, 1958); and Taylor, *Kierkegaard's Pseudonymous Authorship*, pp. 291 ff.

91. *Postscript*, p. 480; 7:471.

92. Ibid., pp. 194-195; 7:182. The notion of God that Kierkegaard develops falls within Hegel's category of the "bad infinite." See above, text corresponding to n. 20.

93. See Crites, *Twilight of Christendom*, pp. 59-60; and Wahl, *Études kierkegaardiennes*, p. 134.

94. *Concept of Dread*, p. 80; 4:359.

or should be akin to God is ancient paganism; but that the individual is God is Christianity, and this individual is called the God-Man."[95]

Kierkegaard sets his adherence to the unmediated positivity of the God-Man in direct opposition to Hegel's view of the Incarnation. For speculative philosophy, "the eternal is *ubique et nusquam*, but concealed by the actuality of existence; in the paradoxical religiousness, the eternal is at a definite place, and precisely this is the breach with immanence."[96] The "pagan" identification of God with the race, or with finitude as a whole, transforms the uniqueness of the historical Incarnation event into "an eternal history," and transmutes the deity in time into "an eternal becoming of the divine." Kierkegaard suggests that the interpretation of "the becoming of the eternal in time" as an "eternal becoming" inevitably leads to a Feuerbachian reduction of theology to anthropology.[97] The sheer facticity of the God-Man establishes Christ as "an exclusive individual man . . . from whom all are closed off."[98] Yet precisely this splendid isolation enables the God-Man to illuminate the nature of spirit and the distinctive character of human existence.

To the despairing individual, mired in sin and separated from the divine, Christ reveals the truth of God and self.[99]

> *The paradoxical religiousness* defines the distinction [between "here" and "hereafter"] absolutely by accentuating paradoxically what it is to exist. For as the eternal came into the world at a moment of time, the existing individual does not in the course of time come into relation to the eternal and deliberate over it . . . , but *in time* one comes into relation with the eternal *in time*; so that the relation is within time, and this relationship conflicts equally with all thinking, whether one reflects upon the individual or upon the deity.[100]

---

95. *Training in Christianity*, p. 84; 12:79.

96. *Postscript*, p. 506; 7:497.

97. For Kierkegaard's development of this point see *Postscript*, pp. 512-515; 7:500-504.

98. These are the words Hegel uses to describe the view of the Savior held by the early Christian community, which, he believes, must be overcome if the truth implicit in Christ is to become explicit.

99. By stressing the Christological character of Kierkegaard's anthropology, I distinguish my argument from Professor Elrod's line of analysis. As is evident from *Kierkegaard's Pseudonymous Authorship*, I am in agreement with much of Elrod's interpretation of Kierkegaard's view of the personality. But I reject his claim that "Kierkegaard's conception of the self does not depend upon any Christian *Weltanschauung*" (p. 65). Such a position simply cannot find textual support. In his haste to discover a generalized ontology in Kierkegaard's writings, Elrod overlooks the significant interplay between the notion of the God-Man and the Kierkegaardian view of individual selfhood. See his *Being and Existence in Kierkegaard's Pseudonymous Works* (Princeton: Princeton University Press, 1975).

100. *Postscript*, pp. 505-506; 7:496. Kierkegaard adds: "The apprehension of the distinction 'here' and 'hereafter' is at bottom the apprehension of what it is to *exist*, and the

Since the temporal individual does not enjoy an immanent relation to the divine, but stands over against transcendent infinitude, any relation to God must arise in time, the life-time of the particular self. The overriding question addressed in both *Philosophical Fragments* and *Concluding Unscientific Postscript* is: "Is an historical point of departure possible for an eternal consciousness; how can such a point of departure have any other than a merely historical interest; is it possible to base an eternal blessedness upon historical knowledge?"[101] Through the persona of Johannes Climacus, Kierkegaard not only answers this question affirmatively but maintains that such an affirmation forms the essence of the Christian religion.

> I scarcely suppose that anyone will deny that it is the Christian teaching in the New Testament that the eternal blessedness of the individual is decided [*afgjøres*] in time, and is decided through the relationship to Christianity as something historical. . . . To avoid distraction again, I do not wish to bring forward any other Christian principles; they are all contained in this one, and may be consistently derived from it, just as this determination also offers the sharpest contrast with paganism.[102]

Because truth does not lie within the individual, it must encounter him from without. For Kierkegaard, realization of spirit does not involve the recognition or recollection of antecedent actuality but requires the volitional enactment or repetition of conceived possibility. In the "Christianity" of Christendom and of speculative philosophy,

> there is no historical starting-point. The individual merely discovers in time that he must assume he is eternal. The moment in time is therefore *eo ipso* swallowed up by eternity. In time the individual recollects that he is eternal. This contradiction lies exclusively within immanence. It is another thing when the historical is outside and remains outside, and the individual who was not eternal now becomes such, and so does not recollect what he is, but becomes what he was not, becomes, be it observed, something which possesses the dialectic that as soon as it is, it must have been, for this is the dialectic of the eternal. This proposition inaccessible to thought is: that one can become eternal, although one was not such.[103]

So understood, the moment of the Incarnation assumes a significance matched only by the importance of the moment in which the individual's eternal destiny is decided through his response to the

---

other distinctions converge about this—if one is careful to notice that Christianity is not a doctrine, but an existence-communication."

101. *Philosophical Fragments*, title page. Throughout this study, I render the Danish *Salighed* by "blessedness" rather than by the more common translation "happiness."

102. *Postscript*, p. 340; 7:319.

103. Ibid., p. 508; 7:500.

irrevocable either-or posed by the God-Man. Such a decisive encounter between the divine-human object and the individual subject can occur only in the situation of contemporaneity (*Samtidighed*).

Contemporaneity

While the interpretation of the discontinuous moment represents an account of the fullness-of-time alternative to Hegel's pregnant present, and the insistence on the irreducibility of the Absolute Paradox is directed against Hegel's implicitly rational Mediator, Kierkegaard develops the notion of contemporaneity to correct what he regards as problematic implications of the Hegelian sociocultural and philosophical mediation of the God-Man's positivity. It will be recalled that Hegel's teleological hermeneutic leads to the conclusion that in contrast with the spiritual results of the process of historical and conceptual mediation, Christianity, when carried back to its first appearance, is virtually "brought down to the level of spiritlessness." Kierkegaard inverts Hegel's dialectic of historical development by arguing that the history of Christendom is a story of the fall from spirit to spiritlessness. To recover the vision of authentic spirit, it is necessary to retreat from the spiritless nineteenth century to a direct confrontation with the Absolute Paradox. "Out with history," Kierkegaard declares. "In with the situation of contemporaneity. This is the criterion: as I judge anything contemporaneously, so am I. All this subsequent chatter is a delusion."[104] A polemic against the eighteen-hundred-year mediation of Christianity which culminates in bourgeois Protestant Christendom runs throughout Kierkegaard's diverse writings. "For him who is not contemporary with the Absolute," Kierkegaard argues, "for him the Absolute has no existence. And since Christ is the Absolute, it is easy to see that with respect to him, there is only one situation: that of contemporaneity. The five, the seven, the fifteen, the eighteen hundred years are neither here nor there; they do not change him, neither do they in any way reveal who he was, for who he is, is revealed only to faith."[105]

The Absolute Paradox forces an "absolute decision"—*either* believe *or* be offended. There is no middle ground, no mean between

---

104. *Journals and Papers*, 69; 9:A 76. It is helpful to recall Kierkegaard's discussion of "chatter" as symptomatic of spiritlessness. See above, chap. 2, 2d sec. ("Dissipation"), 1st subsec. ("Society and Politics: Leveling Crowd").

105. *Training in Christianity*, p. 67; 12:60.

these extremes. Christianity demands decision, an "eternal decision in time" which "is the most intensive intensity, the most intensive leap."[106] The necessity for decisive response is a function of the absurdity of the God-Man. Paradoxically, divine revelation is at the same time God's self-concealment. "The absurd is—that the eternal truth has come into being in time, that God has come into existence, has been born, has grown up, and so forth, precisely like any other individual human being, quite indistinguishable from other individuals."[107] By presenting himself in the form of a particular person, God assumes an "incognito," an "absolute unrecognizableness [*Ukjendeligheden*]" that is "impenetrable to the most intimate *observation*."[108] Though joined in a single person, overt humanity and covert divinity stand opposed, thereby making Christ "the sign of contradiction."[109] The bifurcation of inward essence and outward appearance renders every age equidistant from the Absolute Paradox. In relation to the absolute or eternal fact, Kierkegaard argues, "it would be a contradiction to suppose that time had any power to differentiate the fortunes of men . . . in any decisive sense."[110] In another context, he explains this central point in greater detail:

> The Christian fact has no history, for it is the paradox that God once came into existence in time. This is the offense, but also it is the point of departure; and whether this was eighteen hundred years ago or yesterday, one can just as well be contemporary with it. Like the polar star, this paradox never changes its position and therefore has no history, so this paradox stands immovable and unchanged; and though Christianity were to last for another ten thousand years, one would get no farther from this paradox than the contemporaries were. The distance is not to be measured by the quantitative scale of time and space, for it is qualitatively decisive by the fact that it is a paradox.[111]

In relation to this absurdly paradoxical event, later generations might appear to enjoy an advantage over earlier generations of potential believers. With the passing of years and the expansion of Christendom, the tension present in the Absolute Paradox gradually

---

106. *Journals and Papers*, 4806; 10-1A: 329.
107. *Postscript*, p. 188; 7:176.
108. *Training in Christianity*, p. 27; 12:24. Emphasis added.
109. Ibid., p. 127, 135; 12:118, 126.
110. *Philosophical Fragments*, p. 125; 4:263.
111. *On Authority and Revelation*, trans. W. Lowrie (New York: Harper and Row, 1966), pp. 60-61.

relaxes and the incongruity of the Incarnation event is "naturalized."
As a result of widespread acceptance, the God-Man becomes inoffen-
sive and the transition from nonbelief to belief seems to be facilitated. But Kierkegaard completely rejects this dissolution of the
Christian paradox and the correlative domestication of human existence. In order to defend his position on this issue, he develops an
extended critique of the "proof of the centuries," or the appeal to
the results of the eighteen hundred years since Christ lived. He cites
four fundamental reasons for rejecting the historical mediation of
Christian belief.[112]   In the first place, there can be no appeal to
results in establishing faith, for the results are still outstanding.
History is not complete but is an ongoing process composed of free
events that bring unexpected twists and unforeseen turns. The effect
of this open-endedness is retroactive, for it means that consequences
and results of previous events are incomplete and thus intrinsically
unknowable. Second, human knowledge of the historical process is
only approximate. Man's angle of vision is necessarily limited and his
awareness inevitably circumscribed. Unable to comprehend everything *sub specie aeterni*, the existing individual is forced to admit the
partiality and inadequacy of his knowledge. Third, the essentially
religious lies in hidden inwardness, and therefore cannot be directly
manifested in outward historical events. As the Absolute Paradox,
Christ is "an extremely unhistorical person," who

> is not, and for nobody is he willing to be, one about whom we have learned
> to know something merely from history (i.e., world-history, secular history,
> in contrast to sacred history); for from history we can learn to know
> nothing about him, because there is absolutely nothing that can be
> "known" about him. He declines to be judged in a human way by the
> consequences of his life, that is to say, he is and would be the sign of
> offense and the object of faith. To judge him by the consequences of his life
> is mere mockery of God; for, seeing that he is God, his life (the life that he
> actually lived in time) is infinitely more decisively important than all the
> consequences of it in the course of history.[113]

---

112. See *Postscript*, pp. 126 ff.; 7:116 ff.
113. *Training in Christianity* p. 26: 12:24. In the *Postscript*, Kierkegaard explains the
relevance of this point for his difference from Hegel. "The Hegelian philosophy culminates
in the proposition that the outward is the inward and the inward is the outward. With this
Hegel virtually finishes. But this principle is essentially an aesthetic-metaphysical one, and in
this way the Hegelian philosophy is happily finished, or is fraudulently finished by lumping
everything (including the ethical and the religious) indiscriminately in the aesthetic-
metaphysical. . . . The religious posits decisively an opposition between the outward and
the inward, posits it decisively as opposition. . . . If our age had not the distinction of

The world-historical speculator who attempts to ascertain the results of the impact of the God-Man on the development of the race becomes entangled in externalities that have nothing to do with matters religious. He loses himself in the observation of the spectacle unfolding before him and forgets what it means to be a concrete individual for whom religion is a live existential option. Fourth and finally, the appeal to results or the consequences of the eighteen hundred years indicates a basic misunderstanding of the nature of religious faith. Even if the outcome of the historical drama were available and expressible in objective historical terms, it could not affect the personal decision in which the individual faithfully appropriates the historical figure of Jesus as the God-Man. For Kierkegaard, "if inwardness is truth, results are only rubbish with which we should not trouble each other."[114]   All efforts to mediate the Incarnation through incorporation within the historical process seek to mitigate the risk involved in the radical decision posed by the God-Man. The advantage of later generations is illusory, actually a disadvantage. Temporal distance from the offensive paradox creates an "optical illusion" in which the difficulties of belief and the tensions of authentic selfhood are obscured.

Confusion is only compounded by the attempt to mediate the God-Man by means of rational or philosophical reflection. The Absolute Paradox is not intrinsically rational but is inherently self-contradictory and irreducibly absurd. Rather than revealing the omnipotence of reason and the rationality of actuality, the God-Man confronts human reason with its limitations, establishes its boundaries, and irrevocably separates the rational and the actual. Faith and reason, religious belief and philosophical knowledge, are not implicitly one but are antithetical. The individual must believe "against reason," for the object of faith is an "offense" to reason, the "shipwreck" of reason, the "crucifixion" of understanding.[115]   In relation to the God-Man the task of reason is thoroughly negative. Reason must make it clear that the Absolute Paradox cannot be

---

simply ignoring the duty of existing, it would be inconceivable that such wisdom as the Hegelian could be regarded as the highest, as maybe it is for aesthetic contemplators, but not either for ethical or for religious existers" (pp. 263-264 n.; 7:254 n).

114. *Postscript*, p. 216; 7:203.

115. Unlike Hegel, Kierkegaard does not distinguish reason and understanding. My analysis of Hegel suggests that he would regard Kierkegaard's description of the relationship between reason and faith as typical of the perspective of Verstand or of the reflective philosophy of subjectivity. As we have seen, however, Hegel insists that Vernunft rationally mediates the opposites established and maintained by Verstand.

understood, and hence help the individual to see that the paradox really is a paradox. To explain the paradox is, in the final analysis, to deny its paradoxicality by reducing it to a relative moment that is sublated through rational comprehension. The attempted philosophical mediation of Christian faith misconstrues religious belief. It mistakenly regards faith as the result of cognitive reflection instead of the outcome of volitional appropriation.[116]

In a manner analogous to Kierkegaard's indirect existential maieutic, the God-Man poses an unavoidable choice.

> When one says, "I am God; the Father and I are one," that is direct communication. But when he who says it is an individual man, quite like other men, then this communication is not just perfectly direct; for it is not just perfectly clear and direct that an individual man should be God— although what he says is perfectly direct. By reason of the communicator, the communication contains a contradiction, it becomes indirect communication, it puts to you a choice, whether you will believe him or not.[117]

The response to this either-or is decisive for an individual's eternal destiny. Through the decisions that constitute personal history, the self defines itself, assumes a concrete and unique identity by which one differentiates oneself from all other selves. Since the individual is not internally related to God, the God-self relationship must come into existence in time, through the response of the solitary self to the temporalized deity. Faith is a radical venture, an unmediated leap in which the self transforms itself. Through belief, one "does not recollect what he is, but becomes what he was not." In the moment of faith, the individual, singled out from all others and standing alone before the wholly other God, is completely responsible for the self he freely becomes. When a person responds faithfully, the truth of the God-Man is inwardized, assumes subjective vitality. The self actualizes possibility and *becomes* faithful. This transformative resolution happens at a depth of inwardness which is incommensurable with outward expression. The faith of the believing subject, like the divinity of the believed object, is an "incognito." Time and eternity meet in the moment of faith as the *temporal* individual gains *eternal* blessedness through free decision. "Faith," in other words, "is as

---

116. Kierkegaard's view of faith and reason has been the subject of extensive, but rarely insightful, consideration. For helpful studies see James Collins, "Faith and Reflection in Kierkegaard," in *A Kierkegaard Critique*, pp. 141-155, and N. H. Søe, "Kierkegaard's Doctrine of the Paradox," ibid., pp. 207-227.

117. *Training in Christianity*, p. 134; 12:126.

paradoxical as the paradox."[118]   Unlike the Incarnation, however, faith is not a once-and-for-all occurrence but must be repeated ever again. Becoming spirit is the task of a lifetime.

The moments of Incarnation and faith are mirror images of each other: "The paradox unites contradictories, and is the historical made eternal, and the Eternal made historical."[119]   The eternal God becomes temporal in the moment of Incarnation and the temporal individual becomes eternal in the moment of faith. In the fullness of time, spirit is revealed to spirit through the contemporary encounter between God and self brought about when the individual overleaps spiritless Christendom to meet the God-Man face to face. Authentic spirit is a coincidentia oppositorum in which contraries are brought together in the passion of free resolution. Put differently, the God-Man is the prototype in whose image the faithful individual constantly seeks to form his self. Christ leaves behind "footsteps" to guide those who journey to selfhood. Kierkegaard's sojourner is a solitary pilgrim who settles in no earthly city and is at home in no worldly kingdom. Obedient to his transcendent Lord, the wayfarer wanders through a confusing world in ceaseless search of spirit. "This is how Christianity presents it," Kierkegaard writes. "Before you lies an eternity—your fate is decided in this life, by how you use it. You have perhaps thirty years left, perhaps ten, perhaps five, perhaps one, perhaps, perhaps only one month, one day: frightful earnestness."[120]

---

118. *Philosophical Fragments*, p. 81; 4:230.
119. Ibid., p. 76; 4:226.
120. *Journals and Papers*, 4807; 11-1:A 399.

|5|

STRUCTURES OF SPIRIT

Without Contraries is no progression. Attraction and Repulsion, Reason and Energy, Love and Hate, are necessary to Human existence.
—*Blake*

I am the strife, for the strife is just this conflict, which is not any indifference of the two as diverse, but is their being bound together. I am not one of these two taking part in the strife, but I am both the combatants, and am the strife itself. I am the fire and the water which touch one another, and am the collision and unity of what flies apart, and this very collision, is this double, conflicting relation, as the relation of what now is separated, fragmented, and now is reconciled in unity with itself.
—*Hegel*

The view that sees life's doubleness (dualism) is higher and deeper than that which seeks or "pursues studies toward unity" (an expression from Hegel about all the endeavors of philosophy); the view that sees the eternal as *telos*, and the teleological view in general, is higher than all immanence or all talk about *causa sufficiens*. The passion that saw paganism as sin and assumed eternal torment in hell is greater than the *summa summarum* of the thoughtlessness (that is disheveled) which sees everything within immanence.
—*Kierkegaard*

To a spiritless age, plagued by personal and social fragmentation or suffering the dissipation of concrete individuality, the person and life of Christ offer an image of authentic spiritual existence. "The God-Man," as Kierkegaard puts it, "wants to show what it is to be a man."[1] For Hegel, the Mediator represents the inherently rational reintegration of the opposites that rend unhappy consciousness. The central symbol of Christian faith neither obscures the reality of conflicting contraries nor denies the passion of spiritual tension. Christ reveals reconciliation *in the midst of* estrangement. Spirit, Hegel insists, finds itself through the process of dismembering and remembering. From Kierkegaard's point of view, the Absolute Paradox reestablishes the contrasts and reaccentuates the distinctions that form authentic individuality. The God-Man discloses the passionate coincidence of opposites which must be repeatedly reconstituted in the life of the self. Spiritual sojourners remain distended between the conflicting extremes they struggle to join.

We have seen that Hegel and Kierkegaard maintain that the God-Man "absolutely contradicts the understanding." Within Hegel's system, understanding (Verstand) is the form of thought which is governed by the principle of abstract identity formulated in traditional logic. According to understanding, everything is what it is, and is not another; the laws of identity, difference, and noncontradiction are inviolable. Any coincidence of opposites is, in principle, unintelligible or absurd. Understanding, therefore, cannot grasp the conceptual truth implicit in the Incarnation. Although Hegel recognizes the importance of this mental activity, he stresses that Verstand can easily become unreasonable and even dogmatic. "Dogmatism," he explains, "consists of holding fast to the one-sided determinations of the understanding to the exclusion of their opposites. It is generally the strict *either-or*: for instance, the world is *either* finite *or* infinite, but only one of these two."[2] By leaving contraries unreconciled, undialectical understanding both manifests and perpetuates estrangement. To overcome this alienating opposition, dialectical reason must attempt to demonstrate that everything is inherently self-contradictory. Hegel is convinced that "neither in heaven nor on earth, neither in the world of spirit nor of nature, is there anywhere such an

---

1. *Journals and Papers*, 82; 11-1:A 236.
2. *Lesser Logic*, par. 32; 8:98-99. This text suggests that Hegel is thinking of Kant's antinomies of pure reason. Elsewhere Hegel writes: "It is the fashion of youth to dash about in abstractions, but the man experienced in life steers clear of the abstract *Either-Or* and holds to the concrete" (par. 80; 8:172).

abstract either-or as the understanding maintains."[3] Adequate comprehension of the truth revealed in the God-Man requires a revision of the fundamental logical principles that lie at the base of western reflection. In place of the analytic logic of Verstand, Hegel proposes a speculative logic of Vernunft. Reason sublates the oppositional either-or of understanding and apprehends the dialectical character of thought and the relationality of being. By grasping "opposites in their unity," speculative reason uncovers the structure of spirit revealed in Christ.

In *Philosophical Fragments*, Kierkegaard's pseudonym Johannes Climacus insists that

> at bottom it is an immovable firmness with respect to the Absolute, with respect to absolute distinctions, that makes a man a good dialectician. This is something that our age has altogether overlooked, in and by its repudiation of the principle of contradiction, failing to perceive what Aristotle nevertheless pointed out, namely that the proposition: the principle of contradiction is annulled, itself rests upon the principle of contradiction, since otherwise the opposite proposition, that it is not annulled, is equally true.[4]

Over against Hegel's speculative revision of the principles of identity, difference, and contradiction, Kierkegaard reaffirms traditional logic as originally defined by Aristotle. He believes that Hegel's effort to mediate opposites actually collapses distinctions essential to concrete existence. From the Kierkegaardian perspective "the view that sees life's doubleness (dualism) is higher and deeper than that which seeks or 'pursues studies toward unity.' "[5] In place of an inclusive dialectic of relationality, Kierkegaard proposes an exclusive dialectic of coincidence. In Kierkegaard's hands Hegel's mediation of opposites, which leads to the internal relation of "both-and," reverts to a disjunction of opposites which issues in the external relation of "either-or." Put differently, while Hegel criticizes the unmediated Kierkegaardian antitheses sustained by Verstand, Kierkegaard rejects the Hegelian mediation of opposites effected by Vernunft. Kierkegaard maintains that the structure of spirit becomes apparent only through the precise delineation and careful contraposing of the qualitative opposites paradoxically conjoined in the God-Man.

Despite their basic disagreement about the nature and function

---

3. Ibid., par. 119; 8:246.
4. *Philosophical Fragments*, pp. 136-137; 4:270.
5. *Journals and Papers* 704; 4:A 192.

of logical principles, Hegel and Kierkegaard describe the formal structure of spirit in remarkably similar terms. Spirit, according to Hegel, "is essence, or that which has *being in itself*; it is that which *relates itself to itself* and is *determinate*, it is *other-being* and *being-for-self*, and in this determinateness, or in its self-externality, abides within itself; in other words, it is *in and for* itself." Hegel proceeds to identify spirit with self, and then argues that "the self is the sameness and simplicity that relates itself to itself [*das Selbst die sich auf sich beziehende Gleichheit und Einfachheit ist*]."[6] In his most concise definition of spirit, Kierkegaard writes: "Man is spirit. But what is spirit? Spirit is the self [*Selvet*]. But what is the self? The self is a relation that relates itself to its own self [*der forholder sig til sig selv*], or is that in the relation by which the relation relates itself to its own self; the self is not a relation, but that the relation relates itself to its own self."[7] These central passages suggest that Hegel and Kierkegaard see spirit as essentially an activity of self-relation. Moreover, they agree that through this self-relating activity, opposites are brought together. In both Hegelian and Kierkegaardian anthropology, authentic human spirit, like the God-Man, is a union or a coincidence of finitude and infinitude, reality and ideality, necessity and possibility, temporality and eternity, and individuality and universality. Beneath this common definition of the structure of spirit, however, lie significant differences that distinguish the two interpretations of the self. The effort to discern the similarities joining and differences separating their formal accounts of the nature of genuine selfhood revealed in Christ brings us into contact with some of Hegel's and Kierkegaard's most perplexing texts. In the course of our analysis it will become apparent that these extremely abstract writings grow out of, and are addressed to, the concrete existential problem of overcoming estrangement. They seek to remedy spiritlessness.

RELATIONSHIP: BOTH-AND

Identity, Difference, and Contradiction

As early as the *Differenzschrift*, Hegel recognizes that the fragmentation of modern experience can be surmounted only by means

---

6. *Phenomenology*, pp. 14, 12; 24, 22.
7. *Sickness unto Death*, p. 146; 11:127-128.

of a form of reconciliation that involves a "union of union and nonunion." In order to reintegrate opposites in a way that does not negate the progress resulting from the process of differentiation, Hegel must, as Professor Fackenheim points out, "be both unyieldingly realistic in [his] acceptance of non-union and unyieldingly idealistic in [his] assertion . . . of union."[8] The preoccupation with religion persuades Hegel that the Christian drama of Incarnation, Crucifixion, and Resurrection represents just such a differentiated reconciliation of opposites, and therefore symbolizes the way that must be followed if spirit is to achieve self-realization. The successful completion of this journey presupposes the rational comprehension of the dialectical structure of spirit. As we have observed, Hegel believes this task is impossible in terms of traditional analytical reflection. A logic built upon the abstract rules of identity, difference, and noncontradiction can neither penetrate the most fundamental features of concrete actuality nor grasp the ideality of spirit. In an effort to arrive at a speculative logic capable of rationally articulating the contradictions inherent in experience and the dialectical structure of spirit, Hegel recasts the basic principles of western rationalism. The most significant step in this lengthy argument is a reinterpretation of the notions of identity, difference, and contradiction. Hegel develops the internal relation between identity and difference in such a way that each term passes into the other, and both join in the principle of contradiction. This logical revision uncovers the structure of identity-within-difference which is definitive of authentic spirit, and is the formal foundation of the entire Hegelian system. Hegel's effort to construct a dialectical logic capable of conceptually expressing the reintegration of opposites necessary for reconciliation begins during his years in Jena and culminates in his mature *Science of Logic.*[9]

The heart of Hegel's extraordinarily complex *Logic* is his consideration of the "Determinations of Reflection" at the beginning of the second book, "The Doctrine of Essence."[10] In this section of his

---

8. Fackenheim, *Religious Dimension*, p. 229.

9. For an excellent account of the development of Hegel's thought on this central issue see Bonsiepen, *Begriff der Negativität*.

10. In stressing the centrality of this part of Hegel's argument I follow the lead of Dieter Henrich. See especially his "Hegels Logik der Reflexion," in *Hegel im Kontext*, pp. 157-186, and "Formen der Negation in Hegels Logik," *Seminar: Dialektik in der Philosophie Hegels*, ed. Rolf-Peter Horstmann (Frankfurt: Suhrkamp Verlag, 1978), pp. 213-229. Stanley Rosen (*G. W. F. Hegel: An Introduction to the Science of Wisdom*

analysis Hegel presents an extensive criticism of the abstract either-or of analytic understanding. Contrary to commonsense reflection, Hegel maintains that "a consideration of everything that is shows that *in its own self* everything is in its selfsameness different from itself and self-contradictory, and that in its difference, in its contradiction, it is self-identical, and is in its own self this movement of transition of one of these categories into the other, and for this reason, that each is in its own self the opposite of itself."[11] To establish the conversion of identity and difference into one another and their dialectical union in contradiction, Hegel first examines each term independently. He argues that identity is simple selfsameness, which usually is regarded as exclusive of difference. Hegel points out, however, that when such self-relation is considered more carefully, it becomes apparent that abstract self-identity is actually inseparable from absolute difference.

> In other words, identity is the reflection-into-self that is identity only as internal repulsion [*innerliches Abstossen*], and is this repulsion as reflection-into-itself, repulsion which immediately takes itself back into itself. Thus it is identity as difference that is identical with itself. But difference is only identical with itself insofar as it is not identity, but absolute non-identity. But non-identity is absolute insofar as it contains nothing of its other but only itself, that is, insofar as it is absolute identity with itself. Identity, therefore, is *in its own self* absolute non-identity.[12]

The self-relation that forms identity is necessarily mediated by opposition to otherness. Consequently, in the act of affirming itself, identity negates itself and becomes its opposite, difference. "*Identity is difference*," for "*identity is* different from difference."[13]

Conversely, difference *as* difference, pure or absolute difference, is indistinguishable from identity. Difference defines itself by opposition to its opposite, identity. Since Hegel has argued that identity is inherently difference, he claims that in relating itself to its apparent opposite, difference really relates to itself. Relation to other turns out to be self-relation. In the act of affirming itself, difference likewise negates itself and becomes its opposite, identity. Hegel

[New Haven: Yale University Press, 1974]) presents a useful elaboration of some of Henrich's primary points. Rosen's placement of Hegel's logical investigation within the context of ancient philosophy is particularly helpful. Compare Hans-Georg Gadamer, "The Idea of Hegel's Logic," in *Hegel's Dialectic: Five Hermeneutical Studies*, trans. P. C. Smith (New Haven: Yale University Press, 1976), pp. 75-99.

    11. *Logic*, p. 412; 6:40.
    12. Ibid., p. 413; 6:40-41.
    13. Ibid., p. 413; 6:41.

contends that "difference in itself is self-related difference; as such, it is the negativity of itself, the difference not of an other, but *of itself from itself*; it is not itself but its other. But that which is different from difference is identity. Difference is, therefore, itself and identity. Both together constitute difference; it is the whole, and its moment."[14]

Identity, in itself difference, and difference, in itself identity, join in contradiction, which Hegel defines as the identity of identity and difference. Stanley Rosen underscores the importance of Hegel's interpretation of contradiction when he writes: "Hegel's greatest innovation is to develop a new doctrine of contradiction and negativity, the core of his 'dialectic,' which attempts to resolve the *aporiai* of classical rationalism at a higher, more comprehensive and so genuinely rational level."[15] Inasmuch as identity and difference necessarily include their opposites within themselves, they are inherently self-contradictory.

> Each has an indifferent self-subsistence of its own through the fact that it has within itself the relation to its other moment; it is thus the whole, self-contained opposition. As this whole, each is mediated with itself *by its other* and *contains* it. But further, it is mediated with itself by the *non-being of its other*; hence it is a unity existing on its own account and it *excludes* the other from itself. . . . It is thus contradiction.[16]

In Hegel's system, such contradiction is the root of all movement and vitality; it is the universal life pulse.

It is essential to recognize that for Hegel, the dialectical relation between identity and difference results in neither the absorption of difference in identity nor the dissolution of identity in difference. Hegel walks the fine line between the extremes of undifferentiated monism and abstract dualism or pluralism.[17] Throughout the *Logic*,

---

14. Ibid., p. 417; 6:46-47. Findlay maintains that the dialectical relation of identity and difference is the "governing idea of Hegel's system" ("Reflexive Asymmetry: Hegel's Most Fundamental Methodological Ruse," in *Beyond Epistemology: New Studies in the Philosophy of Hegel*, ed. F. G. Weiss [The Hague: Martinus Nijhoff, 1974], p. 155).

15. Rosen, *Science of Wisdom*, pp. xvii-xviii. Marcuse also gives a helpful account of Hegel's doctrine of contradiction (*Reason and Revolution*, pp. 147 ff.). Even in his earliest philosophical reflection, Hegel recognizes the importance of the principle of contradiction. The first thesis of his *Habilitationsschrift* reads: *Contradictio est regula veri, non contradictio falsi.*

16. *Logic*, p. 431; 6:65.

17. For this reason, it is incorrect to label Hegel a philosopher of identity. He himself stresses that "unity is a bad expression; it is an abstraction of empty understanding. Philosophy is not a system of identity" (*History of Philosophy*, 2:149; 19:163). As we shall see, Kierkegaard views Hegelianism as a philosophy of identity in which difference is

he attempts to give rational expression to a reconciliation of opposites sustained within an internally differentiated totality. This is the
truth of spirit which is manifested in Christ: three-in-one and one-in-
three, multiplicity-in-unity and unity-in-multiplicity, the union of
union and nonunion, the identity of identity and difference.

Hegel's grasp of the interplay of identity, difference, and contradiction leads to his recognition of the internality of relationship. The
identity of *both* identity and difference is constituted and maintained by relation to otherness. "In the first place, then, each *is, only
insofar as the other is*; it is what it is, through the other, through its
own non-being; . . . second, it is, *insofar* as the other is not; it is
what it is, through the non-being of the other."[18] In more general
terms, relations are not external and accidental to antecedent identity but are internal and essential to unique particularity. Hegel's
idealistic denial of the opposition between thought and being suggests the ontological implications of his logical analysis. Being, like
thought itself, is inherently dialectical, essentially relational, or fundamentally social. To be is to be related, and to fall out of relation is
to fall into the indeterminateness of nonbeing. "Everything that
exists," Hegel argues, "stands in relation, and this relation is the
truth of each existence. In this way, the existent [*das Existierende*]
is not abstractly for-itself, but is only in an other. In this other,
however, it is in relation [*Beziehung*] to itself, and the relation
[*Verhältnis*] is the unity of relation to self and relation to other." [19]
In spite of appearances to the contrary, relation to other is mediate
self-relation. Dialectical reason demonstrates that "something
through its own nature relates itself to the other, because otherness is
posited in it as its own moment; its being-within-self includes the
negation within it, by means of which alone it now has its affirmative
determinate being."[20] In Hegel's onto-logic, all identity is co-relative

---

absorbed or dissipated in unity. Analysts of the Hegel-Kierkegaard relation have tended to
accept uncritically Kierkegaard's misinterpretation of Hegel. See, for example, Thulstrup,
Kierkegaards forhold til Hegel, and Wahl, *Études kierkegaardiennes*, p. 351. Findlay puts it
more accurately: "Hegel has a self-pluralizing monism and a self-unifying pluralism"
("Reflexive Asymmetry," p. 162).

    18. *Logic*, p. 425; 6:57.

    19. *Lesser Logic*, par. 135; 8:267. Although Kevin Wall identifies the centrality of
Hegel's view of relation, his discussion of Hegel's position is brief and is obscured by the
attempted comparison with the Thomistic analysis of relation: see his *The Doctrine of
Relation in Hegel* (Fribourg: Albertus Magnus Press, 1963).

    20. *Logic*, p. 125; 5:135. For further discussion of this problem see Mark C. Taylor,
"Toward an Ontology of Relativism," *Journal of the American Academy of Religion*
46 (1978), 41-61.

with difference. On the one hand, relata are bound in an internal relation of mutual constitution and definition. On the other hand, relationality is the self-subsistent structure that assumes concrete actuality in and through the particularities whose determinate identities it establishes and maintains. From this perspective, relation is the essence or ground of being. This important point becomes clearer when the nature of relationship is considered in more detail.

One of the guiding principles of Hegel's system is that negativity is the structure of constitutive relationality. Determinate identity emerges through a process of double negation in which opposites become themselves through relation to one another. Affirmation and negation are inseparable. Instead of "to be *or* not to be," the sum of the matter for Hegel is to be *and* not to be, for to be is not to be, and not to be is to be. Hegel agrees with Jacob Böhme's definition of the speculative task as the effort "to grasp the no in the yes and the yes in the no."[21]

To understand Hegel's position on this complex issue, it is necessary to return to his interpretation of the relation between identity and difference. According to Hegel, the law of identity defined by abstract understanding and enshrined in traditional logic asserts that everything is identical with itself. Stated concisely: A = A. What usually remains unnoticed, however, is that this principle of identity is inherently self-contradictory. Those who attempt to affirm such abstract identity "do not see that in this very assertion, they are themselves saying that *identity is different*; for they are saying that *identity* is different from difference; while this must at the same time be admitted to be the nature of identity, their assertion implies that identity, not externally, but in its own self, in its very nature, is this, to be different."[22] Since Hegel acknowledges the coimplication of identity and difference, he recognizes that determinate identity establishes itself through the negation of otherness. The other, however, is itself the negation of the determinate identity *it* opposes. Each member of the relationship becomes itself through the negation of its own negation. "Each therefore *is*, only insofar as its *non-being is*, and is in an identical relationship with it."[23] In more abstract terms, the assertion "A is A" necessarily

---

21. Hyppolite, *Genesis and Structure*, p. 148. Throughout his career Hegel greatly admired the work of Böhme. For Hegel's most extensive discussion of Böhme's thought see *History of Philosophy*, 3:188-216; 20:91-119.

22. *Logic*, p. 413; 6:41.

23. Ibid., p. 425; 6:57.

entails the claim that A *is not* non-A: $A = -\overline{A}$. A is the negation of its own negation, and hence is double negation. The same analysis, of course, must be applied to non-A. Non-A becomes itself through relation to its opposite, A. But A has shown itself to be $-\overline{A}$. Thus non-A also forms itself through a process of double negation: $-A = -(-\overline{A})$.

In sum, the structure of constitutive relationality is negativity, understood as a process of double negation through which opposing relata coinhere. "If I say I am for myself," Hegel explains, "I not only am, but I negate all other in me, exclude it from me, insofar as it appears external. As the negation of other being [*Anderssein*], which is negation over against me, being-for-self is the negation of negation, and thus is affirmation; and this is, as I call it, absolute negativity."[24] The specific example Hegel chooses to illustrate his point suggests the close connection between his logical and theological analyses. "Father is the other of son, and son the other of father, and each only *is* as this other of the other; and at the same time, the one determination only is, in relation to the other; their being is a *single* subsistence."[25]

The structure of double negativity, which sustains identity-in-difference by simultaneously distinguishing and reconciling opposites, is in the final analysis both infinite and absolute. Through double negation or self-referential negativity, opposites relate *to themselves* in otherness. Viewed speculatively, absolute negativity not only is the ground of difference but also establishes "infinite unity."[26] The reason Hegel describes this unity of opposites as "infinite" is that neither member of the relationship is burdened by unreconciled otherness. When negativity is adequately grasped in its infinity and absoluteness, it reveals itself to be the essence, the *Wesen* or *Inbegriff*, of everything.[27]

---

24. *History of Philosophy*, 1:302-303; 18:356-357.
25. *Logic*, p. 441; 6:77. See above, chap. 4, text corresponding to n. 44. For post-Freudians, Hegel's argument also carries interesting psychological implications.
26. Ibid., p. 233; 5:271.
27. Professor Henrich stresses the importance of Hegel's theory of double negation when he notes a remark made by Hegel in an obscure book review: "I observe in the first place that one finds in this idea [of Solger's] the logical concept, which constitutes the basis for all speculative knowledge—the 'only true affirmation,' namely grasped as the negation of negation. . . . The superficial inspection of any of my writings, starting with the *Phenomenology of Spirit*, which appeared in 1807, and, even more, my *Logic*, which was published in 1811 ff., would show that all the forms, whether they might be taken as forms of existence or of thought, resolve themselves into the same concept" (*Berliner Schriften*, pp. 185, 188): Henrich, "Autonomous Negation" Lecture delivered at Oxford University.

Hegel defines essence as

> the self-subsistent [*Selbständige*], which *is* as self-mediated through its
> negation, which negation essence itself is; it is therefore the identical unity
> of absolute negativity and immediacy. The negativity is negativity in itself;
> it is its relation to itself and is thus in itself immediacy; but it is negative
> self-relation, a negating that is a repelling of itself, and the inherent immedi-
> acy is thus negative or *determinate* in regard to it. But this determinateness
> is itself absolute negativity, and this determining, which is, as determining,
> immediately the sublating of itself, is a return-into-self.[28]

In other words, essence is pure negative activity that relates itself to
itself in otherness. "The reflection-into-self," therefore, "is equally
reflection-into-another, and vice versa."[29] The other through which
essence realizes itself is appearance. Hegel maintains that "essence is
not *behind* or *beyond* [*hinter oder jenseits*] appearance [*Erscheinung*]."[30] To the contrary, appearance is the manifestation or
revelation (*Offenbarung*) of essence; it is essence in its existence.
Within Hegel's system, essence is the infinite process of self-differentiation and reintegration. Essence realizes itself through active self-
negation in which it posits itself as other, that is, as determinate
being, and returns to itself from this otherness by negating its own
negation. Concrete particularity is the *Par-ousia*, the appearance of
essence, the embodiment or *incarnation* of essentiality. When determinate being is comprehended as the self-determination of essence, it
is re-collected (*Erinnerung*) or resurrected in the eternity of essential
becoming. Through this process, essence becomes actual and actuality becomes essential.[31] Expressed in the theological language Hegel
is attempting to conceptualize, God reveals himself through the
Word. In the eternal life-process of spirit, Father becomes incarnate
in Son, and Son is resurrected in Father.

Fall 1973). For further consideration of Hegel's view of negation see Bonsiepen, *Begriff der
Negativität*. This topic has been of particular interest to members of the Frankfurt School.
See, for instance, Theodor Adorno, *Negative Dialectics*, trans. E. B. Ashton (New York:
Seabury Press, 1973), and Marcuse, *Reason and Revolution*, pp. 127 ff.

    28. *Logic*, p. 398; 6:22.

    29. *Lesser Logic*, par. 121; 8:248.

    30. Ibid., par. 131; 8:261-262. Hegel's account of appearance (Erscheinung) con-
stantly plays on the nuances of *Schein*, which can mean appearance, illusory being, apparent
being, or shining forth. Appearance, therefore, is the shining forth of essence. This particular
text is further illuminated by recalling Hegel's critique of the insistence on the *Jenseits* of
God in the reflective philosophy of subjectivity. See above, chap. 2, 1st sec. ("Fragmentation"), 3d subsec. ("The Reflective Philosophy of Subjectivity").

    31. As we shall see in chap. 7, this is the basis of Hegel's solution to the problem of
nihilism he believes inherent in all forms of dualism.

There are thus three distinct moments: *essence, being-for-self* which is the otherness of essence and for which essence is, and *being-for-self*, or the knowledge of itself *in the other*. Essence beholds only its own self in its being-for-self; in this externalization is only with itself; the being-for-self that shuts itself out from essence is *essence's knowledge of its own self*. It is the word which, when uttered, leaves behind, externalized and emptied, him who uttered it, but which is as immediately heard, and only this hearing of its own self is the existence of the Word. Thus the distinctions made are immediately resolved as soon as they are made, and are made as soon as they are resolved, and what is true and actual is precisely this circular movement.[32]

Hegel's analysis of the internal relation of identity and difference in terms of double negation culminates in the notion of essence. When interpreted speculatively, essence discloses the structure of authentic spirit. In the definition of spirit with which we began, Hegel directly identifies essence and spirit. "Spirit," he writes, "is essence, or that which has *being in itself*; it is that which *relates itself to itself* and is *determinate*, it is *other-being* and *being-for-self*, and in this determinateness, or in its self-externality, abides within itself; in other words, it is *in and for itself*."[33] In terms by now familiar, spirit is an identity-within-difference in which opposites are *both* distinguished *and* united. It is "the being that is the movement of retaining its self-identity in its otherness."[34] Hegel believes that genuine spirit or authentic selfhood arises through the activity of self-relation in which the subject expresses (*äussern*) itself in determinate thoughts and deeds, and reconciles itself with otherness by reappropriating difference as its own self-objectification. Summarizing the moments of this process, Hegel explains that spirit, self, or subject is

pure, *simple negativity*, and is for this very reason the bifurcation [Entzweiung] of the simple; it is the doubling that sets up an opposition, and then again [is] the negation of this indifferent diversity and of its opposition. Only this self-*restoring* identity, or this reflection into otherness within itself—not an *original* or *immediate* unity as such—is the true. It is the process of its own becoming, the circle that presupposes its end as its aim,

---

32. *Phenomenology*, p. 465; 534-535.
33. Ibid., p. 14; 24. See above, text corresponding to n. 6.
34. Ibid., p. 459; 528. Compare: "Spirit, in fact, simply means that which comprehends itself in an infinite way in antithesis or opposition" (*Philosophy of Religion*, 2:352; 17:208). Having reached this point in his argument, Hegel equates spirit and subject, or self. Consequently I have used and shall continue to use these terms interchangeably.

having its end also as its beginning; and only by being worked out to its end is it actual.[35]

The life of spirit is the infinite process of self-differentiation and reintegration, the eternal activity of procession and epistrophe.[36]

From Hegel's point of view, spirit cannot be completely comprehended until it is recognized as divine. As the creative essence of all that is, spirit is absolute. The absolute, Hegel argues, is "the absolute form which, as the bifurcation of itself, is utterly identical with itself, the negative *as* negative, or that unites with itself, and only thus is it the absolute identity-with-self which is equally *indifferent to its differences*, or is absolute *content*."[37] The Hegelian absolute is an all-encompassing whole, an inwardly variegated totality within which each member becomes itself through reciprocal relation to otherness. The realization of reconciliation presupposes that

> there is nothing in the whole which is not in the parts, and nothing in the parts which is not in the whole. The whole is not abstract unity, but unity as a diverse multiplicity; but this unity as that in which the elements of multiplicity relate themselves to one another is the determinateness of each element through which it is a part. Thus the relation has an inseparable identity and only one self-subsistence.[38]

It should be evident that such an absolute is neither abstractly other nor radically transcendent. Hegel's God is not a *deus absconditus*, but is incarnate in the natural-historical process. Determinate being, therefore, really is a moment in the divine life. The actualization of absolute spirit is inseparable from the absolutization of actual spirit. Spirit enacts the eternal drama of Incarnation, Crucifixion, and Resurrection on the stage of world history. Spirit reveals itself to

---

35. *Phenomenology*, p. 10; 20.

36. I borrow this term from Abrams's discussion of Plotinus (*Natural Supernaturalism*, p. 148). Hegel's interpretation of spirit is deeply influenced by the Neoplatonic tradition. For his discussion of the importance of Neoplatonism see *History of Philosophy*, 2:374 ff.; 19:403 ff.

37. *Logic*, p. 536; 6:194. Recall Hegel's definition of God as spirit: "God is this, to differentiate himself from himself, to be an object to himself, but in this differentiation, to be absolutely identical with himself—this is spirit" (see above, chap. 4, text corresponding to n. 42). For an extensive and helpful discussion of Hegel's view of the absolute see Rosen, *Science of Wisdom*, pp. 229 ff.

38. *Logic*, pp. 515-516; 6:169. As will become clear when we consider the relation of time and eternity in the next section and the unfolding of spirit charted in the *Phenomenology* in the next chapter, Hegel's absolute is not a static totality but is historically emergent. The appreciation of the significance of historical development is one of the chief factors that distinguishes Hegel's position from that of many of his Romantic contemporaries with whom he otherwise shares so much.

spirit in the life and death of the God-Man. The divine descends to the human and the human ascends to the divine, creating reconciliation in the midst of estrangement, the union of union and nonunion.

Spiritual Tensions

Although Hegel acknowledges the infinite pain and suffering wrought by fragmentation and bifurcation, he insists that spirit overcomes alienation by reconciling, without dissolving, the opposites between which spiritlessness is torn. Most important for purposes of comparison with Kierkegaard's pneumatology is Hegel's claim that spirit is the identity-within-difference of finitude and infinitude, reality and ideality, actuality and possibility, necessity and freedom, time and eternity, and particularity and universality. A consideration of each of these binary opposites sheds additional light on the undergirding structural principle of double negativity and further specifies Hegel's notion of spirit.

Analytic understanding regards finitude and infinitude as opposed to one another and as mutually exclusive. We have seen that Hegel believes this view of the matter leads to a problematic finitizing of the infinite and infinitizing of abstract finitude.[39] If the finite and the infinite are regarded as merely antithetical, the infinite is limited by the finitude over against which it stands. The finite, therefore, appears to be independent and self-subsistent, and the *in*-finite seems to be dependent on and conditioned by firmly established finitude. According to Hegel's dialectical reason, the finite is neither independent nor self-subsistent, but is inherently dependent and inwardly self-contradictory. Since finitude does not itself possess aseity, its being necessarily entails the being of another, which is its opposite, infinitude. *"The being of the finite,"* Hegel explains, *"is not only its being*, but is also the being of the infinite."[40] Finitude includes within itself its opposite as the indispensable presupposition and essential ground of its being. The determinate identity of finitude comprehends its own difference (infinitude) in such a way that relationship to otherness is a dimension of self-relation requisite for self-realization. Hegel maintains that

> the finite itself in being elevated into the infinite is in no sense acted upon by an alien force; on the contrary, it is its nature to be related to itself as

---

39. See above, chap. 4, 1st sec. ("Mediation"), 1st subsec. ("The Fullness of Time: The Present").
40. *Philosophy of Religion*, 3:254; 17:437.

limitation, both limitation as such and as an ought, and to transcend such limitation and to be beyond it. It is not in the sublating of finitude as a whole that infinity in general comes to be; the truth is rather that the finite is only this, through its own nature to become itself the infinite.[41]

The finite, in other words, includes the infinite as a moment of itself. Through dialectical reason, the self-contradiction implicit in the abstract identity of finitude becomes explicit, and the fully relational nature of finitude's concrete self-identity is disclosed.

Infinitude, by contrast, contains finitude in its own being. While the finite realizes itself in and through the infinite, infinitude renders itself infinite in relation to finitude. The finite is not merely other than or opposed to the infinite but is an essential dimension of the infinite itself. To be truly infinite, infinitude cannot be limited by finitude and must include otherness within itself as a necessary moment of self-determination. The infinite becomes itself through its other, finitude. In the process of establishing its identity by contrast with difference, infinitude sublates the otherness of its other and makes finitude an intrinsic aspect of its own being. The infinite, therefore, "is on its own account just as much finite as infinite."[42] So interpreted, infinitude is unfettered by alien finitude, and consequently is true rather than spurious. Hegel summarizes the conclusion of his argument:

> Thus both finite and infinite are this *movement* in which each returns to itself through its negation; they *are* only as *mediation* within themselves, and the affirmative of each contains the negative of each and is the negation of the negation. They are thus a *result*, and hence not what they are in the determination of their *beginning*; the finite is not a *determinate being* on *its* side, and the infinite a *determinate being* or *being-in-itself* beyond the determinate being, that is, beyond the being determined as finite. . . . They occur . . . only as moments of a whole and . . . come on the scene only by means of their opposite, but essentially also by means of the sublation of their opposite.[43]

Hegel believes that his analysis of the dialectical relation of finitude and infinitude implies the mediation of the second spiritual polarity we have identified: reality and ideality. "Spirit," he argues, "is *as well* infinite *as* finite, and *neither* merely the one *nor* merely

---

41. *Logic*, p. 138; 5:150, For an elaboration of this and related points see Mark C. Taylor, "*Itinerarium Mentis in Deum*: Hegel's Proofs of God's Existence," *Journal of Religion* 57 (1977), 211-231.
42. *Logic*, p. 153; 5:170.
43. Ibid., p. 147; 5:162.

the other; in making itself finite it remains infinite, for it sublates finitude within itself; nothing in it is fixed, simple affirmative being, but rather everything is only an ideality, only an appearance."[44] As infinitude in itself is finitude and vice versa, so ideality is inherently real and reality is essentially ideal. For Hegel,

> ideality [*Idealität*] is not something that is outside of and next to reality [*Realität*]; the notion of ideality lies explicitly in its being the *truth* of reality. That is to say, reality, posited as what it is in itself, proves itself to be ideality. Hence ideality does not receive its proper estimate, if one allows that reality is not all in all, but that an ideality outside of it must still be recognized. Such an ideality next to or even above reality, in fact, would be only an empty name. Ideality has a content only when it is the ideality of something. But then this something is not a mere indeterminate this or that, but is determinate being [*bestimmtes Dasein*] which, if held fast for itself, possesses no truth.[45]

Against the bifurcating propensity of Verstand, Hegel insists that the ideal and the real are not separated by an unbridgeable abyss, but are inseparably bound in a relation that is mutually constitutive. Ideality is not a transcendent abstraction, an ever elusive *ought*, but is an active potency immanent in what *is*. The comprehension (*Begriff*) of the dialectical interplay of ideality and reality involves the re-cognition that the ideal is real and the real is ideal.[46] Without this reintegration of opposites, spirit remains spiritless. Entangled in nonideal reality, the self yearns for unreal ideality.

Hegel uses the term *actuality* (*Wirklichkeit*) to define the rational unity-within-distinction of reality and ideality.[47] With the introduction of this concept, a further opposition arises which reason must mediate. Understanding contraposes possibility and actuality and leaves unexplained the transition from one to the other. Hegel attempts to solve the puzzle created by Verstand by showing that actuality and possibility are coimplicates whose inextricable unity constitutes necessity. It seems self-evident that the actual is possible, for were it impossible, it could not be actual. Actuality, therefore,

---

44. *Philosophy of Spirit*, par. 386; 10:37.
45. *Lesser Logic*, par. 96; 8:204.
46. This expresses succinctly the heart of Hegel's idealism. He writes: "The proposition that the finite is ideal [*ideell*] constitutes idealism." Again: "The ideal is the finite as it is in the true infinite—as a determination, a content, which is distinct, but is not *independent, self-subsistent* being, but only a moment" (*Logic*, pp. 154, 149-150; 5:172, 149).
47. See especially *Logic*, pp. 755 ff.; 6:462 ff. It is important to stress that *Wirklichkeit* does not signify empirical reality per se, but reality grasped as the concretion of ideality.

must be implicitly identical with possibility. Hegel's effort to demonstrate that possibility is inherently actual is more complex. His argument turns on a distinction between formal and real possibility. According to the notion of formal possibility, *"everything is possible that is not self-contradictory."*[48] Having argued that *everything* is inherently self-contradictory, Hegel contends that such an abstract interpretation of possibility unwittingly leads to the absurd conclusion that nothing is possible or everything is impossible. To overcome this impasse, he proposes to define "real possibility [*reale Möglichkeit*]" as the *"totality of conditions"* presupposed by a certain actuality.[49] Hegel's line of thought is readily accessible when formulated generally. If A is the set of conditions that constitutes the real possibility of B, then A in itself is the possibility of B. Given the actuality of A, B must likewise be actual. In other words, the *real* possibility of B is the actuality of A. "When all the conditions of something are completely present, it enters into actuality; the completeness of the conditions is the totality as the content, and *the something itself* is this content determined as being as actual as possible."[50] Hegel insists that not only is actuality in itself possibility, but real possibility in itself is actuality, "for it is real insofar as it is also actuality."[51]

The spiritual unity of possibility and actuality eventuates in necessity. Necessity, for Hegel, is "the sublatedness [*Aufgehobensein*] of actuality in possibility, and conversely [of possibility in actuality]; because it is the *simple conversion* of one of these moments into the other, it is also their *positive unity* since each, as we saw, unites *only with itself* in the other."[52] Inasmuch as possibility and actuality assume determinate identity only through interrelation, their dialectical unity is necessary. Each is inevitably bound to the other and relates itself to itself in its other. This insight prepares the way for the final conclusion Hegel draws from his analysis of

---

48. *Logic*, p. 543; 6:203.

49. Ibid., p. 547; 6:209.

50. Ibid., p. 548; 6:210. Elsewhere Hegel asserts: "Substance is the *Absolute*, the actuality that is in and for itself—*in itself* as the simple identity of possibility and actuality, absolute essence containing all actuality and possibility *within itself*; and *for* itself, being this identity as absolute *power* or purely self-related *negativity*" (ibid., p. 578; 6:246).

51. Ibid., pp. 548-549; 6:210. As we shall see, Kierkegaard believes this argument illustrates the tautologous reasoning characteristic of speculative logic. His own interpretation of the relation of possibility, actuality, and necessity is an effort to overcome the problem he sees in Hegel's position. See below, 2d sec. ("Coincidence: Either-Or"), 2d subsec. ("Spiritual Tensions").

52. Ibid., p. 551; 6:214.

possibility and actuality: implicitly, necessity is freedom. Alternatively phrased, "freedom reveals itself as the *truth of necessity*." [53] This unlikely result becomes more understandable when we realize that for Hegel, freedom is precisely the self-relation in difference which is born of "*pure* self-recognition in absolute otherness." [54] Oppositions necessarily bound in a relationship of coimplication are, in fact, free, for they are unencumbered by otherness and undisturbed by determination *ab extra*. Apart from reconciliation with otherness, freedom is impossible and heteronomy unavoidable. Hegel maintains that

> the process of necessity is of such a nature that it overcomes the fixed externality that is at first present, and reveals it [i.e., otherness or outwardness] as its own inwardness. Through this it appears that the elements bound together are not alien or foreign [*fremd*] to one another, but are only moments in *one* whole, and each in the relation to the other is at home with itself and goes together with itself [*ist bei sich selbst ist und geht mit sich selbst zusammen*]. This is the transfiguration of necessity into freedom. This freedom is not the empty freedom of abstract negation, but rather is concrete and positive freedom. From this it becomes clear what a mistake it is to regard freedom and necessity as mutually exclusive. [55]

From Hegel's perspective, freedom is necessity rationally comprehended. He concludes that possibility and actuality join in necessity, which in itself is freedom. Such rational freedom, however, presupposes the reconciliation of time and eternity.

The distention suffered by unhappy consciousness culminates in the opposition of time and eternity created by the separation of temporal individuality and eternal universality. Spirit heals the wound of spiritlessness by revealing the intrinsic reconciliation of time and eternity and the inherent unity of individuality and universality. Drawing on insights derived from his logical rendering of the Christian drama of Incarnation, Crucifixion, and Resurrection, Hegel maintains that time is the manifestation of eternity, the process of appearance through which eternity reaches completion. In the Hegelian system, the eternal is *actus purus* that, properly understood, is infinite self-referential negativity. The dialectical relation of double negation constitutes the essential structure and substantial ground of all concrete reality. This way of viewing eternity establishes its

---

53. Ibid., p. 578; 6:246.
54. *Phenomenology*, p. 14; 24.
55. *Lesser Logic*, par. 158; 8:303.

inseparability from temporality. As the embodiment of an eternal logical structure, time is the concrete *instant*-iation of eternity. In itself the eternal is temporal, and time is implicitly eternity. Eternity and time form an identity-within-difference sustained by internal relation. Hegel states his point concisely: time "is the existent notion itself [*der daseinede Begriff selbst*]." Put differently, time "is the arising and passing away which does not itself arise and pass away, but is 'in itself,' and constitutes the actuality and the movement of the life of truth."[56] In order to become itself, eternity negates itself through its own temporalization, and returns to itself by the negation of this negation. Figuratively expressed (*Vorstellungsweise*), divine spirit is the eternal process in which the Father negates himself by becoming incarnate in the historical particularity of the Son, and returns to himself through the negation of this negation in the Crucifixion and Resurrection. By means of dialectical logic, Hegel believes he can discern the *Logos* of the fullness of time to be the rational unity within distinction of temporality and eternity. "*History*," he argues,

> "is a *conscious* self-*mediating* process—spirit externalized in time; but this externalization is equally an externalization of itself; the negative is the negative of itself. This becoming presents a slow-moving succession of spirits, a gallery of images, each of which, endowed with all the riches of spirit, moves thus slowly just because the self has to penetrate and under- stand this entire wealth of its substance. Since its fulfillment consists in perfectly *knowing* what *it is*, in knowing its substance, this knowing is its *withdrawal into itself* in which it abandons its outer existence and gives its existential shape over to recollection.[57]

Recollection (*Er-Innerung*) inverts eternity's self-externalization (*sich Ent-Äusserung*) by re-membering dismembered temporal moments through the sublation of *external* particularity in *internal* relational-

---

56. *Phenomenology*, p. 27; 38, 39. The most helpful discussions of Hegel's view of the relation of time and eternity include Kojève, *Introduction to the Reading of Hegel*, pp. 100-149; Rosen, *Science of Wisdom*, pp. 130 ff.; and Andries Sarlemijn, *Hegel's Dialectic*, trans. P. Kirschenmann (Boston: D. Reidel Publishing Co., 1975), part 3.

57. *Phenomenology*, p. 492; 562. Such passages suggest the kenotic character of Hegel's Christology. It must be stressed that Hegel's interpretation of the dialectical relation between time and eternity *does not*, as many commentators insist, imply the end of history, in any ordinary meaning of this term. To the contrary, the historicity of the eternal assumes the eternity of the historical. The eternal process of self-related negativity realizes itself ever again in constantly changing historical circumstances. This process completes itself in specu- lative philosophy only in the sense that its abiding nature is conceptually comprehended. Kierkegaard's objections to the contrary notwithstanding, Hegel maintains that systematic thought does not presuppose actual historical finality.

ity. This twofold process involves *both* the temporalization of the eternal *and* the eternalizing of the temporal. This wedding of heaven and earth consummates the union of Heilsgeschichte and Bildungs-geschichte and brings to birth *das Reich Gottes*.

Individual and Community

Hegel summarizes the conclusion of his analysis of the structure of spirit:

> Spirit is not a motionless something, but rather is absolute unrest, pure activity, the negating or ideality of all fixed determinations of the under-standing, not abstractly simple, but in its simplicity at the same time a self-differentiation from itself; not an essence that is already complete before its appearance, keeping within itself behind the host of its appear-ances, but the essence that is actual in truth only through the determinate forms of its necessary self-revelation.[58]

Hegel is convinced that when spirit is so conceived, the journey to selfhood can reach completion only in spiritual community. The relational character of identity establishes the sociality of spirit and the intersubjectivity of selfhood. "Spirit," Hegel argues, is " 'I' that is 'we' and 'we' that is 'I.' "[59] Since determinate identity is gener-ated by intercourse with otherness, individuality arises in community with other selves. In the absence of such interrelation, spirit remains completely abstract and utterly indefinable. Rather than abrogating unique individuality, social relations produce concrete selfhood. Fully comprehended, the social web constitutive of individuality is universal. In a manner analogous to each of the other binaries we have considered, spirit unifies universality and particularity to form individuality. Hegel steadfastly maintains that "the individual is the determinate universal."[60] As opposed to abstract universality, the concrete universal

> is the self-identical universal and this, as containing self-repellent negativity, is in the first instance universal, and therefore as yet *indeterminate activity*; but because this is negative relation-to-self, it *determines* itself immediately, giving itself the moment of *particularity*, which, as likewise the *totality of the form reflected into itself*, is *content as against the posited* differences of

58. *Philosophy of Spirit*, par. 378; 10:12.
59. *Phenomenology*, p. 110; 140.
60. *Logic*, p. 620; 6:298.

the form. Equally immediately this negativity, through its relation-to-self, is absolute reflection of the form into itself and individuality.[61]

Dialectical reason sees individuality and universality as thoroughly co-relative. The dissolution of one necessarily entails the destruction of the other, and the realization of one presupposes the actuality of the other.[62] Not only is concrete universality in itself individual, but concrete individuality is in itself universal. The individual self, Hegel argues, is an

"I," which is *this* and no other "I," and which is no less immediately a *mediated* or sublated *universal* "I." It has a *content* which it *differentiates* from itself; for it is pure negativity or the bifurcation of itself, it is *consciousness*. In its difference, this content is itself the "I," for it is the movement of sublating itself, or the same pure negativity that the "I" is. In it, as differentiated, the "I" is reflected into itself; the content is *comprehended* only when the "I" is at home with itself in its being other. Stated otherwise, this content is nothing else than the very movement just spoken of, for the content is spirit that traverses its own self and does so *for itself* as spirit by the fact that it has the shape of the notion in its objectivity.[63]

The self-consciousness of such spiritual individuality, however, is socially and historically mediated. Since Hegel defines the goal of the journey to selfhood as "absolute knowledge, or spirit that knows itself as spirit,"[64] he insists that authenticity is impossible apart from self-conscious membership in the ongoing life of spiritual community.

"Spirit," Hegel remarks, "is, in a much deeper sense this *one thing*, the negative unity in which its determinations interpenetrate

---

61. Ibid., p. 741; 6:446. For a description of the Trinitarian God which is homologous to this account of concrete universality see above, chap. 4, text corresponding to n. 45.

62. Hegel's view of the intersubjectivity of spirit is the basis of his conviction that selfhood is most fully realized in the social life of a free people objectified in the institution of the modern state. In contrast with a commonly accepted caricature of Hegel, it should be apparent from my analysis of the foundational principle of identity-in-difference that the Hegelian state is not in any way totalitarian. Universality grounds, and does not absorb, individuality. Hegel conceives the state as the social matrix within which unique particularity is nourished. Karl Popper's misguided attack on Hegel has been instrumental in creating widespread confusion concerning the Hegelian view of the state. See Popper, *The Open Society and Its Enemies*, vol. 2, *The High Tide of Prophecy, Hegel, Marx, and the Aftermath* (London: George Routledge and Sons, 1945). Shlomo Avineri's account of Hegel's political theory is much more balanced and corrects many of the errors that pervade Popper's argument: see his *Hegel's Theory of the Modern State*.

63. *Phenomenology*, p. 486; 556-557.

64. Ibid., p. 493; 564.

one another."[65] When interpreted according to the principles of speculative logic, spirit appears to reconcile, without dissolving, the opposites left sundered in spiritlessness. The rational comprehension of spirit overcomes the fragmentation characteristic of spiritlessness and completes the mediation of the truth revealed in the God-Man. Hegel confesses:

> I am the strife, for the strife is just this conflict, which is not any indifference of the two as diverse, but is their being bound together. I am not one of these two taking part in the strife, but I am both the combatants, and am the strife itself. I am the fire and the water which touch one another, and am the collision and unity of what flies apart, and this very collision is this double, conflicting relation, as the relation of what is separated, fragmented, and now reconciled in unity with itself.[66]

This reconciliation in the midst of estrangement brings peace that passes all Verstand.

COINCIDENCE: EITHER-OR

Identity, Difference, and Contradiction

During the years in which Kierkegaard was completing his prolonged university education and was gathering materials for the extraordinary literary output he soon would begin, Hegel's philosophy in general and logic in particular were topics of extensive and often heated debate in Copenhagen.[67] Throughout the late 1830s and early 1840s Hegel's logic attracted special attention in Danish intellectual circles. At this time, the primary representatives of Hegelianism in Denmark were the philosopher-playwright J. L. Heiberg and the theologian and onetime tutor of Kierkegaard, H. L. Martensen.[68] During the fall of 1837, Martensen delivered his *Forelæsn-*

---

65. *Logic*, p. 498; 6:147.

66. *Philosophy of Religion*, 1:63-64; 16:69.

67. For a survey of this chapter of intellectual history see Thulstrup, *Kierkegaards forhold til Hegel*, pp. 23 ff. Thulstrup presents his main points more concisely in two related essays: "Kierkegaards Verhältnis zu Hegel," *Theologische Zeitschrift* 13 (1957), 200-226, and "Le désaccord entre Kierkegaard et Hegel." At several points I have drawn on Thulstrup's account in developing these brief remarks on the intellectual milieu of Kierkegaard's Denmark.

68. Martensen, it should be noted, was not an uncritical follower of Hegel. As an outstanding representative of the Hegelian right wing, he proposed to "go beyond Hegel" (a claim that provoked Kierkegaard's endless ridicule) by revising the system to include a personal God and individual immortality. See H. L. Martensen, *Christian Dogmatics*, trans. W. Urwick (Edinburgh: T. and T. Clark, 1890). The only study of Martensen's theology available in English is R. L. Horn, "Positivity and Dialectic: A Study of the Theological Method of Hans-Lars Martensen" (Th.D. thesis, Union Theological Seminary, 1969).

inger over Indledning til Speculative Dogmatik, in which he devoted considerable attention to Hegel's *Science of Logic*.[69] Martensen concentrated on the Hegelian doctrine of essence and insisted that Hegel's major contribution was the development of a speculative notion of negation. As the first comprehensive presentation of Hegelianism in Denmark, Martensen's lectures occasioned widespread philosophical and theological discussion. The major anti-Hegelian spokesman to emerge from this debate was a teacher of Kierkegaard, F. C. Sibbern. In an 1838 monograph entitled *Undersøgelser fornemmelig betreffende Hegels Philosophie*, Sibbern subjected major tenets of Hegel's philosophy to critical review. Most importantly, he maintained that Hegel's speculative logic dissolves the contrast between identity and difference and nullifies the notion of contradiction. This position, Sibbern contended, is self-destructive, for it must simultaneously deny the principle it seeks to affirm. In the face of such speculative confusion, Sibbern believed it necessary to reassert that the law of noncontradiction "must hold completely throughout all thinking"[70] and that the rule of identity and the principle of the excluded middle must never be violated. This argument proved to be of interest beyond the narrow confines of the academic community. Since it gave philosophical precision to misgivings expressed less rigorously in the critique of Martensen's theology formulated by the well-known and highly influential Bishop Mynster, Sibbern's work enjoyed a rather wide public audience.[71]

Although not initially an active participant in these discussions, it is clear that Kierkegaard followed the debate with interest and was fully aware of the complexity and the significance of the relevant issues. Kierkegaard derived his basic understanding of the principles of traditional logic from Sibbern's *Logik som Tænkelaere*. His sketchy knowledge of the fundaments of Hegelian logic, acquired largely from the writings of Heiberg and Martensen, deepened considerably when he heard Karl Werder's lectures, *Logik: Als Commentar und Ergänzung zu Hegels Wissenschaft der Logik*, during his stay in Berlin (1841-42). Shortly after this extensive exposure to Hegel, Kierkegaard began his study of Trendelenburg. Staunchly anti-

69. Kierkegaard attended the early lectures in this series and followed the remainder of the course through notes taken by fellow students.

70. Sibbern, *Maanedsskrift for Litteratur*, 19:425. For an account of Sibbern's thought see Jens Himmelstrup, *Sibbern* (Copenhagen: J. H. Schultz Forlag, 1934).

71. The book in which Mynster elaborates his critique is *Rationalism and Superrationalism*. Mynster was the pastor and confidant of Kierkegaard's troubled father and a regular guest in the family home.

Hegelian in matters of logic, Trendelenburg based his critique upon a reexamination and reaffirmation of the principles of Aristotelian logic.[72] In the writings of Trendelenburg, Kierkegaard found a sophisticated articulation of his own nascent criticism of Hegel which proved decisive for his intellectual development. In fact, at one point Kierkegaard goes so far as to declare that "there is no modern philosopher from whom I have learned so much as from Trendelenburg."[73] Armed with his understanding of Aristotle and appreciation for Trendelenburg, Kierkegaard joins forces with Sibbern and Mynster against Heiberg and Martensen.

In *Concluding Unscientific Postscript*, Kierkegaard suggests the continuing significance of this debate for his overall interpretation of human existence and for his critique of Hegel's philosophical anthropology.

> Everyone is familiar with the fact that the Hegelian philosophy has rejected the principle of contradiction. Hegel himself has more than once sat in solemn judgment upon those thinkers who remain in the sphere of reflection and understanding, and therefore insist that there is an either-or. . . . Here in Denmark the Hegelians have several times been on the warpath, especially after Bishop Mynster, to gain the brilliant victory of speculative thought. Bishop Mynster has more than once become a vanquished standpoint, though as such he seems to be doing very well, and it is rather to be feared that the tremendous exertion incident to the winning of the victory has been too much for the unvanquished victors.[74]

Kierkegaard acknowledges that "Hegel is utterly and absolutely right in asserting that viewed eternally, *sub specie aeterni*, in the language of abstraction, in pure thought and pure being, there is no either-or."[75] But he refuses to admit that the speculative mediation of

---

72. The most significant works of Trendelenburg for Kierkegaard were *Logische Untersuchungen; Die logische Frage in Hegels System; Elementa logices Aristotelicae;* and *Erläuterungen zu den Elementen der aristotelischen Logik*. Although frequently noted, Kierkegaard's relation to Trendelenburg rarely has been examined with any care. For a helpful discussion see James Collins, *The Mind of Kierkegaard* (Chicago: Henry Regnery Co., 1967), pp. 226 ff.

73. *Journals and Papers*, 5978; 8-1:A 18.

74. *Postscript*, p. 270; 7:261. The translators point out that in his manuscript, Kierkegaard identifies the Danish Hegelians as Martensen and Heiberg. Hegel, of course, does *not* reject the principle of contradiction. As we have seen, it is essential to his entire philosophical and theological position. It will become evident, however, that Hegel and Kierkegaard interpret contradiction differently.

75. Ibid., p. 270; 7:261. In light of the strictures Kierkegaard believes to be imposed upon human existence by its inescapable finitude, it is not clear that he is, on his own terms, justified in making this concession. Moreover, as we have previously noted, Kierkegaard does not seem to realize that this position actually reduces freedom to a subjective illusion created by the limitation of the human perspective.

opposites applies to concrete existence or can disclose the nature of human selfhood. "Hegel is equally wrong," Kierkegaard continues, "when, forgetting the abstraction of his thought, he plunges down into the realm of existence to annul the double *aut* with might and main. It is impossible to do this in existence, for in so doing, the thinker abrogates existence as well."[76] The concretely existing individual is firmly situated in a limited perspective within which contradictions are irresolvable and oppositions irrevocable. As self-conscious and freely active, the self faces an indefinite future, which constantly poses unmediated alternatives. For such an individual the attempt to mediate the opposites or to resolve the contradictions inherent in finite spirit through speculative reflection inevitably "ignores the concrete and the temporal, the existential becoming, the distress of the existing individual arising from his being a synthesis of the temporal and the eternal situated in existence."[77] Speculative philosophy exacerbates the malady of spiritlessness plaguing Christendom by dissipating concrete existence in fantastic abstractions of pure thought. The Hegelian philosopher, like the comfortably settled bourgeois citizen, becomes absentmindedly forgetful of himself and therefore personally falls into the self-contradiction he believes he has reflectively overcome. For Kierkegaard, "the existential expression of abrogating the principle of contradiction is to be in contradiction to oneself. The creative omnipotence implicit in the passion of absolute disjunction which leads the individual resolutely to make up his mind is transformed into the extensity of prudence and reflection—that is, to be nothing at all. The principle of contradiction strengthens the individual in faithfulness to himself. . . ."[78]

Not only is Hegel's speculative rendering of the principles of identity, difference, and contradiction existentially problematic, it is also logically indefensible. Following the lead of Sibbern, and in adherence to supposedly surpassed Aristotelian logic, Kierkegaard argues that "the proposition: the principle of contradiction is annulled, itself rests upon the principle of contradiction, since other-

---

76. Ibid., p. 271; 7:261-262. T. H. Croxall recognizes the importance of the issue of identity and contradiction in Kierkegaard's relation to Hegel. But he accepts the Kierkegaardian caricature of Hegel as a philosopher of identity and therefore misrepresents the nature of the problem he attempts to consider. See "An Assessment," in *Johannes Climacus; or, De Omnibus Dubitandum Est, and A Sermon*, trans. T. H. Croxall (Stanford: Stanford University Press, 1967), pp. 77-83.

77. *Postscript*, p. 267; 7:258.

78. *Two Ages*, p. 97; 8:70. This remark underscores the close relationship between these extremely abstract logical problems and the concrete existential preoccupations of both Hegel and Kierkegaard.

wise the opposite proposition, that it is not annulled, is equally true."[79] As the existential expression of the abrogation of the rule of contradiction is to be in contradiction to oneself, so the attempt to annul the maxim of contradiction in speculative logic is itself based upon the principle of contradiction. Giving an unacknowledged Hegelian twist to the argument, Kierkegaard contends that contradiction affirms itself in the attempt to negate it.

In addition to this, Kierkegaard is convinced that Hegel's apparent mediation of opposites actually remains suspended between the horns of an irresolvable dilemma and hence fails to effect the reconciliation it promises. According to Kierkegaard, Hegelian mediation both demands and destroys otherness. In terms of the foundational structure of identity-within-difference, Kierkegaard maintains that *either* difference is real and reconciliation with otherness is not actual, *or* reconciliation with other is actual and difference is not real. On the one hand, if difference is real, as it must be on Hegel's own terms, opposites cannot be mediated, but must remain independent of, or in unmediated antithesis to, one another. On the other hand, if Hegel's mediation of contraries is actual, opposites are merely apparently opposite and are really identical. Kierkegaard concludes that the *choice* is between a monism in which otherness and difference are epiphenomenal and a dualism in which otherness and difference are abiding features of experience which finally can be overcome, if at all, only eschatologically.[80]

There is no doubt in Kierkegaard's mind about which alternative Hegel chooses. Efforts to the contrary notwithstanding, Hegel collapses the distinctions and dissolves the oppositions ingredient in concrete human existence and necessary for authentic spirit. Essence absorbs existence, infinitude encompasses finitude, ideality incorporates reality, necessity unravels freedom, eternity engulfs time, universality dissipates individuality, self is lost in society.

> On behalf of speculative thought, it is usual to say that the absoluteness of the principle of contradiction is an illusion of the understanding, and that it vanishes for thought. Just so. But then again it must be remembered that the abstraction as a result of which the principle vanishes, is itself a phantom that vanishes before the reality of existence. For the abrogation of the principle of contradiction, if it really means anything, and is not merely

---

79. *Philosophical Fragments*, p. 137; 4:270.
80. As we have seen, it is just this exclusive dilemma that Hegel's speculative logic seeks to resolve.

a literary conceit born of an adventurous imagination, means for an existing individual that he has ceased to exist.[81]

Kierkegaard chooses the other horn of the Hegelian dilemma. He argues that "the view that sees life's doubleness (dualism) is higher and deeper than that which seeks or 'pursues studies toward unity' (an expression from Hegel about all the endeavors of philosophy)."[82] In order to reestablish the possibility of truly spiritual existence, it is necessary to redefine the exclusive opposites and to rearticulate the absolute qualitative distinctions lost in speculative thought. Amidst the spiritless dissipation of modernity, "purity lies not in the blending-into-one . . . , but in distinction."[83] While Hegel is engaged in the struggle to mediate bifurcated opposites, Kierkegaard seeks to differentiate undifferentiated contrasts through the exercise of what he labels "absolute distinction." "That the principle of identity is in a certain sense higher, in that it is basic to the principle of contradiction," Kierkegaard explains,

is not difficult to see. But the principle of identity is merely the limit; it is like the blue mountains in the distance, or like the line that the artist calls his base line: the figure is what is important. The principle of identity therefore determines a lower point of view than the principle of contradiction, which is more concrete. Identity is the *terminus a quo*, but it is not a *terminus ad quem* for existence. An existing individual may arrive at identity as a maximum, and may repeatedly arrive at it, but only by abstracting from existence. But since ethics regards every existing individual as its bond servant for life, it will absolutely and in every moment forbid him to begin upon such an abstraction. Instead of identity annulling the principle of contradiction, it is contradiction that annuls [*ophæve*] identity. . . . Mediation proposes to make existence easier for the existing individual by leaving out the absolute relationship to the absolute *telos*. The exercise [*Indøvelsen*] of the absolute distinction makes life absolutely strenuous, precisely when the individual remains in the finite and simultaneously maintains an absolute relation to the absolute *telos* and a relative relationship to the relative.[84]

---

81. *Postscript*, p. 310; 7:301.

82. *Journals and Papers*, 704; 4:A 192. Jann Holl correctly points out that Kierkegaard's dualism returns to important features of Kant's philosophy. This insight underscores the similarity between Kierkegaard's position and the reflective philosophy of subjectivity that Hegel attempts to sublate. See Jann Holl, *Kierkegaards Konzeption des Selbst: Eine Untersuchung über die Voraussetzungen und Formen seines Denkens* (Meisenheim: Anton Hain, 1972), p. 27.

83. *Journals and Papers*, 4435; 7-1:B 192. Elsewhere Kierkegaard stresses that "exclusion [*Udelukkelse*] is precisely the opposite of mediation" (*Either-Or*, 2:178; 2:157).

84. *Postscript*, p. 377; 7:365-366.

For Kierkegaard, determinate identity is not generated by internal relation to otherness but emerges from the encounter between
and among mutually exclusive individuals. To mitigate the externality of this relationship is to dissipate concrete particularity in undifferentiated oneness. Faced with Hegel's effort to sublate logical
atomism and existential monadicism, Kierkegaard queries: "Is not
the individual an ἄτομον, which in no way can be regarded as a mode
or affection of another?"[85] In the final analysis, Kierkegaard insists,
"it is immovable firmness with respect to absolute distinctions that
makes a man a good dialectician."[86] Only by replacing Hegel's
integrative dialectic of internal relationality with a disintegrative
dialectic of exclusive individuality and oppositional coincidence does
Kierkegaard believe it possible to discern the structure of spirit. In an
extremely important journal entry he writes: "All relative contrasts
can be mediated [mediere]; we do not really need Hegel for this,
inasmuch as the ancients point out that they can be distinguished.
Personality will for all eternity protest against the idea that absolute
contrasts can be mediated (and this protest is incommensurable with
the assertion of mediation); for all eternity it will repeat its immortal
dilemma: to be or not to be—that is the question (Hamlet)."[87]

The disagreement between Hegel and Kierkegaard about fundamental logical principles forms the basis of essential differences lying
beneath the surface of their ostensibly similar formulations of the
structure of spirit. We have noted that Kierkegaard follows Hegel in
interpreting spirit as the activity of self-relation in which opposites
join. In the most complex passage in all his writings Kierkegaard
argues:

> Man is spirit [Aand]. But what is spirit? Spirit is the self [Selvet]. But what
> is the self? The self is a relation which relates itself to its own self, or is that
> in the relation by which the relation relates itself to its own self; the self is
> not a relation, but that the relation relates itself to its own self. Man is a
> synthesis [Synthese] of the infinite and the finite, of the temporal and the
> eternal, of freedom and necessity, in short, a synthesis. A synthesis is a
> relation between two. So regarded, man is not yet a self. In the relation
> between two, the relation is the third as a negative unity, and the two relate

85. *Journals and Papers*, 2023; 10-2:A 480.
86. *Philosophical Fragments*, p. 136; 4:270.
87. *Journals and Papers*, 1578; 2:A 454. "But," Kierkegaard admits, "to understand
the greatest oppositions together, and to understand oneself existing in them, is very
difficult. Let anyone merely observe himself, and take note of how men speak, and he will
perceive how rarely this task is successfully realized" (*Postscript*, p. 316; 7:307).

themselves to the relation, and in the relation to the relation; such a relation is that between soul and body, when man is determined as soul. If, on the contrary, the relation relates itself to its own self, the relation is then the positive third, and this is the self. Such a relation which relates itself to its own self (that is to say, a self) must either have constituted itself or have been constituted by another. If this relation which relates itself to its own self is constituted by another, the relation doubtless is the third, but this relation (the third) is, in turn, a relation relating itself to that which constituted the whole relation. Such a derived, constituted, relation is the human self, a relation which relates itself to its own self, and in relating itself to its own self relates itself to another.[88]

The Hegelian language in which Kierkegaard ironically couches his description of spirit tends to obscure the unique contours of selfhood he highlights. Therefore this pivotal text must be interpreted with extreme care.

Kierkegaard begins by defining spirit in terms that are virtually quoted from Hegel: "The self is a relation that relates itself to its own self." In his alternative phrasing of this point, however, Kierkegaard already subtly indicates a departure from the Hegelian view of spirit and suggests the distinctiveness of his own anthropology: the self is "that in the relation by which the relation relates itself to its own self; the self is not the relation, but that the relation relates itself to its own self." Both the negative and the positive points are essential to Kierkegaard's argument. "The self *is not* the relation." Kierkegaard is convinced that in Hegel's notion of spirit, the self *is* simply the relation, and that this relation is a *negative* unity. Or as he expresses it later in the text: "In the relation between two, the relation is the third term as a negative unity, and two relate themselves to the relation, and in the relation to the relation." We have seen that for Hegel, the structure of spirit is essentially self-referential negativity that binds together coimplicated opposites. Kierkegaard denies that contraries are identical in their difference, or that opposites are related in such a way that each in itself is at the same time its other. His adherence to the rules of traditional logic persuades him that opposites are mutually exclusive and actually

---

88. *Sickness unto Death*, p. 146; 11:127. This text has driven more than one commentator to despair! Even as perceptive a student of Kierkegaard as Louis Mackey declares: "The rationale for the 'gobbledygook' is now clear enough: . . . the force of Kierkegaard's paradoxes is to define human nature by pointing to the impossibility of defining it" (*Kierkegaard*, p. 137). To the contrary, this passage, which is Kierkegaard's most complete and explicit definition of the structure of selfhood, becomes intelligible through its intended contrast with Hegel's view of spirit.

antithetical. Consequently spirit, as the structure of self-relation within which opposites meet, cannot be the "negative unity" of internal relationality, but must be a "positive third" constitutive of a genuine *coincidentia oppositorum*. In other words, since opposites are not implicitly identical or necessarily related, they must be contingently conjoined.

Kierkegaard distinguishes his view of spirit from that of Hegel with greater precision when he further explains that "man is a synthesis of the infinite and the finite, of the temporal and the eternal, of freedom and necessity, in short, a synthesis."[89] While this formulation again recalls Hegel's notion of spirit, the carefully chosen term *synthesis* is calculated to introduce a distinctive characteristic of the Kierkegaardian self. Although Hegel's dialectic is commonly understood as a tripartite structure of thesis, antithesis, and synthesis, Hegel scrupulously avoids this terminology. In the *Logic*, Hegel explains that "the very expression *synthesis* easily recalls an *external* unity [*äusserliche Einheit*] and mere combination [*blosse Verbindung*] of entities which are *in and for themselves separate* [*an und für sich getrennt*]."[90] As my analysis of Hegel's speculative logic suggests, "mediation" rather than "synthesis" describes the relation of opposites within the system. However, what makes the notion of mediation attractive and the term *synthesis* problematic for Hegel makes the concept of synthesis attractive and the category of mediation problematic for Kierkegaard. "We have an old respectable terminology," Kierkegaard writes,

> thesis, antithesis, synthesis. They [speculative philosophers] invent a newer one in which mediation occupies the third place. Is this to be considered such an extraordinary step in advance? Mediation is equivocal, for it designates at once the relation between two terms and the result of the relation, that in which they stand related to one another as having been brought into relationship; it designates movement, but at the same time rest. Whether this is a perfection only a far deeper dialectical test will decide; but for that unfortunately we are still waiting. They abolish synthesis, and say "mediation."[91]

---

89. As is evident later in this passage, Kierkegaard adds another polarity to this list: body and soul. This binary, however, is functionally equivalent to the relation between the more inclusive terms "necessity and possibility" and therefore does not play a significant role in his analysis of the structure of spirit. It should be noted that Hegel also describes spirit as the unity of body and soul. See *Logic*, p. 757; 6:465; and *Philosophy of Spirit*, par. 387 ff; 10:38 ff.

90. *Logic*, p. 589; 6:261. Hegel's emphasis.

91. *Concept of Dread*, p. 11; 4:283.

Kierkegaard, by contrast, seeks to abolish mediation and to reinstate synthesis. A synthesis involves the conjunction of two mutually exclusive opposites effected by a "positive third." Kierkegaard argues that "a synthesis is unthinkable if the two are not united in a third."[92] Thus, "if there is no third, there really is no synthesis."[93] The positive third that creates the synthetic coincidence of opposites is spirit itself, "for that which combines [det Forbindende] is precisely spirit."[94] Kierkegaard clarifies his point when he explains that "the synthesis is a relationship, and it is a relationship which, though it is derived, relates itself to itself, which means freedom. The self is freedom [Selvet er Frihed]."[95] Or as he puts it elsewhere: "But what, then, is this self of mine: If I were to define this, my first answer would be: It is the most abstract of all things, and yet at the same time it is the most concrete—it is freedom."[96] Through the freedom of spirit or of the self, infinitude and finitude, possibility and necessity, eternity and time, come together in the concrete life of the individual. Opposites are synthesized by means of the individual's free self-conscious activity. For Kierkegaard, free resolution overcomes the dissolution endemic to speculative philosophy and to Christendom.

It is important to recognize that within Kierkegaard's anthropology, the true shape of finite spirit can emerge only over against the wholly other God who is decisively revealed through unique Incarnation in the God-Man. Since Kierkegaard believes that the Hegelian dialectic of identity-within-difference finally dissipates otherness in undifferentiated unity, he insists that Hegel's identification of divine and human spirit fails to sustain the distinction between self and God, and ends in the pantheistic dispersion of the divine and dissipation of the human. "The only consistent position outside Christianity," Kierkegaard contends,

> is that of pantheism, the taking of oneself out of existence by way of recollection into the eternal, by which all existential decisions become a mere shadow-play beside what is eternally decided from behind. The apparent decisiveness of speculative philosophy is, like all *apparent* decisiveness, a piece of nonsense; for decisiveness is precisely the eternal protest against all

92. Ibid., p. 39; 4:315.

93. Ibid., p. 76; 4:355. Compare Elrod, *Being and Existence in Kierkegaard's Psuedonymous Works*, pp. 39 ff.

94. *Concept of Dread*, p. 44; 4:319.

95. *Sickness unto Death*, p. 162; 11:142. It is important to remember that Kierkegaard identifies spirit and self (p. 146; 11:127).

96. *Either-Or*, 2:218; 2:192. Emphasis added.

fictions. The pantheist is eternally set at rest from behind; the struggle of existence in time, the seventy years, is a vanishing.[97]

In an effort to overcome the profanation of the divine and the disintegration of the human, Kierkegaard reaffirms the infinite qualitative difference between God and man. In the present context, this difference manifests itself as the contrast between the omnipotent Creator and the dependent creature. Spirit, which for Kierkegaard is essentially human spirit, must *"either* have constituted itself *or* have been constituted by another."* Kierkegaard is of the opinion that the self, in all its inner complexity, is created and sustained by its almighty Lord. Any minimization of the radical difference between self and wholly other God simply distorts the structure of spirit. From this perspective, "the more conception of God, the more self; and the more self, the more conception of God."[98] Authentic spirit presupposes obedient acknowledgment of the transcendent power upon which the self is ontologically dependent.

Kierkegaard's involved argument leads to the conclusion that human spirit, like the God-Man, is a freely sustained coincidence of opposites. Freedom, be it human or divine, synthesizes antitheses. Kierkegaard's exploration of the spiritual tensions resulting from the self's synthetic self-relating activity completes his interpretation of the structure of selfhood.

Spiritual Tensions

Kierkegaard expresses the diastatic and synthetic[99] rhythms of spirit by means of a series of homologous polarities. The self is a synthesis of ideality and reality, infinitude and finitude, possibility and necessity, eternity and time, universality and individuality. The precise meaning given to each of these terms and the exact nature of the relationship between these opposites further distinguish Kierkegaard's interpretation of the self from Hegel's notion of spirit.

When viewed as free self-relating activity, Kierkegaard argues, spirit must be regarded as both conscious and self-conscious. Freedom presupposes, but is not simply identical with, self-conscious-

---

97. *Postscript*, p. 203; 7:190.
98. *Sickness unto Death*, p. 211; 11:192.
99. Paul Sponheim organizes much of his discussion of Kierkegaard around these two terms. Sponheim, however, is more concerned with the relation between God and man than with the nature of selfhood. See *Kierkegaard on Christ and Christian Coherence*.

ness.[100]   Expressing this point in a Hegelian manner, Kierkegaard claims that "consciousness is spirit."[101]   More precisely, consciousness is the synthesis of reality and ideality. The term *reality* in Kierkegaard's lexicon designates the world as such—the immediate, sensual, empirical given (*datum*) of experience. *Ideality*, by contrast, is the conceptuality of thought articulated in language. Kierkegaard explains: "Immediacy is reality [*Realiteten*]. Language [*Sproget*] is ideality [*Idealiteten*]. Consciousness is opposition and contradiction."[102]

The synthesizing activity of consciousness is impossible apart from the clear delineation of the opposition between reality and ideality. Kierkegaard maintains that "the moment spirit posits itself, it posits the synthesis, but to posit the synthesis, it must first permeate it differentially [*adskillende*]."[103]   Borrowing a term from Hegel, Kierkegaard defines this activity of discriminating opposites as "reflexion."[104]   Against the integrative propensity of Hegelian Vernunft, "the determinations of reflexion are always *dichotomous* [*dichotomiske*]: e.g., ideality and reality, soul and body . . . and so on."[105]   By differentiating contraries, reflexion creates the *possibility* of their relationship. Since, however, these opposites are not internally related—the real is not ideal and the ideal is not real—their relation can become actual only when they are conjoined by a third. This third is spirit, understood as consciousness. Kierkegaard makes his point concisely: "Reflexion is the *possibility of relationship*, consciousness *is* the relationship, whose first form is opposition." [106]

---

100. Failure to maintain the distinction between freedom and self-consciousness confuses Kierkegaard's position and completely obscures his essential difference from Hegel on the issue of the structure of spirit. Mackey, for instance, falls prey to this error, when he maintains that freedom and self-consciousness are "finally synonymous in Kierkegaard" (*Kierkegaard*, p. 135).

101. *De Omnibus Dubitandum Est*, p. 151; *Papirer*, 4:148.

102. *Ibid.*, pp. 148-149; 4:146.

103. *Concept of Dread*, p. 44; 4:319.

104. See above, chap. 2, 1st sec. ("Fragmentation"), 3d subsec. ("The Reflective Philosophy of Subjectivity"). Hegel, of course, would contend that Kierkegaard's synthetic activity of consciousness does not move beyond Verstand to the rational integration of opposites. Kierkegaard would acknowledge the accuracy of Hegel's observation but would interpret the apparent criticism as supportive of his own alternative to speculative confusion. Kierkegaard's and Hegel's critiques of and responses to one another form the substance of chap. 7. In this context it is essential to note Kierkegaard's distinction between "reflexion" and "reflection." While reflexion differentiates previously undifferentiated opposites, reflection abstracts from concrete existence by dispassionate speculation.

105. *De Omnibus Dubitandum Est*, p. 150; *Papirer*, 4:147.

106. Ibid., p. 150; 4:147.

Through the activity of consciousness, immediate sensual reality and conceptual ideality join to form concrete human awareness. Kierkegaard concludes that "consciousness implies collision and then contradiction inevitably appears. Reality is not consciousness, any more than ideality is. And yet consciousness is not present without both, and this opposition or contradiction between reality and ideality is the origin and essence of consciousness. This is the first pain of becoming."[107] But no more than the *first* pain of becoming.

In *The Sickness unto Death*, Kierkegaard contends that "generally speaking, consciousness, i.e., consciousness of self, is the decisive criterion of the self. The more consciousness, the more self; the more consciousness, the more will, and the more will, the more self."[108] Consciousness, turned back upon itself, becomes self-consciousness and creates the possibility of free becoming. Becoming "consists in moving away from oneself infinitely by the process of infinitizing oneself, and in returning to oneself infinitely by the process of finitizing oneself."[109] The Kierkegaardian self, like Hegelian spirit, joins finitude and infinitude. For Kierkegaard, however, finitude is not a particular moment in the self-realization of an all-encompassing infinite spiritual totality. Rather, "the finite is limitation, and the infinite is expansion" in individual spirit.[110] Finitude identifies the temporally conditioned dimension of selfhood. In a more modern idiom, it is the self's historical facticity. Infinitude refers to the capacity of the individual so situated to transcend this givenness in imaginative reflection. According to Kierkegaard, the "imagination is the medium of the process of infinitizing; it is not one faculty on a par with others, but, if one would so speak, it is the faculty *instar omnium*. What feeling, knowledge, or will a man has depends in the last resort upon what imagination he has. . . . Imagination is the reflection of the process of infinitizing."[111]

Kierkegaard clarifies his understanding of the finitude and infinitude of spirit by his analysis of the parallel polarity designated "necessity and possibility." He explains that "just as finitude is the limiting factor in relation to infinitude, so in relation to possibility it

107. Ibid., pp. 149-150; 147. For an extensive discussion of the place of consciousness in Kierkegaard's overall philosophical position see Adi Schmuëli, *Kierkegaard and Consciousness*, trans. N. Handelman (Princeton: Princeton University Press, 1971).
108. *Sickness unto Death*, p. 162; 11:143.
109. Ibid., pp. 163-164; 11:143.
110. Ibid., p. 163; 11:143-144.
111. Ibid., pp. 163-164; 11:144.

is necessity that serves as a check. . . . The self κατὰ δύναμιν is just as possible as it is necessary; for though it is itself, it has to become itself. Inasmuch as it is itself, it is the necessary, and inasmuch as it has to become itself, it is a possibility."[112] By identifying the given aspects of concrete individuality, necessity specifies the determinate limitations the self's finitude imposes. Our consideration of the interpretation of the relation of possibility and necessity which Kierkegaard develops in *Philosophical Fragments* suggests that such conditionedness is not necessary in the sense that it could not have been otherwise. But having emerged historically, particular features of determinate spirit cannot be otherwise. The self's necessity is the concrete givenness from which all becoming proceeds.

The limitation imposed by such necessity does not, however, entangle spirit in a deterministic web. As a self-conscious being, the individual is able to discriminate the real self that is from the ideal self that ought to be. Through reflective imagination, spirit can project and apprehend multiple possibilities that form its own potentiality. While necessity describes what the self is or has become, possibility depicts what the self is not but might become. Confrontation with one's own protean possibilities evokes the dread that is inseparable from authentic selfhood.[113] From Kierkegaard's perspective the polarities of finitude and infinitude and of necessity and possibility delineate opposites separated by an abyss that can be bridged only by a third factor. This third is spirit or the self, now comprehended as freedom. Kierkegaard summarizes his long and complex argument: "The self is composed of infinitude and finitude. But the synthesis is a relationship, and it is a relationship which, though it is derived, relates itself to itself, which means freedom. The self is freedom. But freedom is the dialectical element in terms of possibility and necessity."[114] By means of free resolution embodied in individual decision, spirit conjoins reality and ideality, finitude and infinitude, necessity and possibility. Freedom is the κίνησις

---

112. Ibid., p. 168; 11:148. It might be helpful to note that on the one hand, Heidegger's terms *facticity* and *being-ahead-of-itself-in-already-being-in-a-world* parallel Kierkegaard's *finitude* and *necessity*, and on the other hand, *potentiality for being* and *anticipatory resoluteness* are basically equivalent to *infinitude* and *possibility*. See *Being and Time*, trans. J. Macquarrie and E. Robinson (New York: Harper and Row, 1962).

113. This, of course, is the central theme of *The Concept of Dread*. Kierkegaard writes: "He who is educated by dread is educated by possibility, and only the man who is educated by possibility is educated in accordance with his infinity. Possibility is, therefore, the heaviest of all categories" (pp. 139-140; 4:422).

114. *Sickness unto Death*, p. 162; 11:142.

through which the self realizes itself and spirit becomes actual. The self's free realization of possibility defines its actuality.

Although not readily apparent, Kierkegaard's position on this point represents a significant critique of Hegelian anthropology. It will be recalled that for Hegel, possibility and actuality join in necessity, which in itself is freedom. Kierkegaard retains these terms but reorders their relationship. He argues that necessity and possibility join in actuality, which is constituted by freedom. Kierkegaard believes that the speculative mediation of possibility and actuality through the category of necessity ends by denying freedom and rendering becoming illusory. "The fact that modern speculative thought has imported necessity into the historical process has caused much confusion; the categories of possibility, of actuality, and of necessity have all been compromised."[115] Kierkegaard's reexamination of necessity, possibility, and actuality, and his reinterpretation of the nature of their relationship represent his effort to overcome this confusion and to clarify the intricate structure of spirit.[116]

The kairotic character of the coincidentia oppositorum constitutive of authentic selfhood becomes apparent in Kierkegaard's account of spirit as the momentary synthesis of time and eternity. "The moment [Øjeblikket] is that ambiguity in which time [Tiden] and eternity [Evigheden] touch one another, and by this posit the temporal [Timelighed], where time constantly intersects eternity and eternity constantly penetrates time."[117] Kierkegaard carefully distinguishes time and temporality. In contrast to tensed temporality, time is "infinite succession, a passing by [Forbiganget]" that is not tensed; it therefore lacks spiritual tension. Time represents undifferentiated flux from which consciousness is excluded. Temporality emerges only when eternity touches time in the moment of self-conscious reflection and deliberate decision. Over against what he takes to be Hegel's retrospective relation to the eternal discovered by cognitive recollection, Kierkegaard proposes a prospective relation to the eternal established by volitional repetition. Stressing the parallel between this and other existential polarities, Kierkegaard maintains that "the past is actuality; the future is possibility. Eternally the

---

115. *Postscript*, pp. 306-307; 7:297.
116. It should be emphasized that unlike Hegel, for whom spirit characterizes objective as well as subjective reality, Kierkegaard restricts finite freedom to the sphere of human being, and thus establishes a qualitative opposition between self and world, or subject and object.
117. *Concept of Dread*, p. 80; 4:358.

eternal is the eternal; in time the eternal is possibility, the future."[118] Within a Kierkegaardian framework, the future is not merely the projection or result of the past. As possibility is not inherently necessary, so futurity is not completely immanent in what has been. The future holds unforeseen possibilities incommensurable with the past, and hence is discontinuous with antecedent actuality. As Merleau-Ponty explains, "the future is not prepared behind the observer, it is a brooding presence moving to meet him like a storm."[119] Inbreaking futurity invades the present and penetrates the past by posing radically new possibilities that shatter the deterministic chain of immanent development. The ground of such infinite possibility is the eternal God. According to Kierkegaard, "God *is* that all things are possible, and that all things are possible *is* God; and only the man whose being has been so shaken that he became spirit by understanding that all things are possible, only he has had dealings with God."[120] Futurity is the absence that masks the divine presence that forms the horizon of experience for the existing individual.

Possessed by the conviction that "things need not always be as they are or have been,"[121] Kierkegaard inverts the Hegelian dialectic of temporal development. Rather than viewing present and future as the result of the past, Kierkegaard claims that present and past are posited by the future. Futurity is the *decisive* mode of temporality— spirit lives out of the future. Anticipating insights of twentieth-century existentialism, Kierkegaard argues that

> in a certain sense, the future signifies more than the present and the past; for the future is in a sense the whole of which the past is a part, and in a sense the future may signify the whole. This is due to the fact that the eternal means first of all the future, or that the future is the incognito in which the eternal, as incommensurable with time, would nevertheless maintain its relations with time.[122]

---

118. *Works of Love*, trans. Howard and Edna Hong (New York: Harper and Row, 1962), p. 234; 9:238. For alternative discussions of Kierkegaard's view of the relation of time and eternity see Crites, *Twilight of Christendom*, pp. 66 ff.; Elrod, *Being and Existence*, pp. 65 ff.; and Schrag, *Existence and Freedom*, pp. 119 ff.

119. Merleau-Ponty, *Phenomenology of Perception* (London: Routledge and Kegan Paul, 1966), p. 441. This is a particularly apt remark, for it recalls Hegel's claim that spirit necessarily unfolds "behind the back" of unscientific consciousness.

120. *Sickness unto Death*, pp. 173-174; 11:153.

121. John Miles, "Witnesses and Catholics," *Commonweal* 105 (1978), 818-819.

122. *Concept of Dread*, p. 80; 4:359. Only with such a conception of time does Kierkegaard think it is possible to make sense out of central Christian concepts such as forgiveness, redemption, rebirth, and conversion. His position on this point presents an interesting anticipation of the recent theology of hope. See Mark C. Taylor, "Kierkegaard as a Theologian of Hope," *Union Seminary Quarterly Review* 28 (1973), 225-233.

Accumulating past and impending future join in the present to form Øjeblikket—the moment of decision which is the fullness of time for the existing individual. The liminality of the present is the ambiguous tension-filled frontier that is the passageway between past and future, the point at which time and eternity meet. Since time and eternity are not inherently identical or necessarily interrelated, they too must be contingently conjoined by the self. Spirit synthesizes eternity and time by actualizing possibilities in free decision. The self-conscious and freely active individual confronts an uncertain future composed of unmediated alternatives, in the face of which he must reappropriate his past and redefine his actuality through his own resolution. As the mirror image of the moment of divine Incarnation in the God-Man, this crucial moment of decision is also fraught with eternal significance. It is the hinge upon which history, the personal history of the individual, swings. In Øjeblikket, the self self-consciously defines itself and freely accepts responsibility for itself in its "eternal validity."

Spiritual tensions culminate in the existential "passion" of the fullness of time, thereby rendering transparent the structure of authentic selfhood.[123] For Kierkegaard, as for Blake, "without Contraries is no progression. Attraction and Repulsion, Reason and Energy, Love and Hate, are necessary to Human existence."[124] Opposites collide through the self's free self-relating activity. Authentic selfhood is a coincidentia oppositorum in which contraries are brought together in the passion of free resolution. Expressed differently, spirit is the synthesis of opposites in which the *self* becomes *itself*. This is genuine repetition by which spirit becomes actual—actually Christ-formed because genuinely cruciform. This spiritual coincidence, however, is only "momentary," and must be reestablished "repeatedly." Consequently, becoming spirit is an unending task, a task coterminous with life itself. "Existence," writes Kierkegaard, "is the child that is born of the infinite and the finite, the

---

123. For Kierkegaard, passion is created by the conjunction of opposites. The passion of the individual's crisis of decision reflects the passion of the God-Man's Crucifixion. For a useful account of the oppositional nature of the Kierkegaardian self see Louis Dupré, "The Constitution of the Self in Kierkegaard's Philosophy," *International Philosophical Quarterly* 3 (1963), 506-526. Josiah Thompson stresses that in the eyes of Kierkegaard, "to exist in the most eminential sense is to raise contradiction to its highest intensity by attempting to live a paradox" ("The Master of Irony," in *Kierkegaard: A Collection of Critical Essays*, p. 154).

124. William Blake, *The Marriage of Heaven and Hell* (New York: Oxford University Press, 1975).

eternal and the temporal, and therefore is a *constant* striving." [125] Existence is profoundly unsettling, for spirit again and again is called from a comfortable and secure present to an uncertain and insecure future. To settle along the way is to forsake the journey to selfhood. To remain under way is to immerse oneself ever more deeply in the ineluctable ambiguities, the irresolvable contradictions, and the irreconcilable oppositions of concrete existence. Kierkegaard does not deny that the way of spirit brings passion and suffering. Life *is* lived in the "middest," acted out at the *cross*-roads, betwixt'n between past and future, beginning and end, Genesis and Apocalypse, creation and redemption. The tension generated by the recurrent crisis of decision is the cross upon which authentic spirit hangs.

Individual or Community

Kierkegaard is convinced that when spirit is so conceived, the journey to selfhood cannot culminate in spiritual community but must be a solitary sojourn that separates self from other. Against Hegel's insistence on the sociality of spirit, Kierkegaard asserts that "to become spirit means to become the single individual [*den Enkelte*]; isolation is a *conditio sine qua non*, an indispensable condition." [126] Since identity does not arise from internal relation with otherness, but is a function of contrast with or opposition to otherness, "spirit is exactly this: not to be like others." [127] The Kierkegaardian "formula" for authentic selfhood "constantly is: individual in opposition to the others." [128] Rather than forming concrete selfhood, social relations abrogate unique individuality. In direct opposition to Hegel, Kierkegaard argues that "this precisely is spirit, that everyone is an individual before God, that 'community' [*Fælledsskab*] is a lower category than 'the single individual,' which everyone can and should be." [129]

It is apparent that Kierkegaard must reject Hegel's contention that authentic selfhood presupposes membership in spiritual commu-

---

125. *Postscript*, p. 85; 7:73. Emphasis added.

126. *Journals and Papers*, 2074; 11-1:A 518. The word *Enkelte* emphasizes singularity. See Gregor Malantschuk, *Fra Individ Til Den Enkelte: Problemer omkring Friheden og det etiske hos Søren Kierkegaard* (Copenhagen: C. A. Reitzels Boghandel, 1978).

127. *Attack upon Christendom*, p. 286; 14:355.

128. Ibid., p. 167; 14:201.

129. *Training in Christianity*, p. 218; 12:204. As will become apparent in chap. 6, Kierkegaard does not intend his argument to lead to the simple abnegation of social relations in a "monkish flight" from the world. His position is considerably more dialectical. Whether he can maintain this dialectical tension, however, remains to be seen.

nity. Instead of being the fulfillment of selfhood, life in community with others is a concession to the human weakness of being unable to bear the isolation of spiritual individuality. "Society cannot be deduced from 'spirit,'" Kierkegaard maintains, and "the church exists precisely because we are not truly spirit or pure spirit. 'The congregation' is an accommodation, a concession in view of how little we are able to endure being spirit."[130] Equally problematic is the inability of the spiritual community to mediate the divine presence necessary for individual authenticity. For Kierkegaard, "intercourse with God is, in the deepest sense, absolutely non-social [*ubetinget uselskabelig*]."[131]

Kierkegaard does not deny that there are social dimensions of selfhood. As a matter of fact, he agrees with Hegel's characterization of spirit as at once universal and individual. "The deepest reason for this is to be discovered," Kierkegaard explains, "in the essential characteristic of human existence, that man is an individual and as such is at once himself and the whole race, in such a way that the whole race has part in the individual, and the individual has part in the whole race."[132] But over against what he believes to be the tendency of Hegelian philosophy and modern Christendom to dissipate concrete individuality in abstract universality, or to lose self in the crowd, Kierkegaard resolutely maintains that "the individual as the individual is higher than the universal, is justified over against it, is not subordinate but superior. . . . This position cannot be mediated, for all mediation comes about precisely by virtue of the universal; it is and remains to all eternity a paradox."[133] The birth of such spiritual individuality requires severing the umbilical cord of sociality through the difficult labor of differentiating self and other. The one who undertakes this spiritual pilgrimage ever remains a lonely wayfarer.

---

130. *Journals and Papers*, 4341; 10-4:A 226.
131. *Christian Discourses*, trans. W. Lowrie (New York: Oxford University Press, 1962), p. 334; 10:24.
132. *Concept of Dread*, p. 26; 4:300.
133. *Fear and Trembling*, trans. W. Lowrie (Princeton: Princeton University Press, 1970), p. 66; 3:106. Here, as elsewhere, Kierkegaard's reading of Hegel is problematic and is designed to advance his own argument. In elaborating Kierkegaard's interpretation of the structure of spirit, it has been necessary to take into account important elements of his critique of Hegel's point of view. The adequacy of Kierkegaard's representation of Hegel and the relative merits of their alternative positions will be considered in chap. 7.

|6|

WAYFARING

Great spirits now on earth are sojourning. . . .
                                            —*Shelley*

The goal, absolute knowledge, or spirit that
knows itself as spirit, has for its way [*Weg*] the
recollection of the spirits as they are in themselves, and as they complete the organization of
their *Reich*. Their preservation, regarded from
the side of their free existence appearing in the
form of contingency, is history; but regarded
from the side of their comprehended organization, it is the science of appearing or apparent
knowledge; the two together comprehend history; they form the inwardizing of the Golgotha of absolute spirit, the actuality, truth,
and certainty of his throne, without which he
would be lifeless and alone. Only "from the
chalice of this kingdom of spirits [*Geisterreich*],
foams forth for Him his own infinitude."
                                            —*Hegel*

But he knows also that higher than this there
winds a solitary path, narrow and steep; and he
knows that it is terrible to be born outside the
universal, to walk without meeting a single traveler. He knows very well where he is and how
he is related to men. Humanly speaking, he is
mad and cannot make himself intelligible to
anyone.
                                            —*Kierkegaard*

In the aesthetic education Hegel and Kierkegaard prescribe, Christ is envisioned as the Way, and life as wayfaring—a pilgrimage from the city of man to the city of God, from sin to salvation, from bondage to freedom—the journey to selfhood. If wayfaring pilgrims are to be cured of the sickness unto death, they must follow the stations or stages of the way from inauthenticity to authenticity revealed in the person and life of the God-Man. The alternative interpretations of the nature of spiritlessness and the structure of spirit developed by Hegel and Kierkegaard imply contrasting beginnings and endings for their respective spiritual sojourns. We have seen that for Hegel, the ills of fragmentation and disintegration can be remedied only through the rational reintegration of the oppositions and mediation of the conflicts sundering modern man's personal and social life. Kierkegaard maintains that overcoming the dissipation of concrete existence requires decisively distinguishing self and world. In other words, while Hegel describes the movement from oppositional differentiation to reconciliation of self and other, Kierkegaard stresses the need to advance from the nondifferentiation to the differentiation of self and other. Hegel begins where he thinks Kierkegaard ends, and Kierkegaard begins where he believes Hegel ends. Despite these differences, Hegel's *Stationen des Weges* and Kierkegaard's *Stadier paa Livets Vei* share important features. To discern the differences and to identify the similarities between the Hegelian and Kierkegaardian journeys to selfhood, it is necessary to consider the specific courses they chart in the *Phenomenology of Spirit* and the pseudonymous writings.[1]

---

1. Clearly the scope of this essay neither permits nor requires a detailed commentary on Hegel's *Phenomenology* and Kierkegaard's pseudonymous writings. My purpose in the following pages is to consider the general structure, major stages, and overall direction of Hegel's and Kierkegaard's contrasting ways to selfhood. This discussion, of course, is guided by the overriding concern to establish a comparison of the positions of Hegel and Kierkegaard and is not intended to deny the validity of other approaches to these unusually difficult works. The most helpful commentary on the *Phenomenology* remains Hyppolite's *Genesis and Structure of Hegel's Phenomenology of Spirit*. Other works that are useful include: Howard P. Kainz, *Hegel's Phenomenology, Part 1: Analysis and Commentary* (University: University of Alabama Press, 1976); Pierre-Jean Labarrière, *Structures et mouvement dialectique dans la Phénoménologie de l'esprit de Hegel* (Paris: Aubier-Montaigne,˙ 1968); Quentin Lauer, *A Reading of Hegel's Phenomenology of Spirit* (New York: Fordham University Press, 1976); Jacob Löwenberg, *Hegel's Phenomenology: Dialogues of the Life of the Mind* (La Salle, Ill.: Open Court, 1965); Rosen, *Science of Wisdom*, pp. 123-160; and Charles Taylor, *Hegel* (New York: Cambridge University Press, 1975), pp. 127-213. For a more complete analysis of Kierkegaard's stages of existence see Mark C. Taylor, *Kierkegaard's Pseudonymous Authorship*, chaps. 3-7.

STATIONS OF THE WAY

In a summary statement prepared for a publisher's advertisement, Hegel offers a concise description of the structure and movement of the *Phenomenology:*

> It includes the various shapes of spirit within itself as stages in the progress through which spirit becomes pure knowledge or absolute spirit. Thus, the main divisions of this science, which fall into further subdivisions, include a consideration of consciousness, self-consciousness, observational and active reason, as well as spirit itself—in its ethical, cultural, and moral, and finally religious forms. The apparent chaos of the wealth of appearances in which spirit presents itself when first considered is brought into a scientific order, which is exhibited in its necessity, in which the imperfect appearances resolve themselves and pass over into the higher ones constituting their proximate truth. They find their final truth first in religion and then in science, as the result of the whole.[2]

Unfortunately the structure and dialectical progression of Hegel's notoriously complex work have rarely been so clear to perplexed readers. As a matter of fact, many analysts despair of finding a unifying thread that binds together Hegel's argument, and insist that the book does not form an organic totality, but remains a patchwork that was quickly composed during a short period of personal turmoil and circumstantial pressure. This point of view has been developed most completely by Theodor Haering in a widely influential address delivered before the 1933 Hegelkongress.[3] Haering argues that Hegel radically revised the plan of the *Phenomenology* during the course of its composition. Although initially intending only an analysis of consciousness, self-consciousness, and reason, Hegel is supposed to have expanded the work to include the examination of what he later identifies as historically emergent forms of objective spirit. Until recently, most scholars have followed Haering in denying the overall unity of the *Phenomenology*. This point of view, however, has been seriously challenged by Otto Pöggeler's careful analysis of the relationship between the *Phenomenology* and philosophical investiga-

---

2. *Intelligenzblatt der Janaischen Allgemeinen Litteraturzeitung*, 28 October 1807. Quoted by M. J. Petry in the introduction to his translation of *Hegel's Philosophy of Subjective Spirit* (Boston: D. Reidel Publishing Co., 1978), p. lxvii.

3. Theodor L. Haering, "Die Entstehungsgeschichte der *Phänomenologie des Geistes*," in *Verhandlungen des dritten Hegelkongresses vom 19. bis 23. April 1933 in Rom*, ed. B. Wigersma (Tübingen: J. C. B. Mohr, 1934), pp. 118-138.

tions Hegel conducted during his years in Nuremberg and Jena.[4]
Pöggeler demonstrates conclusively that the *Phenomenology* was not
the product of a brief outburst of creative energy which grew beyond
the bounds originally established by its author. Nor is it a palimpsest,
repeatedly revised to fit changing intentions and to include newly
found materials. To the contrary, the argument of the *Phenomenology* represents a deliberate refinement and systematic elaboration of insights Hegel first advanced in his philosophical *Propae-
udeutic*, written while he was still in Nuremberg. Pöggeler further
underscores the conceptual coherence of the *Phenomenology* by
correlating its dialectical progression with the categorial structure of
the speculative logic Hegel formulates in his Jena *Realphilosophie*.[5]
Although it is impossible to enter into the details of this debate in
this context, it should be noted that Pöggeler's painstaking reconstruction of the historical genesis and logical structure of the
Phenomenology strongly suggests the unity of this extraordinarily
complicated work.

Our investigation of the pedagogical purpose of the *Phenomenology* offers further support for the coherence of Hegel's argument.
We have seen that Hegel attempts to provide a cure for the modern
malaise of spiritlessness by developing a therapeutic aesthetic education that will lead the reader from inauthentic to authentic selfhood.
Proper educational technique requires Hegel to begin from the standpoint of the pupil and to proceed to disclose the internal inconsistencies and contradictions of the learner's perspective in such a way
that the student is enabled to move through the stages from error
and bondage to truth and freedom. The point of departure for
Hegel's educational journey, therefore, must be the modern experience of self-alienation. Hegel believes the quintessential expression of
spiritlessness to be the isolation of self from other typified by the
opposition between subjectivity and objectivity. As is by now
apparent, the bifurcation of subject and object is not simply the
narrowly epistemological issue so important in modern philosophy,
but is a polymorphic problem with psychological, social, cultural,
religious, and philosophical aspects. Hegel's keen awareness of the
multidimensionality of contemporary fragmentation *forces* him to

---

4. Otto Pöggeler, "Zur Deutung der *Phänomenologie des Geistes*," *Hegel-Studien*
1 (1961), 254-294.

5. While Fulda disagrees with the exact logical underpinnings Pöggeler identifies, he
agrees that Hegel's logic provides the unifying substructure of the *Phenomenology*. See
Fulda, *Problem einer Einleitung*.

consider the full range of experience probed in the *Phenomenology*.
Fulfillment of his mission as the Volkserzieher who restores the
unity of man is impossible apart from the mediation of all the
oppositions among which the self is torn. Hegel's salvific pedagogy
attempts to overcome disintegration by sublating isolated particularity through the reunion of self and other. Put differently, aesthetic
education leads to the actualization of spiritual individuality through
the re-cognition of particularity as a concrete moment of an all-
encompassing universal totality within which subject and object are
reconciled. From Hegel's perspective, the movement from spiritlessness to spirit involves the incremental reintegration of subject and
object, and the correlative realization of definitive internal relations
among specific objects and the constitutive interrelation of particular
subjects.[6]

Although the stations of the way identified by Hegel represent
contrasting forms of experience, the journey to selfhood passes
through three distinct stages, each of which is triply subdivided.[7]
Natural selfhood, inclusive of consciousness, self-consciousness, and
reason, depicts the human struggle to reintegrate subject and object
through theoretical reflection and practical action. Ethical selfhood,
which falls into the moments of substantial, self-estranged, and
self-certain spirit, recounts the differentiation and reintegration of
the particular self and the universal sociocultural totality.[8] Religious
selfhood, expressed in natural, artistic, and revealed religion, represents the gradual realization of the reconciliation of the divine and
human. Hegel's pedagogy culminates in absolute knowledge that
conceptually articulates the mediation of opposites which gradually
emerges in the course of spirit's journey. Though not at first evident
to the wayfaring self, the movement within and among the different
forms of experience or shapes of spirit constitutes an immanent
progression that unfolds necessarily. End is implicit in beginning, and
beginning is explicit in end.[9] The individual who undertakes the

---

6. Hyppolite correctly emphasizes that "the opposition between the universal and the
specific—and more profoundly, at a different level, between the universe and the I—is the
theme of Hegel's philosophy. It is the separation that must be overcome without either of
the terms being swallowed up by the other" (*Genesis and Structure*, p. 238).

7. Every substage, of course, is defined more precisely by the discrimination of
further dialectical moments.

8. When used in this general way, the term *ethical* encompasses both Hegel's *Sittlichkeit* and *Moralität*.

9. See *Phenomenology*, p. 10; 20. Throughout the remainder of this chapter, the
references to the *Phenomenology* are given in the body of the text.

journey to selfhood recollects, and therefore inwardizes, the formative stages (Bildungsstufen) through which universal spirit has
passed in the course of its own self-actualization. The *Phenomenology*, Hegel stresses, should be "regarded as the path of the natural
consciousness which presses forward to true knowledge; or as the
way of the soul which journeys through the series of its own
configurations as though they were stations appointed for it by its
own nature, so that it may purify itself for the life of spirit, and
achieve finally, through a completed experience of itself, the
awareness of what it really is in itself" (49; 67).

Natural Selfhood

The first major station in the pilgrimage of Hegelian spirit
includes the dialectically related moments of consciousness, self-
consciousness, and reason. As I have suggested, passage through this
stage involves the sublation of the apparent opposition of subject and
object by means of cognitive reflection and volitional action. On the
one hand, through the interrelated processes of sense-intuition,
perception, and understanding, the knowing subject discovers itself
in the known object. Consciousness of the object reveals itself to be
self-consciousness of the subject. Self-consciousness, on the other
hand, necessarily involves consciousness of self as object. Put differently, self-consciousness is impossible apart from self-objectification.
While consciousness entails the subjectification of objectivity, self-
consciousness implies the objectification of subjectivity. Reason, for
Hegel, is the dialectical union of consciousness and self-consciousness
through which subject and object join to form an identity-within-
difference.

Broadly conceived, Hegel's phenomenology of spirit charts the
way from "natural consciousness" to "absolute knowledge." "The
standpoint of consciousness which knows objects in their opposition
to itself and itself in opposition to objects," Hegel points out, "is for
science the opposite of its own standpoint" (15; 25). Since he is
convinced that opposites coinhere, Hegel insists that absolute knowledge is implicit in natural consciousness. Absolute knowledge's dialectical inversion (*Umkehrung*) of natural consciousness, therefore, is simultaneously natural consciousness's necessary conversion
(*Umkehrung*) to redemptive absolute knowledge. To reach this end,
Hegel begins with an examination of the experience of consciousness
which, he argues, is characterized by the alienation of subjectivity

and objectivity. This bifurcation of subject and object is the distinctive feature of post-Cartesian philosophy and is the basis of the
epistemological aporias of the reflective philosophy of subjectivity
most significantly expressed in Kant's critical writings.[10] In consciousness, subject and object, self and other, person and world,
certainty and truth are contraposed. The conscious subject believes
itself to be confronted *ab extra* by a world of alien objects
(*Gegen-stände*).

Hegel further specifies the starting point of his analysis by
qualifying primal consciousness as "natural." He explains that "it is
precisely externality [*die Äusserlichkeit*] which is characteristic of
nature, that is, differences are allowed to fall outside of one another
[*auseinanderfallen*] and to appear as indifferent existences."[11] The
significance of this point for Hegel's analysis of human experience
becomes evident when it is recognized that "naturalness has . . . this
further determination: that the natural man is a single or particular
individual [*ein Einzelner*] as such, for nature generally lies in the
bonds of separation and isolation [*Vereinzelung*]."[12] The qualifier
natural, then, implies mutual externality sustained by separation and
isolation.[13]   Such unmediated opposition to or division from otherness Hegel labels *im-mediacy*. Immediacy (*Unmittelbarkeit*) is the

---

10. In the *Encyclopaedia*, Hegel claims that "the Kantian philosophy can be described
most accurately as having viewed spirit as consciousness" (*Philosophy of Spirit*, par. 415;
10:202). Thus the position of a commentator such as Richard Norman, who argues that the
program for the *Phenomenology* is "the overcoming of the Kantian skepticism, the demon-
stration of the possibility of knowing things in themselves," is not incorrect. But analysts
rarely recognize the close relation between the issue of epistemology and Hegel's broader
concerns: see above, chap. 2, 1st sec. ("Fragmentation"). As a result of this oversight,
Hegel's reason for considering the diversity of experience explored in the *Phenomenology*
remains opaque. See Norman, *Hegel's Phenomenology: A Philosophical Introduction* (New
York: St. Martin's Press, 1976), p. 10; compare Ivan Soll, *An Introduction to Hegel's
Metaphysics* (Chicago: University of Chicago Press, 1969), pp. 47 ff.

11. *Philosophy of Nature*, par. 249; 9:31.

12. *Lesser Logic*, par. 25; 8:90-91. It is significant that Hegel makes this point in the
context of an account of the fall. By way of anticipation it is helpful to note that while
Hegel begins with the separate Einzelnen and attempts to reach the intersubjectivity of
spiritual community, Kierkegaard begins with a self dispersed in the social totality and
endeavors to arrive at the isolated *Enkelte*.

13. It is important to stress that in the *Phenomenology*, Hegel begins with an analysis
of natural *consciousness*. As is apparent from his anthropological explorations in the
Philosophy of Spirit (pars. 388-412), he postulates a state antecedent to consciousness in
which self and other (subject and object) remain undifferentiated. This condition, however,
is strictly unconscious (*bewusstlos*). For conscious beings, such a state (represented as a
paradisiacal or infantile innocence) is always present as lost and can never be regained. See
Philosophy of Religion, p. 278; 17:146. Jacques Derrida has recently developed this idea in
an imaginative way in his notion of "erasure": see his *Of Grammatology* trans. G. C. Spivak
(Baltimore: Johns Hopkins University Press, 1976).

condition of disintegration (*Auseinanderfallen*) that results from the abstract opposition of atomistic particulars.[14] "Knowledge in its first phase, or *immediate spirit* [*der unmittelbare Geist*]," Hegel asserts, "is spiritless [*Geistlose*], *sense-consciousness*" (15; 26). The progression from natural to ethical selfhood sublates immediacy through the mediation of subject and object, and the recognition of constitutive interrelations among specific objects and determinate subjects.

From Hegel's point of view, the most rudimentary form of natural consciousness is sense-certainty, in which a particular subject, isolated from all other subjects, confronts an alien object, separated from all other objects. At this initial stage of awareness, the subject regards objectivity as the locus of essential truth and believes knowledge to be the result of determination by, or passive reception of, external data of sensible intuition. Although this type of consciousness apparently is the richest form of knowledge, "it proves itself to be the most abstract and poorest *truth*" (58; 79). Since determinate identity is born of intercourse with otherness, *im*mediacy or *un*mediatedness is completely *in*determinate. This indefiniteness leaves sense-certainty ineffable, utterly inexpressible. As soon as the subject attempts to express sense-certainty, the immediacy of isolated particularity is sublated and the object is posited as a universal. Hegel maintains that sense-certainty cannot say what it means (*meint*), for language negates immediacy by elevating particularity to universality. The object intended (*gemeint*) by sense-certainty is a unique particular. When actually expressed, however, the object turns out to be a universal—a pure "This," formed by the spatio-temporal unity of a universal "here," composed of multiple particular "heres," and a universal "now," composed of a plurality of particular "nows." Hegel concludes that "sense-certainty has demonstrated in its own self that the truth of its object is the universal" (61; 82).[15] The knowing subject likewise shows itself to be a universal (an I), which incorporates a plurality of particulars (multiple sensations). It is clear that the universality of both object and

---

14. *Philosophy of Religion*, 2:123; 17:9. My analysis of Hegel's Christology should lead us to suspect that Unmittelbarkeit is the opposite of the truth revealed in *der Mittler*.

15. For a very helpful account of Hegel's discussion at this point see Charles Taylor, *Hegel*, pp. 127-147; and idem, "The Opening Arguments of the *Phenomenology*," in *Hegel: A Collection of Critical Essays*, ed. A. MacIntyre (New York: Doubleday and Co., 1972), pp. 151-186.

subject is dialectically related to and inclusive of, rather than firmly opposed to and abstracted from, particularity. In themselves, subject and object already reveal the essential structure of unity-in-multiplicity or identity-within-difference.[16]

In the effort to express its object, consciousness necessarily moves beyond sense-certainty to perception (*Wahrnehmung*). Perception is the commonsense attitude in which a subject attempts to apprehend an object that is conceived as *a* thing with *multiple* properties, that is, a oneness that is also a plurality. The definitive qualities of the thing both distinguish it from and relate it to other things. The determinate identity of the concrete object is a function of its relation to other such objects. Hegel argues that the object

> is only a *thing*, or a one that exists on its own account, insofar as it does not stand in this relation to others; for this relation establishes rather its continuity with others, and for it to be connected with others is to cease to exist on its own account. It is just through the *absolute character* of the thing and its opposition that it *relates* itself to *others*, and is essentially only this relating. The relation, however, is the negation of its self-subsistence, and it is really the essential property of the thing that is its undoing. . . . The thing is posited as being *for itself*, or as the absolute negation of all otherness, therefore as purely *self*-related negation; but the negation that is self-related is the sublation of *itself*; in other words, the thing has its essential being in another thing. . . . With this, the last *insofar* that separated being-for-self from being-for-another falls away; on the contrary, the object is *in one and the same respect the opposite of itself: it is for itself, so far as it is for another, and it is for another, so far as it is for itself.* [76; 98-99]

When the negation of the isolated particularity of the object of consciousness is recognized, it becomes apparent that the object's essential identity is constituted by its internal relation to other determinate objects. The structure of relation which forms the essential identity of the object is, however, inaccessible to sense awareness. It is the *supersensuous* object of understanding.[17]

Through the activity of understanding, the cognitive subject

---

16. Throughout the remainder of his analysis of consciousness, Hegel is primarily concerned with the changing nature of the object. The corresponding consideration of the subject is elaborated in his discussion of self-consciousness.

17. The concept by which Hegel makes the transition from perception to understanding is force. When conceived as the expression or manifestation (*Aüsserung*) of force, the object appears to be an inwardly differentiated totality that stands in reciprocal relation with other such objects.

transcends the world of sense perception in an attempt to ascertain the essence of things. By virtue of such creative knowing, "the inner, or supersensible beyond [*das übersinnliche Jenseits*], has *arisen*: it *comes from* appearance which has mediated it; in other words, appearance is its essence and, in fact, its completion. The supersensible is the sensuous and the perceived [*das Wahrgenommene*], posited [*gesetzt*] as it is *in truth*; but the *truth* of the sensuous and the perceived is to be *appearance*. The supersensible is therefore *appearance as appearance*" (89; 113). In contrast to sense-certainty, for which sensuous particularity is both essential and true, understanding grasps sensuous particularity as the outward appearance of inward essence. Understanding comprehends this inner essence as a law (*Gesetz*) that *conceptually* articulates the substance of the object. As our investigation of the logical doctrine of essence has shown, Hegel maintains that essence and appearance are inseparably bound in a relation of unity-in-distinction. Essence is not a fixed beyond or a wholly other noumenon, eternally opposed to the phenomenal world of everyday experience. To the contrary, essence, understood as law, and appearance are internally related to each other: law is the law *of* appearance, and appearance is the appearance *of* law. Each presupposes the other and contains its opposite within itself, creating what Hegel calls the "inverted world." As Professor Rosen explains,

> the effort to affirm the world by analytic thinking immediately transforms the reality or essential significance of the world into concepts or laws: into analytic thinking and its products. The sensuous world is transformed by thinking into the supersensuous world. On the other hand, the supersensuous world is itself derived from the sensuous world, which is consequently the *essence* of the supersensuous world. The sensuous gives substance to, exhibits, renders accessible the supersensuous. But this exhibition, precisely as it succeeds, at the same time negates itself, or results in the inversion of the sensuous into the supersensuous. Conversely, every effort to explain the essence or substance of the supersensuous immediately inverts it into the sensuous. This reciprocal oscillation is the dialectic of the inverted world.[18]

By grasping objectivity as lawful appearance, understanding discloses the identity-within-difference of the object and the subject

---

18. Rosen, *Science of Wisdom*, p. 145. Gadamer's essay "Hegel's 'Inverted World' " (in his *Hegel's Dialectic*, pp. 35-53) is also instructive.

of consciousness. The object is a unified plurality and a pluralized unity, which is a concrete instantiation of the essential structure of double negativity. According to Hegel,

> law completes itself in an immanent necessity, and all the moments of appearance are taken up into the inner world. That the simplicity of law is infinity means . . . (a) that it is self-*identical*, but it is also in itself *different*; or it is the selfsame that repels itself from itself or sunders itself into two. . . . (b) The bifurcation, which represents the parts thought of as in the *law*, exhibits itself as subsistent. . . . (c) But through the notion of inner difference, these unlike and indifferent moments . . . are a *difference* which is no *difference*, or only a difference of what is *selfsame*, and its essence is unity. . . . The two differentiated moments both subsist; they are *in themselves* and are *opposites in themselves*, i.e., each is the opposite of itself; each has its other within it and they are only one unity. [99-100; 124-25]

When conceptually comprehended, it becomes apparent that the object is formally homologous with the structure of subjectivity uncovered in our analysis of Hegel's interpretation of spirit. In view of this isomorphism, the subject's cognition of the object is simultaneously its recognition and re-cognition of itself. Though at first convinced of the irrefutable otherness of the object, consciousness passes from sense-intuition and perception to understanding in which it realizes that its relation to the object is, in fact, self-relation.

> Raised above perception, consciousness exhibits itself closed in a unity with the supersensible world through the mean [*die Mitte*] of appearance, through which it gazes into this background. The two extremes, the one of the pure inner world, the other that of the inner being gazing into this pure inner world, now have converged, and just as they, as extremes, have vanished, so too the mean as something other than the extremes, has also vanished. This curtain [*Vorhang*] hanging before [*vorhanden*] the inner world is therefore drawn away, and we have the inner [the subject] gazing into the inner [of the object] —the vision of the undifferentiated selfsameness, which repels itself from itself, posits itself as an inner being containing differentiated moments, but for which equally these moments are immediately *not* different—*self-consciousness*. [103; 128-129] [19]

---

19. Hegel acknowledges that this result is implicit in Kant's notion of the "transcendental unity of apperception." But Kant fails to draw the radical conclusion implied in his own argument. By reifying the separation of subjectivity and objectivity in the doctrine of the thing-in-itself, Kant makes genuine knowledge impossible and self-alienation unsurpassable. See above, chap. 2, 1st sec. ("Fragmentation"), 3d subsec. ("The Reflective Philosophy of Subjectivity").

Through immanent dialectical development, consciousness of the object reveals itself to be self-consciousness of the subject.

While consciousness begins with a belief in the essentiality of the object and the inessentiality of the subject, self-consciousness initially assumes the essentiality of the subject and the inessentiality of the object. Throughout the circuitous course of its education (Bildung), self-consciousness attempts to achieve satisfaction by giving objective expression to its subjective certainty.[20] In the course of objectifying itself, self-consciousness reveals its internal relation to consciousness.

The most primitive form of self-consciousness is desire. The desiring subject seeks to assert its own substantiality and independence, and to establish the insubstantiality and dependence of that which opposes it by negating its object. "Certain of the nothingness of this other, it explicitly affirms that this nothingness is *for it* the truth of the other; it destroys the independent object and thereby gives itself the certainty of itself as a *true* certainty, a certainty that has become explicit for self-consciousness itself *in an objective manner*" (109; 139). Desire, however, is always frustrated and inevitably fails to achieve complete satisfaction. It is insatiable, perpetually requiring another object through whose negation it can assert itself. Furthermore, such intended self-affirmation is actually self-negation. In quest of fulfillment, the desiring subject annuls its self-sufficiency and demonstrates its reliance on the object of desire. The once seemingly dependent object now appears to be independent of the subject. In light of this independence Hegel concludes that self-consciousness "can achieve satisfaction only when the object itself effects the negation within itself." The *self*-negation of the other upon which the truth of self-consciousness depends can be brought about solely by a self-conscious being. In other words, "*Self-consciousness achieves its satisfaction only in another self-consciousness*" (110; 139). This insight forms an essential link in Hegel's dialectical analysis of spirit.

"Self-consciousness," Hegel argues, "exists in and for itself when, and by the fact that, it so exists for another; that is, it exists only in being recognized" (111; 141). In order to establish the objective truth of its subjective certainty, a self-conscious subject must confront another self-conscious agent and win from that other the

---

20. Satisfaction (*Befriedigung*), for Hegel, is not the banal fulfillment of pleasure but is the subject's communion with itself in the object.

acknowledgment of the subject's own substantiality and independence. The recognition granted by the other presupposes the other's own self-negation as an autonomous individual. Since the other is also a self-conscious being, however, he is an equal partner in the struggle for recognition and seeks the same acknowledgment from the subject confronting him. Consequently, the endeavor of each self-conscious subject to affirm itself by exacting the self-negation of its other involves the effort to accomplish the negation of its own negation. In the language of speculative logic, the self-identity of the participants in the struggle for recognition is mediated by the negation of negation. Determinate subjects are bound together in an internal relation of double negativity. "Each is for the other the mean, through which each mediates itself with itself and unites with itself; and each is for itself, and for the other, an immediate being on its own account, which at the same time is such only through this mediation. They *recognize* themselves as mutually recognizing one another" (112; 143). Each subject becomes itself through relation to the other, and hence includes the other within it as constitutive of its own being. As we have seen, the relationship of double negativity which sustains identity-within-difference is the essential structure of spirit. Self-consciousness's struggle for recognition, therefore, discloses the intersubjectivity of selfhood definitive of genuine spirit. Hegel maintains that "with this, we already have before us the notion of *spirit*. What still lies ahead is for consciousness to experience what spirit is—this absolute substance which is the unity of the different independent self-consciousnesses which in their opposition enjoy perfect freedom and independence: 'I' that is 'we' and 'we' that is 'I' " (110; 140).[21]

It is obvious, however, that if carried to completion, the struggle for recognition is self-destructive. Realizing that self-consciousness presupposes life, one contestant concedes the recognition sought by the other. By so doing, the vanquished subject (*sub-jectum*) becomes a slave, and the victor the lord and master. Apparently the master has established the truth of his own independence, or his being for self. Correlatively, the slave seems to be completely dependent upon the master, or merely to possess being for another. But as always, appearances are deceptive. Since one can be a master only in relation

---

21. Observed consciousness itself is not yet fully aware of the nature and significance of this "spiritual unity." This point is reached at the conclusion of Hegel's discussion of reason and forms the transition to his analysis of ethical selfhood.

to a slave, the master is dependent upon the slave for his mastery, and the slave is, in fact, master of the master. The lord *needs* the obedient acknowledgment and servile labor of his bondsman. In himself, the master is a slave—a slave to his own slave. Initially the bondsman is unaware of his implicit mastery. In the face of the omnipotent lord, the servant is gripped by fear and trembling, and believes himself absolutely dependent upon the fortuitous grace of the other. For Hegel, this "fear of the lord is indeed the beginning of wisdom" (117-118; 148). Having confronted its own nothingness, servile consciousness "has trembled in every fibre of its being, and everything solid and stable has been shaken to its foundations. But this pure universal movement, the absolute melting-away of every-thing stable, is the simple essence of self-consciousness, absolute negativity, *pure being-for-self*, which consequently is implicit in this consciousness" (117; 148).[22] As the seemingly independent master is inherently for another, so the ostensibly dependent slave is essentially for self.[23]

The bondsman becomes aware of his independence through the discipline of labor. Unlike desire, work is not the thoroughgoing negation of objectivity, but is the subject's transformation of the object into its own self-image. The product of labor is the objectifica-tion of the self. In the labor process, the subject alienates itself from itself by positing itself as an object, and returns to itself by reappro-priating this object as its own self-objectification. Hegel explains:

> In the lord, the being-for-self is an other for the bondsman, or is only *for*
> him [i.e., is not his own]; in fear, the being-for-self is present in the
> bondsman himself; in forming the thing, he becomes aware that being-for-
> self belongs to *him*, that he himself exists essentially and actually in his own
> right. The form does not become something other than himself through
> being posited outside him; for it is precisely this shape that is his pure

---

22. Kojève correctly identifies, though he overstresses, the importance of the fear of death in the formation of self-consciousness. This suggests many interesting connections between Hegel and twentieth-century existentialists. See *Introduction to the Reading of Hegel*, esp. chap. 1. It is important to note that Hegel's purpose in this context is not to describe actual historical events, though history amply illustrates the dialectic he identifies. He intends to analyze the significance of the generic experience of struggling for recognition and of mastery and servitude for the education of the self. In a similar manner, when Hegel later considers stoicism and skepticism, he is not primarily concerned with particular philosophical movements but is interested in typical experiences essential to the formation of spirit.

23. G. A. Kelly properly emphasizes that the master-slave dialectic refers to intra- as well as to intersubjective experience. See "Notes on Hegel's 'Lordship and Bondage,'" in *Hegel: A Collection of Critical Essays*, pp. 189-217.

being-for-self, which in this externality is seen by him to be the truth. Through this rediscovery of himself by himself, the bondsman realizes that it is precisely in his work, in which he seemed to have only an alienated existence, that he acquires a mind of his own. [118-119; 149]

This self-relation in otherness reconciles subject and object, and constitutes the essential freedom of self-consciousness through which bondage is sublated. For Hegel, *die Arbeit macht frei.*

With the subject's recognition of itself in the object, a new shape of spirit emerges which, "as the infinitude of consciousness or as its own pure movement, is aware of itself as essential being, a being which *thinks* or is a free self-consciousness" (120; 151). Hegel identifies this station along the way to selfhood as stoicism. Though remaining in bondage, stoic consciousness turns inward and apprehends itself free in thought. From Hegel's perspective, however, this freedom is thoroughly abstract and completely unreal (i.e.,unrealized). It possesses no definite content and lacks the fullness of life. In a way analogous to the desiring subject, the stoic attempts to affirm independence through negative relation to otherness. But in this process, the stoic falls into self-contradiction. We have established that according to Hegel's dialectic of double negation, the effort to assert independence by negative relation to otherness negates itself and confirms dependence upon and relation to otherness. When the dialectical reversal of stoic experience becomes explicit, the calm self-certitude of stoicism gives way to the restless uncertainty of skepticism.

Realizing the contradictions implicit in stoicism, the skeptic acknowledges that the self

is in fact nothing but a purely accidental entanglement, the dizziness of a perpetually self-engendered disorder. It is itself aware of this; for it itself maintains and creates this restless confusion. Hence it also admits to it, it owns to being a wholly contingent, single, and separate consciousness—a consciousness that is *empirical*, that takes its guidance from what has no reality for it, which obeys what is for it not an *essential* being, which does those things and brings to realization what it knows has no truth for it. [124-125; 156-157]

The self-conscious subject, which recognizes its inevitable involvement in the endless flux of mundane experience, knows itself to be both independent and dependent, and thus becomes the "doubly contradictory consciousness of unchangeableness and identity, and of utter contingency and non-identity" (125; 157-158). At this stage of the self's educational sojourn, these extremes remain antithetical, forming what Hegel describes as "bifurcated, inwardly fragmented, unhappy consciousness" (126; 158).[24]

Rent by ceaseless oscillation between conflicting opposites, the subject contraposes the peace (*Friede*) of unchangeableness to its own restive (*unzufrieden*) mutability. The divided self believes the unchangeable "to be essential being [*Wesen*]; but the other, the protean changeable, it takes to be the inessential. The two are, for unhappy consciousness, alien to and estranged from one another; and because it is itself the consciousness of this contradiction, it identifies itself with the changeable consciousness, and takes itself to be the inessential" (127; 159). Unhappy consciousness represents the unchangeable as wholly other, an "absolute object" that is radically transcendent and totally beyond the particular subject. In this form of experience, the self believes the object to be the independent locus of essential truth and regards itself as dependent upon and passively determined by this alien other. To the observant eyes of the phenomenological teacher and pupil, it is clear that this "transcendent" object actually is born of the subject's own conception.[25] As in the labor process, the self alienates itself from itself, but now reifies the object and fails to reappropriate it as its own production. Unhappy *consciousness*, therefore, is the dialectical inversion of the starting point of self-consciousness and represents a return to the perspective of consciousness. Casting a backward glance from a later stage of spirit, Hegel explains that unhappy consciousness "externalized its independence and struggled to make its *being for self* into a *thing*. Through this it reverted from self-consciousness to consciousness, i.e., to the consciousness for which the object is something that merely *is*, a thing" (208; 252). Whereas self-consciousness begins its journey with the twofold conviction of its own essentiality and the inessentiality of the object, it ends by confessing its own insubstantiality and the substantiality of the object standing over against

---

24. In an important sense, Hyppolite is correct when he argues that "unhappy consciousness is the fundamental theme of the *Phenomenology*" (*Genesis and Structure*, p. 190). We have seen that the overall aim of Hegel's phenomenological pedagogy is to overcome the spiritless fragmentation of unhappy consciousness. Compare Wahl, *Le malheur de la conscience dans la philosophie de Hegel*.

25. For a discussion of the distinction between observing and observed consciousness, see above, chap. 3, 1st sec. ("Theoria"). Observed consciousness reaches the insight here anticipated by observing consciousness only after passing through the stage of religious selfhood.

it. Hegel concludes that consciousness discloses itself to be implicit self-consciousness, and self-consciousness reveals itself to be inherently consciousness. Consciousness and self-consciousness, in other words, are inseparably bound, for each contains the other within itself. The subject's consciousness of the object is its own self-consciousness, and self-consciousness presupposes consciousness of self as object. Surveying the stations so far traversed, Hegel writes: "There appeared two aspects, one after the other: one in which the essence or the true had for consciousness the determinateness of *being*, the other in which it had the determinateness of being only *for consciousness*. But the two reduced themselves to a single truth, viz. that what *is* or the in-itself [*das Ansich*] *is* only insofar as it is *for* consciousness, and what is *for* consciousness is also *in itself*" (141; 177). The explicit union of consciousness and self-consciousness in which subject and object are reconciled is reason.

Purified by the struggle between subjectivity and objectivity enacted by consciousness and self-consciousness, reason emerges "certain that it is itself reality, or that everything actual is none other than itself" (139; 176).[26] Reason, however, *forgets* the purgatorial path along which it has traveled and must, in its own way, reenact the drama whose conclusion it forms. Accordingly, rational spirit realizes itself in two distinguishable though dialectically related moments: as theoretical or observing reason, it retraces at a higher level the steps of consciousness; and as practical or active reason, it recollects the phases of self-consciousness.

Observing reason no longer supposes the domain of objectivity to be a totally alien and completely inaccessible "beyond" that remains an impenetrable thing-in-itself. The rational subject is confident that through careful observation it is possible to discover the *logos* of inorganic, organic, and human nature, and thereby to rediscover subjectivity in objectivity, or to discern self in thing. Through the long course of its development, theoretical reason finally accomplishes its aim. But the achievement of this end leads to an unexpected result. In the curious "science" of phrenology, reason reaches

---

26. This claim constitutes the heart of Hegelian idealism. It is essential to reemphasize that Hegel does not collapse subjectivity and objectivity in undifferentiated oneness. We have seen that subject and object form an identity-within-difference. Hegel explains: "But now this category or *simple* unity of self-consciousness and being possesses difference *in itself*; for its essence is just this, to be immediately self-identical in *otherness*, or in absolute difference. The difference therefore *is*, but is perfectly transparent, and a difference that at the same time is none" (142; 235).

the improbable conclusion that "the *being of spirit is a bone*" (208; 252).[27] In more general and less provocative terms, the rationality of objectivity entails the objectivity of rationality. In finding the thing to be like itself, spirit finds itself to be like a thing—thoroughly ossified. Theoretical reason, Hegel argues, "turns the actuality of spirit into a thing [*Ding*] " (208; 252). The conclusion of theoretical reason is one-sided and, taken by itself, misleading. To redress this imbalance, the self turns from the effort to discover itself to the attempt "to produce itself through its own activity" (209; 253). With this shift, theoretical reason becomes practical.

Hegel briefly summarizes the way of practical reason: "To begin with, this active reason is aware of itself merely as an individual and as such must demand and produce its reality in an other. Then, however, its consciousness having raised itself into universality, it becomes *universal* reason, and is conscious of itself as reason, as a consciousness that is already recognized in and for itself, which in its pure consciousness unites all self-consciousness" (211; 256). Through this progression, spirit completes the transition from natural to ethical selfhood. The dramatis personae of the initial stages of practical reason's sojourn represent various forms of individualism: the hedonist searching for pleasure, the frenzied reformer protesting the established order, the utopian dreamer judging the way of the world. Gradually the active individual realizes that selfhood can reach completion only within a social community formed by mutually recognizing and freely acting subjects. The goal of practical reason, Hegel contends, is "the self-consciousness that is recognized and acknowledged and which has its own self-certainty in the other free self-consciousness, and possesses its truth precisely in that other" (212; 256).

Hegel's long and involved analysis turns upon his argument for the intersubjectivity of practical reason. The active self simultaneously sublates the antithesis of subjectivity and objectivity and overcomes opposition among particular agents. When poised for action, the subject faces objective reality that represents the potential for the subject's own self-realization. In Hegel's terms, objectivity is the in-itself of subjectivity. This is manifest in the interest the object evokes in the subject. The subject, conversely, is the in-itself

---

27. The only way to make sense out of Hegel's inordinately long discussion of phrenology is by understanding the way in which the primary assertion of this pseudoscience advances the dialectical progression of his argument.

of the object. This becomes evident in the subject's action on the object. In practical activity, the subject posits itself in actuality in such a way that it also discloses the essence of the object by uncovering its latent potential. Subject and object join in a relation of mutual self-revelation in which their implicit identity-within-difference becomes explicit.[28]

In order to secure this point, Hegel analyzes action in terms of three dialectically related moments. Subjective purpose is the abstract moment of indeterminate intention (universality). Purpose is realized (i.e., made real) by means of efficacious effort in which general intention assumes specific expression (particularity). The third moment closes the circle of action by recognizing purpose accomplished and intention embodied (individuality or concrete universality). At this point, the subject realizes its unity with the object by self-consciously appropriating objectivity as the objectification of its own subjectivity. So understood, practical activity is a process of double negation in which the subject negates its abstract indeterminacy by expressing (*äussern*) itself in the object, and then negates this negation by reappropriating this other as itself. "Reason is *purposive activity*." Furthermore, Hegel explains,

> purpose [*Zweck*] is what is immediate and *at rest*, the unmoved which is also *self-moving*, and as such is subject. Its power to move, taken abstractly, is *being for self* or pure negativity. The result is the same as the beginning, only because the *beginning* is *purpose*; or the actual is the same as its notion only because the immediate, as purpose, or concretely existing actuality, is movement and unfolded becoming; but it is just this unrest that is the self; and the self is like that immediacy and simplicity of the beginning because it is the result, that which has returned into itself, the latter being similarly just the self. And the self is the identity and simplicity that relates itself to itself. [12; 22]

The analysis of Hegel's view of the logical structure of spirit leads to the suspicion that the bond joining the active subject to its determinate expression in specific action or particular experience is not a simple identification but forms a differentiated unity that preserves distinction. The self is not merely this, or any other single determination. As an active agent, the subject is immanent in, though distinguishable from, the determinations predicated of it. Thus, while Hegel admits that "the work produced is the reality which conscious-

---

28. The thrust of Hegel's argument is illuminated by the double significance of the words *object* and *objective*, which can mean aim (intention) or thing.

ness gives itself, . . . that in which the individual is explicitly for himself what he is implicitly or in himself," he insists that the subject also differentiates itself from the objectivity with which it identifies (242; 290). "The consciousness that withdraws from its work is, in fact, the universal consciousness in contrast with its work, which is *determinate* or *particular*—and it is universal because it is absolute negativity or action in this opposition" (243; 291). Hegel's point is that the self is a unified plurality and a pluralized unity in which universality and particularity are reconciled in concrete individuality.

The distinction of the subject from the product of its activity becomes clearer with the recognition that the self's self-objectification necessarily involves its being for others. The self can be for itself only insofar as it is for others. Hegel stresses that "the work [i.e., the subject's self-objectification] *is*; that is, it exists for other individualities, and is for them an alien actuality, which they must replace by their own in order to obtain through *their* action the consciousness of *their* unity with actuality" (243; 291). Action elicits counteraction. The self's realized purpose presents itself to other agents as an occasion for action by establishing a possibility through whose negation they can realize themselves. The object produced in the process of the subject's self-actualization is possessed of potentiality that necessarily remains unrealized by the acting subject. Such possibility can be actualized only through the agency of other selves. Consequently, the complete determination of the object upon which the concrete actuality of the subject depends presupposes a community of active selves engaged in common labor. Given this insight, Hegel proceeds to argue that the self can become itself only through relation to other selves. Relation to other, therefore, is mediate self-relation that is creative of determinate identity. This internal and mutually constitutive relation of self and other forms the spiritual community within which authentic selfhood is born.

Hegel defines the corporate practical activity sustained by and generative of individual spirit with the multivalent term *die Sache selbst*. Although usually translated "the fact of the matter," "the thing itself," or "the matter at hand," Royce's use of "cause" is a more accurate rendering of this problematic category.[29] Since Hegel conceives practical reason to be universal (*allgemein*), his meaning might be better expressed by the term *common cause*.[30] The

---

29. Royce, *Modern Idealism*, pp. 136 ff. Hegel's selection of the expression *die Sache* is calculated to strike a contrast with *das Ding* with which theoretical reason ends.

30. *Allgemein* can mean "common" as well as "universal."

common cause is the joint activity of a community of subjects through which each participant assumes unique individuality. The nature of the common cause, Hegel maintains, is "such that its *being* is the *action* of the *single* individual and of all individuals, and whose action is immediately for others, or is a cause . . . only as the action of *each* and *everyone*: the essence which is the essence of all beings—the spiritual essence [*das geistige Wesen*]" (251-252; 300). In other words, *die Sache selbst* is "substance permeated by individuality; the *subject* in which there is individuality just as much *qua* individual, or *qua this particular individual*, as *qua all* individuals; and it is the universal which has being only as this action of all and each, and [is] an actuality through the fact that *this particular* consciousness knows it to be its own individual actuality and the actuality of all" (252; 300). This spiritual organism, which both posits and is posited by its members, is an internally differentiated totality within which identity is created and sustained by relation to difference. Whole, as well as part, exhibits the essential structure of spirit— double negativity. Through active participation in the common cause, practical reason achieves its aim of self-recognition in otherness.

Practical reason is the culmination of spirit's journey through the stage of natural selfhood and marks the transition to the ethical form of life. Having set out from the perspective of natural consciousness in which a particular subject, isolated from all other particular subjects, confronts an alien object, separated from all other objects, spirit has developed an awareness of the thoroughly dialectical relation of subjectivity and objectivity, and has recognized the internal relations among objects and the intersubjectivity of selfhood. Passage through the first major station of the way brings the wayfaring self to "the *absolute cause*, which no longer suffers from the opposition of certainty [subjectivity] and its truth [objectivity], of universal and individual [*Einzelne*], of purpose and its reality, but whose existence is the *actuality* and *activity* of self-consciousness. This cause, therefore, is the ethical substance [*sittliche Substanz*], and consciousness of it is *ethical* consciousness" (253; 301-302).

Ethical Selfhood

With the advance to ethical selfhood, Hegel's aesthetic education explicitly enters the domain of spirit. "Reason is spirit," Hegel explains, "when its certainty of being all reality has been raised to truth, and it is conscious of itself as its own world, and of the world as itself" (263; 312). The movement through the ethical stage involves an increasingly precise articulation of the relationship between the individual self and the sociocultural totality. This multi-faceted issue represents a further dimension of the pervasive subject-object problem that runs throughout Hegel's phenomenological investigation. After examining the relation of the particular subject to both natural objects and other specific selves, Hegel turns his attention to the relationship between the subject and objective social substance. This social substance is "the absolute spiritual *unity* of the essence of individuals in their independent *actual existence*; it is an inherently universal self-consciousness which is actual in another consciousness, in such a way that this has complete independence, or is looked on as a thing, and it is precisely therein that the universal self-consciousness is aware of its *unity* with it, and only in this unity with this objective being is it self-consciousness" (212; 256). Hegel's analysis of consciousness, self-consciousness, and reason demonstrates that the awareness of social substance emerges from the evolution of antecedent forms of experience. In the process of unfolding itself, natural selfhood reveals that in itself, it is ethical. Since it is the immanent telos of the natural stage of human existence, ethical selfhood is the presupposition of prior shapes of spirit. In order to grasp Hegel's interpretation of ethical experience, it is essential to understand that he regards social substance as the shared life of a free people embodied in generally accepted cultural, moral, and religious norms, and objectified in public institutions designed to serve both personal interest and common good. The relation between the individual subject and the sociocultural totality develops dialectically. In progressing through the ethical stage, spirit passes three way stations: true or substantial spirit, self-estranged spirit, and self-certain spirit. Each station represents both a phase in the development of western history and a necessary moment in the education or formation of individual spirit.[31] Corporate and

---

31. Understood from a historical point of view, Hegel's analysis describes: (1) the ancient world of Greece and Rome, in which unified life in the polis gives way to imperial oppression; (2) the movement from medieval Catholicism and feudalism through the emergence of modern Europe, most dramatically expressed in the French Revolution; (3) significant developments in postrevolutionary Europe. Given the focus of our investigation, it is not possible to discuss the historical aspects of Hegel's argument. This ground is well covered by other commentators. (For helpful summaries see Hyppolite, *Genesis and Structure*, pp. 321 ff., and Lauer, *A Reading of Hegel's Phenomenology*, pp. 177 ff.) Our concern is to identify the importance of the typical forms of experience Hegel explores for the formation of authentic spirit. Little is lost by concentrating on this aspect of the argument, for, as our consideration of Hegel's pedagogical method and his speculative logic suggests, the education of the universal and individual subjects is actually two dimensions of a single developmental process.

personal history display an advance from the unreflective identification of self and sociocultural world, through their explicit opposition to a self-conscious reconciliation of subject and social substance.[32] Hegel insists that "everything turns upon grasping and expressing the true, not only as *substance*, but equally as *subject*" (10; 19). The accomplishment of this end concludes spirit's ethical sojourn and forms the transition to the religious stage.

In Hegel's dialectical analysis, ethical existence first appears as *Sittlichkeit*. This form of experience is characterized by the absence of opposition between self and sociocultural world, and by the subject's failure to recognize the inner complexity of social substance.[33] In this situation, the individual completely and unquestionably identifies with the customs (*Sitte*) of his people (*Volk*). The person is integrated with the social organism to such an extent that he "is not aware of being a pure individuality on his own account" (214; 259). In addition to this, the self remains ignorant of the internal differentiation of the social sphere. The social whole, Hegel emphasizes, has not yet "resolved itself into its *abstract* moments" (214; 259). Consequently the acting subject is unconcerned with drawing distinctions among contrasting laws, multiple customs, competing authorities, and different institutions. Unlike so many of his Romantic contemporaries, Hegel does not see this happy state as the complete realization of spirit. To the contrary, achievement of authentic selfhood requires the loss of simple, undifferentiated harmony and the attainment of complex, differentiated reconciliation. This end can be reached only through the cultivation of spirit's self-consciousness. If spirit is to "advance to the consciousness of what it is immediately," Hegel argues, it "must leave behind it the beauty of ethical life, and by passing through a series of shapes, attain to a knowledge of itself" (265; 315).

The immediate rapport of the subject with its social world, and undifferentiated ethical substance, both dissolve as a result of the self's own activity. Hegel contends that in the act of realizing itself, spirit "forces its moments outside of one another. *Action* separates it into substance, as well as consciousness of the substance, and divides the substance as well as consciousness" (266; 317). In this brief remark, Hegel identifies three essentially interrelated consequences

---

32. The structure of the argument at this point further illustrates the lasting influence that Schiller's *On the Aesthetic Education of Man* had on Hegel's view of personal and social history. See above, chap. 3.

33. This shape of spirit, of course, is best illustrated by life in the Greek polis. The place assigned to Sittlichkeit in the overall phenomenological progression underscores Hegel's conviction of the impossibility of recovering this primitive form of experience.

of action. First, there is the separation of subject from substance; second, the scission of the substance within itself; and third, the division of the subject within itself. Initially the action of the subject is not based upon self-conscious deliberation but is an immediate response that grows out of direct acceptance of social custom. Since the unreflective agent does not recognize that the social totality is composed of different laws governing distinguishable spheres of human life, he mistakes the rule he believes applicable to his particular situation for the law of the whole. The error of his way and the partiality of his vision are revealed through the action itself. As in the realm of interacting forces, the subject's action evokes a reaction on the part of another agent whose life is immediately ruled by an alternative law. For instance, a man's obligation to public life and human law collides with woman's devotion to family life and divine law.[34] The tragic conflict that results from the unconscious absolutizing of particularity unravels the social fabric by setting selves in opposition to one another and by creating conflict between the individual self and universal social life. On the one hand, subjects who no longer are harmoniously joined now "exist as persons for themselves, and exclude any continuity with others from the rigid unyieldingness of their atomicity" (293; 346). On the other hand, social substance, with which the self previously identified, begins to appear alien to, and externally imposed upon, subjective desire and purpose.

As a result of the separation of self and substance brought about by the activity of the particular agent, the subject becomes aware of itself as distinct from the sociocultural totality within which it had been absorbed. Such self-knowledge is mediated by the contrast between the individual and the social world. At this juncture, "personality . . . has emerged from the life of ethical substance" (290; 343). This stage of development marks a decisive moment in the formation of spirit. The previously unselfconscious subject becomes aware of itself as a unique center of knowledge and action. And yet Hegel, always the dialectician, insists that this crucial gain inevitably is accompanied by significant loss. With the disintegration of substantial spirit and the accompanying development of atomized individuality, the self apprehends itself as insubstantial (*substanzlos*) and inessential (*wesenlos*). Recognizing its alienation from essential sub-

---

34. The example is Hegel's and represents his reading of the relation between Creon and Antigone.

stance or substantial essence, the subject "is *driven back into itself*" and "ponders its inessentiality" (293; 346). In the course of its own development, substantial spirit necessarily becomes self-estranged.

Hegel describes the fundamental difference between the first two moments of the ethical stage when he points out that substantial spirit

> neither thinks of itself as *this particular exclusive self*, nor has substance the significance of a determinate existence excluded from it, with which it would have to become united only by alienating itself from itself and at the same time producing the substance itself. But the spirit whose self is an absolute discrete unit has its content confronting it as an equally hard unyielding reality, and here the world has the character of being something external, the negative of self-consciousness. This world is, however, a spiritual entity, it is in itself the interpenetration of being and individuality; its existence is the *work* of self-consciousness, but it is also an alien reality already present and given, a reality that has a being of its own and in which it does not recognize itself. [294; 347]

Spirit's progression from self-estrangement to self-certainty involves the interrelated elevation of particular individuality to universality, and the return of alien objectivity to creative subjectivity. Through this double process, substance becomes subject and subject becomes substantial.

Having suffered the dissolution of substantial spirit, the *particular* self finds itself contraposed to *universal* social substance. "Although this world [i.e., the social whole] has come into being through individuality, it is for self-consciousness immediately an alienated world that has the form of a fixed and immovable reality over against it. But at the same time, certain that this world is its substance, it [i.e., self-consciousness] sets about making it its own" (299; 352). The activity by which the subject attempts to divest itself of its particularity in order to establish unity with what it believes to be objective social substance, Hegel defines as culture—*Bildung*. Self-cultivation presupposes the sublation of idiosyncratic particularity through identification with essential universality. " 'Culture,' " as Hyppolite observes, "and 'alienation' are akin in meaning: the determinate individual cultivates himself, and forms himself to essentiality, through alienation of his natural being."[35]

_____

35. Hyppolite, *Genesis and Structure*, p. 384. Werner Marx notes that elsewhere Hegel describes education as the individual's effort "to elevate his singleness to his universal nature" (*Hegel's Phenomenology of Spirit*, p. 31).

The central figures in this act of the phenomenological spectacle are "noble [*edelmütig*] and base [*niederträchtig*] consciousness." Hegel defines these forms of life by distinguishing two typical responses of the individual to objective political and economic structures. "Base consciousness," he explains, "sees in the sovereign power [*Herrschergewalt*] a fetter and a suppression of its own *being-for-self*, and thus hates the ruler, obeys only with a secret malice, and . . . is always on the point of revolt." Noble consciousness, conversely, "sees in public authority what is in accord with itself, sees in it its own simple *essence* and the factual evidence of it, and in the service of that authority, its attitude towards it is one of actual obedience and respect" (305; 358-359). By means of "the heroism of service," noble consciousness attempts to express its belief in the essentiality of social substance concretely embodied in common political and economic life. The individual so disposed sacrifices his own particular ends to the universal aims of society. In actualizing itself, however, each of these forms of consciousness discloses its inherent identity with its opposite. In itself, noble consciousness is base, and ignoble consciousness is implicitly noble. Noble consciousness's overt self-denial is really covert self-assertion that unravels, rather than binds, the social fabric. While noble consciousness "behaves as if it were *conforming* to the universal power, the truth about it is rather that in its service it retains its own being-for-self, and that in the genuine renunciation of its personality, it actually is the sublation and complete sundering [*Zerreissen*] of the universal substance" (312; 366). The loyal service of noble consciousness seems to promote the good of society as a whole but really seeks personal advantage at the expense of the well-being of others.

Hegel identifies a related consequence of this "devoted" labor. Although noble consciousness avows the essentiality of objective political and economic structures, its activity exposes the insubstantiality of social substance and uncovers the substantiality of active subjectivity. In a manner reminiscent of the master-slave dialectic, Hegel argues that since the

> spirit proper of state power consists in its obtaining actuality and nourishment from the sacrifice of action and thought by noble consciousness, it is an *independence that is self-alienated*; noble consciousness, the extreme of *being-for-self*, receives back the other extreme, that of *actual universality*. . . ; the power of the state *has passed* to noble consciousness. In it, that

power is first made truly effective; in the *being-for-self* of noble consciousness it ceases to be the *inert essence* which it appeared to be as the extreme of abstract being-in-itself. Considered as it is *in itself*, state power that is reflected into itself, or has become spirit, simply means that it has become a moment of self-consciousness, i.e., it exists only as *sublated*. [311-312; 366]

Deceptively self-assertive and passionately devoted to what, in fact, is inessential, noble consciousness evidently is base. Base consciousness, by contrast, demonstrates its intrinsic nobility by resisting obedience to insubstantial social structures and by rejecting spurious public authority. Upon the basis of this dialectical reversal Hegel concludes that "the consciousness of each of these moments, the consciousness judged as noble and as base, are [sic] rather in their truth just as much the reverse of what these characterizations are supposed to be; the noble consciousness is base and depraved, just as the depraved consciousness changes round into the nobility that characterizes the most highly developed freedom of self-consciousness" (317; 371).

When the self becomes aware of the implicit identity of noble and base consciousness, it recognizes its inherently self-contradictory nature and confesses the inner discord plaguing its existence. "Lacerated consciousness [*das zerrissene Bewusstsein*]" emerges as the "consciousness of the inversion [*Verkehrung*], and, moreover, of the absolute perversion [*Verkehrung*]" (317; 372). Like unhappy consciousness, lacerated consciousness remains impaled upon unreconciled opposites. This inward dismemberment marks the outer limit of spirit's self-estrangement. Hegel describes two closely related, though seemingly opposite, responses to lacerated consciousness: faith and pure insight. These forms of experience represent respectively the negative and the positive sides of the contradiction into which spirit has fallen.

The faithful subject attempts to escape the dissolute world of culture by fleeing to a transcendent realm of perfection, undisturbed by antagonism and discord. This strategy ultimately fails to resolve the existential dilemma of estranged spirit and actually constitutes a further dimension of self-alienation. The ostensibly wholly other sphere in which fulfillment is believed to be possible remains inseparably bound to and conditioned by the fragmented world of lacerated consciousness. As a matter of fact, the believer's heaven is nothing more than an imaginative projection created by a dialectical inversion of the world within which self-alienated spirit suffers.[36] In faith, according to Hegel,

> the world of this spirit dis-integrates into two. The first is the world of reality or of its self-alienation; but the other is that which spirit, rising above the first, constructs for itself in the aether of pure consciousness. This second world, standing in opposition to estrangement, is, for that very reason, not free from it; on the contrary, it is really only the other form of that estrangement which consists precisely in being conscious of the two different worlds, and which embraces both. [296-297; 350]

Enlightened pure insight sees through faithful dissemblance.[37] Insisting that spirit's journey through the world of culture finally discloses the insubstantiality of objectivity and the substantiality of subjectivity, pure insight asserts that the believer's consciousness of the object of belief is really the self's consciousness of itself. "As faith is the tranquil pure *consciousness* of spirit as *essence*, so pure insight is the *self*-consciousness of spirit as essence; it therefore knows essence, not as being, but as absolute *self*. Thus it seeks to sublate every kind of independence other than that of self-consciousness, whether it be the independence of what is actual, or of what possesses being in itself, and to make it into the *notion*" (326; 382). This insight reveals culture (Bildung) to be the product of the self's education or cultivation (Bildung) of itself, rather than an independent objective domain.[38] The movement from the initial stage of self-estranged spirit to insight repeats at a higher level the progression from consciousness to self-consciousness. The insightful person assumes a utilitarian attitude in which objectivity, particularly the objectivity of social substance, is essentially being for an other, that is, being for the self.[39] In pure insight, "self-consciousness sees right

---

36. This argument anticipates analyses of religious awareness developed by left-wing Hegelians such as Feuerbach and Marx. Unlike his followers, however, Hegel subtly distinguishes religion from faith. The former is not subject to the same critique as the latter. The basis of this distinction will become clearer in the next section. For a helpful account of Hegel's relation to Marx on this and related issues see Louis Dupre, *The Philosophical Foundations of Marxism* (New York: Harcourt, Brace and World, 1966).

37. Hegel interprets the Enlightenment in terms of the conflict between superstitious faith and pure insight.

38. At this stage, self-consciousness's interpretation of the relation between active subjectivity and objective social structures is still undialectical. The belief in the immovable objectivity of social substance gives way to the equally one-sided view of the substantiality of subjectivity and the accidental character of the social totality. Hegel's analysis attempts to overcome the imbalance of both of these perspectives.

39. This interpretation of utilitarianism recalls Hegel's analysis of desire. Utilitarian spirit is distinguished from desiring spirit by increased self-consciousness and by the social nature of the intended object.

into [*ein-sieht*] the object, and this insight [*Einsicht*] contains the *true* essence of the object (which is to be something that is penetrated [by consciousness], or to be for an other)" (355; 413).

With the achievement of pure insight, spirit returns to itself from its self-alienation. Hegel stresses that "this insight, as the self which *apprehends* itself, completes [the stage of] culture; it apprehends nothing but self and everything as self, i.e., it *comprehends* everything, abolishes the objectivity of things, and converts all being *in itself* into a being *for itself*" (296; 349). The immanent dialectical progression of self-estranged spirit further illustrates the coimplication of opposites. Having begun with the conviction of the essentiality of universal social substance and the inessentiality of its particular subjectivity, the self discovers the essentiality and universality of its own subjectivity. For the self that has reached this station of the way, "the world is simply its will, and this is a universal will" (356-357; 415). Stated otherwise: "Substance is essentially subject"—"spirit's own possession." This revolution of consciousness initially can find only negative expression, and thus remains incomplete. When spirit realizes its absolute freedom, it "stands on the very edge of this innermost abyss, of this bottomless depth, in which all stability and substance have vanished" (315; 369-370). While substantial spirit entails the loss of subjectivity in objectivity (i.e., of the particular self in universal social substance), insightful spirit dissolves objectivity in subjectivity (i.e., absorbs social substance in universal self-consciousness). In both cases, difference collapses into undifferentiated identity, thereby rendering unrealizable the identity-within-difference definitive of authentic spirit.

Hegel suggests the implications of this stage of spirit's educational journey when he writes: "This movement is thus the interaction of consciousness with itself in which it lets nothing break loose to become a *free object* standing over against it. It follows from this that it cannot achieve anything positive, either universal works of language or of actuality, either of laws and general institutions of *conscious* freedom, or of deeds and works of a freedom that *wills* them" (358; 417). The "terrifying" consequences of this type of experience become apparent when it is recognized that since spirit's absolute freedom "can produce neither a positive work nor deed, there is left for it merely *negative* action; it is only the *fury* of destruction" (359; 418). Spirit attempts to affirm its independent self-identity and absolute freedom by the thoroughgoing negation of otherness. The concrete expression of this supposed self-sufficiency

and negative freedom is revolutionary activity that seeks to disman-
tle, but is unable to reconstruct, social structures. In Hegel's eyes,
this shape of selfhood is simply *"abstract self-consciousness*, which
annihilates all difference within itself. It is as such that it is objective
to itself; the *terror* of death is the vision of its negative being" (361;
419).[40] It is obvious, however, that like the desiring subject and the
assertive master, this form of spirit finally negates itself in its attempted self-affirmation. Sustained by the essential structure of
double negativity, the struggle to establish independence of and
freedom from otherness by negation of difference reveals the internal
relation to otherness and the necessary coinherence of difference.
What the subject previously had regarded as inessential turns out to
be essential to its own being. Hegel claims that "absolute freedom as
pure self-identity of the universal will has within it *negation*; but this
means that it contains *difference* in general, and this again it develops
as an *actual* difference" (361; 420). Social substance that has passed
into the subject must reemerge as the necessary *other* in which the
subject recognizes itself. Hegel unfolds the progression to the final
realization of spirit in his analysis of the third moment of ethical
selfhood.

Weaned from the security of substantiality, spirit is left to roam
the strange and uncertain world of culture. At the end of this
sojourn, spirit returns from estrangement to find certainty of itself:
self-alienated spirit becomes moral.[41] The last phase of the ethical
stage of the journey to selfhood takes up into itself the two antecedent moments from which it results. From the moral point of view,

> substance is just as *immediate* as it is absolutely *mediated*. . . . It is *immedi-
> ate*, like the ethical [*sittliche*] consciousness which knows its duty and does
> it, and is bound up as with its own nature. . . . It is *absolute mediation*, like
> the consciousness that cultivates itself, and the consciousness that believes;
> for it is essentially the movement of the self to sublate the abstraction of
> *immediate determinate existence*, and to become itself a universal—and yet
> to do so neither by the pure alienation and laceration of itself and of
> actuality, nor by fleeing from it. Rather, it is *immediately present* to itself
> in its substance, for this is its knowledge, is the intuited pure certainty of

---

40. Quite clearly, Hegel here is thinking of the degeneration of the French Revolution
into the Reign of Terror.
41. Hegel distinguishes Moralität from Sittlichkeit upon the basis of the self-
consciousness of the subject present in the former but absent in the latter. It is essential to
note that in the analysis of self-certain spirit, Hegel first is concerned with moral *consciousness* and only subsequently considers moral *activity*.

itself; and just *this immediacy* which is its own actuality is all actuality for
the immediate is *being* itself, and it is *being* in general, or *all* being. [364;
423-424]

Not only immediacy and mediation but also subject and substance,
and particularity and universality, meet explicitly in moral consciousness. Substance is apprehended as pure universal duty that no longer
is viewed as externally or heteronomously imposed but is believed to
be inherent in the consciousness of the autonomous moral subject. [42]
At this station of the way, "self-consciousness knows duty to be
absolute essence. It is bound only by duty, and this substance is its
own pure consciousness, for which duty cannot receive the form of
something alien" (365; 424). Particularity, by contrast, refers to the
natural being of the subject, manifest most clearly in sensuous
inclination. Since pure universal duty is regarded as essential and
particular natural inclination as inessential, the self appears to be a
contradictory coincidence of opposites—both identical with and different from essentiality, and identical with and different from inessentiality. "From this determination is developed a moral view of the
world which consists in the relation between the absoluteness of
morality and the absoluteness of nature. This relation is based, on
the one hand, on the complete *indifference* and independence of
nature towards moral purposes and activity, and, on the other hand,
on the consciousness of duty alone as what is essential, and of nature
as completely dependent and inessential" (365-366; 425). Morality
inwardizes (*erinnert sich*, i.e., both recollects and internalizes) the
struggle enacted by self-alienated spirit in the sphere of culture. The
moral subject seeks self-reconciliation by attempting to sublate particularity in universality. Through the cultivation of duty, the self
tries to elevate natural inclination to moral ideality, and, correlatively, to give moral ideality actual expression.

But the moral view of the world finally founders upon its own
presuppositions. The starting point and continuing assumption of the

---

42. Although here, as elsewhere, Hegel is describing a typical form of experience in
the education of the self, it is evident that the paradigm of this stage is Kant's moral
philosophy. While the overall phenomenological investigation begins with puzzles posed by
Kant's first *Critique*, Hegel's interpretation of ethical experience concludes with a discussion
of the Kantian practical philosophy. Resolution of these contradictions, anticipated in the
third *Critique* and suggested by post-Kantian philosophers, leads to the completion of
spirit's journey. As our consideration of Hegel's view of his age has shown, Kant and his
followers simultaneously typify the problem and point to the solution of the modern
experience of spiritlessness. See above, chap. 2, 1st sec. ("Fragmentation"), 3d and 4th
subsecs. ("The Reflective Philosophy of Subjectivity" and " 'The Need of the Time' ").

moral perspective is that contraries are merely antithetical or are completely indifferent. Morality, nonetheless, requires the mediation of opposites such as duty and desire, substance and subject, and universality and particularity. In an effort to escape self-contradiction, moral consciousness resorts to a series of postulates designed to reunite the opposites between which the self is suspended. The moral subject represents (*stellt vor*) the reconciliation of opposites in the form of a "kingdom [Reich] of ends" which is constituted by free selves engaged in effective moral activity. The perpetual conflict of obligation and inclination, however, infinitely delays the coming of this kingdom and makes the telos of moral activity an end that can be approached only asymptotically. Hope for the realization of the moral commonwealth, therefore, entails two further assumptions. In the first place, the possibility of achieving the conformity of duty and desire presupposes the immortality of the individual agent. Second, the accomplishment of moral purpose requires a divine sovereign who can effectively mediate universal duty and particular circumstance. To overcome the confusion created by the tension between pure duty or abstract moral law and the self's concrete situation, the individual postulates a consciousness "in which universality and particularity are absolutely one." Within the moral Weltanschauung, God is envisioned as a transcendent moral legislator, "a master [*Herr*] and ruler of the world, who brings about the harmony of morality and happiness, and at the same time sanctifies duties in their multiplicity" (370; 430).

These postulates, however, prove unable to resolve the aporias created by moral consciousness, and further entangle wayfaring spirit in self-contradiction. Though intended to preserve moral selfhood from disintegrating in unreconciled opposites and to safeguard the possibility of accomplishing duty, these postulates really negate the moral actuality of the subject and make the fulfillment of the moral law impossible. This development converts morality into its opposite, immorality. By representing moral perfection as lying in an unrealized kingdom of ends and by imagining the harmony of universality and particularity as a holy being beyond reality, the subject simultaneously renders morality nonactual and its own actuality nonmoral. On the one hand, both the moral legislator and the moral commonwealth exist only in the mind of the actor. Their being "is a *representation*," a mere "*imagining* [*Vorstellen*]." The concrete self, on the other hand, cannot effect the lasting mediation of opposites constitutive of moral actuality. "This self-consciousness," Hegel contends,

> is thus left with the lack of harmony between the consciousness of duty and actuality, and indeed of its own actuality. Accordingly, the proposition now runs: "There is no *moral, perfect, actual self-consciousness;*" and, since the moral sphere is at all, only insofar as it is perfect, for duty is the *pure* unadulterated being in itself, and morality consists only in conformity to this pure in itself—the second proposition runs: "There is no moral actuality." [373; 433]

Continually aware of the inward strife between what is and what ought to be and always sensitive to the schism of reality and ideality, moral consciousness admits its imperfection in the very act of longing for perfection. Hegel concisely summarizes the conclusion to which the moral view of the world is driven: "Morality, then, in the moral consciousness is unfulfilled or imperfect; this is now what is put forward. But it is the essence of morality to be only the *perfectly pure*; incomplete or imperfect morality is thus impure, or is immorality" (380; 440).

Hegel insists, however, that moral consciousness misrepresents moral activity—word distorts deed, and deed belies word. Conscientious (*gewissenhafte*) action unmasks the dissemblance (*Verstellung*) of the moral imagination (*Vorstellung*), and restores spirit's self-certainty (*Selbst-Gewissheit*). "Action, therefore, in fact directly fulfills what was asserted could not take place, what was supposed to be only a postulate, merely a beyond [*Jenseits*]. Consciousness expresses through its deed that it is not in earnest in making its postulate, because the meaning of the action is really this, to make into a present reality what was not supposed to exist in the present" (375; 435). With the shift from moral awareness to moral activity, the contradiction of the moral attitude is resolved. Opposites that had been regarded as essentially antithetical now appear to be internally related. Hegel identifies conscience as the structure of awareness that brings together contraries otherwise held apart. In conscience (*Gewissen*), the self, in its particularity, is certain (*gewiss*) of its identity with universal moral law or absolute essence. Since duty no longer is purely abstract but is concretely embodied, conscientious action sublates both the nonactuality of morality and the immorality of actual subjectivity. Substance and subject as well as universality and particularity join in an identity-within-difference to form the concrete individuality of self-certain spirit. In Hegel's view, "this self of conscience" is "spirit that is directly aware of itself as absolute truth and being" (384; 445).

The truth of conscience's certainty of its universality and absoluteness presupposes recognition and acknowledgment by other selves. "Conscience has not abandoned pure duty or the *abstract in itself*; duty is the essential moment relating itself as *universality*, to another. Conscience is the common or mutual [*gemeinschaftlich*] element of the two self-consciousnesses, and this element is the substance in which the act has an *enduring reality*, the moment of being *recognized* and *acknowledged* by the other" (388; 450). Personal conviction inevitably draws the conscientious subject into a struggle for recognition which reenacts the contest for self-consciousness at the level of moral awareness. Conscience (*con-scientia*) is, by definition, a knowing with, which is grounded in the mutual recognition and universal acknowledgment of a community of free moral subjects. The essential intersubjectivity of conscience assumes "self-consciousness which is recognized and acknowledged, and which has its own self-certainty in the other free self-consciousness, and possesses its truth precisely in that other" (212; 256). This interpretation of the conscientious actor brings Hegel's analysis of spirit full circle. The reconciliation of consciousness and self-consciousness in the concrete universality of self-conscious social substance makes explicit the implications of the common cause (*die Sache selbst*) in which reason culminated and with which ethical selfhood began. This important point can be clarified by a more detailed consideration of the contest for recognition in which the conscientious subject necessarily engages.

The initial phase of this struggle is marked by the individual's failure to win the recognition of opposing moral agents. Though the subject is certain of the universal validity of its act, self-objectification in particular deed always retains "the blemish of determinacy" and consequently goes unacknowledged by other conscientious actors. Instead of recognizing the individual's action as a concrete expression of universal ethical purpose, others tend to view it as inexpugnably contingent, arbitrary, and idiosyncratic. From the perspective of the conscientious subject, it is the others' response that appears tainted by particularity and devoid of universality. In a final effort to convince (*überzeugen*) others of its moral probity and hence to gain desired recognition, the self verbally affirms the conviction (*Überzeugung*) of the essentiality and substantiality of its deed.

"The content of the language of conscience is the *self that knows itself as essential being*. This alone is what it expresses, and this expression is the true actuality of the act, and the validity of the action. Consciousness declares its *conviction*; it is in this conviction alone that the action is a duty; it is valid as duty solely through the conviction being expressed" (396; 459). Other selves, however, remain unconvinced by the assurances of the self-proclaimed conscientious subject. The recognition that "what is valid for that self-consciousness is not the *action* as a *determinate existence*, but the *conviction*, made actual in language, that it is a duty," confirms the suspicion of the inessentiality of the act and underscores the perceived disparity between expressed intention and actual deed.

Increasingly aware of "the opposition between what it is for itself and what it is for others," the conscientious subject turns from active engagement with other selves to the contemplation of its own inner purity. This introversion of consciousness creates a new shape of spirit which Hegel labels "the beautiful soul."[43] Having forsaken resolute participation in the outward world, the beautiful soul

> lacks the power of externalization or alienation [*Entäusserung*], the power to make itself into a thing, and to endure being. It lives in dread of defiling the splendour of its inwardness by action and determinate existence; and, in order to preserve the purity of its heart, it flees from contact with actuality, and persists in its self-willed powerlessness to renounce its self, which is reduced to the extreme of ultimate abstraction, and to give itself substantiality, or to transform its thought into being and put its trust in the absolute difference. [399-400; 462-463]

When a person is unwilling to express conviction in action, his life is reduced to mere judging, a judging of himself and of others. The subject attempts to reassure itself of its own purity by judging other selves impure. The beautiful soul steadfastly insists that its rejection at the hands of others is the result of selfish motives that arise from an unwillingness to renounce private interest for common weal. From the viewpoint of the judged self, the judging beautiful soul

---

43. While moral consciousness is most adequately represented by Kant's practical philosophy, the beautiful soul is best illustrated by romantic literati such as the Schlegels and Tieck, by a philosopher like Jacobi, and by a theologian such as Schleiermacher. For an account of Hegel's discussion of these figures in their historical context, and of his view of the relationship of their thought to the rise of speculative philosophy, see chap. 2, 1st sec. ("Fragmentation"), 3d and 4th subsecs. ("The Reflective Philosophy of Subjectivity" and " 'The Need of the Time' ").

appears not only hypocritical but actually evil. Still involved in moral struggle, the condemned subject insists that "duty without deeds is utterly meaningless." For the active self, the beautiful soul represents "the hypocrisy that wants its judging to be taken for an *actual* deed, and instead of proving its rectitude by actions, does so by uttering fine sentiments. Its nature, then, is altogether the same as that which is reproached with making duty a mere matter of words" (403; 466). Furthermore, the judgment by which the beautiful soul attempts to confirm its purity really affirms the evil that attaches to its character and its actions. Through "hardhearted judgment [*Ur-teil*]," the self separates itself from, and opposes itself to, an other subject. Rather than establishing the beautiful soul's universal validity and the inadequacy of other particular subjects, unacknowledged judgment reveals the persistent particularity of the judging self which is a product of abiding opposition to otherness.

Hegel is persuaded that the conflict between self and other can be overcome only in an act of *mutual* recognition. As a result of their interrelationship, each subject gradually acknowledges the tenability of the viewpoint of the other, and thereby comes to recognize *itself* in the other. The judging self admits the insufficiency of words without deeds, and the judged self accepts the inevitable partiality of its acts. This self-awareness, which is mediated by relation to other, involves both the confession of the self's guilt and the forgiveness of the opposing subject. The twofold deed of confession and forgiveness brings about the concrete actualization of spirit toward which the wayfaring self has ineluctably been moving. As we have seen, spirit is "*pure* self-recognition in absolute otherness"—"it is that which *relates itself to itself* and is *determinate*, it is *other-being* and *being-for-self*, and in this determinateness, or in its self-externalization, abides within itself." Through forgiveness, self and other emerge from the suffering of separation and opposition to discover their identity-within-difference. This reconciliation is the true life of spirit.[44] Hegel concludes: "The word of reconciliation [*das Wort der Versöhnung*] is concretely existing spirit, which beholds the pure

---

44. In his *Early Theological Writings*, Hegel asserts that "genuine love excludes all oppositions" (304; 379). His mature view of love, which is based upon his understanding of forgiveness, is considerably more sophisticated. By the time of the *Phenomenology*, Hegel recognizes that true love endures opposition and overcomes separation without destroying difference. This is the spiritual love revealed in Christ, and is ultimately divine. In short, Hegel believes that "God is love, and anyone who lives in love lives in God, and God lives in him" (1 John 4:16).

knowledge of itself as *universal* essence, in its opposite, in the pure knowledge of itself as absolute *individuality* in itself—a mutual recognition which is *absolute* spirit" (408; 471).[45]

For Hegel, "spirit is all the greater, the greater the opposition from which it has returned to itself" (206; 250). Having lost immediate harmony created by direct identification with social substance, spirit is forced to wander through the alien world of culture (Bildung). Although painful, this sojourn proves to have educational value (*Bildungswert*). The subject overcomes self-estrangement and achieves self-certainty that is mediated by internal relation to otherness. This identity-within-difference of self and other is the end (both *Zweck* and *Ende*) of the ethical stage and the beginning of the religious station of the way. As natural selfhood, through immanent dialectical development, passes over into ethical selfhood, so the ethical subject discloses itself to be inherently religious. "The reconciling *Yea*, in which the two I's let go of their oppositional *existence*, is the *concrete existence* of the *I* which has distended into dualism, and therein remains identical with itself, and, in its complete externalization [Entäusserung] and opposite, possesses the certainty of itself: it is God in the midst [*mitten*] of those who know themselves in the form of pure knowledge" (409; 472).

Religious Selfhood

At the penultimate stage of Hegel's aesthetic education, it becomes clear that the journey to selfhood is actually the *Itinerarium Mentis in Deum*.[46] Overcoming the fragmentation characteristic of spiritlessness requires the reconciliation of the human subject and the divine object, or the reintegration of spirit and absolute spirit. The authenticity toward which the pilgrim has been steadily progressing is unattainable apart from the reunion of self and God. With the mediation of this last opposition, the wayfarer returns home.

Hegel defines religion in general as "the self-consciousness of spirit" (410; 473). In religion, spirit represents (*stellt vor*) itself to

---

45. It appears that the double entendre of *das Wort* is intended. It is also important to notice the etymological relation between *die Versöhnung* and *der Sohn*.

46. This is the title of St. Bonaventure's famous mystical tract. My analysis of Hegel's position should suggest his deep affinities with this mystical strand of western theology. At one point, Hegel goes so far as to claim that "speculative truth . . . means very much the same as what, in special connection with religious consciousness and its content, used to be called mysticism" (*Lesser Logic*, par. 82; 8:178). For an elaboration of this aspect of Hegel's thought see Mark C. Taylor, "*Itinerarium Mentis in Deum*: Hegel's Proofs of God's Existence."

itself. Passage through the religious stage results in an increasingly adequate self-representation of spirit, and correspondingly, the incremental reconciliation of the human subject and the divine object. The goal of this progressive revelation is spirit's self-recognition in otherness. "Since spirit lives in the difference of its consciousness and its self-consciousness," Hegel submits, "the aim of the movement [through various religious configurations] is to sublate this primary distinction and to give the object of consciousness the form of self-consciousness" (417; 481-482). The stations along the way of religious selfhood reenact the dialectical development of previous moments of experience. Natural, artistic, and revealed religion represent religious awareness in the respective forms of consciousness, self-consciousness, and reason. The first shape of religious life is

> *immediate*, and therefore *natural religion*. In this, spirit knows itself as its object in a natural or immediate shape. The second actuality, however, is necessarily that in which spirit knows itself in the shape of *sublated naturalness*, or of *the self*. This, therefore, is *artistic religion*, for the shape raises itself to the form of the self through the creative activity of the self by which this [subject] beholds in its object its act or the self. Finally, the *third* actuality sublates the one-sidedness of the first two; the self is just as much an *immediacy* as the *immediacy* is the *self*. In the first, spirit in general is in the form of consciousness, and in the second, in that of self-consciousness, and in the third it is in the form of the unity of both. It has the shape of *being in and for itself*, and when it is thus represented as it is in and for itself, this is *revealed religion*. [416; 480][47]

The distinctive feature of natural religion is spirit's consciousness of itself in the shape of a natural object. The three forms of experience in which natural religion realizes itself and passes over into artistic religion reproduce at a spiritual level the moments of sense-certainty, perception, and understanding through which consciousness becomes self-consciousness. As in the immediate consciousness of sense-certainty, the religious subject initially regards its object as essential and its own self as inessential. The devotee first represents absolute spirit as omnipotent substance. "In virtue of this determination, this 'shape' is the pure, all-embracing and all-pervad-

---

47. Each of these three primary shapes of religious selfhood is typical of a particular historical religious tradition: Natural religion is characteristic of the East, especially of Persia, India, and Egypt; artistic religion is represented in Greece; and revealed religion is realized in Christianity. In this context, as in the *Phenomenology* as a whole, Hegel is less concerned with the details of the historical development of religion than with the logos of religious experience as it moves from less complete to more complete forms of expression.

ing *essential light* of sunrise, which preserves itself in its formless substantiality" (419; 484). At this stage of the religious quest, particular selves lack substance, "have no will of their own," and consequently become "merely superfluous messengers" of divine substance's "power, visions of its majesty [*Herrlichkeit*], and voices of its praise" (419-420;484). The utter indeterminacy of the religious object is overcome when the divine no longer is imagined to be shapeless substance but is pictured as definable natural form. In totemism, the believing subject divinizes a particular species of plant or animal life. Although the totem serves as a source of tribal and personal identity, natural form cannot fully represent spiritual reality.

The shortcomings of natural religion are surmounted when the religious person ceases to identify absolute spirit with a given shape of natural life and starts to represent the divine in an object that bears the impress of spiritual activity. Natural religion begins to give way to artistic (*künstlerisch*) religion when the natural object of veneration is replaced by an artificial (*künstlich*) object. Like the unknowing activity of the understanding self, the action of the religious subject on the religious object is at first unconscious. "Spirit, thus, here appears as an *artificer*, and its action through which it produces itself as object, but without having yet grasped the thought of itself, is an instinctive work, like the building of a honeycomb by bees" (421; 487). This form of religious experience is essentially transitional. Repeating the dialectical development from consciousness to self-consciousness, the instinctive artisan inevitably becomes the intentional artist.

In artistic religion, the creative subject becomes self-conscious.[48] The different forms of artistic religiosity illustrate an ever closer correlation between the active subject and the object of belief. As we have noted, the objective artistic "shape raises itself to the form of the self through the creative activity of consciousness, by which this [subject] beholds in its object its act or the self" (416; 480). The conclusion of this movement is an identification of subject and object in which divine substance is taken up into the creative activity of the human subject. In Hegel's dramatic words: "This form [of experience] is the night in which substance was betrayed and made itself into subject" (426; 492).

---

48. In his mature system, Hegel separates his analysis of art from his interpretation of religion.

Hegel argues that "the first work of art, as immediate, is abstract and individual [*einzeln*]. As for itself, it has to move away from this immediate and objective mode towards self-consciousness, while self-consciousness, on the other hand, in the cult seeks to sublate the difference by which it distinguishes itself at first from its spirit, and by so doing to produce a work of art which is in its own self animate" (427; 493). The original object of devotion in artistic religion is a concrete statue created by the deliberate activity of a human agent. Although this object represents "nature transfigured by thought," it remains abstract in two important senses. In the first place, the inanimate figure of plastic art is unable to picture the animation of spirit. The repose of bronze or marble cannot capture the movement and unrest vital to spirit. Second, statuesque stasis fails to re-present artistic activity. The work of art does not satisfactorily express the work of the artist. "The [artistic] work is not, therefore, actually an inspired work; it is a *whole* only together with its becoming. The common element in a work of art, viz. that it is begotten in consciousness and is made by human hands, is the moment of the notion existing as notion, which stands in contrast to the work" (429; 495). Though he has objectified self in thing, the artist finds it difficult to rediscover subject in substance. When creation confronts creator as alien, "the artist learns that in his work, he did not produce a being *like himself*" (429; 495).

The movement from the abstract to the living work of art involves the interrelated vitalization of the object of belief, and identification of believing subject and believed substance. The simultaneous sublation of abstract divine being and abstract human being is effected in cultic activity. Through this process, divine substance and human subject directly identify.

> Man thus puts himself in the place of the statue as the shape that has been raised and fashioned for perfectly free *movement*, just as the statue is perfectly free *repose*. . . . He is an inspired and living work of art which matches strength with its beauty; and on him is bestowed, as a reward for his strength, the decoration with which the statue was honored, and the honor of being, in place of the god in stone, the highest bodily representation among his people of their essence. [438; 505]

While this type of religious experience marks a considerable advance over lifeless abstraction, "living corporeality" is in the end an incomplete representation of spirit. Whether in the form of frenzied cultic animation or mere bodily presence of a human deemed divine, the living work of art lacks the inwardness of genuine spiritual being. Spirit, consequently, remains dumb, inarticulate, unexpressed— wordless.

Spirit manifest as word creates the spiritual work of art, which forms the culmination of artistic and the prefiguration of revealed religion. "Language," Hegel maintains, "is the perfect element in which inwardness is just as outward as outwardness is inward" (439; 505). The self undergoing the forms of experience described in the final stage of artistic religion repeats at a higher level antecedent moments of religious life. In the words of the epic poet, the classical tragedian, and the ancient comedian, creative subjectivity becomes transparently objective to itself. The movement through the epic, tragic, and comic stations of the way results in the gradual return of substance to subject. The universal divine object discloses its inherent identity with the particular human self. At the beginning of this progression, the creative artist is absorbed in his work; poet is lost in poem. The minstrel attempts to efface himself in order to sing the praises of the gods he believes essential and the heroes he seeks to immortalize. This bard "is the individual and actual spirit from whom, as a subject of this world, it [the world] is produced and by whom it is borne. His pathos is not the deafening power of nature, but is Mnemosyne, recollection and a gradually developed inward- ness, the remembrance of essence that formerly was directly present. He is the organ that vanishes in its content; what counts is not his own self, but his Muse, his universal song" (440-441; 507). Through immanent dialectical development, this form of experience turns into its opposite—comedy.[49]

The human subject's increasing appreciation of its own powers of creativity is inversely proportional to its recognition of the divine object's creative power. In comic awareness, creative subjectivity becomes self-certain. The comedian insists that "the self is absolute being" (453; 521). The gods, by contrast, are mere "clouds, an evanescent mist," "imaginary representations."[50] The wordless body of the living work of art becomes the bodiless word of the spiritual work of art. "Comedy has, therefore, above all, the aspect that actual self-consciousness exhibits itself as the fate of the gods" (450; 516).

---

49. The middle term joining the extremes of epic and comedy is tragedy. We have already considered the main features of Hegel's interpretation of tragedy in our discussion of the dissolution of Sittlichkeit.

50. Hegel's passing reference to "clouds" is an allusion to Aristophanes' comedy entitled *Clouds*.

Hegel summarizes the way to this conclusion when he points out that in artistic religion, the

> incarnation of the divine being starts from the statue which wears only the *outer* shape of the self, the *inwardness*, the self's activity, falling outside of it. But in the cult the two sides [divine and human] have become one; and in the result of artistic religion, this unity in its completion has even gone right over at the same time to the extreme of the self. In spirit that is completely certain of itself in the individuality of consciousness, all essentiality is absorbed. [453; 521]

As the necessary propaedeutic to the Christian form of experience, comic awareness represents the precise inversion of the initial form of natural religion. No longer convinced of the essentiality of the divine object and the inessentiality of the human subject, the comic asserts the essentiality of human subjectivity and the inessentiality of divine substance. According to Hegel,

> what this self-consciousness beholds is that whatever assumes the form of essentiality over against it, is instead dissolved in it—in its thinking, its existence, and its action—and is at its mercy. It is the return of everything universal into the certainty of itself which, in consequence, is this complete loss of fear and of essential being on the part of all that is alien. This self-certainty is a state of spiritual well-being and repose such as is not to be found anywhere outside of this comedy. [452-453; 520]

But such professed self-assurance is, after all, *comic*. The truly comical character of comic awareness becomes explicit with the recognition of its intrinsically self-contradictory nature.[51] The apparent happy consciousness of the comic subject, is, in fact, unhappy.[52] "Unhappy consciousness," Hegel argues,

> constitutes the reverse side of the fulfillment of comic consciousness that is perfectly happy within itself. Into this latter, all divine being returns, or it is the complete *alienation* [*Entäusserung*] of *substance*. Unhappy consciousness, on the other hand, is, conversely, the tragic fate of the certainty of self that aims to be absolute. It is the consciousness of the loss of all *essential* being in this *certainty of itself*, and of the loss even of this knowledge about itself—the loss of substance as well as of the self, it is the grief which expresses itself in the hard saying that "God is dead." [454-455; 523]

---

51. It is precisely this dialectical twist that atheistic and humanistic interpretations of Hegel's position such as those developed by Kojève, Lukács, and Marcuse fail to appreciate. Consequently, the joke is really on them.

52. From the perspective of observing consciousness it would not be incorrect to describe the whole phenomenological progression prior to absolute knowledge as a "comedy of errors."

As we have seen, however, in Hegel's dialectical vision, negation and affirmation are inseparable. The self-certainty of comedy negates itself in the act of affirming itself, and thus generates the uncertainty of unhappy consciousness. Unhappy consciousness, in turn, contains its negation within itself, and therefore points to the negation of negation in which subjectivity's self-certainty is represented as objectively true in the form of determinate self-conscious spirit. In order to resolve the twofold abstraction of wordless body and bodiless word, the Word must become flesh: spirit embodied and body enspirited, giving rise to the unity-in-difference of substance and subject, the reintegration of consciousness and self-consciousness.[53] Unhappy consciousness, Hegel claims, "stands impatiently expectant round the birthplace of spirit as it becomes self-consciousness." "The infinite sorrow of grief and longing" is the "birth pang" of spirit becoming conscious of itself as self-conscious spirit (456-457). Having risen in the East, the sun sets in the West, creating the dark night in which substance is betrayed and makes itself into subject, arising as Son, the true light of the world.

Revealed religion "overcomes the one-sidedness" of natural and artistic religion by uniting the consciousness and self-consciousness of spirit. At this decisive station of the way, spirit at last is conscious of itself as concretely existing self-conscious spirit. Spirit is thoroughly actualized when absolute spirit becomes self-conscious and self-conscious spirit becomes absolute—"it is only spirit that gives birth to spirit." The rational comprehension and appropriation of the reconciliation of opposites represented in revealed religion brings the full realization of spirit which completes the journey to selfhood.

In the eyes of the believer, "God is immediately and sensuously beheld as a self, as an actual individual man; only so *is* God self-consciousness" (459; 528). Hegel maintains that "this incarnation of the divine being, or the fact that it essentially and immediately has the shape of self-consciousness, is the simple content of the absolute religion. In this religion, the divine being is known as spirit, or this religion is the consciousness of the divine being that it is spirit" (459; 528). In the consummate moment of religious experience, divine substance and human subject are reconciled in the self-conscious identity-within-difference of God and man. Subject and substance,

---

53. Although historically demonstrable, the necessity to which Hegel is pointing lies in the internal development of religious consciousness. For a discussion of the historical dimension of Hegel's analysis, see above, chap. 4, 1st sec. ("Mediation"), 1st subsec. ("The Fullness of Time: The Present").

self and other, humanity and divinity are internally related in such a way that each becomes itself through the other, and therefore each includes difference within itself as constitutive of its own identity. This dialectical mediation of opposites forms genuine spirit, "for spirit," Hegel insists, is "the knowledge of oneself in the externalization of oneself; the being that is the movement of retaining its self-identity in its otherness" (459; 528). The dialectical activity definitive of spirit involves the inseparable, though distinguishable, moments of subjectifying substantiality and substantializing subjectivity. "Spirit has in it two sides," Hegel explains:

> one is this, that *substance* alienates itself from itself and becomes self-consciousness; the other is the converse, that *self-consciousness* alienates itself from itself and gives itself the nature of a thing, or makes itself into the universal self. Both sides have in this way encountered each other, and through this encounter their true union arises. The externalization of substance, its growth into self-consciousness, expresses the transition into the opposite . . . ; in other words, that substance is *in itself* self-consciousness. Conversely, the externalization of self-consciousness expresses this, that it is *in itself* the universal being or essence, or—since the self is pure being-for-self which in its opposite remains at home with itself—that it is just because substance is self-consciousness *for the self* that it is spirit. [457; 525]

In the original form of revealed religion, the nature of authentic selfhood or the true structure of spirit is manifest in sensuous immediacy. Although apparently concrete, this revelation is actually abstract. The object of devotion, the Mediator in whom the most extreme opposites between which the self is torn are reconciled, is regarded as separate from and other than the devoted subject. "Spirit, in the immediacy of self-consciousness, is this *particular* self-consciousness, the opposite of *universal* self-consciousness. It is an exclusive one which has the still unresolved form of a *sensuous other* for the consciousness for which it is immediately present" (461; 530). Like all immediacy, this abstraction can be overcome only through the sublation of the isolated particularity of the sensuous "here and now" in concrete universality, and the reintegration of bifurcated subjectivity and objectivity in a mutually formative relationship.[54] In other words, the immediacy of the truth embodied in

---

54. So understood, the unfolding of the final stage of spirit's journey repeats the dialectical progression of the very first station of the way.

the Mediator must be mediated.[55] This mediation arises through the universalization of the particular self-consciousness of the sensuous other brought about by the believing subject's recognition that in its consciousness of the believed object, it is likewise self-conscious. This inversion (*Umkehrung*) of consciousness into self-consciousness is the "conversion [*Umkehrung*] of consciousness" which creates the awareness of "absolute reconciliation," "the consciousness of the reconciliation óf man and God." For Hegel, "Christ, man as man, in whom the unity of God and man has appeared, has in his death, and his history generally, himself presented the eternal history of spirit—a history which every man has to accomplish in himself in order to exist as spirit, or to become a child of God, a citizen of his kingdom."[56] The reconciliation of opposites incarnate in the Mediator reveals the inherent or implicit nature of all individuals. The truth of the particular divine man is appropriated as the universal truth of selfhood when the subject becomes aware of the identity-within-difference of *its own self* and the divine. This redemptive self-consciousness is thoroughly intersubjective, for it is mediated by the Mediator.

This station of the way brings the pilgrim to the foot of the cross. The wayfaring self discovers that the *Itinerarium Mentis in Deum* is at the same time the *Descensus Dei in Mundum*. The ascent of the self and the descent of God are two sides of one complex process: the divinization of the human is the humanization of the divine, and the humanization of the divine is the divinization of the human; the infinitizing of the finite is the finitizing of the infinite, and the finitizing of the infinite is the infinitizing of the finite; the eternalizing of the temporal is the temporalizing of the eternal, and the temporalizing of the eternal is the eternalizing of the temporal. The particular human subject now grasps itself as a finite, temporal moment in the universal, infinite, and eternal life of the divine. God, by implication, is no longer regarded as wholly other or radically transcendent, but is apprehended as active subjectivity that realizes

---

55. As our consideration of Hegel's Christology has shown, this mediation is an extraordinarily complex process that involves not only religious but also historical and philosophical factors. There is no need to repeat the previous analysis in this context. Our present concern is to understand the place of revealed religion in Hegel's overall phenomenological investigation and thus to see its significance for the realization of authentic selfhood. For further discussion of this part of Hegel's argument see chap. 4, 1st sec. ("Mediation").

56. *Philosophy of History*, p. 328; 12:397.

itself through the eternal drama of Incarnation, Crucifixion, and Resurrection enacted in the concrete natural-historical process. God and self are joined in a relation of coimplication in which each becomes itself through the other. The reunion of divinity and humanity, infinitude and finitude, and eternity and time reconciles the final opposites sundering selfhood.

Journey's End

The telos of Hegel's aesthetic education is absolute knowledge— "spirit that knows itself as spirit." In the introduction to the *Phenomenology*, Hegel explains that "the *goal* is as necessarily fixed for knowledge as the serial progression; it is the point where knowledge no longer needs to go beyond itself, where knowledge finds itself, where notion corresponds to object and object to notion. Hence the progress toward this goal is also unhalting, and short of it no satisfaction is to be found at any of the stations on the way" (51; 69). Absolute knowledge, therefore, sublates the estrangement of subject and object which is the distinctive feature of spiritlessness, and realizes the reconciliation of opposites which forms authentic selfhood. The malaise of spiritlessness can be cured only by the mediation of all the opposites fragmenting the self. As the final station of the way, absolute knowledge is the self's complete awareness of itself as the identity-within-difference of subjectivity and objectivity, reality and ideality, actuality and possibility, necessity and freedom, particularity and universality, individuality and sociality, appearance and essence, finitude and infinitude, time and eternity, humanity and divinity. "To know opposition in unity, and unity in opposition," Hegel asserts, "this is *absolute knowledge*; and science is the knowledge of this unity in its whole development by means of itself."[57]

"The *goal*, absolute knowledge, or spirit that knows itself as spirit, has for its way the recollection of the spirits as they are in themselves and as they complete the organization of their kingdom" (493; 564). Way and goal, means and end, however, are not separable but are implicitly identical. Goal *is* way and end *is* means. "The way to science is already *science*, and hence, in virtue of its content, is the science of the *experience* [*Erfahrung*] *of consciousness*" (56; 74).[58]

---

57. *History of Philosophy* 3:551; 20:460.
58. It is important to recall the etymological relation between *Erfahrung* and *fahren*, which means "to travel."

The content of absolute knowledge, in fine, is nothing less than the complete aesthetic education that Hegel elaborates in the *Phenomenology*.[59] Absolute knowledge arises through the rational recollection and reflective inwardization of the entire course of experience through which spirit forms, cultivates, or educates itself. From the perspective of journey's end, the wayfarer recognizes the necessity of the way stations. Hegel's aesthetic education "is the circle that returns into itself, the circle that presupposes its beginning and reaches it only at the end" (488; 559). Coleridge might well have been describing Hegel's *Bildungsroman* when he wrote: "The common end of all *narrative* . . . is to make those events, which in real or imagined History move in a *straight* Line assume . . . a *circular* motion—the snake with its Tail in its Mouth."[60] Hegel's educational therapy cannot be otherwise, for he is convinced that the true "is the process of its own becoming, the circle that assumes its end as aim, having its end also as its beginning, and only by being worked out to its end is it actual" (10; 20). End is beginning truly comprehended. Beginning, conversely, is implicit end. Omega reveals Alpha, and Genesis harbors Revelation. Teacher and pupil together affirm:

> We shall not cease from exploration
> And the end of all our exploring
> Will be to arrive where we started
> And know the place for the first time.[61]

Absolute knowledge completes the pilgrimage from spiritlessness to spirit by recognizing that "the rose in the cross of the present" stems from the union of union and nonunion, the identity of identity and

---

59. For this reason Hegel devotes most of the last chapter of the *Phenomenology* to a summary of the argument he has developed in the text as a whole. Charles Taylor makes a similar point when he suggests: "Absolute knowledge, one might be tempted then to say, is simply the whole content of the *PhG*; the last chapter has meaning only as a recapitulation of the rest" (*Hegel*, p. 214). These remarks should not obscure the distinction between the *Phenomenology* and the complete system. Having sublated the opposition between subjectivity and objectivity in the *Phenomenology* Hegel presupposes their identity-in-difference in the system. The system, therefore, does not seek to demonstrate the unity of subject and object but elaborates the implications of their interrelation. In the introduction to the *Science of Logic*, Hegel writes: "The notion of pure science and its deduction is therefore presupposed in the present work insofar as the *Phenomenology of Spirit* is nothing other than the deduction of it. Absolute knowing is the *truth* of every mode of consciousness because, as the course of the *Phenomenology* showed, it is only in absolute knowing that the separation of the *object* from the *certainty of itself* is completely eliminated: truth is now equated with certainty and this certainty with truth" (49; 43).

60. Letter to Joseph Cottle, 1815. Quoted in Abrams, *Natural Supernaturalism*, p. 141.

61. T. S. Eliot, *Little Gidding*, p. 220.

difference. This is the realization of reconciliation *in the midst of estrangement*. Spirit "wins its truth only when *in* utter dismemberment, it finds itself" (19; 30). Spiritlessness overcome, dismemberment healed by remembering.

Here ends Hegel's journey to selfhood. Wayfaring over, the prodigal returns. "I am at home in the world," Hegel confesses, "when I know it."[62] In Hegel's pedagogy, knowledge is salvific,

> for thinking is the meeting of the self with *itself* in the other. This is a *deliverance* which is not the flight of abstraction, but consists in what is actual having itself not as something else, but as its own being and creation in the other actuality with which it is bound together by the force of necessity. As existing for self, this deliverance is called *I*; as unfolded to its totality, it is *free spirit*; as feeling, it is *love*; as enjoyment, it is *blessedness* [*Seligkeit*].[63]

Rational knowledge cures spiritlessness and restores the unity of man.[64] No longer "a sordid solitary thing, Mid countless brethren with a lonely heart," the individual becomes "The whole one Self! Self, that no alien knows!... This is Faith! This the Messiah's destined victory!"[65] By inwardizing the apocalyptic drama represented in the God-Man, aesthetic education consummates the wedding of Heilsgeschichte and Bildungsgeschichte which gives birth to authentic selfhood.

STAGES ON LIFE'S WAY

Writing in his Journal in 1846, Kierkegaard admits: "My contemporaries cannot grasp the design of my writing. *Either-Or* divided into four parts or six parts and published separately over six years would have been all right. But that each essay in *Either-Or* is a part

---

62. *Philosophy of Right*. Elsewhere Hegel stresses that "freedom is to be at home with yourself in your other" (*Lesser Logic*, par. 24; 8:84.). As I have suggested, the progression from spiritlessness to spirit can also be viewed as the movement from bondage and heteronomy to freedom and autonomy.

63. *Lesser Logic*, par. 159; 8:305-306. The German *Seligkeit*, like its Danish equivalent, *Salighed*, which is so important for Kierkegaard, can be translated "blessedness," "happiness," or "salvation." "Blessedness" seems to be the word that best captures the intention of both authors.

64. It should now be apparent that the ambiguity of the word *man* in this phrase is appropriate for Hegel's purposes. The term, of course, can refer to the individual or to the race as a whole. Upon the basis of his interpretation of the intersubjectivity of spirit, Hegel insists that individual reconciliation and racial reunification are inseparable.

65. Samuel Taylor Coleridge, "Religious Musings," lines 146 ff., in *The Poems of Coleridge* (New York: John Lane, n.d.).

of a whole, and then the whole of *Either-Or* a part of a whole: that, after all, think my bourgeois contemporaries, is enough to drive one daft."[66] The passing of years has done little to clarify this situation. For many "disciples at second hand," the coherence of Kierkegaard's pseudonymous writings remains as obscure as the overall structure of Hegel's *Phenomenology*. The problem of discerning the unity in the multiplicity of Kierkegaard's writings is, in some ways, more difficult than discovering the thread that ties together Hegel's complex argument. Kierkegaard develops his phenomenology of spirit in a series of diverse works written over an extended period and published under different pseudonyms. Each pseudonymous author and character represents a distinctive form of life that seems to stand in no *necessary* relation to other points of view. Nevertheless, Kierkegaard insists that these widely contrasting works actually "constitute stages in the realization of an idea I had conceived."[67]

The recognition of Kierkegaard's pedagogical purpose suggests an angle of vision from which the coherence of the pseudonymous writings becomes apparent. We have seen that Kierkegaard, like Hegel, attempts to provide a cure for spiritlessness by developing a therapeutic aesthetic education that will lead the reader from inauthentic to authentic selfhood. Kierkegaard's understanding of the nature of spirit requires him to employ an educational method that constantly respects the integrity of the individual. Like Hegel, Kierkegaard decides that spiritlessness can be overcome most effectively by the depiction of alternative forms of life that provide the occasion for the reader's self-examination and self-judgment. The personae of the pseudonymous writings form the cast of characters with which Kierkegaard stages his version of the journey to selfhood. Kierkegaard's pedagogy also begins with the modern experience of self-estrangement. According to Kierkegaard, however, spiritlessness involves the dissipation of concrete human existence brought about by a relaxation of the spiritual tensions characteristic of authentic selfhood. From this perspective, Hegel's attempted cure seems to feed the disease. Through "the abrogation of the passionate disjunction of subjectivity and objectivity," speculative philosophy obscures

---

66. *Journals and Papers*, 5095; 7-1:A 118.
67. *Postscript*, p. 240; 7:228. Johannes Climacus makes this remark in the context of his survey of the pseudonymous production. Despite the wealth of secondary literature devoted to the pseudonymous writings, Kierkegaard's own commentary in the *Postscript* remains one of the most reliable guides. See "A Glance at a Contemporary Effort in Danish Literature," pp. 225 ff.; 7:211 ff.

the decisive opposition between self and other.[68] "The systematic idea," Kierkegaard explains, "is the subject-object, the oneness of thought and being. Existence, on the other hand, is their separation. It does not by any means follow that existence is thoughtless; but it has brought about, and brings about, a separation [*Spatierer*] between subject and object, thought and being."[69] As should be evident by now, Kierkegaard, like Hegel, does not limit the problem of the relation between subjectivity and objectivity to the narrow confines of epistemology. This multifaceted issue has not only philosophical but also psychological, social, cultural, and religious dimensions. Kierkegaard's fulfillment of his mission as a "reformer," whose "whole life is an epigram to make men aware," is impossible apart from the redefinition of the full range of opposites and the rearticulation of the qualitative distinctions lost in the spiritlessness of the age. Kierkegaard's radical cure attempts to overcome the dissipation of concrete existence by decisively distinguishing subjectivity and objectivity. In place of Hegel's rational mediation of internally related contraries, Kierkegaard proposes the qualitative discrimination of mutually exclusive opposites. From Kierkegaard's point of view, the movement from spiritlessness to spirit involves an incremental differentiation of self and other which culminates in spirit's awareness of itself as a unique coincidentia oppositorum, constituted by the individual's passionate decision.

While important differences separate these alternative spiritual pilgrimages, the Kierkegaardian stages on life's way and the Hegelian stations of the way share significant similarities.[70] For Kierkegaard, as for Hegel, the journey to selfhood passes through a natural, an ethical, and a religious stage.[71] In his consideration of natural

---

68. *Two Ages*, p. 103, 8:96.

69. *Postscript* p. 112; 7:101.

70. The parallel is deliberate. In formulating his conception of the stages of existence Kierkegaard draws freely on Hegel's analysis of the development of selfhood elaborated in the *Phenomenology* and the *Philosophy of Spirit*. His understanding of Hegel's position on this point is heavily dependent on the Hegelian psychology of Karl Rosenkranz presented in *Psychologie oder die Wissenschaft von subjektivem Geist*. The only other commentator to have suggested the similarity between Kierkegaard's and Hegel's stages of development is Gregor Malantschuk (*Kierkegaard's Thought*, pp. 150 ff.). Malantschuk, however is more interested in attempting to demonstrate the way in which Kierkegaard's dialectic can subsume Hegel's position than in a careful comparison of these two points of view. In addition to this, Malantschuk's contention that Kierkegaard's pseudonymous writings include an "abstract line" (*Philosophical Fragments*, *Postscript*, and *The Concept of Dread*) and a "concrete line" (*Either-Or, Repetition, Fear and Trembling*, and *Stages on Life's Way*) obscures the overall coherence of Kierkegaard's position and finally falls prey to the dangers of reductive genetic analysis.

71. We shall see that Kierkegaard regards the religious stage as the end of the self's sojourn. Consequently his existential dialectic has no equivalent to Hegel's absolute knowledge. Kierkegaard sees this as a crucial difference between his position and that of Hegel.

selfhood, Kierkegaard examines the progression from the condition of nondifferentiation between self and other to the situation in which the subject is aware of itself as distinct from the natural and social totality within which it had been immersed. The ethical stage of existence explores the self's effort to define itself through deliberate decisions that concretely embody universal moral principles in the life of the particular conscientious actor. Religious selfhood, expressed in what Kierkegaard calls religion A, universal religiosity, and religion B, Christianity, represents the full realization of spirit in which the temporal self, isolated from all other selves, freely defines its unique individuality. By developing a dialogue among themselves and with the reader, Kierkegaard's pseudonymous personae reveal the characteristics, the tensions, and the contradictior.s definitive of contrasting forms of life. The stages Kierkegaard identifies are dialectically related in such a way that each successive stage displaces its predecessor from a position of centrality, yet preserves prior determinants of experience in a relativized form. As opposed to Hegel's phenomenology of spirit, in which different moments are necessarily related by immanent dialectical development Kierkegaard's stages of existence represent distinct forms of selfhood that can be realized only through the contingent resolution of the individual's free will. Kierkegaard stresses that "from the abstract point of view there is no decisive conflict between the standpoints, because abstraction precisely removes that in which the decision inheres: *the existing subject*. But in spite of this consideration, the immanent transition [of speculative philosophy] is a chimera, is imaginary, as if it were possible for one standpoint necessarily to determine itself into an other; for the category of transition is itself a breach of immanence, a *leap*."[72] This leap, Kierkegaard insists, "is neither more nor less than the most decisive protest against the inverse procedure of the Method."[73]

Natural Selfhood

Kierkegaard probes the outstanding aspects of natural selfhood in his description of aesthetic existence. He defines the initial stage of the journey to selfhood by distinguishing two types of aestheticism: immediacy and reflection. The common feature of these apparently antithetical forms of experience is the absence of genuine decision. This lack of free resolution results either from unreflective immer-

---

72. *Postscript*, p. 262; 7:253.
73. Ibid., p. 96; 7:85. "The Method," of course, is Hegel's speculative mediation of opposites.

sion in sensuous inclination and social life or from dispassionate absorption in abstract reflection. Since Kierkegaard regards spirit as the synthesis of opposites created and sustained by the individual's free decision, aesthetic existence represents the most extreme form of spiritlessness. Apart from personal decision, the self remains dissipated—lost in indeterminacy and plagued by inauthenticity. For Kierkegaard, "the more consciousness, the more self; the more consciousness, the more will; and the more will, the more self."[74]

Generally conceived, Kierkegaard's phenomenology of spirit charts the subject's movement from undifferentiated identification with its environment, through increasing differentiation from otherness, to complete individuation in which the self becomes a concrete individual, eternally responsible for itself. Kierkegaard explains that in contrast with Hegel, whose analysis "has the conflict between the *I* and the world as the first stage," his own interpretation of spirit begins with the situation in which the individual "has not separated himself from his surroundings ('me')."[75] Despite this important difference, Kierkegaard follows Hegel in describing the most rudimentary form of natural consciousness as "immediacy." Moreover, Kierkegaard agrees with Hegel's contention that immediacy is "indeterminate" or "indefinite." In an ironic reversal of Hegel's position, however, Kierkegaard argues that such indeterminateness is not the result of the abstract isolation of atomistic particulars but is a function of the *lack* of concrete particularity created by the nondifferentiation of self and other.[76] Kierkegaard maintains that in immediacy, the self "is in immediate connection with the other [*i umiddelbar Sammenhæng med det Andet*], and thus is within the compass of the temporal and worldly and has only the illusory appearance of possessing in it something eternal."[77] The nondifferentiation of self and other typical of immediacy involves the subject's direct identification with its natural and social world. Unconscious of its unique individuality and personal responsibility, the self is ruled by natural desire and social custom.[78] This condition "of

---

74. *Sickness unto Death*, p. 162; 11:142.

75. *Journals and Papers*, 4398; 1:C 126.

76. This disagreement is rooted in their alternative views of the genesis of concrete identity. While Hegel sees identity as arising from internal relation with otherness, Kierkegaard regards concrete determination as a function of difference from and opposition to otherness.

77. *Sickness unto Death*, p. 184; 11:163.

78. The progression Kierkegaard charts in his account of the aesthetic stage parallels the view of the emergence of consciousness from its natural matrix which Hegel develops in his discussion of "anthropology" in the *Philosophy of Spirit*, and the analysis of the

not being conscious of oneself as spirit is despair, which is spiritless."[79]

At the beginning of its sojourn, the self, by virtue of complete immersion in the sensuous "here and now," is "in immediate unity with its natural condition." In an essay entitled "The Immediate Stages of the Erotic," Kierkegaard develops a careful analysis of desire, by means of an imaginative interpretation of Mozart's *Figaro*, *The Magic Flute*, and *Don Juan*. Sounding quite Hegelian, Kierkegaard describes the three stages of sensual immediacy:

> The different stages taken together constitute the immediate stage, and from this we may perceive that the individual stages are rather a revelation of a predicate, so that all the predicates steer a course toward the wealth of the last stage, since this is the real stage. The other stages have no independent existence; for themselves, they are only representations [*Forestillingen*], and from this one may see their accidental character as over against the last stage.[80]

The movement through the immediate stages of the erotic is marked by the progressive differentiation of desire and its object. In the first moment of immediacy, there is virtually no distinction between subject and object. Carried along in a stream of sensuality, the self is "not a single individual" but is thoroughly indefinite—a ceaseless flux of indeterminate sensation. In this primal form of experience, the object of desire has not yet emerged. Desire and desired, subject and object, self and other, remain bound in undifferentiated oneness.

At the second stage of immediacy, desire, in the strict sense of the word, awakens. Kierkegaard points out that "only when the object exists does the desire exist, only when the desire exists does the object exist; desire and its object are twins, neither of which is born a fraction of an instant before the other."[81] The development of desire creates the original bifurcation of self and other. This weaning of subject from object begins the long labor that eventually gives birth to individual selfhood. The "movement of the sensuous,

---

subject's differentiation from its social milieu elaborated in the consideration of the dissolution of Sittlichkeit in the *Phenomenology*. Hegel's formative influence on the ideas that lie behind the interpretation of aesthetic experience is especially evident in the account of Socrates which Kierkegaard presents in *The Concept of Irony* (see esp. pp. 241 ff.; 13:242 ff.).

79. *Sickness unto Death*, p. 178; 11:157.

80. *Either-Or*, 1:73; 1:56. Compare the Danish *Forestilling* and the German *Vorstellung*.

81. Ibid., p. 78; 1:61. The word Kierkegaard uses for desire, *Attraaen* (cf. *Attraktion*), suggests the presupposition of the separation of subject and object. Only what is differentiated can experience the power of attraction.

this earthquake, splits desire and its object infinitely asunder for the moment; but as the moving principle appears a moment separating, so it again reveals itself as wishing to unite the separated. The result of this separation is that desire is torn from its substantial repose within itself, and consequently the object no longer falls under the qualifications of substantiality, but disperses itself in a manifold." [82] While this moment represents a dawning awareness of the difference between self and other, objectivity is still completely indefinite. The object of desire is not specific but is a manifold of sensible intuition. In the final form of immediacy, this manifold is consolidated into a concrete object. Here desire is fully present. Again echoing Hegel, Kierkegaard gives what is at once a brief summary of the relationship among the three stages of immediacy and a clear characterization of the third stage:

> The contradiction in the first stage lay in the fact that desire could acquire no object, but without having desired was in possession of its object, and therefore could not reach the point of desiring. In the second stage, the object appears in its manifold, but since desire seeks its object in this manifold, it still has, in a deeper sense, no object; it is not yet posited as desire. In *Don Juan*, on the other hand, desire is absolutely determined as desire; it is, in an intensive and extensive sense, the immediate unity of the two preceding stages. The first stage desired the one ideally, the second stage desired the particular under the determination of the manifold; the third stage is a unity of these two. Desire has its absolute object in the particular, it desires the particular absolutely.[83]

It is essential to recognize that even at the final stage of immediacy, the self has not arrived at consciousness. The distinction between subject and object is affective rather than cognitive. In addition to this, the self is not yet an autonomous individual who stands in relation to the particular object but is a restless embodiment of purely natural force. Although desire has been distinguished from its object, neither self-consciousness nor self-determination through free decision has developed. Kierkegaard suggests that the leading character in Mozart's *Don Juan* ideally represents the life of sensual immediacy. Don Juan is "the sensuous erotic genius" who is nothing less than "flesh incarnate, or the inspiration of the flesh by

---

82. Ibid., pp. 78-79; 1:62. Kierkegaard's argument represents a remarkable anticipation of modern theories of personality development. I have considered this matter in more detail elsewhere: see *Kierkegaard's Pseudonymous Authorship*, pp. 127 ff., and "Psychoanalytic Dimensions of Kierkegaard's View of Selfhood."

83. *Either-Or*, 1:83; 1:66-67.

the spirit of the flesh."[84] Kierkegaard underscores the lack of individuation in immediacy when he writes: "If I imagine a particular individual, if I see him [Don Juan] or hear him speak, then it becomes comic to imagine that he has seduced 1,003; for as soon as he is regarded as a particular individual, the accent falls in quite another place. When, on the contrary, he is interpreted in music, then I do not have a particular individual, but I have the power of nature."[85] When sunk in sensual immediacy, selfhood is dissipated in the transient moods and multiple pleasures of the effervescent moment.

From Kierkegaard's perspective, such dissolute selfhood is not only typical of sensuous eroticism but characteristic of its apparent opposite—the decorous life of the complacent bourgeois citizen. While the sensuous erotic genius is a reflex of natural forces, the crowd-man is directly identified with the social matrix and is completely ruled by predetermined social custom. Though more refined than the pleasure-seeking dilettante, the crowd-man is no less immediate. He "finds it too venturesome a thing to be himself, far easier and safer to be like the others, to become an imitation, a number in the crowd."[86] Such a person might gain the world, but "by being entirely finitized, by having become instead of a self, a number, just one more man, one more repetition of the everlasting *Einerlei*," he loses his own self.[87] In this form of existence, the subject is dissipated in the objective life of society.

The spiritlessness of immediacy can be described in alternative terms. At the beginning of the first stage on life's way, the self is not a creative synthesis of the opposites ingredient in authentic spirit. To the contrary, the subject is stuck in finitude, reality, necessity, and time, and is unaware of infinitude, ideality, possibility, and eternity. Hopelessly entangled in the natural-social environment, the self is a prisoner of its own facticity. The chains of immediacy can be broken only by the emergence of reflection.

In a manner reminiscent of Hegel's interpretation of the transition from the immediacy of sense-certainty to the mediacy of per-

---

84. Ibid., pp. 86, 87; 1:69, 70.

85. Ibid., p. 91; 1:73-74.

86. *Sickness unto Death*, p. 167; 11:147. Since we have considered Kierkegaard's interpretation of the spiritlessness of the crowd-man in the context of our analysis of social leveling, it is unnecessary to describe this shape of experience in detail at this point. See above, chap. 2, 1st sec. ("Fragmentation"), 1st subsec. ("Society and Politics: Disintegrating *Reich*").

87. Ibid., p. 166; 11:146.

ception, Kierkegaard contends that "what annuls immediacy is language."[88] However, over against Hegel's emphasis on the propensity of language to sublate abstract particularity, Kierkegaard stresses the capacity of language to negate indeterminateness by articulating determinate distinctions. "Language," he argues, "involves reflexion, and cannot, therefore, express the immediate. Reflexion destroys the immediate, and hence it is impossible to express the musical in language; but this apparent poverty of language is precisely its wealth. The immediate is really the indeterminate, and thus language cannot apprehend it; but the fact that it is indeterminate is not its perfection, but an imperfection."[89] Reflexion, as we have seen elsewhere, is the cognitive activity through which contraries are identified and opposites are defined.[90] Kierkegaard maintains that "the determinations of reflexion are always *dichotomous*, e.g. ideality and reality, soul and body, God and world, . . . and so on."[91] The discriminating discernment of reflexion negates the utter indefiniteness of immediacy by defining contrasts and differentiating opposites. When understood in this way, reflexion is the necessary presupposition of consciousness and self-consciousness. Consciousness entails the precise articulation of the difference between subject and object which is only vaguely felt in the last moment of immediacy. Through reflexion, the self further differentiates itself from its world. "Here there is, in fact, a certain degree of self-reflexion, and so a certain degree of observation of oneself. With this certain degree of self-reflexion begins the act of discrimination [*Udsondrings-Akt*] by which the self becomes aware of itself as something essentially different from the environment, from externalities and their effect upon it."[92] For Kierkegaard, reflexion not only draws a distinction between person and world but also enables the self to distinguish itself from itself. Consciousness, turned back upon itself, becomes

---

88. *De Omnibus Dubitandum Est*, p. 149; *Papirer*, 4:146.

89. *Either-Or* 1:68-69; 1:52. Kierkegaard believes that only music can capture the sheer immediacy of sensuality. This point is based upon his appropriation of Hegel's interpretation of the inseparability of artistic form and content. Nowhere is Hegel's influence on Kierkegaard's theory of aesthetics more evident than in "The Immediate Stages of the Erotic." For a very useful discussion of Hegel's aesthetics see Charles Karelis, introduction to *Hegel's Introduction to Aesthetics*, trans. T. M. Knox (New York: Oxford University Press, 1979). The best account of Hegel's influence on Kierkegaard's view of art is Crites's introduction to his translation of *Crisis in the Life of an Actress*.

90. See chap. 5, 2d sec. ("Coincidence: Either-Or"), 2d subsec. ("Spiritual Tensions").

91. *De Omnibus Dubitandum Est*, p. 150; 4:147.

92. *Sickness unto Death*, p. 188; 11:166.

self-consciousness.[93] When reflexion becomes self-reflexive, the subject cognitively differentiates its reality and ideality, necessity and possibility, and finitude and infinitude. No longer lost in the fleeting present, the wayfarer becomes aware of the past from which he has come and the future toward which he can proceed. Even though reflexion effectively draws distinctions, it is unable to synthesize differentiated opposites. In overcoming the spiritlessness of immediacy, reflexion creates the possibility of another form of inauthentic selfhood—reflective aesthetic existence.[94]

Standing between the sensuality of immediacy and the decisiveness of ethical existence, the reflective aesthete is absorbed in the infinity of abstract reflection. As a self-conscious human being, the subject is no longer simply an extension of natural force and social custom. But since the person still has not become a self-determining agent, he is not yet a concrete individual. This stage on life's way represents an "imagination existence [*Phantasie-Existents*]," which, Kierkegaard explains, is "an existential possibility tending toward existence, and brought so close to it that you feel how every moment is wasted as long as it has not come to a decision." The reflective aesthete "keeps existence away by the most subtle of all deceptions, by thinking; he has thought everything possible, and yet he has not existed at all."[95]

Within Kierkegaard's phenomenology of spirit, reflection is the dialectical inversion of immediacy. Having distinguished himself from his surroundings and from given determinants in his own being, the reflective aesthete "becomes intoxicated, as it were, by the infinity of possibles," and seeks "to cancel all actuality and set in its place an actuality that is no actuality."[96] Whereas immediacy is the despair of finitude and necessity due to the lack of infinitude and possibility, reflection is the despair of infinitude and possibility due to the lack of finitude and necessity. These contrasting forms of experience are two variations of the same malaise, spiritlessness. Neither the imme-

---

93. Kierkegaard's phenomenological progression, therefore, is formally, though not substantively, parallel to Hegel's: from sensual immediacy, through consciousness, to self-consciousness.

94. Here as elsewhere, it is important to note the distinction between reflexion and reflection. It will be recalled that while reflexion differentiates previously undifferentiated opposites, reflection abstracts from concrete existence by dispassionate speculation. See above, chap. 5, 2d sec. ("Coincidence: Either-Or"), 2d subsec. ("Spiritual Tensions").

95. *Postscript*, p. 226; 7:213. Kierkegaard uses the German word *Phantasie*, which is a cognate of *phantastisk*.

96. *The Concept of Irony*, pp. 279, 306; 13:335, 361.

diate nor the reflective aesthete achieves the genuine coincidence of opposites definitive of authentic selfhood. Describing the shortcomings of reflective aestheticism, Kierkegaard writes: "That the self looks so and so in the possibility of itself is only half truth; for in the possibility of itself the self is still far from itself, or only half itself. So the question is how the necessity of the self determines it more precisely. . . . Instead of summoning back possibility into necessity one runs after possibility—and at last he cannot find his way back to himself."[97]

Kierkegaard elaborates his interpretation of the reflective form of aesthetic existence by developing a vignette of a "reflective seducer." In "The Seducer's Diary," Kierkegaard presents a figure named Johannes, who is the reflective counterpart of the sensuous erotic genius. In contrast with Don Juan's sensual frenzy, which overpowers 1,003 women, Johannes devotes himself to an imaginative romantic intrigue whose sole aim is the seduction of a single maiden—Cordelia Wahl.[98] What engages Johannes even more than anticipated erotic satisfaction is the sheer pleasure created by the free play of his imagination. Fascinated by the plurality of possibilities, Johannes attempts to create interesting situations he can observe with detachment. "Life for him is a drama, and what engrosses him is the ingenious unfolding of this drama. He is himself a spectator, even when performing some act."[99] Preoccupied with reflection and unwilling to take definitive action, Johannes remains an enigma to himself and to others. By means of agile mind and quick wit, he translates every decisive either-or into an equivocal both-and. The ethical Judge Wilhelm explains to his young friend: "For the polemical result which resounds in all your songs of triumph over existence has a strange resemblance to the pet theory of the newer philosophy, that the principle of contradiction is dissolved."[100] Although Johannes has much to do with reality, Kierkegaard insists that he does not belong to the real world. Drawn to possibility and away from actuality, Johannes avoids involvement in concrete existence. In fact, he never really enters into an actual relationship with Cordelia, but manipulates her in such a way that she forms herself in

---

97. *Sickness unto Death*, p. 170; 11:150.
98. The irony of the name Wahl (German: "choice" or "selection") is, no doubt, intentional.
99. *The Concept of Irony*, p. 300; 13:355.
100. *Either-Or*, 2:174; 2:154. Since the Judge is convinced that Johannes has yet to face up to the seriousness of life, he regularly addresses him as "my young friend."

his own image. "What she must learn," Johannes admits in the privacy of his diary, "is to go through all the movements of infinity, to sway, to lull herself in her moods, to confuse poetry and actuality, truth and romance, to toss herself about in the infinite." [101] By the end of his "psychological experiment," Johannes is convinced that "he has developed the many-tongued reflection within her, that he has developed her aesthetically so far that she no longer listens humbly to one voice, but is able to hear many voices at one time." [102] Multiple voices, however, are cacophonous, and protean possibilities perplexing. Deserted by her erstwhile lover, Cordelia is left "to struggle with the doubt as to whether the whole affair was not a figment of the imagination." [103]

In the final analysis, the seducer is also seduced, not by confused Cordelia, but by his own confusing imagination. Increasingly detached from actuality, the reflective aesthete finally loses touch with the "mainland of reality" and drifts into the fantasy world of unreal possibility.

> Possibility then appears to the self ever greater and greater, more and more things become possible, because nothing becomes actual. At last it is as if everything were possible—but this is precisely when the abyss has swallowed up the self. . . . At the instant something appears possible, and then a new possibility makes its appearance, at last this phantasmagoria moves so rapidly that it is as if everything were possible—and this is precisely the last moment, when the individual becomes for himself a mirage [*Luftsyn*]. [104]

It becomes apparent that Kierkegaard's vignette of Johannes is really a "shadowgraph." "In such a dream of imagination, the individual is not an actual figure but is a shadow, or rather the actual figure is invisibly present and therefore is not content with casting one shadow, but the individual has a multiplicity of shadows, all of which resemble him and for the moment have an equal claim to be accounted himself." [105] Reflection turns out to be just as spiritless as immediacy. Kierkegaard's sojourner overcomes the dissipated life of sensuality only to be anaesthetized by the ether of pure possibility. As Judge Wilhelm points out, the self of the aesthete, be he immediate

---

101. Ibid., 1:387; 1:359.

102. Ibid., p. 305; 1:281.

103. Ibid., p. 303; 1:279.

104. *Sickness unto Death*, p. 169; 11:149. R. D. Laing's *The Divided Self: A Study in Sanity and Madness* (London: Tavistock Publications, 1959) presents a vivid account of this form of experience. See esp. pp. 70 ff.

105. *Repetition*, p. 58; 3:194.

or reflective, "is like a plot of ground in which all sorts of herbs are planted, all with the same claim to thrive; his self consists of this multiplicity, and he has no self that is higher than this."[106]

Drawing on Hegel's interpretation of unhappy consciousness, Kierkegaard concludes his examination of the aesthetic stage by arguing that the reflective aesthete is really "the unhappiest man."[107] When absent to and estranged from the present because of constant reflection on the past and speculation about the future, the self "lives as one already dead." Remembering that for which he ought to hope and hoping for that which he ought to remember, the unhappiest man "cannot become old, for he has never been young; he cannot become young, for he is already old. In one sense of the word, he cannot die, for he has not really lived; in another sense, he cannot live, for he is already dead."[108] One of the *symparane-kromenoi*, the unhappiest man finally confesses: "I lie stretched out, inactive; the only thing I see is emptiness, the only thing I move about in is emptiness."[109] The aesthetic stage on life's way ends in what Kierkegaard calls "melancholy [*Tungsind*]." The melancholy person is aware of the meaninglessness of his life but takes no steps to resolve the existential impasse into which he has fallen.[110] Although this malaise is a symptom of the sickness unto death, Kierke-

---

106. *Either-Or*, 2:229; 2:202.
107. The barb in Kierkegaard's irony, of course, is that it is precisely Hegel who is the paradigm of the unhappiest man.
108. *Either-Or*, 1:224; 1:200.
109. Ibid., p. 36; 1:21.
110. The mood of melancholy pervades the "Diapsalmata" with which *Either-Or* begins. Kierkegaard stresses the complexity of this affection when he notes the peculiar attraction melancholy is capable of exercising. "In addition to the rest of the numerous acquaintances, I still have one intimate confidante—my melancholy. In the midst of my joy, in the midst of my work, she beckons to me and calls me aside, even though physically I do not budge. My melancholy is the most faithful mistress I have known; what wonder, then, that I love in return" (*Either-Or*, 1:20; 1:5). In one of his most poignant aphorisms, Kierkegaard places greater emphasis upon the distress wrought by melancholy. "Is there anything that could divert me? Aye, if I might behold a constancy that could withstand every trial, an enthusiasm that endured everything, a faith that could remove mountains, a thought that could unite the finite and the infinite. But my soul's poisonous doubt is all-consuming. My soul is like the Dead Sea, over which no bird can fly; when it has flown midway, then it sinks down to death and destruction" (p. 36; 1:21). This text is particularly instructive, for it suggests Kierkegaard's proposed remedy for melancholy. It is important to note that Kierkegaard uses two words for melancholy: *Tungsind* and *Melancholi*. The translation of both words as "melancholy" loses a distinction important for Kierkegaard. Melancholi is more light-hearted and attractive, while Tungsind is a darker mood that involves brooding self-preoccupation. For a helpful discussion of this distinction see Vincent McCarthy, *The Phenomenology of Moods in Kierkegaard* (The Hague: Martinus Nijhoff, 1978), pp. 54-56.

gaard insists that it is not without therapeutic value. Melancholy is "the hysteria of spirit" which is a "presentiment of a metamorphosis." Kierkegaard is convinced that there comes a moment in the life of the self when "spirit would collect itself, as it were, out of this dissipation and explain itself to itself—the personality would become conscious of itself in its eternal validity."[111] Reflection alone cannot effect this spiritual metamorphosis. Aesthetic dissolution can be overcome only through ethical resolution. The "way of reflection is unending, and can come to an end only if the individual arbitrarily breaks it off by bringing something else into play, a resolution of the will, but in so doing the individual brings himself under ethical determinations, and loses aesthetic interest."[112]

Ethical Selfhood

In one of his lengthy epistles to Johannes, Judge Wilhelm writes: "But what is it to live aesthetically, and what is it to live ethically? What is the aesthetic in a man, and what is the ethical? To this I would reply: the aesthetic in a man is that by which he is immediately what he is; the ethical is that by which he becomes what he becomes."[113] The becoming that is essential to ethical selfhood arises through the subject's free decision. In contrast with the aesthetic avoidance of decision as a result either of identification with sensuous inclination and social custom or of preoccupation with abstract reflection, self-conscious decision is the nerve of ethical existence. "The act of choosing," declares Kierkegaard's ethical persona, "is a proper and stringent expression of the ethical" (170; 151). Such deliberate decision is an essential moment in the process of individuation and marks a crucial stage of the journey to selfhood. The ethicist "has himself as a task." Unwilling merely to be swayed by passing mood or contingent circumstance and disillusioned with the "world of possibilities, glowing with imagination and dialectically organized," the ethical person assumes responsibility for becoming himself. Expressing dismay over aesthetic dissipation, Judge Wilhelm queries, "Can you think of anything more frightful than that it might end with your nature being resolved into a multiplicity, that you

---

111. *Either-Or*, 2:193; 2:170.

112. Ibid., p. 178; 1:157.

113. Ibid., 2:182; 2:161. Throughout this section, citations to the second volume of *Either-Or* are given in the body of the text.

really might become many, become, like those unhappy demonics, a legion, and you thus would have lost the inmost and holiest thing of all in a man, the unifying power of personality?" (164; 146). The ethicist attempts to quell aesthetic despair by means of resolute activity in which he "consolidates himself [*consolidere sig*]" or "collects himself [*samler sig*] out of dissipation." No longer a bundle of conflicting desires or an array of fantastic possibilities, the self becomes a concrete individual through its own free will. In ethical action, the subject gains a history that is unified by the coherence and consistency of purposeful striving. This personal history is the self's "revelation [*Aabenbarelse*]" of itself to itself and to others. Temporality, therefore, is the medium of the subject's self-expression. Released from unreflective immersion in the present and abstract reflection on the past and the future, the ethicist creatively joins past and future in "the true present, which is a unity of hope and recollection." The freely acting temporal subject negates the abject spiritlessness of aestheticism and points toward the authentic form of spirit realized in religious existence.

Judge Wilhelm maintains that his form of life is *decisively* different from the point of view of his young friend and from the philosophy whose embodiment he believes Johannes to represent— Hegelianism. The Judge carefully distinguishes his concrete either-or, in which contraries are contrasted, from the allegedly abstract aesthetic principle of both-and, in which opposites are mediated. While readily admitting that "there are situations in life where it would be ridiculous or a species of madness to apply an either-or," he insists that "there are also men whose souls are too dissolute to grasp what is implied in such a dilemma, whose personalities lack the energy to say with pathos, either-or" (161; 141). This is no minor point for Judge Wilhelm. Were he to admit the validity of what he understands to be the perspective of speculative philosophy, he believes, the foundation upon which his world rests would crumble. "If we concede mediation," he argues, "then there is no absolute choice, and if there is nothing of that sort, then there is no absolute either-or" (177; 157).

But one must always be wary of taking a pseudonym at his word, even a law-abiding character like the Judge. More often than not, they fail to comprehend completely what they are saying. When fully examined, Judge Wilhelm's form of life is remarkably similar to its apparent opposite—the shape of selfhood Hegel unfolds in his interpretation of spirit's progression from Sittlichkeit to the self-certain conscientious moral actor.[114] Though the consistent emphasis on individual resolution is a distinctive feature of Kierkegaard's ethical analysis, the form of selfhood actualized by this self-conscious decision is extremely Hegelian. In light of this intentional parallel, Kierkegaard's insistence that the wayfarer must move beyond the ethical stage to reach authenticity is not surprising. The Judge clearly recognizes that the realization of genuine selfhood requires the joining of contraries through free decision. But he lacks sufficient appreciation of the depth of the antitheses the self must synthesize, and consequently does not achieve the coincidence of opposites definitive of spirit.

The unique contours of ethical selfhood begin to emerge with a careful consideration of the Judge's understanding of choice. From the ethical viewpoint, choice or decision[115] is not a simple phenomenon but is a complex activity comprising a plurality of interrelated factors. In the most comprehensive sense, ethical decision involves "the choice of oneself in one's eternal validity [at vælge sig selv i evige Gyldighed]." The Judge distinguishes this central ethical category from the aesthetic maxim concisely expressed by Socrates: "Know thyself." As we have noted, over against the aesthetic, which is that by which a person is immediately what he is, the ethical is that by which one becomes what he becomes. Paradoxically, however, the initial moment of self-formative becoming is the free choice of what one is. In the first instance, the self's choice of itself in its eternal validity is the decision to decide, the choice to choose. In Kierkegaardian anthropology, self-consciousness is a necessary but not sufficient condition of authentic selfhood. One must will to will. At this point, "it is not yet a question of the choice of something in particular, it is not a question of the reality of that which is chosen, but of the reality of the act of choice" (180; 160). Prior to the possibility of reaching specific decisions, the self must consciously recognize and freely appropriate itself as a self-determining being. Judge Wilhelm writes: "But what, then, is this self of mine? If I were

---

114. This emphasis on the Hegelian character of Kierkegaard's ethical stage stands in tension with the usual interpretation of the Judge as a thoroughgoing Kantian moralist. While there is an undeniable Kantian flavor to Kierkegaard's ethical world, the influence of Kant is mediated by Hegel.

115. Kierkegaard makes no systematic distinction between choice (valg, at vælge) and decision (beslutning, at beslutte).

required to define this, my first answer would be: It is the most abstract of all things, and yet at the same time it is the most concrete—it is freedom" (218; 192).

As soon as a person accepts responsibility for himself as a free agent, other dimensions of selfhood come into sharp focus. Most importantly, the subject clearly distinguishes what it is from what it ought to be by differentiating its givenness and its possibility, its reality and its ideality. The self that the ethicist wills to become "is not an abstract self which passes everywhere and hence is nowhere, but [is] a concrete self which stands in living reciprocal relation with these specific surroundings, these conditions of life, this natural order. This self which is the goal [*Formaalet*] is not merely a personal self, but a social, a civic self. He has, then, himself as a task for an activity in which, as this definite personality, he grasps the relations of life" (267; 235). The ethicist is completely aware of the natural and social determinants of being that immediately dominate aesthetic experience. Through prolonged self-scrutiny, he "becomes conscious of himself as this definite individual, with these talents [*Gave*], these dispositions, these instincts, these passions, influenced by these definite surroundings, as this definite product of a definite environment. But being conscious of himself in this way, he assumes responsibility for all this" (255; 225). The free act of self-choice effectively mediates aesthetic immediacy. The ethicist simultaneously annuls complete determination by, and appropriates (*ophæve*) his dependence upon, the given natural and social aspects of selfhood. Kierkegaard contends that "in choosing itself, the personality chooses itself ethically and excludes absolutely the aesthetic, but since he chooses himself and since he does not become another by choosing himself but becomes himself, the whole of the aesthetic comes back again in its relativity" (182; 161).

Having accepted the finite limits of its facticity, the subject is in a position to assess realistically the possibilities it might realize or the ideality it might strive to actualize. "This self the individual knows," Kierkegaard stresses, "is at once the real self and the ideal self that the individual has outside himself as the picture in likeness to which he has to form himself and which, on the other hand, he nevertheless has in him since it is the self. Only within him has the individual the goal after which he has to strive, and yet he has this goal outside him, inasmuch as he strives after it" (263; 232). As the ambiguous "being which is nevertheless a non-being," the ideal self represents what the subject essentially is, yet actually is not. The ethicist expresses the dialectical relation of essence and existence by distinguishing universality and particularity. In the opinion of Judge Wilhelm,

> only when the individual himself is the universal is it possible to realize the ethical. This is the secret of conscience, it is the secret that the individual life shares with itself, that it is at once an individual life and at the same time the universal, if not immediately as such, yet according to its possibility. He who regards life ethically sees the universal, and he who lives ethically expresses the universal in his life, he makes himself the universal man, not by divesting himself of his concretion, for then he becomes nothing, but by clothing himself with it and permeating it with the universal. [260; 229]

At Kierkegaard's ethical stage on life's way, as in Hegel's moral view of the world, the self both acknowledges the existential disparity between universal moral law and the particular acting subject, and initially insists upon the possibility of a harmonious reconciliation of these opposites. The self-confident actor attempts to bring about this integration of contraries by elevating his idiosyncratic particularity to universality. Convinced of the essentiality of universality, "the task the ethical individual sets himself is to transform himself into the universal individual [*almene Individ*]" (265; 234). The Judge speaks for all ethicists when he states: "The truly extraordinary [*ualmindelige*] is the truly ordinary [*almindelige*] man. The more of the universally human an individual is able to realize in his life, the more extraordinary he is. The less of the universal he is able to take up in his life, the more imperfect he is. He is then an extraordinary man to be sure, but not in a good sense" (333; 294).[116] The realization of the universally human, or the transformation of oneself into the universal individual, "is only possible if I already have this [universality] in myself *kata dunamin*"[117] (265-266; 234). In ethical action the individual freely actualizes his latent possibilities by self-consciously enacting the universal moral law. Since this law not only transcends the conscientious subject as the telos toward which he moves but also is immanent in him as his own ideal or essential self, the autonomous moral actor really "has his teleology in himself, has inner teleology, is himself his teleology. His self is thus the goal toward which he strives" (279; 246). Within the ethical framework,

---

116. Kierkegaard's point turns on a pun lost in translation. *Almindelig* can mean "universal," as well as "ordinary" or "common." By way of anticipation, it is important to note that from the religious point of view, the ethical expression of universality appears to abolish, rather than to sublate, particularity.

117. Kierkegaard borrows this term from Aristotle.

of course, such self-realization presupposes the cultivation of the social relations within which the individual stands. "In the movement toward himself, the individual cannot relate himself negatively toward his surroundings, for if he were to do so, his self would be an abstraction and remain such. His self must be opened in relation to his entire concretion; but to this concretion belong also the factors which are designed for taking an active part in the world. So his movement, then, is from himself through the world, to himself" (279; 246). The precise nature of this movement to one's self by way of relation to other can be clarified by analyzing the ethicist's interpretation of duty.

The universality the ethical agent seeks to actualize is not abstract and indefinite, but is present to the self in the form of its particular duty.

> Duty is the universal which is demanded of me; so if I am not the universal, I am unable to perform duty. On the other hand, my duty is the particular [*det Enkelte*], something for me alone, and yet it is duty and hence the universal. Here personality manifests itself in its highest validity. It is not lawless, neither does it make laws for itself, for the definition of duty holds good; but personality reveals itself as the unity of the universal and the particular. [268; 236]

As Judge Wilhelm unfolds his understanding of duty, it becomes apparent that his point of view represents a latter-day version of Luther's doctrine of earthly vocation which Kierkegaard believes typical of the "healthy-minded"[118] this-worldliness of Christendom.[119] The Judge identifies two primary domains of duty: *Liebe und Arbeit*.[120]

As a dedicated civil servant, the Judge is persuaded that every person has a calling. "The ethical thesis that every man has a calling,"

---

118. For a penetrating psychological analysis of this form of experience see William James, *Varieties of Religious Experience* (New York: The New American Library, 1958). Particularly relevant for our purposes is James's contention that Hegelianism represents this type of religious experience. Though this description might be accurate for some of Hegel's less dialectical followers, my analysis should make us suspicious of its applicability to Hegel's own position. By failing to recognize Hegel's insistence on the "power of the negative," James seems to support the common caricature of Hegelianism as a philosophy of identity. This misreading of Hegel is especially common among and attractive to interpreters who are of a Kierkegaardian persuasion.

119. It is important to recall the significance Hegel attributes to this Lutheran doctrine in the mediation of truth revealed in the God-Man. See above, chap. 4, 1st sec. ("Mediation"), 3d subsec. ("Mediation").

120. This is the phrase Freud uses to define the two spheres of life in which satisfaction must be achieved if the personality is to be healthy.

he explains, "is the expression for the fact that there is a rational order of things in which every man, if he will, fills his place in such a way that he expresses at once the universally human and the individual" (297; 262). Not only does earthly vocation lend meaning to an otherwise meaningless life, it also plays an essential role in the individual's self-cultivation. Through free participation in the objective social order, the subject attempts to sublate its particularity and to realize its potential universality. Implicitly drawing on Hegel's analysis of the master-slave dialectic, the Kierkegaardian ethicist contends that "it is precisely by working that man makes himself free, by working he becomes lord over nature, by working he shows that he is higher than nature" (286-287; 253). In the labor process, the ethicist alienates himself from himself in the act of self-objectification, and returns to himself by consciously recognizing and freely reappropriating self in other. Fulfillment of duty both generates the objective, universal social substance, and actualizes the individual subject. In this way, the movement of the ethical agent is, as Kierkegaard has noted, "from himself through the world, to himself." At the ethical stage of existence, relation to other is conceived as mediate self-relation.

The paradigm of ethical life is to be found in love and marriage. In a phrase that recalls Hegel's account of his *Phenomenology of Spirit*, the domesticated Judge Wilhelm defines marriage as the self's "most important voyage of discovery."[121] The essential intersubjectivity of ethical selfhood is most concretely realized in marital love. The Judge describes his relation to his wife in thoroughly Hegelian terms: "What I am through her, that she is through me, and we are neither of us anything by ourselves, but only in union."[122] When singing the praises of marriage, the usually sober and prosaic Judge waxes poetic. In one of his more lyrical effusions, he proclaims:

> Marriage is "the fullness of time." . . . Such is marriage. It is divine, for love is the miracle; it is of the world, for love is nature's profoundest myth. Love is the unfathomable bottom which is hidden in obscurity, but resolution is the victor which like Orpheus fetches love out to the light of day, for resolution is love's true form, its true transfiguration, hence marriage is holy

---

121. *Stages on Life's Way*, p. 97; 6:87. The aesthete sighs: "Sometimes I have considered taking a decisive step, compared with which all my preceding ones would be only childish tricks—of setting out on the great voyage of discovery. As a ship at its launching is hailed with the roar of a cannon, so would I hail myself. And yet. Is it courage I lack? If a stone fell down and killed me, that would be a way out" (*Either-Or*, 1:36; 1:21).

122. *Stages on Life's Way*, p. 101; 6:91.

and blessed by God. It is civic, for thereby the lovers belong to the state and the fatherland and the concerns of fellow citizens. It is poetic, ineffably poetic, as love is, but resolution is the conscientious translator who translates enthusiasm into reality, and this translator is so precise, oh, so precise! . . . Such is marriage.[123]

As the "fullness of time," marriage is the harmonious integration of the contraries inherent in the self. It is the wedding of universality and particularity, subject and society, infinitude and finitude, eternity and time, freedom and necessity, divinity and humanity. This harmony, of course, is not immediate but is mediated by the free resolution of consenting subjects. For the ethicist, marriage is a moral duty. Yet this is no onerous obligation, for it is the "precise translation," the "true transfiguration," of love.

In attempting to convince Johannes of "the aesthetic validity of marriage," Judge Wilhelm argues that love is a "unity of contradictions." "It is the unity of freedom and necessity. The individual feels drawn to the other individual by an irresistible power, but precisely in this is sensible of his freedom. It is a unity of the universal and the particular [Særegne];" "it is sensuous and yet spiritual; it is in the moment, is definitely in the present tense, and yet it has in it an eternity" (46, 61; 42; 55). At first, however, love is fortuitous, contingent, accidental—after all, one *falls* in love. The integration of contraries constitutive of immediate love is unstable and is always subject to disintegration. Love, the ethicist argues, is "an unreal *an sich*" (95-96; 86),[124] whose explicit realization presupposes the dutiful resolve of the lovers. By transforming love into duty, lovers seek to arm love against the threat of dissolution. Duty, therefore,

> comes as an old friend, an intimate, a confidant, whom the lovers mutually recognize in the deepest secret of their love. And when he speaks, it is nothing new he has to say; and when he has spoken, the individuals humble themselves under it, but at the same time are uplifted just because they are assured that what he orders is what they themselves wish, and that his commanding is merely a more majestic, a more exalted, a divine way of expressing the fact that their wish can be realized. [149; 132][125]

According to Judge Wilhelm, the public marriage vow is the resolution through which immediate love is transfigured from abstract

---

    123. Ibid., p. 121; 6:113. In interpreting this passage, it is necessary to recall the difference between Hegel's and Kierkegaard's views of the Christian fullness of time. See chap. 4, 1st sec. ("Mediation"), 1st subsec. ("The Fullness of Time: The Present"); and 2d sec. ("Paradox"), 1st subsec. ("The Fullness of Time: The Moment").
    124. Kierkegaard uses the German term that is so important for Hegel.
    125. Hardly the words of a Kantian moralist!

unreality into concrete actuality. In the face of Johannes's protest to the contrary, the Judge asserts and reasserts that marriage consummates rather than annihilates love. "And now I invert everything and say: the aesthetic does not lie in the immediate, but in the acquired—but marriage is precisely the immediacy that has mediacy in itself, the infinity that has finitude in itself, the eternal that has the temporal in itself" (96; 86). This is the aesthetic validity of the ethical, and the ethical validity of the aesthetic—a freely willed union in which self and other seem to form a unity-in-difference, both within and between themselves.

But the Judge does not stop here. Within the ethical Weltanschauung, marriage also has religious validity. We have seen that duty "is merely a more majestic, a more exalted, a *divine* way of expressing the fact that their [the lovers'] wish can be realized." Reveling in the harmony of terrestrial and celestial spheres, Judge Wilhelm exorts his reader: "Harken and be amazed at the harmonious accord of these different spheres. It is the same thing, except that it is expressed aesthetically, religiously, and ethically" (60-61; 55).[126] The ethical God is no strict and demanding moral legislator but is a humane, lenient father who asks only what his children wish. At the ethical stage of existence, the unity of desire and duty and the harmony of human and divine intention is so complete that any conflict between these spheres is unthinkable.[127] For Judge Wilhelm, God does not "torment men with the most terrifying collisions—and hardly could a more frightful thing be conceived than that there might be a collision between love for God and love for the persons for whom love has been planted by Him in our hearts" (249; 220). The ethicist sees the aesthetic, ethical, and religious dimensions of experience as "three great allies." The belief in the harmonious accord of the different spheres of life leads the Kierkegaardian ethicist to agree with the Hegelian assessment of all forms of otherworldly spirituality as essentially "unhappy." The Judge explains: "Marriage I regard as the highest *telos* of individual existence, it is so much the highest that the man who goes without it cancels with one stroke the whole of earthly life and retains only eternity and spiritual interests—which at first glance seems no slight thing, but in the long run is very exhausting and also in one way or another is the

---

126. At some points, Kierkegaard uses the term *sphere* (*Sphærer*) instead of *stage* (*Stadier*) to describe aesthetic, ethical, and religious aspects of existence.

127. As will become apparent in what follows, the religious person believes this to be the de facto death of God. Such a humane deity is nothing other than humanity regarded as divine. This is the Feuerbachianism that is supposed to lie at the heart of Hegelianism.

expression of an unhappy existence."[128] If religious obligation were
to conflict with ethical duty and personal desire, the equilibrium
[*Ligevægt*] for which the ethicist strives would be upset. Moreover,
the entire temporal process would be reduced from an end in itself to
a mere "time of probation [*Prøvetid*] in which again and again one is
put to the test without anything really resulting from it, and without
the individual getting further than he was at the beginning" (254;
224). The Judge believes that his profession and marriage protect
him from such unhappiness. "When the ethical is rightly viewed," he
maintains, "it makes the individual infinitely secure in himself" (259;
229). Moral duty and religious obligation do not create insatiable
yearning by turning the individual's eyes toward an ever transcendent
telos. The ethical view of the world "affords peace, assurance, and
security, for it constantly calls to us: *quod petis, hic est*—what you
seek is here" (328; 290). Through *Liebe und Arbeit*, Judge Wilhelm
establishes a "heartfelt sense of community" that overcomes the
unsettling feeling of being "a stranger, and an exile [*en Fremmed og
Udlænding*] in the world" (86; 77). Apparently released from the
disease of homelessness, the ethicist feels completely at home in the
world.

But what if this form of life is the domestication, not the
realization, of spirit; what if the end of life is not secure, meaningful
occupation and a *hyggelig*[129] family life; what if self is not fully
actualized in community; if individuality is not best expressed in
universality; what if eternity is not within time; if infinitude is not in
finitude; what if desire and duty conflict; what if God *does* create
dreadful collisions; if God demands renunciation, not consummation,
of love; if God requires lover to forsake beloved; if God orders the
sacrifice of a son, perhaps his own son, perhaps the son of another;
what if . . . ; what if . . . ; what if . . . ? Frightful uncertainty, terrible
insecurity—*horror religiosus*. Of this the ethicist knows nothing; but
he suspects. And this gnawing suspicion slowly unravels the fabric of
ethical life.

---

128. *Stages on Life's Way*, p. 107; 6:98. In "Observations about Marriage in Reply to
Objections," which forms the second part of *Stages*, the Judge presents the *possibility* of a
valid "religious exception" to ethical obligation. The ethicist, however, remains skeptical
about the likelihood of such an exception becoming actual and is critical of the form of life
that would result from such a situation. Thus, while in *Either-Or* the Judge defends his form
of life against Johannes's aesthetic critique, in *Stages on Life's Way* the ethical perspective is
under attack from both the aesthetic and the religious points of view.

129. *Hyggelig* continues to be an extremely important word in Danish life and
culture. It has no precise English equivalent, but connotes coziness, comfortableness, and
homeyness. It captures precisely the atmosphere of Kierkegaard's ethical world.

Within the context of Kierkegaard's overall dialectic of existence, the ethical stage is "only a transitional sphere" between aesthetic and religious forms of life. Although ethical existence sublates important features of the indeterminateness and dissipation of aestheticism, moral selfhood finally negates itself in the struggle to affirm itself. Kierkegaard argues that "ethics points to ideality as a task and assumes that man is in possession of the conditions requisite for performing it. In this way, ethics develops a contradiction, precisely by making the difficulty and the impossibility clear."[130] Unlike Hegel's conscientious subject whose actions disclose the inherent identity of opposites, Kierkegaard's ethicist gradually discovers the depth of the oppositions, the disparity of the differences, and the exclusivity of the contraries within the self. "The aesthetic sphere is that of immediacy," Kierkegaard explains, "the ethical is that of requirement, and this requirement is so infinite that the individual always goes bankrupt."[131] When ethical obligation is grasped with total seriousness, and ethically it can be taken in no other way, its fulfillment appears more and more impossible—ideality seems unrealizable, possibility unactualizable, infinitude unattainable, eternity transcendent. The more earnestly one struggles, the deeper the disparity becomes, until at last the self acknowledges a persistent conflict between the opposites it ought to synthesize.[132] The awareness of this failure to fulfill the ethical task brings with it a sense of the self's guilt. Kierkegaard's ethical stage does not culminate in beautiful souls contemplating their own divinity but in the guilty individual painfully conscious of his separation from and opposition to the absolute.

For the individual who apprehends himself as guilty, the naive self-confidence with which the ethical sojourn began appears humorous. "Humor," Kierkegaard maintains, "is the last stage of existential inwardness prior to faith."[133] Kierkegaardian humor, however, is no Hegelian comedy. Unlike the comedian who is completely self-certain and regards his own subjectivity as absolute essence, the humorist, plagued by self-doubt, is convinced of his own inessentiality. "As the border of the religion of hidden inwardness, humor

---

130. *Concept of Dread*, p. 15; 4:288.

131. *Stages on Life's Way*, p. 430; 6:443.

132. In some contexts Kierkegaard underscores the Pauline and Lutheran roots of his interpretation of the relation between (ethical) law and Gospel. For example: "What is said of the Law applies to ethics, that it is a severe schoolmaster, which in making a demand, by its demand only condemns, does not give birth to life" (*Concept of Dread*, p. 15; 4:288).

133. *Postscript*, p. 259; 7:249.

comprehends guilt consciousness as a totality."[134] This recognition of guilt reveals the abiding contradictions of moral selfhood, and profoundly unsettles wayfarers who dwell at the ethical stage on life's way. Humor, therefore, is at once the limit of the ethical and the "boundary of the religious." This border forms the frontier of a wilderness that leads to Moriah, or perhaps even to Golgotha. To sojourn in this land of promise, the pilgrim must leave behind wife and family, mother and father, and journey alone.

Religious Selfhood

Under the guise of the religious Anti-Climacus, Kierkegaard asserts that "to be a self is the greatest concession made to man, but at the same time it is eternity's demand upon him."[135] The true proportions of this demand and the significance of this concession become clear at the final stage on life's way. In the religious form of life, the spiritless dissipation of concrete existence is completely overcome, and authentic selfhood is fully realized. In contrast with Hegel's *absolute knowledge*, in which opposites are rationally mediated through cognitive recollection, Kierkegaard's phenomenology of spirit culminates in the paradoxical *coincidentia oppositorum*, created and sustained by the faithful individual's *absolute decision*. Faith is the free activity of self-relation in which the self becomes itself by simultaneously differentiating and synthesizing the opposites ingredient in its being. In this kairotic moment of decision, a person who is fully conscious of the responsibility he bears for his own life constitutes his unique individuality by decisively distinguishing himself from other selves and by defining his eternal identity in the face of the wholly other God. The authenticity toward which the pilgrim has been progressing is unattainable apart from the passionate resolution that "holds together the discontinuities of existence."

From the religious point of view, "when the individual by his guilt has gone outside the universal, he can return to it only by virtue of having come, as the individual, into an absolute relationship with the absolute."[136] As Johannes de Silentio suggests, the existential dilemma with which the ethical stage concludes can be resolved only if the *solitary* self establishes an unconditional relation to the

---

134. Ibid., p. 489; 7:480. For a more complete discussion of Kierkegaard's view of humor see Mark C. Taylor, "Humor," in *Bibliotheca Kierkegaardiana*, ed. Niels and Marie Thulstrup (Copenhagen: C. A. Reitzels Boghandel, 1978 ff.).

135. *Sickness unto Death*, p. 154; 11:135.

136. *Fear and Trembling*, p. 108; 3:145.

absolute. Having become convinced that "intercourse with God is in the deepest sense and absolutely non-social," the religious person insists that "to become spirit means to become the single individual [*den Enkelte*] ; isolation is a *conditio sine qua non*, an indispensable condition."[137] So understood, the religious form of life represents a dialectical inversion of ethical existence. Whereas the ethicist's task is to express particularity in universality,

> faith is precisely this paradox, that the single individual [den Enkelte] , as the individual is higher than the universal, is justified over against it, is not subordinate but superior—yet in such a way, be it observed, that it is the single individual who, after he has been subordinated as the individual to the universal, now through the universal becomes the individual who as the single individual is superior to the universal, for the fact that the individual as the single individual stands in an absolute relation to the absolute. This position cannot be mediated, for all mediation comes about precisely through the power of the universal; it is and remains to all eternity a paradox, inaccessible to thought.[138]

To become such a spiritual individual, the self must pass through the two forms of experience Kierkegaard describes in his account of the religious stage of existence. In religion A, the subject attempts to express an absolute relation to the absolute by dying to the world through a process Kierkegaard labels "infinite resignation." The end of the journey to selfhood is religion B, or Christianity, in which the self becomes a genuine coincidence of opposites by means of the faithful response to the Absolute Paradox. By virtue of belief in the God-Man, the individual anticipates the enjoyment of eternal blessedness and reappropriates the temporal world. Taken together, religion A and religion B constitute the imitation of Christ, through which the believer freely inwardizes and existentially repeats the God-Man's Crucifixion and Resurrection, death and rebirth. The one who follows the Way *becomes* the truth—spirit—the *imago Christi*.

Religion A is the outgrowth of and response to the disintegration of ethical self-confidence. Ever more sensitive to his failure to realize authentic selfhood, the ethicist at last repeats the confession of the Jutland priest, whose sermon concludes *Either-Or*: "As against God, we are always in the wrong." The consciousness of guilt eventually leads to the desperate admission of the self's alienation from God and from itself. According to the pseudonymous author of the

---

137. *Christian Discourses*, p. 334; 10:25; *Journals and Papers*, 2074; 11-1:A 518.
138. *Fear and Trembling*, p.66; 3:106.

Postscript, Johannes Climacus, "between God and a human being (for let speculative philosophy keep *humanity* to play tricks with), there is an absolute difference. In man's absolute relationship to God this absolute difference must, therefore, come to expression, and any attempt to express an immediate likeness becomes impertinence, frivolity, effrontery, and the like."[139] The struggle to give concrete expression to this absolute difference between God and self forms the substance of religion A. This type of religiosity is a thoroughly dialectical form of experience in which the self attempts to establish an absolute relation to the absolute by maintaining a negative relation to itself and its world. "In the religious sphere," Kierkegaard argues, "the positive is recognizable by the negative."[140] Through the act of "infinite resignation," in which the self dies to [*afdøe*] the world of finite experience, the believing subject freely confesses both its own powerlessness and the omnipotence of the object of belief. At this stage on life's way, religious self-denial displaces ethical self-assertion. "Religiously it is the task of the individual to understand that he is nothing before God, or to become wholly nothing and to exist thus before God; this consciousness of impotence he requires constantly to have before him, and when it disappears, the religiosity also vanishes."[141]

Kierkegaard imaginatively probes the nature of such obedient devotion in Johannes de Silentio's dramatic interpretation of Abraham, the progenitor of faith and prefiguration of Christ. Abraham's God is no permissive father who finally is indistinguishable from human desire and social custom. The Abrahamic God is the all-powerful Lord and Master who demands nothing less than the total obedience of his faithful servants. The transcendent otherness of God creates the possibility of a collision between religious commitment and the individual's personal desire and moral duty. Should such a conflict develop, the faithful self must follow Abraham in forgoing desire and suspending duty—even if this means sacrificing one's own son or forsaking one's beloved.[142] From the perspective

---

139. *Postscript*, p. 369; 7:357.
140. Ibid., p. 474; 7:466.
141. Ibid., p. 412; 7:401.
142. Kierkegaard viewed his affair with Regina in terms of Abraham's relation to Isaac. The most tortured testimony to Kierkegaard's own religious crisis is presented in the third part of *Stages on Life's Way*: "Quidam's Diary, 'Guilty?'/'Not Guilty?': A Passion Narrative." Throughout the entire literature, Kierkegaard never relinquishes his conviction that without the prospect of such conflict, religion is merely the deification of human desire and custom. The confusion of the divine and the human produces the illusion upon which Christendom and its philosophy, Hegelianism, rest.

of universally human ethical consciousness, such an action is completely incomprehensible, utterly mad. The conscientious actor pronounces Abraham's conduct indefensible, the work of an insane murderer. Since the command of the transcendent Lord is contrary to every canon of human reason, the religious individual can never be sure that the ethicist's judgment is incorrect. This ineradicable uncertainty breeds the unavoidable insecurity that creates the inescapable fear and trembling of the religious life.

If Abraham's intention to sacrifice Isaac is actually a religious trial and not a base temptation, he must continue to feel fatherly love toward his son and to accept parental obligation for his child. In the Kierkegaardian dialectic, the teleological suspension of desire and duty entails neither their outright rejection nor simple annihilation. Religious conviction both acknowledges and relativizes the aesthetic and ethical spheres of experience. The resulting clash of contraries generates the form of suffering peculiar to religion A. Johannes Climacus stresses that

> this suffering has its ground in the fact that the individual is in his immediacy absolutely committed to relative ends; its significance lies in the conversion of the relationship, the dying away from immediacy, or the expression existentially of the principle that the individual can do absolutely nothing of himself, but is as nothing before God; for here again the negative is the mark by which the God-relationship is recognized, and self-annihilation is the essential form of the God-relationship.[143]

According to Kierkegaard, the free acceptance of the self's ontological dependence on God is essential to personal authenticity. Devout self-negation alone, however, cannot bind the wound of spiritlessness. As the penultimate stage of Kierkegaard's journey to selfhood, religion A points to the full realization of spirit which arises through Christian faith.

Initially, Christian therapy seems to the patient to be as bad as or worse than his disease. The first dose of this bittersweet tonic deepens the discontinuities and exacerbates the oppositions the self struggles to synthesize. From the Christian perspective, the individual is not merely guilty, he is sinful. Through the persona of Anti-Climacus, Kierkegaard clarifies the anthropological significance of the notion of sin.

> The doctrine of sin, the doctrine that we are sinners, you and I, which absolutely disperses the "crowd," fixes then the qualitative distinction

---

143. *Postscript*, p. 412; 7:401.

between God and man more deeply than ever it was fixed anywhere. . . . In no respect is a man so different from God as in the fact that he is a sinner, as every man is, and is a sinner "before God," whereby indeed the opposites are held together in a double sense: they are held together (*continentur*), not allowed to separate from one another; but by being thus held together the differences display themselves all the more strikingly, as when one speaks of holding colors together, *opposita juxta se posita magis illucescunt*.

Kierkegaard believes that in this difference, there is *no* identity. "As a sinner, man is separated from God by a yawning qualitative abyss. And obviously God is separated from man by the same yawning qualitative abyss when he forgives sin."[144]

The acceptance of oneself as sinful and the appropriation of divinely offered forgiveness form the two moments of Christian faith. In the *Postscript*, Kierkegaard provides a concise summary of the overall progression of the spiritual pilgrimage his pseudonymous writings plot, and distinguishes the conclusion of his existential dialectic from the problematic implications he sees in Hegel's philosophical and theological position.

> The stages of existence rank in accordance with the interpretation of what it means to exist. (Speculative philosophy, as abstract and objective, entirely ignores the fact of existence and inwardness; and inasmuch as Christianity accentuates this fact paradoxically, speculation is the greatest possible misunderstanding of Christianity.) *Immediacy, the aesthetic*, finds no contradiction in the fact of existing. . . . *The ethical* finds the contradiction, but within self-assertion. *The religiousness A* comprehends the contradiction as suffering in self-annihilation. . . . *The paradoxical religiousness* breaks with immanence and makes the fact of existing the absolute contradiction, not within immanence, but against immanence. There is no longer any basis for an immanent relationship between the temporal and the eternal, because the eternal itself has entered time and there would constitute the relationship.[145]

The absolute and qualitative difference between God and self renders impossible any immanent relation between the divine and the human. Left to himself, the sinful individual cannot establish the absolute relation to the absolute upon which authentic selfhood depends. Here the self is brought to the utmost extremity where "humanly speaking no possibility exists," where "humanly speaking salvation is the most impossible thing of all." Kierkegaard argues that

---

144. *Sickness unto Death*, pp. 252, 253; 11:231. Not even the believer in religion A recognizes this extremity of the divine-human opposition.

145. *Postscript*, pp. 507-508; 7:499.

the only way out of this desperate impasse is through the belief that "for God, all things are possible! This is the fight of faith, which, if one were so to express it, fights madly for possibility. For possibility is the only salvation [*Frelsende*].... God *is* that all things are possible, and that all things are possible *is* God; and only the one whose being has been so shaken that he became spirit by understanding that all things are possible, only he has had dealings with God."[146] Salvific possibility is neither immanent in the self's actuality nor a continuous projection of the self's past. As the ground of infinite possibility, unfettered by finitude, undetermined by necessity, and unbound by the past, God encounters the individual *ab extra* as the inbreaking future that has the power to transfigure what is by redeeming what has been. The concrete form of divine presence which creates redemptive possibility is the offer of forgiveness extended to the sinful self by the God-Man. The realization of authentic selfhood requires the free appropriation of forgiveness through resolute belief in the Absolute Paradox. For Kierkegaard, "to believe the forgiveness of one's sins is the decisive crisis through which a human being becomes spirit; he who does not believe this is not spirit."[147]

My analysis of Christology has shown that Kierkegaard rejects Hegel's interpretation of Christ as the Mediator who reintegrates opposites in an inherently rational way. He develops an alternative view of the God-Man as the Absolute Paradox, formed by an absurd coincidence of opposites which unyieldingly resists all rational, historical, and religious mediation. Johannes Climacus muses:

> Suppose Christianity to be a mystery and intentionally so, a genuine and not a theatrical mystery, which is revealed in the fifth act of the drama, while a clever spectator sees through it in the course of the exposition. Suppose that a revelation *sensu strictissimo* must be a mystery, and that its sole and sufficient mark is precisely that it is a mystery.... Suppose Christianity never intended to be understood; suppose that, in order to

---

146. *Sickness unto Death*, pp. 171-174; 11:151-154. In his Journal, Kierkegaard writes: "This is the turning point in world history. Christianity is the religion of the *future*" (*Journals and Papers*, 1639; 8-1:A 305). Kierkegaard's emphasis on the discontinuous future that presents possibilities incommensurable with the self's actuality is intended to be a critique of Hegel's insistence on retrospective recollection and immanent historical development.

147. *Papirer*, 8-1:A 673; *Armed Neutrality*, p. 66. It is important to note that over against Hegel's interpretation of forgiveness as essentially an interhuman phenomenon through which divine immanence is recognized, Kierkegaard sees forgiveness as a transaction between the single individual and the transcendent God, brought about through the agency of the God-Man.

express this, and to prevent anyone from misguidedly entering upon the objective way, it declared itself to be the paradox. Suppose it wished to have significance only for existing individuals, and essentially for existing individuals in inwardness, in the inwardness of faith, which cannot be expressed more definitely than in the proposition that Christianity is the absurd, held fast in the passion of the infinite. Suppose it refuses to be understood, and that the maximum of understanding which could come in question is to understand that it cannot be understood. Suppose it accentuates existence so decisively that the individual becomes a sinner, Christianity the paradox, existence the period of decision.[148]

The Absolute Paradox occasions an absolute decision by posing an absolute either-or. *Either* believe *or* be offended. From the Christian perspective, this crucial decision is of eternal significance. In this decisive moment, the self-conscious and freely active individual confronts an uncertain future composed of unmediated alternatives in the face of which he must reappropriate his past and redefine his actuality by means of his own resolution. Through such decision, the self becomes itself, defines itself, assumes a concrete and unique identity by which it differentiates itself from all other selves. Since the individual is not internally bound to God, the God-self relation must come into existence in time through the response of the solitary self to the temporalized deity. Faith is a radical venture, an unmediated leap in which the self transforms itself. Through belief, one "does not recollect what he is, but becomes what he was not."[149] By faithfully responding to the absolutely paradoxical divine presence, the self inwardizes the truth of the God-Man—truth becomes subjective and the subject becomes truthful. Kierkegaard maintains that this "eternal decision in time is the most intensive intensity, the most intensive leap."[150]

Kierkegaard's spiritual pilgrimage culminates in the leap of faith. In this moment, the isolated individual realizes authentic selfhood through the passion of free resolution in which contraries are synthesized to constitute a genuine *coincidentia oppositorum*. Possibility and necessity, infinitude and finitude, eternity and time, meet in Øjeblikket to form the fullness of time for the existing individual. The passion (*Lidenskab*) of faith is the existential repetition of the suffering (*Lidende*) of the God-Man. It is the imitatio Christi that gives birth to spirit. The wayfarer at last can join the young man

---

148. *Postscript*, pp. 191-192; 7:179-180.
149. Ibid., p. 508; 7:499.
150. *Papirer*, 11-1:A 329.

portrayed in *Repetition* to declare: "I am born to myself."[151] But the moment always passes. The genuine coincidence of opposites within the self is only momentary, and must be repeatedly reconstituted. The existing individual, therefore, never *is* spirit; rather he *becomes* spirit. The self's spiritual birth is the labor of a lifetime. The final enjoyment of the fruits of this lifelong labor is eschatological.

Kierkegaard insists that becoming spirit does not require, indeed does not permit, a "monkish flight" from the world. We have seen that the stages of existence are dialectically related in a way that allows each stage to displace and to subsume its predecessor. Thus religious selfhood incorporates, though it subordinates, aesthetic and ethical aspects of experience. By developing an existential analogue to Hegel's speculative principle of double negation, Kierkegaard argues that the believer negates the negation of infinite resignation by reappropriating the world of finite experience as the free creation of the omnipotent Lord. "It is a great thing to grasp the eternal," Kierkegaard writes, "but it is greater still to hold fast to the temporal after having given it up."[152] In a typically humorous passage, Johannes de Silentio describes an imaginary meeting with a faithful individual.

> Here he is. Acquaintance made, I am introduced to him. The moment I set eyes upon him, I instantly push him from me, I myself leap backwards, I clasp my hands and say half aloud, "Good Lord, is this the man? Is it really he? Why, he looks like a tax-collector!" However, it is the man after all. I draw closer to him, watching his least movements to see whether there might not be visible a little heterogeneous fractional telegraphic message from the infinite, a glance, a look, a gesture, a note of sadness, a smile, which betrayed the infinite in its heterogeneity with the finite. No! I examine his figure from tip to toe to see if there might not be a cranny through which the infinite was peeping. No! He is solid through and through.[153]

"This possessing," of course, "is at the same time a relinquishing or an abandoning [*Opgiven*]."[154] In the eyes of the faithful individual for whom "doubleness (dualism) is higher and deeper than that which seeks or 'pursues studies toward unity,'" life is duplicitous,

151. *Repetition*, p. 126; 3:254.
152. *Fear and Trembling*, p. 33; 3:70. Kierkegaard confesses his own inability to make the final movement of faith: "If I had had faith, I would have remained with Regina" (*Papirer*, 4:A 107).
153. *Fear and Trembling*, pp. 49-50; 3:89-90.
154. Ibid., p. 57; 3:97.

appearances deceiving—revelation is concealment, and concealment is revelation. Kierkegaard holds that over against the speculative "maxim that the external is the internal, and the internal the external," "faith is the paradox that inwardness is higher than outwardness. . . . The paradox that there is an inwardness that is incommensurable with the outward."[155] Wrapped in a cloak of unbreakable silence and masked by an impenetrable worldly persona, the faithful individual cannot enter into community and is unable to communicate directly with other selves. At the final stage on life's way, the self is in, though not of, the world. One

> still lives in the finite, but does not have his life in the finite. His life has, like that of others, the various predicates of a human existence, but he is in them as one who is clothed in the borrowed garments of a stranger. He is a stranger in the world of the finite, but does not manifest his heterogeneity, his separation from *worldliness*, by a foreign mode of dress. This would be a contradiction, since he would thereby qualify himself in a worldly manner. He is incognito, but his incognito consists in having an appearance entirely like others. Just as the dentist has loosened the soft tissues about a tooth and cut the nerve, so the roots of his life in the finite have been severed. It is not his task to give the tooth an opportunity to grow fast again, which would be mediation.[156]

The Christian stage of existence is the telos of Kierkegaard's journey to selfhood.[157] Overcoming the dissipation characteristic of spiritlessness requires both distinguishing self from other and simultaneously differentiating and synthesizing the opposites within the self through self-conscious reflexion and free decision. In the moment of faith, the individual, singled out from all others and standing alone before the wholly other God, is completely responsible for the self he becomes. For the spiritual wayfarer, however, wandering never ceases. Throughout his edifying works, Kierkegaard repeatedly stresses that Christians are "pilgrims, strangers, and foreigners in the world." The transcendent God unsettles the sojourner by forever calling him from a secure present to an insecure and uncertain future. To obey this Word is to immerse oneself more and

---

155. *Either-Or*, 1:3; 1:5; *Fear and Trembling*, p. 79; 3:118. For a more detailed consideration of this theme see Mark C. Taylor, "Sounds of Silence," in *Kierkegaard's Fear and Trembling: Critical Appraisals*, ed. R. Perkins (University: University of Alabama Press, 1980).

156. *Postscript*, p. 367; 7:356.

157. Since Kierkegaard insists that faith cannot be mediated, he denies the possibility of sublating belief in knowledge, and relentlessly satirizes speculative philosophers who claim to go beyond faith.

more deeply in the ambiguities, contradictions, paradoxes, and oppositions of human existence. This is the *via crucis* in which passion is the life-pulse of spirit, and the *pathos* of the moment, the decisive realization of selfhood.

Journey's End

In Kierkegaard's pedagogy, the end is at the same time a beginning. This conclusion, of course, does not imply a Hegelian mediation of opposites in which the implicit identity of telos and archē becomes explicit. To the contrary, Kierkegaard's educational therapy seeks to contrapose, not to mediate, opposites—to dissolve the both-and of speculation into the either-or of decision. In an age when people seem to have "forgotten what it means to exist," Kierkegaard attempts to provide an education that recovers the significance of unique individuality and discloses the way to authentic selfhood. As we have seen, this education is aesthetic. Even nonaesthetic forms of existence are presented aesthetically. In the pseudonymous writings, each stage on life's way confronts the reader as an ideal possibility that might be realized. Such abstract ideality can serve as a "mirror" for the "self-examination" that leads to self-knowledge.

Kierkegaard's aesthetic education, however, points beyond itself by teaching that the end of life is not merely aesthetic, but is ethical, and finally religious. Authenticity lies not in knowledge, even absolute knowledge, but in decision, absolute decision. Imaginative recollection (*Erindring*) becomes existential inwardness (*Erindring*) solely through the free repetition of thought in being, possibility in actuality, ideality in reality. "Only when reflection comes to a halt can a beginning be made, and reflection can be halted only by something else, and this something else is something quite different from the logical—it is a decision."[158] Kierkegaard's maieutic calls upon the reader not only to acknowledge what he is but to imagine what he might be and to become what he is not. Though the midwife can attend this birth, the labor is finally the individual's own. As Kierkegaard freely admits in his posthumous "Report to History," the

> result is not in my power; it depends upon so many things, and above all it depends upon whether he will or not. In all eternity it is impossible for me to compel a person to accept an opinion, a conviction, a belief. But one thing I can do: I can compel him to take notice. In one sense this is the first

---

158. *Postscript*, p. 103; 7:92.

thing, for it is the condition antecedent to the next thing, i.e., the acceptance of an opinion, a conviction, a belief. In another sense it is the last—if,
that is, he will not take the next step.[159]

For Kierkegaard, the journey to selfhood winds along "a solitary
path, narrow and steep," where the individual wanders "without
meeting a single traveler." To follow the Way is to embark upon an
extra-ordinary (*u-almindelig*) pilgrimage, a venture that suspends one
"above seventy thousand fathoms of water, many, many miles from
all human help." And yet Kierkegaard is convinced that only such a
journey holds the promise of a radical cure for spiritlessness—the
sickness unto death.

---

159. *Point of View*, p. 55; 13:538.

|7|

PREFATORY CONCLUSION

In my end is my beginning. . . .
    —*T. S. Eliot*

The movement is the circle that returns into
itself, the circle that presupposes its beginning
and reaches it only at the end.
    —*Hegel*

The dialectic of the beginning must be made
clear.
    —*Kierkegaard*

Wayfaring complete, *we* "arrive where we started. And know the place for the first time." The goal with which we began was to bring Hegel and Kierkegaard closer together, so that their differences might emerge more clearly. Our sojourn through the labyrinthine works of these two formidable figures has disclosed remarkable identity in the midst of significant difference. We have seen that throughout their diverse writings, Hegel and Kierkegaard develop alternative phenomenologies of spirit which are designed to lead the reader from inauthentic to authentic selfhood. This common task reflects both a mutual diagnosis of the malaise of modernity as spiritlessness and the shared conviction that cure requires a therapeutic aesthetic education. For both Hegel and Kierkegaard, the central figure of the Christian tradition is revelatory of the true structure of spirit. In order to realize authentic selfhood, the individual must undertake a spiritual pilgrimage that leads along the "highway of despair." The stations or stages on this way mark the pilgrim's progress from sin to salvation, illusion to truth, bondage to freedom, spiritlessness to spirit. The end of the journey is concrete individuality—truly spiritual selfhood.

Renewed appreciation for the similarities between the perspectives of Hegel and Kierkegaard cannot, however, be allowed to obscure the equally important differences between their philosophical and theological positions. By way of conclusion, it is necessary to redefine and to evaluate the contrast between their interpretations of the self.[1] In ending, I offer prefatory suggestions about the way in which the Hegel-Kierkegaard debate illuminates the path along which we must journey to selfhood. Thus as our end was in the beginning, so a beginning is in our end.

ODYSSEUS AND ABRAHAM

In the final analysis, the Hegelian and the Kierkegaardian journeys to selfhood lead to different destinations. Hegel's end is Kierkegaard's beginning, and Kierkegaard's end is Hegel's beginning. What Hegel regards as spirit is for Kierkegaard spiritlessness, and what Kierkegaard sees as spirit is for Hegel spiritlessness. Kierkegaard considers Hegel's journey to selfhood to be a pagan odyssey in which

---

1. My purpose in this context is not to repeat in detail points of comparison that have emerged in the course of the investigation. Rather I shall attempt to underscore the most important differences between Hegel and Kierkegaard in order that we may better judge the relative strengths and weaknesses of their respective positions.

the wayfarer never advances to the stage on life's way in which he confronts the eternally decisive either-or posed by the God-Man. Hegel would view Kierkegaard's journey to selfhood as an Abrahamic sojourn in which the lonely wanderer never returns from Moriah to appropriate the reconciliation implicit in the God-Man.[2] For neither philosopher does the spiritual pilgrimage of the other lead to salvation, the realization of authentic selfhood revealed in the person and life of Christ. Ending where one ought to begin, Hegel becomes Kierkegaard's unhappiest man, Kierkegaard remains Hegel's unhappy consciousness.

From Kierkegaard's point of view, the mediation of opposites definitive of Hegel's notion of spirit actually dissolves difference in identity, creating the dissipation characteristic of spiritlessness. Being is lost in thought, existence in essence, reality in ideality, finitude in infinitude, actuality in possibility, freedom in necessity, particularity in universality, individual in crowd. The result of this seemingly asymmetrical relation is the negation of the decisive significance of temporal becoming and the correlative disappearance of concrete individual selfhood. By interpreting time as the necessary manifestation of an eternal logical process, Hegel renders historical development epiphenomenal—becoming is illusory, temporality unreal. "In spite of all that Hegel says about process," Kierkegaard argues, "he does not understand history from the point of view of becoming, but with the help of the illusion of pastness, understands it from the viewpoint of a finality that excludes all becoming."[3] This conclusion carries with it significant existential implications. Kierkegaard goes so far as to claim that "*speculation* discounts existence; in its eyes the fact of existing amounts to having existed (the past), existence is a transitory factor taken up into the pure being of the eternal. As the abstract, speculation can never be contemporary with existence as existing, but can only see it in retrospect."[4] Hegelian philosophy is not an accurate translation of Christian revelation but is a revival of "pagan reminiscence" in which time is engulfed by eternity and individuality absorbed in universality.[5]

---

2. The Hegelian critique of Kierkegaard developed in this section represents a reconstruction based upon Hegel's analysis of forms of experience similar to Kierkegaard's version of authentic selfhood. In addition to relevant sections of the *Phenomenology*, it is important to recall our consideration of the interpretation of Abraham which Hegel develops in his *Early Theological Writings*. See above, chap. 2, 1st sec. ("Fragmentation"), 2d subsec. ("The Oppression of Objectivity: Religion and Self-alienation").

3. *Postscript*, p. 272 n.; 7:263.

4. Ibid., p. 506; 7:496.

5. Kierkegaard repeatedly charges Hegel with transforming Christianity into paganism.

Hegel's insistence on the coinherence of divinity and humanity not only misrepresents the nature of the infinite, eternal God and of the finite, temporal self but also effectively abrogates the eternal significance of the individual's temporal life. For Hegel, Kierkegaard contends, "existence in time does not have any decisive significance, because the possibility of taking oneself back into eternity through recollection is always there."[6] From this point of view, "all existential decisions become a mere shadow-play beside what is eternally decided from behind. The apparent decisiveness of speculative philosophy is, like all *apparent* decisiveness, a piece of nonsense; for decisiveness is precisely the eternal protest against all fictions."[7]

Within the framework of Kierkegaard's dialectic of existence, when decisions become a "mere shadow-play," the self becomes a "mere shadowgraph." Since decision is definitive of selfhood and constitutive of spirit, the absence of genuine decision leaves the self inauthentic. This is the basis of Kierkegaard's frequently repeated charge that Hegel has forgotten what it means to be an existing individual. If the irreconcilable either-or of decision becomes the mediated both-and of reflection, the tensions of temporal subjectivity are relaxed and spirit becomes spiritless. When a person is either not yet or no longer a center of responsible self-determination, particularity is sacrificed to universality, self lost in society, individual dissipated in crowd. Kierkegaard summarizes his critique of Hegel:

> No, the error lies mainly in this, that the universal, which Hegelianism considers the truth (and the single individual to be the truth by being swallowed up in it), is an abstraction—the state, etc. He does not come to God, the subjective in the absolute sense, or to the truth—that ultimately the single individual is really higher than the universal, namely, the single individual in his God-relationship. How frequently have I sworn that Hegel basically regards men paganly, as an animal race endowed with reason. In an animal race, "the single individual" is always lower than the "race." The human race always has the remarkable character that, just because every individual is created in the image of God, the "single individual" is higher than the "race."[8]

Hegel's "cure" actually feeds the sickness unto death. In Hegel's aesthetic therapy, the individual "disappears from his own eyes like an atom, like a speck of dust, which is simply part and parcel of

---

6. *Postscript*, p. 184; 7:172.
7. Ibid., p. 203; 7:190.
8. *Journals and Papers*, 1614; 10-2:A 426.

man's lot in general, the lot of all mankind, disappears like an infinitely small element of sound in the spherical harmony of existence."[9]

For Kierkegaard, this harmony is merely imagined, not real. Hegel attempts to unite what existence separates. Consequently his system remains completely abstract—an imaginary construction irreconcilably opposed to the concrete actuality it purports to comprehend. Kierkegaard admits that "if Hegel had written his whole logic and had written in the preface that it was only a thought-experiment, in which at many points he still steered clear of some things, he undoubtedly would have been the greatest thinker who has ever lived."[10] But he did not. Hegel, therefore, presents the comical spectacle of a thinker who is supposed to have rationally comprehended everything in heaven and on earth, but is unable "to understand himself by means of his philosophy." Using an image remarkably similar to one with which the young Hegel had described the condition of self-alienation, Kierkegaard writes: "A thinker erects an immense building, a system, a system that embraces the whole of existence and world-history, etc.—and if we observe his personal life, we discover to our astonishment this terrible and ludicrous fact, that he himself personally does not live in this immense high-vaulted palace but in a barn alongside of it, or in a doghouse, or at most in the porter's lodge."[11] Preoccupation with such fantastic philosophical abstractions distracts one from the essential task of becoming a concrete individual.

Hegel, of course, would find Kierkegaard's critique essentially misguided. He would reply that Kierkegaard's contention that rational mediation dissolves difference in identity represents a failure to grasp the dialectical relation of identity-within-difference in which opposites are coimplicated and mutually constitutive. Kierkegaard interprets Hegelian idealism as a philosophy of identity in which difference, multiplicity, and plurality are merely apparent and finally unreal. We have seen, however, that Hegel rejects the abstract non-differentiation of Schellingian idealism and romantic intuitionism as emphatically as he denies the abstract differentiation of philosophical atomism and existential individualism. Hegel insists that the dialectical relation between identity and difference results in neither

---

9. *Stages on Life's Way*, p. 418; 6:430.
10. *Journals and Papers*, 1605; 6:A 73.
11. *Sickness unto Death*, pp. 176-177; 11:156. Compare above, chap. 2, text corresponding to n. 25.

the absorption of difference in identity nor the dissolution of identity in difference. Only a position that walks the fine line between the abstract extremes of monism and pluralism can disclose the truth of spirit.

It is clear, then, that Hegel would resist Kierkegaard's charge that speculative philosophy is a "monkish flight" of abstraction which transports one from the contradictions of actual existence and the tensions of concrete individuality to the tranquil repose of a fanciful world of the imagination. Hegel maintains that dialectical reason enables one to penetrate actuality and to comprehend reality. The speculative mediation of particularity and universality does not dissipate individuality, but demonstrates that unique individuality can arise only within an inwardly differentiated totality in which specific members assume determinate identity through internal relation to one another. Moreover, the realization of the identity-within-difference of time and eternity does not imply that temporal existence has no decisive significance. Quite the opposite, the recognition of the coinherence of the eternal and the temporal, or the revelation of the reconciliation of the divine and the human, makes explicit the eternal validity of time and the infinite value of the finite self. In Hegel's phenomenology of spirit, history is regarded as essential and individual selfhood as absolutely significant.

And yet Hegel's confidence that the Kingdom has come sometimes wavers. He concludes his famous Berlin lectures on the philosophy of religion on a "discordant note" by suggesting that the spiritual community has, in fact, passed away. Hegel does not relinquish his conviction that philosophical knowledge can overcome fragmentation by reconciling opposites and harmonizing discord. Confronted, however, by a world in which "individual opinion and conviction without objective truth have assumed authority, and the pursuit of private rights and enjoyment is the order of the day," Hegel is forced to admit that

> this reconciliation is merely a partial one, without outward universality. Philosophy forms in this connection a separate sanctuary, and those who serve in it constitute an isolated order of priests, who must not mix with the world, and thus guard the possession of truth. How the temporal, empirical present is to find its way out of this discord, and what form it is to take, are questions that must be left to itself to settle, and to deal with them is not the *immediate* practical task and concern of philosophy.[12]

---

12. *Philosophy of Religion*, pp. 150-151; 17:343-344. For other noteworthy expressions of Hegel's despair see *History of Philosophy* 1:52; 18:72; and *Briefe*, 2:219.

For Kierkegaard, these are the despairing words of the unhappiest man.

From Hegel's point of view, the coincidentia oppositorum definitive of Kierkegaard's notion of spirit actually leaves contraries unreconciled, creating the fragmentation characteristic of spiritlessness. Stuck fast in abstractions of finite understanding, Kierkegaard differentiates but cannot reintegrate opposites. Thus Kierkegaardian spirit remains "impaled on the stake of absolute opposition." Self is set against other, subject against object, existence against essence, finitude against infinitude, reality against ideality, actuality against possibility, freedom against necessity, individuality against universality, self against society, time against eternity, man against God. The result of such persistent opposition is the negation of the essential significance of temporal becoming and the disappearance of concrete individuality. By opposing essence to existence and eternity to time, Kierkegaard reduces historical process to inessentiality. Time no longer possesses intrinsic value, but is significant only to the extent that it points beyond itself to a transcendent eternity. In this situation, "consciousness of life, of its existence and activity, is only the agonized suffering over this existence and activity, for therein it is conscious that its essence is only its opposite, is conscious only of its own nothingness."[13] This awareness of one's inessentiality leads to passionate self-negation through which the temporal subject seeks to regain essential being by means of reconciliation with the divine object. The project of faith, however, is destined to fail. Reified dualisms make reunification impossible and self-alienation inevitable. Subject and object, self and other, existence and essence, man and God, remain estranged. Hegel explains that in this form of experience, "there is on the one hand, a going out from my finitude to a Higher; on the other hand, I am determined as the negative of this Higher. The latter remains an Other, which cannot be determined by me, insofar as determination is to have an objective meaning. What is present is only this going out on my part, this aiming to reach what is remote; I remain on this side, and have a yearning after a beyond."[14] For Kierkegaard, this "longing is the umbilical cord of the higher life;"[15] for Hegel, it is the ceaseless sigh of self-estranged spirit.

As Kierkegaard's existential dialectic makes clear, this restless yearning eventually leads to the individual's attempt to establish an

---

13. *Phenomenology*, p. 127; 160.
14. *Philosophy of Religion*, 1:177; 16:171.
15. *Journals and Papers*, 4409; 2:A 343.

absolute relation to the absolute. The journey to meet the alien God carries the wayfarer farther and farther from human community, until at last self is completely isolated from other. Unlike Kierkegaard, Hegel maintains that this "self-maintenance in strict opposition to otherness"[16] does not bring the complete realization of unique individuality. Since spirit is essentially intersubjective, the abrogation of social relations is the negation of concrete individuality. Rather than an accurate representation of the truth implicit in the God-Man, Kierkegaardian faith is a revival of Jewish positivity in which a servile subject is completely obedient to an omnipotent Lord and Master. Kierkegaard's insistence on the absolute qualitative difference between the divine and the human not only misconstrues the nature of the infinite, eternal God and of the finite, temporal self but also effectively negates the eternal significance of the individual's temporal life. Hegel believes Kierkegaard's solitary sojourner to be estranged, "a stranger on earth, a stranger to the soil and to men alike."[17] With Abraham, he is condemned to suffer the homesickness born of perpetual exile and endless wandering in a foreign land.

Kierkegaard, of course, would find Hegel's critique essentially one-sided. He would reply that Hegel's contention that the coincidence of opposites leaves contraries fragmented in mere antithesis to one another represents a failure to grasp the dialectical paradox created and sustained by the synthetic activity of spirit. Although opposites are mutually exclusive, they can be brought together momentarily through the passion of free decision. Since Hegel's integrative vision remains blind to genuine paradox, he mistakenly identifies the penultimate stage on life's way with Kierkegaard's notion of realized spirit. Hegel's Abraham is Kierkegaard's knight of infinite resignation, who "lives dejectedly in worldly sorrow." The knight of faith, by contrast, not only dies to the temporal world but also is reborn to finite experience. Faith is the absurdly paradoxical act of simultaneously resigning and reappropriating, negating and affirming the created order. Kierkegaard explains:

> By faith I make renunciation of nothing, on the contrary, by faith I acquire everything, precisely in the sense in which it is said that he who has faith like a grain of mustard can remove mountains. A purely human courage is required to renounce the whole of the temporal to gain the eternal. . . . But a paradoxical and humble courage is required to grasp the whole of the

---

16. *Early Theological Writings*, p. 186; 246. This is the phrase Hegel uses to describe the spirit of Judaism.
17. Ibid., p. 186; 246.

temporal by virtue of the absurd, and this is the courage of faith. By faith Abraham did not renounce his claim upon Isaac, ... by faith he received Isaac.[18]

The life of faith, therefore, is no "monkish flight" from the world, but calls the wayfarer to ever deeper involvement in concrete existence. In Kierkegaard's phenomenology of spirit, the eternal significance of time and the absolute validity of individual selfhood are nowhere more radically accentuated than in the decisive moment of faith.

And yet Kierkegaard is unable to endure the tension generated by the paradoxical coincidentia oppositorum he identifies with true spirit. Unreconciled opposites collide, only to fly apart again, leaving self sundered. In the throes of his celebrated attack upon Christendom, Kierkegaard confesses:

> The conditions of my own life, as has been said, were the foundation of my knowledge; by the help of them, in proportion as I was developed in the course of years, I became more and more observant of Christianity and of the definition of what it is to become a Christian. For according to the New Testament, what is it to become a Christian? Why the oft repeated warnings not to be offended? Whence the frightful collisions (hating father, mother, wife, child, etc.), in which the New Testament lives and breathes? Surely both are accounted for by the fact that Christianity knows well that to become a Christian is, humanly speaking, to become unhappy for this life, yet blissfully expectant of an eternal blessedness. For according to the New Testament, what is it to be loved by God? It is to become, humanly speaking, unhappy for this life, yet blissfully expectant of an eternal blessedness—in no other way can God who is spirit love a man. He makes you unhappy, but He does it out of love—blessed is he who is not offended! And according to the New Testament, what is it to love God? It is to *will* to become, humanly speaking, unhappy for this life, yet blissfully expectant of an eternal blessedness—in no other way can a man love God who is spirit.[19]

For Hegel, these are the despairing words of unhappy consciousness.

ENDING

Spirit against spirit, spirit against spiritlessness, self against self. *Either* Hegel *or* Kierkegaard? It appears that the journey to selfhood ends with a Kierkegaardian dilemma: an irrevocable choice between

---

18. *Fear and Trembling*, p. 59; 3:98-99.

19. *Attack upon Christendom*, pp. 189-190; 14:227. Numerous other examples could be cited from Kierkegaard's work. The most tortured expressions of such passionate world-negation are to be found in his late Journals. See, for example, *The Last Years, Journals of 1853-1855*, ed. and trans. R. G. Smith (New York: Harper and Row, 1965).

mutually exclusive alternatives. The course we have pursued, however, should make us suspicious of this conclusion. Kierkegaard's notion of realized spirit finally is inadequate. Hegel's dialectical vision offers a more satisfactory perspective from which to comprehend the nature of the self and the dynamics of personal and corporate history. To be convincing, this claim cannot stand as the mere assertion of the superiority of Hegel's position over against Kierkegaard's point of view. It must be shown that Hegel's conception of selfhood is, in fact, implicit in its opposite—Kierkegaardian spirit. Put differently, it must be demonstrated that Kierkegaard's interpretation of authentic selfhood negates itself in the very effort to affirm itself, and necessarily passes over into its opposite— Hegelian spirit.

We have seen that Kierkegaard's phenomenology of spirit culminates in the individual's effort to define personal identity by decisively distinguishing self from other. The Kierkegaardian formula for authentic selfhood "constantly is: individual in opposition to the others."[20] The differentiation of self and other is most completely expressed in the religious form of existence. Faith, for Kierkegaard, is a "paradox that does not permit of mediation, for it is founded precisely upon the fact that the individual is only the individual [*den Enkelte kun er den Enkelte*]."[21] From this point of view, identity appears to be established through self-relation that is independent of relation to otherness. Relations among individuals are conceived as external to antecedently constituted identity and therefore remain accidental to determinate being. Identity and difference are regarded as indifferent. Since Kierkegaard is convinced that identity does not arise through internal relation to otherness, but is a function of contrast with or opposition to difference, he insists that "spirit is exactly this: not to be like others."[22]

Hegel's careful consideration of the dialectical relation of identity and difference discloses the contradiction inherent in Kierkegaard's notion of spirit. The individual's struggle to establish self-identity by affirming independence of or freedom from otherness ultimately negates itself and reveals the necessary and internal relation of self and other. Hegel argues persuasively that

> self-subsistence pushed to the point of the one as a being-for-self is abstract, formal, and destroys itself. It is the supreme, most stubborn error, which

---

20. *Attack upon Christendom*, p. 167; 14:201. See above, chap. 5, 2d sec. ("Coincidence: Either-Or"), 3d subsec. ("Individual or Community").
21. *Fear and Trembling*, p. 80; 3:119.
22. *Attack upon Christendom*, p. 286; 14:355.

takes itself for the highest truth, appearing in more concrete forms as abstract freedom, pure I, and, further, as evil. It is the freedom which so misapprehends itself as to place its essence in this abstraction, and flatters itself that in thus being with itself it possesses itself in its purity. More specifically, this self-subsistence is the error of regarding as negative that which is its own essence, and of adopting a negative attitude toward it. Thus it is the negative attitude toward itself which, in seeking to possess its own being, destroys it, and this its act is only the manifestation of the nothingness of this act. Reconciliation is the recognition that the object of this negative attitude is rather its own essence, and is only the *letting go* of the negativity of *its* being-for-self instead of holding fast to it.[23]

Hegel's recognition of the essential coimplication of opposites enables us to see that the individual is *never* only the individual. To the contrary, concrete individuality arises *only* through the internal relation of self and other. In Hegel's terms, being-for-self *necessarily* entails being-for-other. That which "is equal to itself and is for-itself is such only in its absolute difference from every other. And this difference implies a relation with other things [and other selves], a relation that is the cessation of its being-for-self."[24] Since identity is relational, otherness ceases to be merely other, and difference is no longer indifferent. Relation-to-other is simultaneously mediate self-relation through which concrete individuality is established and maintained. Simple difference and exclusive opposition are abrogated when it is recognized that relations are internal and essential, rather than external and accidental. The self is really "in one and the same respect the opposite of itself: it is for itself, insofar as it is for another, and it is for another, insofar as it is for itself."[25] An important passage from Hegel's *Science of Logic* summarizes the conclusion to which the analysis of the structure and development of the self leads:

> Thus something *through its own nature* relates itself to the other, because otherness is posited in it as its own moment; its being-within-itself includes negation within it, by means of which alone it now has its affirmative determinate being. But the other is also qualitatively distinguished from this and is thus posited outside the something. The negation of its other is now the quality of the something, for it is as this sublating of its other that it is something. It is only in this sublation that the other is really opposed to another determinate being; the other is only externally opposed to the *first* something, or rather, since in fact they are *directly* connected . . . their

23. *Logic*, p. 172; 5:192-193.
24. Hyppolite, *Genesis and Structure*, p. 116.
25. *Phenomenology*, p. 76; 99.

connection is this, that determinate being has *passed over* into otherness, something into other, and something is just as much an other as the other itself is. Now insofar as the being-with-self is the non-being of the otherness which is contained in it, but which at the same time has a distinct being of its own, the something is itself the negation, *the ceasing of an other in it*; it is posited as relating itself negatively to the other and in so doing preserving itself; this other, the being-within-self of the something as the negation of the negation, is its *in-itself*, and at the same time this sublation is *present in it* as a simple negation, namely, as its negation of the other something external to it.[26]

This central insight can be expressed in less technical language. The poet Wallace Stevens points out that "nothing is itself taken alone. Things are because of interrelations or interactions."[27] Relations are ontologically definitive—to be is to be related. In terms of human being, selfhood is essentially social, spirit fundamentally intersubjective. Concrete individuality can arise *only* in community with other free subjects. Apart from such creative interrelation, the self remains totally abstract, utterly indefinite, and completely incomprehensible. Instead of negating unique individuality, social relations constitute determinate selfhood. Kierkegaard's refusal to acknowledge the necessary coinherence of opposites leads to his failure to appreciate the thoroughgoing sociality of selfhood and intersubjectivity of spirit. For Kierkegaard, "sociality is essentially retrogression."[28] The individual's most pressing task, therefore, is "to work oneself out of sociality."[29] "The spiritual man," Kierkegaard writes,

> differs from us men in being able to endure isolation, his rank as a spiritual man is proportionate to his strength for enduring isolation, whereas we men are constantly in need of "the others," the crowd; we die, or despair if we are not reassured by being in the crowd, or of the same opinion as the crowd, etc. But the Christianity of the New Testament is precisely reckoned upon and related to this isolation of the spiritual man. Christianity in the New Testament consists in loving God, in hatred to man, in hatred to oneself, and thereby of other men, hating father, mother, one's own child, wife, etc., the strongest expression for the most agonizing isolation.[30]

---

26. *Logic*, pp. 125-126; 5:135.
27. Wallace Stevens, *Opus Posthumous*, ed. S. F. Morse (New York: Alfred A. Knopf, 1957), p. 163.
28. *Journals and Papers*, 2029; 10-3:A 349.
29. Ibid., 2008; 9:A 316.
30. *Attack upon Christendom*, p. 163; 14:196. For further consideration of this tendency in Kierkegaard's writings see Taylor, *Kierkegaard's Pseudonymous Authorship*, part 3.

Kierkegaard's coincidentia oppositorum inevitably breaks down, leaving spirit fragmented. Torn between exclusive opposites and conflicting contraries, the existing individual yearns for a reconciliation that is ever transcendent, never present. Historical existence becomes a period of exile—the self an estranged wanderer. Rather than representing the realization of authentic selfhood, this form of life is the desperate expression of self-alienated spirit.

Hegel's therapeutic pedagogy offers a remedy for Kierkegaardian estrangement. Properly conceived, the dialectical mediation of opposites reconciles, but does not dissolve, the contraries constitutive of authentic selfhood. Hegel is as sensitive to the dangers of the dissipation of difference in identity as he is to the problems created by the disintegration of identity in difference.[31] Consequently he recognizes that an adequate view of the self must find the mean between the extremes of undifferentiated unity and abstract multiplicity. Hegel correctly maintains that authenticity lies neither in simple identity nor in atomistic difference, but is to be found in concrete individuality formed by the identity-within-difference of self and other. The inability of many of his followers to sustain the dialectical tension involved in this notion of spirit and Kierkegaard's calculated misprision of speculative philosophy have too long obscured the subtlety and intricacy of Hegel's interpretation of selfhood.

In our time, as in Hegel's day, we must continue to ask: "How can we restore the unity of man?" The increasing complexity of the contemporary world makes this question more urgent and its answer less clear. Describing the transition from "early modern" to "modern" religion, sociologist Robert Bellah argues that "the central feature of the change is the collapse of the dualism that was so crucial to all historic religions." Bellah is quick to explain that "this is not to be interpreted as a return to primitive monism: it is not that a single world has replaced a double one but that an infinitely multiplex one has replaced the simple duplex structure."[32] Such pluralization often leads to psychological, intellectual, social, and cultural fragmentation. The fundamental religious, philosophical, and

---

31. While the former way leads to the loss of individuality through totalitarian oppression and social absolutism, the latter path ends with the loss of integrated selfhood through nihilistic relativism and social anarchism.

32. Robert Bellah, *Beyond Belief: Essays on Religion in a Post-traditional World* (New York: Harper and Row, 1970), p. 40. Although Bellah does not acknowledge the fact, his theory of "religious evolution" conforms to the general outline of historical development identified by Hegel.

existential issue facing our time is the perennial problem of the relation between oneness and manyness. How can we mediate unity and plurality within and without?[33] How are we to find the way from fragmentation and disintegration among and within individuals to an intra- and interpersonal unification or integration? For sojourners who seek this way, Hegel remains a trustworthy guide.[34] By faithfully following the difficult course he charts, we gradually discover that *if* reconciliation is to be realized, it must be within, not beyond, the "infinite pain" of fragmented life.

> And all shall be well and
> All manner of things shall be well
> When the tongues of flames are in-folded
> Into the crowned knot of fire
> And the fire and the rose are one.[35]

Unity *within* plurality; being *within* becoming; constancy *within* change; peace *within* flux; identity *within* difference: the union of union and nonunion—reconciliation *in the midst of* estrangement. The end of the journey to selfhood.

---

33. Though not posed in precisely these terms, George Rupp's *Beyond Zen and Existentialism* (New York: Oxford University Press, 1978) is the most significant exploration of this issue to have appeared in recent years. His earlier book, *Christologies and Cultures*, underscores the importance of Hegel's work for contemporary philosophical and theological reconstruction. Rupp's analysis is closely related to another unusually insightful and suggestive study: Wayne Proudfoot, *God and the Self: Three Types of Philosophy of Religion* (Lewisburg, Pa.: Bucknell University Press, 1976). The typology of alternative models of the self which Proudfoot develops bears directly on issues we have probed in our examination of Hegel and Kierkegaard.

34. This does not imply, of course, that it is possible simply to accept Hegel's perspective in its entirety. The appropriation of Hegel's point of view requires a critical recasting of his insights in a way that both responds to his critics and incorporates significant aspects of post-Hegelian thought and experience. Such a creative reinterpretation of Hegel provides the most promising framework within which to approach current philosophical and theological problems. I have attempted to suggest the overall direction of such a line of analysis in a recent article entitled "Toward an Ontology of Relativism," *Journal of the American Academy of Religion* 46 (1978), 41-61. A more complete elaboration of this position must await a later study. Here lies the beginning in our end which renders our conclusion prefatory.

35. T. S. Eliot, *Little Gidding*, p. 223.

BIBLIOGRAPHY

A. PRIMARY SOURCES

1. *Hegel*

Werke. 20 vols. Frankfurt: Suhrkamp Verlag, 1969-1971.

Phänomenologie des Geistes. Edited by J. Hoffmeister. Hamburg: Felix Meiner, 1952.
Schriften zur Politik und Rechtsphilosophie. Edited by G. Lasson. Leipzig: Felix Meiner, 1913.
Theologische Jugendschriften. Edited by H. Nohl. Tübingen: J. C. B. Mohr, 1907.

The Difference between Fichte's and Schelling's System of Philosophy. Translated by H. S. Harris and W. Cerf. Albany: State University of New York Press, 1977.
Early Theological Writings. Translated by T. M. Knox. Philadelphia: University of Pennsylvania Press, 1971.
Faith and Knowledge. Translated by H. S. Harris and W. Cerf. Albany: State University of New York Press, 1977.
Foreword to *Die Religion im inneren Verhältnisse zur Wissenschaft*, by H. F. W. Hinrichs. 1822. Translated by A. V. Miller. In *Beyond Epistemology: New Studies in the Philosophy of Hegel*, edited by Frederick G. Weiss. The Hague: Martinus Nijhoff, 1974.
Lectures on the History of Philosophy. Translated by E. S. Haldane. 3 vols. New York: Humanities Press, 1968.
Lectures on the Philosophy of Religion. Translated by E. B. Speirs and J. B. Sanderson. 3 vols. New York: Humanities Press, 1968.
The Logic of Hegel. Translated by W. Wallace. New York: Oxford University Press, 1968.
Natural Law. Translated by T. M. Knox. Philadelphia: University of Pennsylvania Press, 1975.
Phenomenology of Spirit. Translated by A. V. Miller. New York: Oxford University Press, 1977.
Philosophy of History. Translated by C. J. Friedrich. New York: Dover Publications, 1956.

Philosophy of Mind. Translated by W. Wallace and A. V. Miller. New York: Oxford University Press, 1971.

Philosophy of Nature. Translated by A. V. Miller. New York: Humanities Press, 1970.

Philosophy of Right. Translated by T. M. Knox. New York: Oxford University Press, 1967.

Philosophy of Subjective Spirit. Translated by M. J. Petry. Boston: D. Reidel Publishing Co., 1978.

Political Writings. Translated by T. M. Knox. Oxford: Clarendon Press, 1964.

Science of Logic. Translated by A. V. Miller. New York: Humanities Press, 1969.

2. *Kierkegaard*

Søren Kierkegaards Papirer. Edited by P. A. Heiberg and V. Kuhr. Copenhagen: Gyldendalske Boghandel, 1912.

Søren Kierkegaards Samlede Værker. Edited by A. B. Drachmann, J. L. Heiberg, and H. O. Lange, Copenhagen: Gyldendalske Boghandel, 1901 ff.

Armed Neutrality and An Open Letter. Translated and edited by Howard and Edna Hong. New York: Simon and Schuster, 1969.

Attack upon "Christendom." Translated by Walter Lowrie. Princeton: Princeton University Press, 1968.

Christian Discourses. Translated by Walter Lowrie. New York: Oxford University Press, 1962.

The Concept of Dread. Translated by Walter Lowrie. Princeton: Princeton University Press, 1957.

The Concept of Irony. Translated by Lee M. Chapel. Bloomington: Indiana University Press, 1968.

Concluding Unscientific Postscript. Translated by David F. Swenson and Walter Lowrie. Princeton: Princeton University Press, 1941.

Crisis in the Life of an Actress and Other Essays on Drama. Translated by Stephen D. Crites. New York: Harper and Row, Harper Torchbooks, 1967.

The Difficulty of Being a Christian. Translated by Jacques Colette. English translation by Ralph M. McInery and Leo Turcotte, based on French translation. Notre Dame: University of Notre Dame Press, 1969.

Edifying Discourses. Translated by David F. and Lillian Marvin Swenson. 4 vols. Minneapolis: Augsburg Publishing House, 1943 ff.

Edifying Discourses: A Selection. Translated by David F. and Lillian Marvin Swenson. New York: Harper and Brothers, Harper Torchbooks, 1958.

Either-Or. 2 vols. Vol. 1 translated by David F. and Lillian Marvin Swenson. Vol. 2 translated by Walter Lowrie. Princeton: Princeton University Press, 1971.

Fear and Trembling. Translated by Walter Lowrie. Princeton: Princeton University Press, 1970.

For Self-examination and Judge for Yourselves! Translated by Walter Lowrie. Princeton: Princeton University Press, 1968.

The Gospel of Our Sufferings. Translated by A. S. Aldworth and W. S. Ferrie. Grand Rapids: William B. Eerdmans, 1964.

Johannes Climacus; or, De Omnibus Dubitandum Est, and A Sermon. Translated by T. H. Croxall. Stanford, Calif.: Stanford University Press, 1958.

Journals. Edited and translated by Alexander Dru. New York: Oxford University Press, 1938.

Journals and Papers. Edited by Howard and Edna Hong. Bloomington: Indiana University Press, 1967 ff.

The Last Years: Journals 1853-1855. Edited and translated by Ronald Gregor Smith. New York: Harper and Row, 1965.

Letters and Documents. Translated by H. Rosenmeier. Princeton: Princeton University Press, 1978.

On Authority and Revelation. Translated by Walter Lowrie. New York: Harper and Row, Harper Torchbooks, 1966.

Philosophical Fragments. Translated by David F. Swenson. Revised by Howard V. Hong. Princeton: Princeton University Press, 1967.

The Point of View of My Work as an Author: A Report to History. Translated by Walter Lowrie. New York: Harper and Brothers, Harper Torchbooks, 1962.

Purity of Heart Is to Will One Thing. Translated by Douglas V. Steere. New York: Harper and Brothers, 1948.

Repetition. Translated by Walter Lowrie. New York: Harper and Row, Harper Torchbooks, 1964.

The Sickness unto Death. Translated by Walter Lowrie. Princeton: Princeton University Press, 1970.

Stages on Life's Way. Translated by Walter Lowrie. New York: Schocken Books, 1967.

Thoughts on Crucial Situations in Human Life: Three Discourses on Imagined Occasions. Translated by David F. Swenson. Minneapolis: Augsburg Publishing House, 1941.

Training in Christianity. Translated by Walter Lowrie. Princeton: Princeton University Press, 1967.

Two Ages: The Age of Revolution and the Present Age, a Literary Review. Translated by Howard and Edna Hong. Princeton: Princeton University Press, 1978.

Works of Love. Translated by Howard and Edna Hong. New York: Harper and Row, Harper Torchbooks, 1964.

B. SELECTED SECONDARY SOURCES

1. Hegel

Avineri, Shlomo. *Hegel's Theory of the Modern State.* New York: Cambridge University Press, 1976.

Bloch, Ernst. *Subjekt-Objekt: Erläuterungen zu Hegel.* Frankfurt: Suhrkamp Verlag, 1962.

Bukdahl, Jørgen K. *Introduktion Til Hegel.* Aarhus: Aarhus Universitet, 1977.

Chapelle, Albert. *Hegel et la religion.* Paris: Éditions Universitaires, 1963 ff.

Christensen, B., ed. *Hegel and the Philosophy of Religion.* The Hague: Martinus Nijhoff, 1970.

Dove, Kenley Royce. "Hegel's Phenomenological Method." In *New Studies in Hegel's Philosophy*, edited by W. E. Steinkraus. New York: Holt, Rinehart and Winston, 1971. Pp. 34-56.

Fackenheim, Emil. *The Religious Dimension of Hegel's Thought.* Bloomington: Indiana University Press, 1967.

Findlay, J. N. *Hegel: A Re-examination.* New York: Collier Books, 1962.

––––––––. "Hegel's Use of Teleology." In *New Studies in Hegel's Philosophy*, edited by W. E. Steinkraus. New York: Holt, Rinehart and Winston, 1971. Pp. 92-107.

––––––––. "Reflexive Asymmetry: Hegel's Most Fundamental Methodological Ruse." In *Beyond Epistemology: New Studies in the Philosophy of Hegel*, edited by Frederick G. Weiss. The Hague: Martinus Nijhoff, 1974. Pp. 154-173.

Fulda, H. F. *Das Problem einer Einleitung in Hegels Wissenschaft der Logik,* Frankfurt: Suhrkamp Verlag, 1965.

Fulda, H. and D. Henrich, eds. *Materialien zu Hegels Phänomenologie des Geistes.* Frankfurt: Suhrkamp Verlag, 1973.

Gadamer, H. G. *Hegel's Dialectic: Five Hermeneutical Studies.* Translated by C. Smith. New Haven: Yale University Press, 1976.

Habermas, Jürgen. *Knowledge and Human Interest.* Translated by Jeremy Shapiro. Boston: Beacon Press, 1971.

Harris, H. S. *Hegel's Development toward the Sunlight, 1770-1801.* New York: Oxford University Press, 1972.

Heede, Reinhard. *Die göttliche Idee und ihre Erscheinung in der Religion: Untersuchungen zum Verhältnis von Logik und Religionsphilosophie bei Hegel.* Naumburg: Reinhard Heede, 1972.

Heidegger, Martin. *Hegel's Concept of Experience.* Translated by Kenley Dove. New York: Harper and Row, 1970.

Henrich, Dieter. *Der ontologische Gottesbeweis.* Tübingen: J. C. B. Mohr, 1968.

––––––––. "Formen der Negation in Hegels Logik." In *Seminar: Dialektik in der Philosophie Hegels*, edited by Rolf-Peter Horstmann. Frankfurt: Suhrkamp Verlag, 1978. Pp. 213-229.

––––––––. *Hegel im Kontext.* Frankfurt: Suhrkamp Verlag, 1971.

Horstmann, Rolf-Peter, ed. *Seminar: Dialektik in der Philosophie Hegels.* Frankfurt: Suhrkamp Verlag, 1978.

Hyppolite, Jean. *Études sur Marx et Hegel.* Paris: Librairie Marcel Rivière et Cie, 1955.

––––––––. *Genesis and Structure of Hegel's Phenomenology of Spirit.* Translated by S. Cherniak and J. Heckman. Evanston, Ill.: Northwestern University Press, 1974.

––––––––. "Hegel's Phenomenology and Psychoanalysis." In *New*

Studies in Hegel's Philosophy, edited by W. E. Steinkraus. New York: Holt, Rinehart and Winston, 1971. Pp. 57-70.

Iljin, Ivan Aleksandrovic. *Die Philosophie Hegels als kontemplative Gotteslehre.* Translated by Ivan Iljin. Bern: A. Francke Verlag, 1946.

Kainz, Howard P. *Hegel's Phenomenology, Part I: Analysis and Commentary.* University: University of Alabama Press, 1976.

Kaufmann, Walter. *Hegel: Reinterpretation, Texts and Commentary.* New York: Doubleday and Co., 1965.

_____. "The Young Hegel and Religion." In *Hegel: A Collection of Critical Essays*, edited by A. MacIntyre. New York: Doubleday and Co., 1972. Pp. 61-99.

Kelly, George A. *Hegel's Retreat from Eleusis: Studies in Political Thought.* Princeton: Princeton University Press, 1978.

_____. *Idealism, Politics, and History: Sources of Hegelian Thought.* London: Cambridge University Press, 1969.

Knox, T. M. "Hegel's Attitude to Kant's Ethics." *Kant-Studien* 49 (1957-58), 70-81.

Kojève, Alexandre. *Introduction to the Reading of Hegel.* Translated by J. H. Nicholas. Edited by A. Bloom. New York: Basic Books, 1969.

Küng, Hans. *Menschwerdung Gottes: Eine Einführung in Hegels theologisches Denken als Prolegomena zu einer künftigen Christologie.* Basel: Herder, 1970.

Labarrière, J. P. *Structures et mouvement dialectique dans la Phénoménologie de L'esprit de Hegel.* Paris: Aubier-Montaigne, 1968.

Lauer, Quentin. *A Reading of Hegel's Phenomenology of Spirit.* New York: Fordham University Press, 1976.

Löwenberg, Jacob. *Hegel's Phenomenology: Dialogues of the Life of the Mind.* La Salle, Ill.: Open Court, 1965.

Löwith, Karl. *From Hegel to Nietzsche: The Revolution in Nineteenth-Century Thought.* Translated by D. E. Green. New York: Doubleday and Co., 1967.

Lukács, Georg. *The Young Hegel: Studies in the Relations between Dialectics and Economics.* Translated by Rodney Livingstone. Cambridge, Mass.: MIT Press, 1976.

MacIntyre, A., ed. *Hegel: A Collection of Critical Essays.* New York: Doubleday and Co., 1972.

Marcuse, Herbert. *Hegels Ontologie und die Theorie der Geschichtlichkeit.* Frankfurt: Vittorio Klostermann, 1975.

_____. *Reason and Revolution: Hegel and the Rise of Social Theory.* Boston: Beacon Press, 1960.

Marx, Werner. *Hegel's Phenomenology of Spirit.* Translated by P. Heath. New York: Harper and Row, 1975.

Merleau-Ponty, Maurice. "Hegel's Existentialism." In *Sense and Non-sense*, translated by H. L. and P. A. Dreyfus. Evanston, Ill.: Northwestern University Press, 1964. Pp. 63-70.

Nayen, Franz. *Revolution, Idealism, and Human Freedom: Schelling, Hölderlin, and Hegel and the Crisis of Early German Idealism.* The Hague: Martinus Nijhoff, 1971.

Norman, Richard. *Hegel's Phenomenology: A Philosophical Introduction.* New York: St. Martin's Press, 1976.

Plant, Raymond. *Hegel.* Bloomington: Indiana University Press, 1973.

Pöggeler, Otto. *Hegels Idee einer Phänomenologie des Geistes.* Munich: Alber, 1973.

_____. "Hegels Jenaer Systemkonzeption." *Philosophisches Jahrbuch* 71 (1963-64), 286-318.

_____. *Hegels Kritik der Romantik.* Bonn: H. Bouvier, 1956.

_____."Zur Deutung der *Phänomenologie des Geistes.*" *Hegel-Studien* 1 (1961) 255-294.

Popper, Karl. *The Open Society and Its Enemies.* Vol. 2, *The High Tide of Prophecy: Hegel, Marx, and the Aftermath.* London: George Routledge and Sons, 1945.

Ricoeur, Paul. "Hegel aujourd'hui." *Études théologiques et religieuses* 49 (1974), 335-355.

Ripalda, José Maria. *The Divided Nation: The Roots of a Bourgeois Thinker: G. W. F. Hegel.* Amsterdam: van Gorcum, 1977.

Rosen, Stanley. *G. W. F. Hegel: An Introduction to the Science of Wisdom.* New Haven: Yale University Press, 1974.

Rosenkranz, Karl. *Georg Wilhelm Friedrich Hegel's Leben: Supplement zu Hegel's Werken.* Berlin: Duncker und Humblot, 1844.

Royce, Josiah. *Lectures on Modern Idealism.* New Haven: Yale University Press, 1964.

Rupp, George. *Christologies and Cultures: Toward a Typology of Religious Worldviews.* The Hague: Mouton, 1974.

Sarlemijn, Andries. *Hegel's Dialectic.* Boston: D. Reidel Publishing Co., 1975.

Schrader, George. "Hegel's Contribution to Phenomenology." *The Monist* 48 (1964), 18-33.

Soll, Ivan. *An Introduction to Hegel's Metaphysics.* Chicago: University of Chicago Press, 1969.

Solomon, R. C. "Hegel's Concept of 'Geist,' " *Review of Metaphysics* 23 (1970), 642-666.

Taylor, Charles. *Hegel.* New York: Cambridge University Press, 1975.

Taylor, Mark C. "*Itinerarium Mentis in Deum*: Hegel's Proofs of God's Existence." *Journal of Religion* 57 (1977), 211-231.

Theunissen, Michael. *Hegels Lehre von absoluten Geist als theologisch-politischer Traktat.* Berlin: Walter de Gruyter, 1970.

Wahl, Jean. *Le malheur de la conscience dans la philosophie de Hegel.* Paris: Les Éditions Rieder, 1929.

Yerkes, James. *The Christology of Hegel.* Missoula, Mont.: Scholars Press, 1978.

2. *Kierkegaard*

Allison, Henry E. "Christianity and Nonsense." In *Essays on Kierkegaard*, edited by Jerry Gill. Minneapolis: Burgess Publishing Co., 1969. Pp. 127-149.

_____. "Kierkegaard's Dialectic of the Religious Consciousness." *Union Seminary Quarterly Review* 20 (1965), 225-233.

Barth, Karl. "Kierkegaard and the Theologians." *Canadian Journal of Theology* 13 (1967), 64-65.

Bedell, George C. "Kierkegaard's Conception of Time." *Journal of the American Academy of Religion* 38 (1969), 266-269.

Blass, Josef. *Die Endlichkeit der Freiheit: Untersuchungen zur Konstitution der existierenden Subjektivität bei Søren Kierkegaard.* Cologne, 1962.

Bohlin, Torsten. *Kierkegaards dogmatiska aaskaadning i dess historiska sammanhang.* Stockholm: Svenska Kyrkans Diakonistyrelses, 1925.

Broudy, Harry S. "Kierkegaard's Levels of Existence." *Philosophy and Phenomenological Research* 1 (1940-41), 294-312.

_____. "Kierkegaard on Indirect Communication." *Journal of Philosophy* 58 (1961), 225-233.

Brunner, Emil. "Das Grundproblem der Philosophie bei Kant und Kierkegaard," *Zwischen der Zeiten*, 2, 6 (1924), 31-44.

Buske, T. "Die Dialektik der Geschichte zur Theologie Kierkegaards." *Neue Zeitschrift für systematische Theologie und Religionsphilosophie* 5 (1963), 235-247.

Cavell, Stanley. "Kierkegaard's *On Authority and Revelation.*" In *Must We Mean What We Say?* New York: Charles Scribner's Sons, 1969. Pp. 163-179.

Clair, André. "Médiation et répétition: Le lieu de la dialectique kierkegardienne." *Revue des sciences philosophiques et théologiques* 59 (1975), 38-78.

Cole, J. Preston. *The Problematic Self in Kierkegaard and Freud.* New Haven: Yale University Press, 1971.

Collins, James. *The Mind of Kierkegaard.* Chicago: Henry Regnery Co., 1967.

Crites, Stephen. Introduction to *Crisis in the Life of an Actress and Other Essays on Drama.* New York: Harper and Row, Harper Torchbooks, 1967.

_____. "Pseudonymous Authorship as Art and as Act." In *Kierkegaard: A Collection of Critical Essays*, edited by J. Thompson. New York: Doubleday and Co., 1972. Pp. 183-229.

_____. "The Author and the Authorship: Recent Kierkegaard Literature." *Journal of the American Academy of Religion* 38 (1970), 37-54.

Croxall, T. H. *Kierkegaard Commentary.* London: James Nisbet and Co., 1956.

Deuser, Hermann. "Dialektische Theologie: Studien zu Adornos Metaphysik und dem Spätwerk Kierkegaards." Habilitationsschrift, University of Tübingen, 1978.

_____. *Sören Kierkegaard: Die paradoxe Dialektik des politischen Christen.* Munich: Chr. Kaiser Verlag, 1974.

Diem, Hermann, *Kierkegaard: An Introduction.* Translated by David Green. Richmond: John Knox Press, 1966.

————. *Kierkegaard's Dialectic of Existence*. Translated by Harold Knight. London: Oliver and Boyd, 1959.

Dietrichson, Paul. "Kierkegaard's Concept of the Self," *Inquiry* 8 (1964) 1-32.

Dupré, Louis, *Kierkegaard as Theologian*. New York: Sheed and Ward, 1958.

————. "The Constitution of the Self in Kierkegaard's Philosophy." *International Philosophical Quarterly* 3 (1963), 506-526.

Elrod, John W. *Being and Existence in Kierkegaard's Pseudonymous Authorship*. Princeton: Princeton University Press, 1975.

Fischer, Friedrich Carl. *Existenz und Innerlichkeit: Eine Einführung in die Gedankenwelt Søren Kierkegaards*. Munich: C. H. Beck, 1969.

Geismar, Eduard. *Sören Kierkegaard: Seine Lebensentwicklung und seine Wirksamkeit als Schriftsteller*. Göttingen: Vandenhoeck und Ruprecht, 1929.

Gerdes, Hayo. *Das Christbild Sören Kierkegaards, verglichen mit Christologie Hegels und Schleiermachers*. Düsseldorf: Eugen Dietrichs, 1960.

Gill, Jerry H. "Kant, Kierkegaard, and Religious Knowledge." In *Essays on Kierkegaard*, edited by Jerry H. Gill. Minneapolis: Burgess Publishing Co., 1969. Pp. 58-73.

Henriksen, Aage. *Kierkegaards Romaner*. Copenhagen: Gyldendal, 1969.

Hirsch, Emanuel. *Kierkegaard-Studien*. Gütersloh: C. Bertelsmann, 1930-1933.

Holl, Jann. *Kierkegaards Konzeption des Selbst: Eine Untersuchung über die Voraussetzungen und Formen seines Denkens*. Meisenheim am Glan: Anton Hain, 1972.

Holm, Søren. "L'être comme catégorie de l'éternité." In *Kierkegaard Symposion*. Copenhagen: Munksgaard, 1955. Pp. 84-92.

Holmer, Paul. "On Understanding Kierkegaard." In *A Kierkegaard Critique*, edited by Howard A. Johnson and Niels Thulstrup. Chicago: Henry Regnery Co., 1962. Pp. 46-54.

————. "Kierkegaard and Religious Propositions." *Journal of Religion* 35 (1955) 135-146.

Johnson, Howard A., and Niels Thulstrup, eds. *A Kierkegaard Critique: An International Selection of Essays Interpreting Kierkegaard*. Chicago: Henry Regnery Co., 1962.

Kirmmse, Bruce. "Kierkegaard's Politics: The Social Thought of Søren Kierkegaard in Its Historical Context," Ph.D. dissertation, University of California, 1977.

Lindström, Valter. *Stadiernas Teleologi, en Kierkegaard Studie*. Lund: Haakan Ohlssons, 1943.

Logstrup, K. E. "Le concept de l'existence chez Kierkegaard." *Studia Theologica* 19 (1965), 260-268.

Lowrie, Walter. *Kierkegaard*. New York: Oxford University Press, 1938.

Mackey, Louis. "Kierkegaard and the Problem of Existential Philosophy." *Review of Metaphysics* 9 (1956), 404-419, 569-588.

_____. "The Loss of the World in Kierkegaard's Ethics." *Review of Metaphysics* 15 (1961-62), 602-620.

_____. *Kierkegaard: A Kind of Poet*. Philadelphia: University of Pennsylvania Press, 1972.

McKinnon, Alastair. "Kierkegaard: 'Paradox' and Irrationalism." In *Essays on Kierkegaard*, edited by Jerry Gill. Minneapolis: Burgess Publishing Co., 1969. Pp. 102-112.

_____. *The Kierkegaard Indices*. Leiden: E. J. Brill, 1970-71.

Malantschuk, Gregor. *Frihedens Problem i Kierkegaards Begrebet Angest*. Copenhagen: Rosenkilde og Bagger, 1971.

_____. *Kierkegaard's Thought*. Princeton: Princeton University Press, 1971.

Manheimer, Ronald J. *Kierkegaard as Educator*. Berkeley, Los Angeles, London: University of California Press, 1977.

Nordentoft, Kresten. *Kierkegaard's Psychology*. Translated by B. Kirmmse. Pittsburgh: Duquesne University Press, 1978.

Niedermeyer, Gerhard. *Søren Kierkegaard und die Romantik*. Leipzig: Quelle und Meyer, 1910.

Paulsen, Anna. "Kierkegaard in seinem Verhältnis zur deutschen Romantik: Einfluss und Uberwindung." *Kierkegaardiana* 3 (1959), 38-47.

Prenter, R. "L'homme, synthèse du temps et de l'éternité d'après Søren Kierkegaard." *Studia Theologica* 2 (1948), 5-20.

Price, George. *The Narrow Pass: A Study of Kierkegaard's Concept of Man*. New York: McGraw-Hill Book Co., 1963.

Ricoeur, Paul. "Philosopher après Kierkegaard." *Revue de theologie et de philosophie*, 3d ser. 13 (1963), 303-316.

Rohrmoser, Günter. "Kierkegaard und das Problem der Subjektivität." *Neue Zeitschrift für systematische Theologie und Religionsphilosophie* 8 (1966), 289-310.

Sartre, Jean-Paul. "The Singular Universal." In *Kierkegaard: A Collection of Critical Essays*, edited by J. Thompson. New York: Doubleday and Co., 1972. Pp. 230-265.

Schmied-Kowarzik, Wolfdietrich. "Marx, Kierkegaard, Schelling: zum Problem von Theorie und Praxis, I." In *Schelling Studien: Festgabe für Manfred Schiöter zum 85. Geburtstag*. Munich and Vienna: Oldenbourg, 1965. Pp. 193-218.

Schousboe, Julius. *Om Begrebet Humor hos Søren Kierkegaard: En Filosofisk Afhandlung*. Copenhagen, 1925.

Schrader, George. "Kant and Kierkegaard on Duty and Inclination." In *Kierkegaard: A Collection of Critical Essays*, edited by J. Thompson. New York: Doubleday and Co., 1972. Pp. 324-341.

Schrag, Calvin O. *Existence and Freedom: Towards an Ontology of Human Finitude*. Evanston, Ill.: Northwestern University Press, 1961.

Shmuëli, Adi. *Kierkegaard and Consciousness*. Princeton: Princeton University Press, 1971.

Skjoldager, Emanuel. "Søren Kierkegaards *Enten-Eller.*" *Kierke-gaardiana* 7 (1968), 93-112.

Sløk, Johannes. "Kierkegaard and Luther." In *A Kierkegaard Critique*, edited by Howard A. Johnson and Niels Thulstrup. Chicago: Henry Regnery Co., 1962. Pp. 85-101.

————. "Das existenzphilosophische Motiv im Denken von Kierkegaard." *Studia Theologica* 9 (1955), 116-130.

————. *Die Anthropologie Kierkegaards.* Copenhagen: Rosenkilde and Bagger, 1954.

Solomon, Robert C. "Kierkegaard and Subjective Truth." *Philosophy Today* 21 (1977), 202-215.

Sontag, Frederick. "Kierkegaard and the Search for a Self." In *Essays on Kierkegaard*, edited by Jerry H. Gill. Minneapolis: Burgess Publishing Co., 1969. Pp. 154-166.

Sponheim, Paul. *Kierkegaard on Christ and Christian Coherence.* New York: Harper and Row, 1968.

Stack, George. "Kierkegaard and the Phenomenology of Repetition." *Journal of Existentialism* 7 (1966-67), 111-125.

————. *Kierkegaard's Existential Ethics.* University: University of Alabama Press, 1977.

Swenson, David. *Something about Kierkegaard.* Edited by Lillian Marvin Swenson. Minneapolis: Augsburg Publishing House, 1956.

Taylor, Mark C. "Humor." In *Bibliotheca Kierkegaardiana*, edited by Niels and Marie Thulstrup. Copenhagen: C. A. Reitzels Boghandel, 1978 ff.

————. "Kierkegaard as a Theologian of Hope." *Union Seminary Quarterly Review* 28 (1973), 225-233.

————. "Kierkegaard on the Structure of Selfhood." *Kierkegaardiana* 9 (1974), 84-103.

————. "Language, Truth, and Indirect Communication." *Tijdschrift Voor Filosofie* 37 (1975), 74-88.

————. "Psychoanalytic Dimensions of Kierkegaard's View of Selfhood." *Philosophy Today* 19 (1975), 198-212.

————. "Sounds of Silence." In *Kierkegaard's Fear and Trembling: Critical Appraisals*, edited by R. Perkins. University: University of Alabama Press, 1980.

————. "Time's Struggle with Space: Kierkegaard's Understanding of Temporality." *Harvard Theological Review* 66 (1973), 311-329.

Theunissen, Michael. *Der Begriff Ernst bei Sören Kierkegaard.* Freiburg: Alber, 1958.

Thompson, Josiah. *The Lonely Labyrinth: Kierkegaard's Pseudonymous Works.* Carbondale, Ill.: Southern Illinois Press, 1967.

————. *Kierkegaard*, New York: Alfred A. Knopf, 1973.

————. "The Master of Irony." In *Kierkegaard: A Collection of Critical Essays*, edited by J. Thompson. New York: Doubleday and Co., 1972. Pp. 103-163.

Thulstrup, Niels and Marie, eds. *Bibliotheca Kierkegaardiana.* Copenhagen: C. A. Reitzels Boghandel, 1978 ff.

Wahl, Jean. *Études kierkegaardiennes.* Paris: Fernard Aubier, 1938.

————. "Kierkegaard und das Problem der Zeit." *Schweizer Monatshefte* 43 (1963-64), 197-198.

Widenman, Robert. "Some Aspects of Time in Aristotle and Kierkegaard." *Kierkegaardiana* 8 (1969), 7-21.

Wild, John. *Existence and the World of Freedom.* Englewood Cliffs, N. J.: Prentice-Hall, 1963.

————. "Kierkegaard and Contemporary Existentialist Philosophy." *Anglican Theological Review* 38 (1956), 15-32.

3. Hegel and Kierkegaard

Anz, Wilhelm. *Kierkegaard und der deutsche Idealismus.* Tübingen: J. C. B. Mohr, 1956.

Baeumler, Alfred. "Hegel und Kierkegaard." *Deutscher Vierteljahresschrift für Literaturwissenschaft und Geistesgeschichte* 2 (1924), 116-130.

Bense, Max. *Hegel und Kierkegaard: Eine prinzipielle Untersuchung.* Cologne: Staufen, 1948.

Bogen, James. "Remarks on the Kierkegaard-Hegel Controversy." *Synthese* 13 (1961), 372-389.

Collins, James D. "Kierkegaard's Critique of Hegel." *Thought* 18 (1943), 74-100.

————. "The Mind of Kierkegaard: The Attack upon Hegelianism." *Modern Schoolman* 26 (1949), 219-251.

Crites, Stephen. *In the Twilight of Christendom: Hegel vs. Kierkegaard on Faith and History.* Chambersburg, Pa.: American Academy of Religion, 1972.

Heiss, Robert. *Hegel, Kierkegaard, Marx: Three Great Philosophers Whose Ideas Changed the Course of Civilization.* Translated by E. B. Garside. New York: Delacorte Press, 1975.

Joest, Wilfried. "Hegel und Kierkegaard." *Theologische Literaturzeitung* 75 (1950), 533-538.

Johansen, Udo. "Kierkegaard und Hegel." *Zeitschrift für philosophische Forschung* 7 (1953), 20-53.

Kroner, R. J. "Kierkegaard's Understanding of Hegel." *Union Seminary Quarterly Review* 21 (1966), 233-244.

Leisegang, Hans. *Hegel, Marx, Kierkegaard: Zum dialektischen Materialismus und zur dialektischen Theologie.* Berlin: Wissenschaftliche Editionsgeschellschaft, 1948.

McKinnon, Alastair. "Similarities and Differences in Kierkegaard's Accounts of Hegel." *Kierkegaardiana* 10 (1977), 117-132.

Perkins, Robert L. "Hegel and Kierkegaard: Two Critics of Romantic Irony." In *Hegel in Comparative Literature.* Baltimore: St. John's University Press, 1970. Pp. 232-254.

————. "Kierkegaard and Hegel: The Dialectical Structure of Kierkegaard's Ethical Thought." Ph.D. dissertation, Indiana University, 1965.

————. "Two Nineteenth Century Interpretations of Socrates: Hegel and Kierkegaard." *Kierkegaard-Studiet* (International Edition) 4 (1967), 9-14.

Radermacher, Hans. *Kierkegaards Hegelsverständnis.* Cologne: Hans Radermacher, 1958.

Ramsey, Paul. "Existenz and the Existence of God: A Study of Kierkegaard and Hegel." *Journal of Religion* 28 (1948), 157-176.

Read, Lawrence M. "Hegel and Kierkegaard: A Study in Antithetical Concepts of the Incarnation." Ph.D. dissertation, Columbia University, 1977.

Reuter, Hans. *S. Kierkegaards religionsphilosophische Gedanken im Verhältnis zu Hegels religionsphilosophischen System.* Leipzig: Quelle und Meyer, 1914.

Ritsch, D. "Kierkegaards Kritik an Hegels Logik." *Theologische Zeitschrift* 11 (1955), 437-466.

Taylor, Mark C. "Aesthetic Education: Hegel and Kierkegaard." In *Psychiatry and the Humanities,* edited by J. Smith. New Haven: Yale University Press, 1980.

————. "Journeys to Moriah: Hegel vs. Kierkegaard." *Harvard Theological Review* 70 (1977), 305-326.

————. "Love and Forms of Spirit: Kierkegaard vs. Hegel." *Kierkegaardiana* 10 (1977), 95-116.

Thulstrup, Niels. "Kierkegaard og den filosofiske Idealisme." *Kierkegaardiana* 4 (1962), 88-104.

————. *Kierkegaards Verhältnis zu Hegel: Forschungsgeschichte.* Stuttgart: W. Kohlhammer, 1969.

————. *Kierkegaards forhold til Hegel og til den spekulative Idealisme indtil 1846.* Copenhagen: Gyldendal, 1967.

————. "Le désaccord entre Kierkegaard et Hegel," *Kierkegaard-Studiet* 4 (1964), 112-124.

————. "Søren Kierkegaard, historien de la philosophie de Hegel." *Tijdschrift voor Filosofie* 27 (1965), 521-572.

Wahl, Jean. "Hegel et Kierkegaard." *Revue philosophique de la France et de l'étranger* 112 (1931), 321-380.

————. "Hegel et Kierkegaard." In *Verhandlungen des dritten Hegelkongresses vom 19. bis 23. April 1933 in Rom,* edited by B. Wigersma. Tübingen: J. C. B. Mohr, 1934. Pp. 235-249.

Whittemore, R. C. "Pro Hegel, contra Kierkegaard." *Journal of Religious Thought* 13 (1956), 131-144.

C. RELATED SOURCES

Abrams, M. H. *Natural Supernaturalism: Tradition and Revolution in Romantic Literature.* New York: W. W. Norton and Co., 1971.

Aris, Reinhold. *History of Political Thought in Germany from 1789 to 1815.* London: George Allen and Unwin, 1936.

Barth, Karl. *Protestant Thought from Rousseau to Ritschl.* Translated by Brian Cozens. New York: Simon and Schuster, 1969.

Bloom, Harold. *The Anxiety of Influence: A Theory of Poetry.* New York: Oxford University Press, 1973.

Bruford, Walter H. *The German Tradition of Self-Cultivation: "Bildung" from Humboldt to Thomas Mann.* New York: Cambridge University Press, 1975.

Collins, James. *Interpreting Modern Philosophy.* Princeton: Princeton University Press, 1972.

Dupré, Louis. *The Philosophical Foundations of Marxism.* New York: Harcourt, Brace and World, 1966.

Eliot, T. S. *Collected Poems, 1909-1962.* London: Faber and Faber, 1963.

Fackenheim, Emil. "Schelling's Philosophy of Religion." *University of Toronto Quarterly* 22 (1952), 1 ff.

Forstman, Jack. *A Romantic Triangle: Schleiermacher and Early German Romanticism.* Missoula, Mont.: Scholars Press, 1977.

Gadamer, Hans-Georg. *Wahrheit und Methode: Grundzüge einer philosophischen Hermeneutik.* Tübingen: J. C. B. Mohr, 1965.

Henrich, Dieter. *Fichtes ursprüngliche Einsicht.* Frankfurt: Vittorio Klostermann, 1967.

Horn, Robert L. "Positivity and Dialectic: A Study of the Theological Method of Hans Lassen Martensen." Th.D. thesis, Union Theological Seminary, 1969.

Kant, Immanuel. *Critique of Practical Reason.* Translated by L. W. Beck. New York: Bobbs-Merrill, 1956.

————. *Critique of Pure Reason.* Translated by N. K. Smith. New York: St. Martin's Press, 1965.

————. *The Critique of Judgment.* Translated by J. C. Meredith. New York: Oxford University Press, 1973.

Oskar, Walzel. *German Romanticism.* New York: Capricorn Books, 1966.

Pascal, Roy. " 'Bildung' and the Division of Labor." In *German Studies Presented to Walter Horace Bruford.* London, 1962. Pp. 14-28.

Pfleiderer, Otto. *The Development of Theology in Germany Since Kant.* Translated by J. F. Smith. London: Sonnenschein, 1893.

Ricoeur, Paul. *Freud and Philosophy: An Essay on Interpretation.* Translated by D. Savage. New Haven: Yale University Press, 1970.

————. *The Symbolism of Evil.* Translated by E. Buchanan. Boston: Beacon Press, 1967.

Rosenkranz, Karl. *Psychologie.* Königsberg: Bornträger, 1837.

Rupp, George. *Beyond Existentialism and Zen.* New York: Oxford University Press, 1979.

————. *Culture-Protestantism: German Liberal Theology at the Turn of the Twentieth Century.* Missoula, Mont.: Scholars Press, 1977.

Schiller, Friedrich. *On the Aesthetic Education of Man: In a Series of*

Letters. Translated by E. M. Wilkinson and L. A. Willoughby. New York: Oxford University Press, 1967.

Taylor, Mark C., Carl Raschke, and James Kirk. *Religion and the Human Image*. Englewood Cliffs, N. J.: Prentice-Hall, 1976.

_____. "Toward An Ontology Of Relativism." *Journal of the American Academy of Religion* 46 (1978), 41-61.

Tillich, Paul. "Estrangement and Reconciliation in Modern Thought." *Review of Religion* 9 (1944-45), 5-19.

Trendelenburg, Adolf. *Logische Untersuchungen*. Leipzig: S. Hirzel, 1870.

_____. "The Logical Question in Hegel's System." Translated by T. Davidson. *Journal of Speculative Philosophy* 5 (1871), 349-359.

Walzel, Oskar. *German Romanticism*. Translated by A. E. Lussky. New York: G. P. Putnam's Sons, 1932.

Wellek, René. *A History of Modern Criticism: 1750-1950, The Romantic Age*. New Haven: Yale University Press, 1955.

INDEX

Designer: Serena Sharp
Compositor: Trend Western
Printer: Vail-Ballou
Binder: Vail-Ballou
Text: Journal Roman
Display: Palatino
Cloth: Joanna Arrestox B 19990
Paper: 50 lb. Cream Smooth